Elephant Welfare in Global Tourism

The cover photo highlights the relationship between a mahout and elder of the community and his elephants. The elephants are living in a vast forest habitat and forage for 100% of their own diet.

Mahouts Elephant Foundation is an award-winning not-for-profit organization dedicated to improving the lives of Asian elephants and the communities who coexist with them. The foundation develops community-based tourism projects for elephant observation-only tourism, working collaboratively with local stakeholders to ensure all parties benefit. This illustrates the foundation's philosophy that captive elephants' welfare is dependent on their mahouts and their living conditions and livelihood. Their projects are located in vast areas of forest, enabling elephants to live naturally and forage for 100% of their own diet year round while tourists observe from a safe and respectful distance. Alongside developing innovative solutions to complex problems on the ground, the foundation facilitates research into the behavioural ecology of elephants living in natural habitat, to better inform conservation.

The foundation speaks internationally to inform on the issues of captive elephant tourism and have good relationships with others in the field and tour companies. Through an impeccable reputation for working gently in ethical partnership with Indigenous communities the foundation has become a sought-after partner by many Karen communities.

The foundation currently has two projects, supporting three communities and ten elephants in their care.

Elephant Welfare in Global Tourism

Edited by

Eric Laws

retired Professor of Tourism

David W. Knight

Co-Director US-China Lab for Destination Development, Colorado State University, USA

Timothy Lee

Dean and Professor, Macau University of Science and Technology, Macao SAR, China

Kom Campiranon

Associate Dean for Academic Affairs and Research, College of Innovation, Thammasat University, Bangkok, Thailand

Bongkosh Rittichainuwat

Siam University, Bangkok, Thailand

Ann Suwaree Ashton

Associate Professor, NIDA, Bangkok, Thailand

John Koldowski

Special Advisor, Pacific Asia Travel Association (PATA)

Melody Zhirui Zhou

Research Assistant to Professor Timothy Lee

CABI

CABI is a trading name of CAB International

CABI
Nosworthy Way
Wallingford
Oxfordshire OX10 8DE
UK

Tel: +44 (0)1491 832111
E-mail: info@cabi.org
Website: www.cabi.org

CABI
200 Portland Street
Boston
MA 02114
USA

Tel: +1 (617)682-9015
E-mail: cabi-nao@cabi.org

A catalogue record for this book is available from the British Library, London, UK.

ISBN-13: 9781836990079 (hardback)
9781836990086 (ePDF)
9781836990093 (ePub)

DOI: 10.1079/9781836990093.0000

Commissioning Editor: Claire Parfitt
Editorial Assistant: Helen Elliott
Production Editor: Shankari Wilford

Typeset by Straive, Pondicherry, India
Printed and bound in the UK by CPI Group (UK) Ltd, Croydon, CR0 4YY

Contents

Contributors

Gary Akehurst PhD, Emeritus Professor, Management, University of Winchester and Emeritus Professor, Marketing, Aberystwyth University. Founding Managing Editor of *The Service Industries Journal* (1981–2011). Previously a member of the editorial board of several journals in hospitality, financial services, services management and not for profit marketing. Email: duckpond90@noisyhound.com

Georgina Ashby, MSc (conservation and international wildlife trade), BSc (business management and marketing communications), is a sustainable tourism professional specializing in wildlife tourism and trade. Her academic research and articles focus on developing sustainable elephant welfare policies in South-east Asia. She is currently the Senior Communications Manager at Asian Captive Elephant Standards (ACES), an independent and transparent certification and auditing organization for elephant welfare in tourism. With an environmental, social and governance (ESG) chartered financial analyst (CFA) qualification and a strong background in investor relations, sustainability and public relations, Georgina also advises businesses, policy makers and non-governmental organizations (NGOs) on sustainability and ESG matters. Her interdisciplinary skillset fuels her passion for conservation and sustainability. Email: georgina@elephantstandards.com.

Ann Suwaree Ashton is an associate professor. Ann holds a PhD and Master's degree from the University of Queensland, Australia. She is currently a faculty member at the Graduate School of Tourism Management (GSTM) at the National Institute of Development Administration (NIDA) in Bangkok, Thailand. With extensive experience in the hotel industry, Dr Ashton has also gained valuable teaching experience at universities in Australia and New Zealand. Her research expertise encompasses wellness tourism development, and her passion for health and well-being has driven her to pursue extensive knowledge, becoming a certified yoga master instructor, sound healing therapist and forest bathing therapist which highlights her commitment to promoting wellness tourism activities. She is also deeply interested in elephant tourism and is dedicated to advancing sustainable development goals related to elephant well-being. Email: suwareeashton@hotmail.com.

Liv Baker PhD is a conservation behaviourist and expert in animal well-being. Her research explores human–animal relationships and how animals engage with their environments, focusing on the roles of animals in their social groups and cultures. Baker examines similar patterns of well-being across species, emphasizing animals' desire for agency, autonomy and learning. She argues that eco-social context is crucial, and positive emotions and challenges are integral to life. Her work spans various species, including elephants, primates, arachnids, rodents and macropods. Baker chairs the non-profit PAN Works, serves as research director at Mahouts Elephant Foundation, and teaches at Sarah Lawrence College, New York, USA. Email: lbaker@panworks.io.

Sarah Blaine is the co-founder and chief executive officer (CEO) of Mahouts Elephant Foundation, a UK charity improving welfare for captive working elephants, primarily in Thailand. The foundation collaborates with Karen mahouts and their communities for mutual benefit. Sarah's focus is raising awareness and education of elephant welfare. She frequently visits elephant camps and tourist attractions in Thailand, conducting research on animal welfare and developing educational resources. Her work bridges the gap between elephant conservation, community development and responsible tourism. Sarah's hands-on approach and dedication to collaborative solutions make her a key figure in the field of elephant welfare and sustainable wildlife tourism. Email: sarah@mahouts.org.

Cynthia S. Brown PhD is a plant ecologist who has studied invasive plant ecology and management and restoration ecology for nearly 30 years. She has a passion for finding sustainable solutions to challenging problems wherever they occur. Dr Brown served as a US Peace Corps volunteer in Maitengwe, Botswana from 1986 to1988. She is grateful for the opportunity to collaborate with the local community in north-east Botswana to work towards resolving human–elephant conflict in the region. Email: cynthia.s.brown@colostate.edu.

Richard Butler, a geographer, is Emeritus Professor of International Tourism at the University of Strathclyde, having taught in Canada, the UK and several other countries. He has been a consultant for numerous agencies, governments and the United Nations World Tourism Organization (UNWTO), and published 28 books and over 200 papers and chapters in books. His main research areas are destination development, sustainability, Indigenous tourism and tourism in peripheral areas. He is a founding member and past-President of the International Academy for the Study of Tourism and in 2016 was awarded the UNWTO Ulysses medal for 'excellence in the creation and dissemination of knowledge'. Email: richard.butler@strath.ac.uk.

Kom Campiranon completed his PhD in tourism management from the University of Queensland, Australia. Currently, he is an associate professor in the Service Innovation programme at Thammasat University, Thailand.

His research and teaching interests cover areas in tourism crisis, hotel management, hospitality innovation, travel technologies, service design and service quality management. Dr Kom has published internationally in peer-reviewed journals, books and conference proceedings. In addition, he also served on the editorial board for several international journals. Email: kom@citu.tu.ac.th.

Vorakarn Chalermchaikit PhD, MSc, BBA, is a full-time lecturer at the Department of Tourism and Service Industry, Faculty of Humanities at Kasetsart University, Bangkok. She received her bachelor's degree in business administration from Mahidol University International College, her master's degree in international human resource management from Rennes School of Business and her PhD in hospitality and tourism management from Assumption University, Massachusetts. Her research and article interests focus on inclusive management practices, diversity, gender management and sustainability in hotel and tourism. Also, she is interested in interdisciplinary enhancing positive and practical impacts and motivations to readers. Email: vorakarn.ch.@ku.th.

Chelsea Greer is the director of the Wolf Conservation Program, at Raincoast Conservation Foundation. She champions wolf protection in British Columbia, Canada through research, education and policy reform. Her work focuses on predator welfare and management ethics. She holds a master's degree in geography from the University of Calgary, where she researched rewilded Asian elephants in Thailand using a compassionate conservation model. With a bachelor's degree in applied animal biology from the University of British Columbia (UBC), Chelsea developed a passion for animal ethics and welfare science in wild populations. Her expertise bridges conservation, ecology and animal welfare. Email: chelsea@raincoast.org.

David W. Knight is a Center for Collaborative Conservation Fellow and co-Director of the US-China Lab for Destination Development at Colorado State University. His international multi-disciplinary research on tourism-linked empowerment, poverty alleviation, and destination resilience informs tourism and conservation planning associated with national parks, United Nations Educational, Scientific and Cultural Organization (UNESCO) World Heritage sites, rural regeneration, Chinese tourist behaviour and marine protected areas. Email: david.knight@colostate.edu.

John Koldowski is a researcher devoted to the quantification of the travel dynamics of international visitors to and from destinations in the Asia Pacific region. His involvement with the travel and tourism sector spans more than 35 years and includes positions in the private and public sectors as well as in academia, leading him to work in various states/territories of Australia as well as in Singapore, mainland China and Thailand, where he now resides. Although currently semi-retired, John nonetheless maintains his research interests by serving as a special advisor (research) to the Pacific Asia Travel Association (PATA) and the Mekong Tourism Coordinating Office (MTCO). Email: johnk@patachina.org.

Eric Laws has an MPhil from the University of Surrey, UK, and a PhD from Griffith University, Queensland, Australia. He has retired from full-time academic life. His research interests include tourism service quality, destination management, crisis management and elephant tourism. Eric's publications include nearly 100 journal articles, book chapters and conference papers. *Elephant Welfare in Global Tourism* is Eric's 21st authored or edited book, and his second on elephant tourism. Email: e.laws@runbox.com.

Timothy Lee is a professor and the Vice Dean at Macau University of Science and Technology (MUST) in Macao. He is the Editor-in-Chief of the *International Journal of Tourism Research*, which is listed in the Social Science Citation Index (SSCI) Q1 and A in the Australian Business Deans Council (ABDC). He has published more than 350 research articles in academic journals, books and conference proceedings (including 130 in SSCI-indexed journals, and 120 in A*- or A-ranked journals in the ABDC). He has also hosted many international academic conferences in different countries as the chief organizer. His research interests include medical/wellness/health tourism, food tourism, cultural heritage tourism, and tourism development that incorporates local values. His personal website is: www.proftimothylee.org (accessed 4 March 2025). Email: tjlee@must.edu.mo.

Joy Mositi Life PhD is Co-Director of Lijoka International Seminary and Bible College (Lijoka Investment), Botswana, and is currently an adjunct professor at New Convent International University, Miami, Florida, USA. She is a Botswana Qualification Expert, Assessor and Moderator; a counsellor and a marriage officer; and the author of four Christian books. Dr Life co-founded an orphan care programme in Botswana, Motse wa Tsholofelo, and adopted a primary school in Botswana as an initiative to be there as a mother for a girl child to help her discover her desires, fears, dreams and needs, and help her to be a girl of worth. Previously, Dr Life was Senior visiting Scholar at Central China Normal University, 2017–2018. She gained her PhD in developmental and educational psychology from Central China Normal University, 2009–2012. Email: lifejoy@gmail.com.

Stacy J. Lynn PhD is a social ecologist working at the intersection of people, environment and participatory approaches on issues such as land use change, perceptions of the environment, and sustainable livelihoods and conservation. Her first exposure to human–wildlife conflict was as a US Peace Corps volunteer in Namibia 1994–1996, on weekends working with the Cheetah Conservation Fund. She has continued working in Africa, primarily with pastoralist livestock herding communities in dry rangelands of Tanzania and Kenya. Dr Lynn's work is built on degrees in education, rangeland science and ecology; mixed ecological and social science methods; and core belief in the value of community-engaged participatory approaches to research. Email: stacy.lynn@colostate.edu.

Life Mashumba PhD is currently the Director of Lijoka International Seminary and Bible College (Lijoka Investment), Botswana, and is a Botswana Qualification Expert, an Assessor and Moderator. He is also a counsellor and a marriage officer. Dr Mashumba is Adjunct Professor of New Convent

International University, Miami, Florida, USA. He recently retired from his position as a senior lecturer at Tonota College of Education offering educational psychology. Previously he was a senior research scholar at Tsinghua University, China, 2012–2013; and a senior research scholar at Duquesne University, Pittsburgh, Pennsylvania, USA, 2019–2020. Dr Mashumba obtained his PhD in educational and developmental psychology at Shandong Normal University, China, and an additional PhD in intercultural studies in the USA. Email: lifemashumbabw@gmail.com.

Kerri McCrea is the manager and co-founder of Kindred Spirit Elephant Sanctuary and Foundation in northern Thailand. Driven by her passion for wildlife conservation and animal welfare, she founded the organization to give captive elephants a more natural life while supporting the local communities that surround them. Kerri is committed to promoting ethical elephant tourism and sustainable practices. Holding a bachelor's degree in zoology, she has spent her life working closely with animals. Under her leadership, the foundation provides a natural habitat for elephants and educates visitors and volunteers on the importance of their protection. Email: kselephantsanctuary@gmail.com.

Laura Peoples is the Research and Intern Coordinator at Kindred Spirit Elephant Sanctuary and Foundation. She is dedicated to providing a better life for animals in captivity, promoting positive animal well-being and engaging in sustainable wildlife conservation. She graduated with a bachelor's degree in zoology and later went on to study for a master's degree in ethology with a strong focus on elephant behaviour and cognition with field work in South Africa. Email: laurapeoples5@gmail.com.

Galamoyo Pije is a mature hard-working team player trained in customer service. She works as secretary of the Sustainable Elephant and Ecosystem Community Collaborative in Maitengwe, Botswana, where they work in general maintenance projects, developing visitor attractions, and wildlife observation with an understanding of GIS (Geographic Information System). She acts as liaison for this author team (Chapter 7, this volume) with Maitengwe and the surrounding communities. Email: galamoyopije@gmail.com.

Bongkosh Rittichainuwat, PhD, MH, BA, CIS, CEM, EMD, is director of hotel and tourism management at Siam University, Thailand, where she was the former dean of the International College. Dr Rittichainuwat is secretary of the Asia-Pacific Council on Hotel, Restaurant, and Institutional Education (APacCHRIE) where she served as the director of research (two terms) and director of marketing. She received her bachelor's degree (BA) from Chulalongkorn University, her master's degree in hospitality management from Conrad N. Hilton College, University of Houston, and her PhD in hospitality administration from Oklahoma State University. Her industry designations include an exhibition management degree from the UFI University of Cooperative Education in Ravensburg, Germany, the designation Certified Incentive Specialist (CIS) from the Society for Incentive Travel Excellence, and the designation Certified in Exhibition Management (CEM) from the International Association of Exhibitions and Events. Email: ngamson@gmail.com.

Noel Scott, PhD is Adjunct Professor of Tourism Management in the Centre for Tourism Research, Edith Cowan University, Western Australia, Australia and the Sustainable Research Centre, University of Sunshine Coast, Queensland. He is also a Visiting Professor at Mataram University, Lombok, Indonesia and Taylor's University, Malaysia. His research interests include the study of tourism experiences, and destination management and marketing. He is a frequent speaker at academic and industry conferences. He has over 300 academic publications including 21 books. He has supervised 30 doctoral students to successful completion of their theses. He is on the Editorial Board of 10 journals, a member of the International Association of China Tourism Scholars and a Fellow of the Council for Australasian Tourism and Hospitality Education. Email: n.scott@ecu.edu.au.

Yuchen Ti was a chief instructor on Florida International University's Marriott Tianjin China Program. She obtained her master's degree in hospitality and tourism management from Florida International University in 2013 and obtained her professional diploma in culinary arts from the Ferrandi Institute, Paris in 2015. She has been a PhD candidate in hospitality and tourism management at Macau University of Science and Technology from 2022. She has 5 years' work experience in Europe in fine-dining restaurants such as Restaurant Café de la Paix in Paris and the 3-star Michelin restaurant, Guy Savoy. She was awarded a still wine certification by the Wine & Spirit Education Trust (WSET) in China in 2020. Email: 3220005362@student.must.edu.mo.

Daniel Turner is an environmental biologist who has been working for the advancement of applied animal welfare and nature protection for over 25 years. Taking a more pragmatic approach to the challenges that face the natural world, he has created and led initiatives that have influenced international policy and national legislation, tourism sector standards and best practice guidance. Recognized as a leading figure in animal protection in tourism, in 2018, Daniel co-founded and is Director of ANIMONDIAL, a specialist consultancy supporting tourism businesses on all animal and nature protection matters. Daniel advocates an animal-friendly, nature-positive future, where tourism is part of the solution (more information is available at: https://animondial.com/ (accessed 24 February 2025)). He is also co-creator and author of *Nature Positive Travel & Tourism* (2022, World Travel & Tourism Council) and co-creator and author of the Association of British Travel Agent's (ABTA) *Animal Welfare Guidelines* (2019, 2nd edn). Email: daniel@animondial.com.

Rebecca Winkler is a sociocultural anthropology PhD candidate at the University of Pennsylvania, USA whose research centres on human–elephant relations in northern Thailand. As a visiting scholar at Chiang Mai University (2022–2023) she conducted 16 months of ethnographic and archival fieldwork in Thailand, funded by the Wenner-Gren Foundation. Rebecca collaborates with Thai and Karen scholars at Chiang Mai University, Payap University, Chiang Mai Rajabhat University and non-governmental organization (NGO) collaborators from the Mahouts Elephant Foundation and Indigenous North

West (INW). In Philadelphia she serves as the administrator for the Karen community Association of Philadelphia (KCAP) as a Provost's Academic Engagement Fellow with the Netter Center for Community Partnerships. Email: rwinkler@sas.upenn.edu.

Melody Zhirui Zhou is a PhD candidate in tourism management and a research assistant to Professor Timothy Lee at Macau University of Science and Technology (MUST). Her research spans sustainable tourism, cultural heritage, wellness tourism innovation and wildlife tourism ethics, with a particular focus on animal welfare. She has published in leading Social Science Citation Index (SSCI)-indexed journals such as *Tourism Review*, and serves as a reviewer for the SSCI Q1 journal *International Journal of Tourism Research*. Actively participating in international conferences, Melody is recognized for her interdisciplinary scholarship, growing influence and dedication to advancing research in the field. Email: zhou-zhirui_0213@163.com.

Jing Zhuo was awarded a master's degree in risk management from the University of New South Wales, Australia. He completed his bachelor's degree in hospitality management from Florida International University (FIU). He actively works as a teaching assistant in the Faculty of Hospitality Management at FIU at the Tianjin University of Commerce (TUC) FIU campus in Tianjin, China. His research interests include health and wellness tourism, food tourism and creative tourism. Email: JingZhuo.Aidan@outlook.com.

Foreword

PETER SEMONE

Chairman of the Pacific Asia Travel Association

In 1989 while backpacking through Asia, I travelled to northern Thailand where I participated in a multi-day jungle adventure, which included riding a pachyderm named Bintang. Little did I know that tourists riding elephants would become a frowned upon activity.

That same year, the Thai government banned elephants working in the logging industry, forcing their owners and mahouts to find alternative sources of income to meet the expenses of keeping an elephant, which consumes 150–300 kg of food a day, costs about US$18,000 a year to look after and can live up to 70 years and more.

The tourism industry offered a solution to the dilemma of how to afford to care for an elephant. Camps sprouted across Thailand and proved a lucrative business with one of the highest margins in travel. Today, it is estimated that a venue with 50 elephants, welcoming 500 visitors a day paying 1000 baht per person, can earn as much as US$441 a month with total expenditure of just U$165.

Unfortunately, living conditions in camps were often poor, and images and videos showing mistreatment of elephants were circulated on social media networks causing outrage among tourists. Animal welfare was emerging as an important ethical topic. As a result, some owners of elephant camps took steps to improve the quality level of their respective activities. There were also camps that ceased elephant rides and launched new projects such as walking, bathing or feeding the elephants. As the size of groups visiting the camps decreased, the cost of these activities increased. The shift away from the old circus-type activities provided another level of experience with the elephant, sometimes with closer contact.

Efforts to change tourist behaviour towards elephant riding accelerated in 2010, when World Animal Protection conducted a study titled 'Wildlife on a Tightrope', which researched the welfare of animals used for entertainment in Thailand. In 2016, the Coalition for Ethical Wildlife Tourism was established to advocate for observation-only tourist attractions and it drives industry standards and government legislation to better protect wild animals. Ultimately, the goal is to educate consumers on how to have the most responsible and rewarding elephant experience while on holiday.

In October 2016 TripAdvisor launched its 'no touching of wild animals' policy, no longer selling tickets to attractions where travellers came into physical contact with captive, wild or endangered animals including elephants.

The topic of elephants in tourism is a complex one. Asian elephants are an important part of Asian culture and religion, and are featured in many stories, parables and religious traditions. Communities across Asia seeking blessings still make offerings to elephants in religious ceremonies at temples or major festivals. The elephant is the national symbol of Thailand, symbolizing wealth, wisdom and auspiciousness. White elephants are the most sacred creatures and symbolize the power of the royal family. In Hindu cosmology, the Earth is supported and guarded by elephants and the god Ganesha has the head of an elephant. Unlike many wild animals, elephants possess emotional intelligence and a knack for social bonding creating a deep connection with humans.

Once common throughout Africa and Asia, elephant populations across the globe have experienced significant declines over the last century. The greatest threat to African elephants is poaching for the illegal ivory trade, while Asian elephant populations are most at risk from habitat loss and resulting human–elephant conflict.

Asian elephants once roamed across most of Asia, now they are restricted to just 15% of their original range, in a number of fragmented and isolated populations around South and South-east Asia. Today, there are fewer than 50,000 Asian elephants left in the wild. They are also listed as endangered species on the International Union for Conservation of Nature (IUCN) Red List. This does not include the population of captive elephants that are assumed to live in captive or semi-wild conditions and are typically used for logging, village work, tourism or temple purposes. According to another World Animal Protection study titled 'Taken for a Ride', Thailand has more captive elephants (4400) than wild elephants (2500–3200) and the highest number of elephants in tourism (2200). With 30,711 wild and 3000–4000 captive animals, India has by far the largest number of elephants in Asia with around 350 used in tourism.

Unfortunately, there is little cohesive wildlife tourism policy in the Asia–Pacific region. Enforcement is also challenging, particularly as wildlife conservation and tourism may fall under the jurisdiction of different ministries, involving slow coordination processes. One noteworthy initiative is the Asian Captive Elephant Standards (ACES), which collaborates with the governments, the tourism sector and elephant owners to raise the standard of welfare, safety and management of elephants living under human care across South-east Asia. Guided by standards and online training, the programme provides accreditation to elephant camps, which in turn gives peace of mind to visitors.

Since 2015, the Pacific Asia Travel Association (PATA) has participated in raising awareness and encouraging dialogue about elephants and tourism, and continues to advocate for a balanced approach that considers the economic realities of caring for a domesticated elephant, the difficulty of sending it back to the wild, and the need for animal welfare. Working alongside initiatives like ACES, PATA will continue to work across its member countries in Asia to inspire collaboration and partnership between elephant managers/owners, elephant experts, non-governmental organizations (NGOs), Destination Management Organizations (DMOs) and tour operators to identify locally appropriate ways of improving conditions for elephants. If elephants were given limited hours and a limited payload, maybe only two people, limited numbers of days a week and weeks in a year, and they are managed well and looked after the best way possible, including improving their saddlery, elephant riding can be sustainable and positive for the elephant, the owner, the mahout and the visitor.

At the end of the day, the most important challenge is to avoid at all cost the total extinction of elephants. Otherwise, we must respond to David Attenborough's question, 'Are we happy to suppose that our grandchildren may never be able to see an elephant except in a picture book?' This book is one more step to avoiding that sad scenario.

Glossary

Many words and phrases are used to describe the different aspects of elephant management and care. This can result in confusion and a lack of clarity, particularly when elephant affairs are being discussed at international meetings or in publications. The editors of this book recognize the importance of local terminology, but in the interests of consistency and ease of reading *Elephant Welfare in Global Tourism* we have adopted consistent terms throughout this text as noted here:

ABTA
The Association of British Travel Agents. Issued a set of guidelines for elephant tourism companies, revised in 2019.

Angkus or ankus *see Hook*

Anguli
The finger or two fingers, at the end of an elephant's trunk.

ASEAN
The Association of Southeast Asian Nations (ASEAN), was established in 1967 by the Founding Fathers of ASEAN, namely Indonesia, Malaysia, the Philippines, Singapore and Thailand. Among its objectives is to accelerate the economic growth, social progress and cultural development in the region through joint endeavours to strengthen the foundation for a prosperous and peaceful community of South-east Asian Nations. More information is available at: https://asean.org/about-asean (accessed 26 February 2025).

Breaking *see Phajaan*

Bush knife
A long heavy machete used to cut food for the elephant, clear pathways or cut firewood for the mahout. A bush knife is only used to control the elephant when the hook is dropped or in emergencies where human life is in danger.

Calf
A very young elephant that has not learned to use its trunk. It is protected by the maternal herd; male calves become increasingly independent from 5 years of age, but in the wild, females usually remain in the maternal herd.

Camp, also sanctuary or reserve
A place run as a business, which tourists visit to see and interact with captive, rescued or injured conditioned elephants that perform various acts for their entertainment. Camps are usually located in forests. Two philosophies of elephant camp management have been distinguished: (i) anthropocentric elephant camps, the purpose of which is to profit from tourist interest, but which do little to benefit elephant welfare; and (ii) ecocentric camps, centred on concerns for the elephants' well-being.

Captive elephants
It is incorrect to say that elephants are domesticated animals. They have seldom been bred in captivity and therefore do not exhibit attributes selected for human purposes, in contrast to species such as cattle or dogs. The correct term is captive, as they are taken by force from the wild.

Chair
A heavy steel structure mounted on an elephant's back over a thick pad and upholstered for two tourists to sit on in order to ride the elephant, led by a mahout. Chairs are usually locally made. They can cause lesions, and by wearing them for an entire day an elephant's spine may be damaged. Some camps now use lighter plastic chairs.

CITES
Convention on International Trade in Endangered Species, an international agreement to regulate trade in ivory, skins and other products from wild animals by killing them and endangering the survival of species. More information is available at: https://www.cites.org (accessed 26 February 2025).

Conditioned elephant
A captive elephant which has been trained to be safe with tourists, and to perform various unnatural acts to amuse them, such as playing football, playing musical instruments and painting. Conditioned elephants command a premium price in the inter-camp market. The phrase conditioned elephant was introduced by Daniel Turner and Naut Kusters in 2021:

Turner, D. and Kusters, N. (2021) The paradox of elephant-friendly tourism. In: Laws, E., Scott, N., Font, X. and Koldowski, J. (eds) *The Elephant Tourism Business*. CAB International, Wallingford UK, pp. 259–268. DOI: 10.1079/9781789245868.0259.

Crush
A strong, tight enclosure used to restrain an elephant either during phajaan or as a safety measure when performing veterinary procedures such as trimming their toenails.

Ear halter
A small piece of iron shaped like a fishhook and fastened over the base of the ear with light rope. It is used to lead elephants and also, for very short periods of time, to tether them.

ETV
An Elephant Tourism Venue. These include National or other parks, camps, or entertainment centres. The emphasis is on visitor enjoyment and elephant-themed activities, in contrast with sanctuaries which focus on the welfare of elephants.

HARS
Human–Animal Relations. Scientific studies of human–animal relationships are being developed to better understand the effectiveness of various attempts to improve living conditions for animals (including elephants) as human populations continue to increase and natural habitat is put under increasing pressure by modern technologies.

HEC
Human Elephant Conflict. Negative interactions can arise from close proximity between humans moving intro elephants' traditional ranges, new infrastructure and industrialised agriculture. Injury or death can result but the ill effects can be mitigated by programmes designed to facilitate co-existence.

Hobbles
Rope or steel hobbles are fitted to an elephant's front feet to make it stay still, to slow it down, or to ensure that it cannot cross over broad objects or obstacles. Sometimes hobbles are used to prevent elephants from mating. They can be used on their own or attached to tethering chains.

Hook (angkus or ankus)
A short stick with a sharp, finger-length metal hook at the tip, used to control and direct captive elephants. Experienced mahouts use light pressure to guide the elephant, but inexperienced mahouts tend to hit the elephant with the point if it does not respond quickly enough but this can cause injuries. Mahouts always carry a hook, as elephants are unpredictable.

Howdah
A seat or covered pavilion traditionally placed over a thick pad used to ride on the back of an elephant while hunting animals such as tigers or used in ceremonial events.

Mahout
The trainer, keeper or driver of an elephant who usually walks beside it or sits on its neck. Traditionally, mahouts came from ethnic groups with generations of elephant-keeping experience, and one mahout kept his elephant throughout its working life.

Musth
Adult bull elephants (males) annually cycle between a state of heightened aggressiveness, called musth, and one of non-musth. During the musth cycle the bull elephant is primed to mate, and will fight other male elephants, attack other animals, and sometimes destroy inanimate objects in its way. Visitors are usually kept well away from bull elephants in musth for safety reasons.

PATA
Founded in 1951, the Pacific Asia Travel Association (PATA) is a not-for-profit association that is internationally acclaimed for acting as a catalyst for the responsible development of travel and tourism to, from and within the Asia–

Pacific region. Its member organizations comprise government, state and city tourism bodies, international airlines and airports, hospitality organizations, educational institutions, and hundreds of travel industry companies in the Asia–Pacific region and beyond. Thousands of travel professionals also belong to one (or more) of the 36 local PATA chapters worldwide.

Phajaan, also crush

Phajaan is both a ceremony and a process. The 'ceremony' of phajaan is said to originate in the belief that a tribe's shaman can separate the spirit of an elephant from its body, in effect driving the willful and wild spirit out of an elephant and leaving it under the control of its mahouts.

As a process, it involves people gaining control over elephants by their 'breaking-in'. Traditionally this involved harsh methods such as beatings administered to a young elephant roped in a crush to strong posts and deprived of sleep until it accepts a man riding on its back. Modern training methods are more cooperative and reward based but this potentially leaves the mahout without the ability to control an elephant in an emergency, therefore most camps that allow visitors to be close to elephants also require the handler to carry a hook for reasons of safety. More information is available from Kontogeorgopoulos (2019):

Kontogeorgopoulos, N. (2019). *Making the Best of a Bad Situation. Southeast Asia and Environmental Sustainability in Context*. (pp. 49–64). Lexington Books London.

Range countries

Countries with wild elephant populations. The Asian Elephant Range States Meeting (AsERSM) 2017 attracted delegates from all 13 Asian range countries. In sub-Saharan Africa, there are ten range countries.

Reserve

A large area of prime or secondary forest such as a national park in which wild elephants and other animals are constrained, managed and protected from poachers in near-natural ecological conditions. Tourists can visit to observe them but usually no interaction is permitted.

Rewilding

A conservation philosophy based on cores and corridors. A third feature is to maintain a natural balance by introducing or reintroducing predators. The management of wilderness areas is minimized but monitoring is emphasized, and interpreted scientifically. Local residents are encouraged to participate in rewilding schemes.

Sanctuary

A camp or reserve which specializes in treating injured elephants whether wild or captured. Visitors are welcome at some, as they help to defray their costs.

Tethering

Unless they are corralled in a stockade, elephants are tethered at night to strong trees on chains about 30 m long, allowing them to graze much as they would in the wild, but separating them from other elephants. When a camp has sufficient space, elephants are tethered in a different place every night, allowing the first area to recover.

Introduction

Bongkosh Rittichainuwat*

Siam University, Bangkok, Thailand

This book, *Elephant Welfare in Global Tourism*, aims to create better understanding about welfare for Asian and African elephants. Authors from multiple disciplines have shared their expertise and experiences about elephant welfare. Readers should benefit from learning about contrasting ideas about elephant welfare. Specifically, while this book was being prepared, debates in Germany and the UK about the ban on the import of body parts of elephants hunted for trophies were ongoing. Fortunately, Masisi who supports the sales of a licence for wildlife trophy hunting in Botswana ended his term as president. We hope that the new president of Botswana, elected on 1 November 2024, will discontinue the cruel practice.

Elephant welfare is not just a problem for a particular country, it is a global issue. Elephants and other wild animals share the same planet as humans. Hence, they have a right to live instead of being sold as commodities or executed. Therefore, we hope to see progress to improve elephant welfare in the tourism industry by igniting and spreading understanding of responsible elephant tourism.

The welfare of individual elephants, or of matriarchal herds also has to be considered in the light of the increasingly fast extinction of many animals, birds, fish, insects and plants. Extinctions and the rise of new species have been common since the first cells appeared (Kauffman, 2011). But in the 50 millenia since human contact, and particularly since the Industrial Revolution (Burney and Flannery, 2005), the ability of humans to eradicate species has increased to the extent that we may now be witnessing a sixth mass extinction.

This book consists of four sections. Section 1 raises issues about the problems of human–elephant interactions. In Chapter 1, Laws, Scott and Koldowski introduce the problems of human–elephant interactions and describe the definitions of welfare and exploitation to guide readers about the scope of the book. Asian elephants (*Elephas maximus*) benefit local communities in South and South-east Asia and in some parts of southern China when they have been used during wars, logging, tourist and religious activities. Unfortunately, they have been exploited because of their intelligence and have been forced to work for humans. Now, awareness of elephants' sentience is becoming more widely understood, specifically, when social media shows videos about the elephant taming procedure, 'the phajaan' (Thai: ผ่าจ้าน). This is when elephants are deprived of food and water and are caged in restricted areas to generate fear, depression and confusion for a few weeks, dependent on the time taken for them to surrender to human control. Then, a mahout appears as a hero to unchain them, giving them food and water. This method is cunning, deceiving animals into submission. Such practice is not considered to be wise but evil, when knowledge and experience is used in exploiting animals. Similar to the phajaan, which is related to *Schadenfreude* (pleasure from seeing others' suffer), elephant hunting for trophies and the sales of licences for such practices is a business of *Schadenfreude* as evidenced by the hunt for trophies of African savannah elephants (*Loxodonta africana*) and African forest elephants (*Loxodonta cyclotis*). Although there is support from some local residents and the authorities in Botswana and Namibia to control the overpopulation of wild elephants, such activity is a form of dark tourism derived mainly from *Schadenfreude* (Rittichainuwat, 2008). More importantly, such practice reaps benefits for such tourism operators in the form of retaliation hunting, which takes place following a raid by wild elephants causing damage and death, and this can lead to escalated human–elephant conflict.

Section 2 of the book describes conservation challenges and solutions. To illustrate, Baker and her co-authors point out in Chapter 3 the complexity of foraging behaviour, illustrating best practice by Karen mahouts in allowing tamed elephants to roam freely for forage in the forest near the human communities. Baker also presents research about six elephants that were observed during their voluntary foraging. The result showed that the elephants have a variety of diets that varies depending on the season. Meanwhile, freedom to forage enhances elephant well-being. Such information calls for the need for a diversity of diets for captive elephants. Similar to humans, individual elephants differ in terms of their favourite forage. Thus, elephant welfare is not only limited to the condition of the living space but also the quality and variety of foods available. Chalermchaikit (Chapter 2) describes the difference in perception of elephant welfare between men and women. She also proposes a triple bottom line model on gender perspectives on sustainable elephant tourism. Ashton (Chapter 4) presents a case study of Chitwan National Park in Nepal where elephants are used as a therapeutic means to enhance human well-being. Based on her field study at the park, she emphasizes positive human–elephant interactions as a sustainable way to support elephant welfare.

Section 3 analyses the human and elephant conflict. Zhou and Lee (Chapter 5) present a case study of the Xishuangbanna National Nature Reserve in south-western China as an alternative to save elephants from being killed by the outrage of villagers whose crops were damaged by elephants. The case study uses actor–network theory as a theoretical framework in creating a mutual interdependence model for human–elephant interaction. Likewise, Zhuo, Lee and Ti (Chapter 6) discuss historical anecdotes in which elephants have been used in religious ceremonies in India, China, Thailand and Sri Lanka. Unfortunately, the elephants were also used as a sacrifice in the Yin and Shang dynasties of ancient China and to display wealth for some people, but not all Chinese people value this concept. Together with the World Wide Fund for Nature (WWF), the Chinese government promotes elephant conservation through conservation of habitat such as Xishuangbanna's Wild Elephant Valley where tourists can observe elephants from a distance. Similarly, Mashumba *et al.* (Chapter 7) report another case study in Botswana where local communities rely on elephants as a source of income in exchange for retaliation hunting. In Chapter 8, Laws and Butler discuss the consequences of the coronavirus disease 2019 (COVID-19) pandemic on elephant tourism. Although elephant tourism remains the main support for the local economy in several countries, the lockdown caused by the COVID-19 pandemic led to loss of income for elephant tourism venues (ETVs) resulting in poor living conditions for captive elephants. Yet, the absence of tourists relieved the stress for the elephants working in the tourism industry. Moreover, during the COVID-19 period, national parks became a preferable social-distancing attraction for tourists. Unlike private elephant camps, 'national parks are a designated protected landscape for wildlife' (Pringle, 2017 cited in Suresh *et al.*, 2022, p. 2), and revenue generated from tourist admission fees can be invested in park conservation and compensate farmers whose crops were destroyed by elephants (Suresh *et al.*, 2022).

In Section 4, concerning regulation and legislation, Ashby (Chapter 9) argues that regulation of elephant welfare should not be based on tourist perceptions but rely on the expertise of veterinarians and mahouts due to discrepancy between legal provisions and on-the-ground realities. For instance, the Asian Captive Elephant Standards (ACES) was established as an elephant-auditing organization which works with ETVs to respond to changes in legislation affecting the operation of elephant venues. Indeed, some of the ACES guidelines are similar to the UK zoos' captive elephants regulations (discussed in Chapter 12) which aim to be used as universal standards to improve elephant welfare in zoos with limited space. There are alternatives to zoos that increase the living space provided for elephants, such as national parks using tourist income to compensate for the cost. For instance, research found that local and international tourists were willing to pay between US$1 and US$5 to the elephant funds to mitigate the animal–farmer conflict over elephant crop damage (Suresh *et al.*, 2022). Likewise:

> tourists were willing to pay more for the acquisition [of] an extra square kilometre of land for the park - around USD $1 more. In addition, tourists significantly valued the creation of wildlife corridors (USD $1.60) ... tourists are shown to be willing to contribute around USD $1.50 for habitat quality improvement in the national park ... and are prepared to pay a significant sum (USD $2) as compensation to farmers for crop damage caused by wildlife.
>
> (Suresh *et al.*, 2022, p. 16)

Since tourists are the key stakeholders, whose expenditure is critical for elephant welfare, educating tourists about the management of tourist funds to conserve the elephants is necessary. In fact, the use of admission fees and donations from tourists to improve animal welfare is not a new concept. However, some tourists were concerned about the misuse of tourist funds for activities unrelated to elephant preservation. To solve this issue, each ETV should post the annual report to inform the public about the transparency of the tourist funds in conserving the elephant. Such funds are necessary to: (i) increase the size of the national parks as elephant habitats; (ii) build wildlife corridors connecting other national parks to create a trail for elephant migration; (iii) create water ponds to lure elephants to use the wildlife corridors instead of migrating onto farmland; and (iv) compensate farmers whose lands have been invaded by the elephants (Suresh *et al.*, 2022).

National parks are appropriate places for elephant welfare because elephants can freely roam the forests. However, once the national parks become attractions, they became a problem for human and elephant interaction with potential conflict. As the size of the tourist communities increases, the land to be used for national parks decreases. Thus, the elephants have fewer habitats and are often confronted with the residents in competition for land use. Hence, limiting the number of tourists to meet the minimum carrying capacity of the national parks is necessary for sustainable elephant tourism. Construction of wildlife corridors that link dispersed habitat regions also enables elephants to migrate from one park to another (Suresh *et al.*, 2022).

Laws explains the UK regulations and legislation which will be beneficial to elephant welfare. To illustrate, he cites debates in the UK Parliament about two major changes in British legislation to improve elephant welfare at tourist venues. The Animals (Low-Welfare Activities Abroad) Act 2023 (discussed in Chapter 10) boycotts advertising direct contact between tourists and elephants and circus-elephant activities abroad to prevent cruelty in the taming and training procedures of wild and captive elephants. In Chapter 11 the Hunting Trophies (Import Prohibition) Bill, which is currently under debate, is discussed; it creates public awareness about the sales of licences in countries such as Botswana for hunting wild animals for fun. These two pieces of legislation alert global communities about cruelty towards elephants and call for the end of these tourist activities that are harmful to elephants. For example, the Association of British Travel Agents (ABTA) issued guidance to its outbound tour operators to comply with the bills. Under these pressures, elephant camps in Thailand changed from circus activities towards becoming sanctuaries. Likewise, videos about the abusive taming procedure have been posted on social media platforms such as YouTube by some British tourists and non-governmental organizations (NGOs) to boycott the mistreatment of elephants by making them play football and sit on a chair with their front legs lifted. Due to rising public awareness about the maltreatment of elephants, leading tourist suppliers such as TripAdvisor now boycott attractions which exploit elephants for entertainment. Consequently, some inbound elephant tourist suppliers in Thailand have redesigned their product to meet the requirement of the legislative changes and tourist demand.

Laws' Chapter 12 provides the detailed regulations for captive elephants held in British zoos.

The Conclusion by Campiranon (Chapter 13) presents a review of research about elephant welfare; 1780 articles were published between 1914 and 2022 about global research on elephants (Zakaria *et al.*, 2024 cited by Campiranon in Chapter 13, this volume). Campiranon proposes five themes for future research. The emerging research priorities are: (i) tourist behaviour, education and ethical awareness; (ii) animal welfare literacy among tourist operators; (iii) keeper–animal relationships and human–animal interaction; (iv) impact of tourism on captive elephants and welfare standards; and (v) consensus on ethical practices and conservation strategies. Additionally, Turner (in the Afterword; Chapter 14) calls for the change of practices and public perceptions towards the exploitation of elephants in global communities. He illustrates the case of ANIMONDIAL which promotes multi-stakeholder engagement by providing guidance such as for elephant-viewing practices, and he suggests penalties for ETVs which fail to enhance elephant welfare.

Although *Elephant Welfare in Global Tourism* does not include chapters about other species of wildlife, animals used for tourist consumption such as pangolins and bears, this book is the first step to create awareness about elephant welfare in global tourism. The editors plan to organize an international conference on the welfare of elephants and other kinds of animals used in the tourism industry. We hope to find a solution stemming from the discussion and to disseminate empirical findings to improve the welfare of tourist animals.

Bibliography

Burney, D.A. and Flannery, T.F. (2005) Fifty millennia of catastrophic extinctions after human contact. *Trends in Ecology & Evolution* 20(7), 395–401. DOI: 10.1016/j.tree.2005.04.022.

Kauffman, S.A. (2011) Approaches to the origin of life on earth. *Life* 1(1), 34–48. DOI: 10.3390/life1010034.

Rittichainuwat, B.N. (2008) Responding to disaster: Thai and Scandinavian tourists' motivation to visit Phuket, Thailand. *Journal of Travel Research* 46(4), 422–432. DOI: 10.1177/0047287507308321.

Suresh, K., Wilson, C., Quayle, A., Managi, S. and Khanal, U. (2022) Can a tourist levy protect national park resources and compensate for wildlife crop damage? An empirical investigation. *Environmental Development* 42: 100697. DOI: 10.1016/j.envdev.2022.100697.

Zakaria, N., Juahir, H., Nor, S.M.M., Hanapi, N.H.M., Jusoh, H.H.W. *et al.* (2024) Elephant research challenges and opportunities: a global bibliometric analysis. *Ecological Informatics* 82: 102662. DOI: 10.1016/j.ecoinf.2024.102662.

1 A Problems Analysis of Human–Elephant Interactions

Eric Laws,[1*] Noel Scott[2] and John Koldowski[3]

[1]*retired Professor of Tourism;* [2]*Edith Cowan University, Australia;* [3]*Special Advisor, Pacific Asia Travel Association (PATA)*

Abstract
Elephants face significant contemporary problems, primarily driven by human activities including human population pressure on their natural habitats, intensive industrialized land use often based on monospecies culture, climate change, poaching and hunting. This book documents some effective projects which enhance tourists' enjoyment of temporary proximity to captive elephants, or those living in relative freedom in restricted areas such as national parks. All elephant species are on the International Union for Conservation of Nature (IUCN)'s Red List of Threatened Species. In the early 20th century there were about 12 million African elephants, but by the mid-2020s there were fewer than 400,000. Elephants had probably numbered about a million in the precolonial era in Thailand, but now there are fewer than 40,000. Resolution of human–elephant conflict and promotion of peaceful coexistence requires a simultaneous focusing of management efforts on site-specific considerations and strategic plans at the landscape level.

Introduction[1]

Tourism is part of the problems facing elephants, but elephants face several significant contemporary problems, primarily driven by human activities. Human population pressure on their natural habitats, intensive industrialized land use often based on monospecies agriculture, climate change, poaching, hunting and more all threaten elephants' survival and well-being.

How big is tourism in this context? It is part of the problem but importantly, tourism may be the solution. Is it an essential (necessary and sufficient) part of the future survival of elephants? Tourism provides a crucial interface between humans and elephants, fostering awareness and connection with the species.

*e.laws@runbox.com

DOI: 10.1079/9781836990093.0001

However, for tourism to become a viable conservation tool, it has to be done in a respectful manner (Lee *et al.*, 2024).

> Methodology is the important manifestation of scientific and technological achievements, and symmetrically, problemology is needed by the scientific research community. The problematique is a crucial component of problemology, representing the level of understanding of problems within the scientific research community. Through problematique as a medium, it connects, bridges, and aggregates various links among industry, education, academia, and users, improving the quality and efficiency of institutionalized scientific research.
>
> (Liu and Zhang, 2024, p. 1264)

From this perspective, the research presented in this book documents some effective and encouraging projects which enhance tourists' enjoyment of temporary proximity to captive elephants, or those living in relative freedom in restricted areas such as national parks. But it is increasingly clear that in its present forms, tourism as an industry cannot ensure the survival of endangered Asian and African elephants. Nevertheless, the potential of tourism as a conservation tool has precedent. As seen in whale conservation efforts, tourism has supported whale populations by supporting the survival of whales by enabling tourists to see them close up in their annual migrations past the Australian east coast, an area where they were previously hunted almost to extinction (Scott and Laws, 2013). In this way, if managed ethically and with conservation as a priority, tourism could similarly contribute to protecting elephants, encouraging a model of engagement that respects their ecological and ethical well-being.

This first chapter of *Elephant Welfare in Global Tourism* discusses contexts which frame the ways people understand the contemporary problems confronting elephants.

Current Elephant Populations

Elephant Welfare in Global Tourism examines the welfare and conservation status of the three remaining elephant species, all of which are listed on the International Union for Conservation of Nature (IUCN) Red List of Threatened Species (IUCN, n.d.; Ritchie, 2024; Zakaria *et al.*, 2024). The IUCN Red List now includes 134,425 species of which 37,480 are threatened with extinction. The African savannah elephant and the Asian elephant are classified as endangered. All species face grave threats, primarily from poaching, which fuels the illegal international ivory trade.

The population of Asian elephants is estimated at 41,410–52,345 individuals scattered among fragmented habitats in 13 range countries in Asia, and currently occupying 5% of their historic geographic range (Sukumar, 2006).

In the early 20th century, Africa was home to approximately 12 million elephants. However, due to human-induced pressures, African elephant populations dwindled to fewer than 400,000 by the mid-2020s (Hauenstein *et al.*, 2022; Reid, 2022; Zakaria *et al.*, 2024). Similarly, Asia's precolonial elephant populations, once numbering close to a million in Thailand alone, suffered drastic declines

(Reid, 2022). The continent had around 100,000 Asian elephants at the start of the 20th century, but today, fewer than 40,000 remain (Hankinson and Nijman, 2020). African elephants are also vulnerable due to habitat fragmentation and lack of protection. The population of African elephants is much larger than Asian elephants; estimated at 550,000–700,000 individuals living in 37 range countries in sub-Saharan Africa. Yet more than 70% of their geographic range is unprotected (Chase *et al.*, 2016; Joshi *et al.*, 2020). This lack of security highlights the urgent need for protective conservation measures to preserve their habitats.

Monitoring the numbers of wild species is very challenging, it poses unique challenges, even for animals as large as elephants. Advanced monitoring methods are being developed to improve accuracy. GPS (Global Positioning System) tracking (Jiang *et al.*, 2021; Jue *et al.*, 2024), camera traps (Chanev *et al.*, 2023), drones (Linchant *et al.*, 2015), elephants' own seismic 'rumbles' (Reinwald *et al.*, 2021), and satellite image analysis from low Earth orbit (Duporge *et al.*, 2021) are among the innovative tools employed to gather reliable data on elephant populations and movement patterns.

Current Problems for Elephants

Poaching and the ivory trade

Despite international bans, elephants continue to be poached for their tusks, with ivory sold illegally on black markets. This has led to a dramatic decline in elephant populations, where more than 70% of their geographic range remains unprotected. In the remaining 30% of their range, elephants are generally kept on reserves or elephant tourism venues (ETVs) for their protection, to provide them with veterinary attention following an injury, or when calves are separated from their maternal herd.

Other body parts

Beyond tusks, elephants are also killed for their skin, bones and other body parts, which are used in traditional medicine and as luxury items (Challender *et al.*, 2023), despite the protection afforded by the Convention on International Trade in Endangered Species (CITES) (Bodansky *et al.*, 2008).

Habitat loss and fragmentation

Large-scale deforestation for agriculture, logging and expanding human settlements continues to erode elephant habitats. This habitat loss forces elephants into smaller, fragmented areas with increasingly restricted varieties of fodder, a critical need given their daily intake of approximately 150 kg of food (see Chapter 3, this volume).

> Preserving natural habitats and the wildlife species that depend on them is crucial for generating and maintaining ecosystem services, which provide long-term benefits to humans and the environment. However, conservation efforts can also lead to unintended burdens and disturbances that extend beyond the missed opportunities to exploit natural resources in these habitats.
>
> (Ba *et al.*, 2023)

Similar problems are widespread, but each area differs according to local tradition and contemporary developments, resulting in contrasting scenarios of land use and conflict, as illustrated by the Nepalese Kahalle and Yala projects, discussed here as drawn from Fernando *et al.* (2005).

Kahalle was developed and settled under the Mahaweli irrigation project and the main agricultural practice was irrigated agriculture, with two annual growing seasons. The area was a mosaic of settlements, agriculture and small forest patches with ill-defined human- and elephant-use areas. Elephants ranged within the habitat mosaic year round, occupying remnant forest patches and raiding adjacent crops at night.

In contrast, Yala's land use is more structured, with a large protected area complex and clear segregation between human and elephant zones. Here, slash-and-burn agriculture and rain-fed paddy cultivation prevail, with the protected area providing a seasonal refuge and food source for elephants. Human- and elephant-use areas were well defined and segregated. The protected area provided elephants with a refuge and food during the rainy season, when the single annual crop was grown. During the dry season, elephants moved into slash-and-burn areas and utilized leftover crops and pioneer vegetation in fallow fields.

The land-use pattern and agricultural practices in Yala facilitated coexistence, whereas that in Kahalle led to year-round conflict. Fernanado *et al.* (2005) suggest that areas managed according to traditional land-use practices should be part of an elephant conservation strategy, where people and elephants have to share resources. This contrast illustrates that traditional land-use practices, when thoughtfully managed, can support elephant conservation by creating spaces where humans and elephants can share resources more sustainably.

Infrastructure development

Infrastructure expansion, including the development of roads, railways and urban areas, has transformed and fragmented natural habitats. This expansion disrupts traditional elephant migration routes and leads to increased instances of human–elephant conflict as elephants encounter human settlements more frequently (Pai *et al.*, 2024).

Crop raiding

As their natural habitats decrease, elephants are forced to seek food outside their traditional ranges, increasingly venturing into agricultural areas. This crop raiding often results in significant damage to crops, leading to conflict with local farmers. In some cases, farmers retaliate by harming or killing elephants (Kiffner *et al.*, 2021).

Fatal encounters

The intensification of human–elephant conflict can result in injuries or fatalities of both humans and elephants. Farmers attempting to protect their land may resort to extreme measures, such as shooting, poisoning or electrocuting elephants to safeguard their livelihoods (Natarajan *et al.*, 2023). Local news media report the deaths of elephants trying to cross busy roads or railways (Ahmed *et al.*, 2022).

Climate change and food availability

Climate change plays a crucial role in shaping the ecosystems that sustain elephants. Changes in vegetation distribution and growth patterns, influenced by shifting climate conditions, often force elephants to migrate in search of food, potentially leading to further habitat conflict (Bai *et al.*, 2022).

Water scarcity

Droughts and fluctuating rainfall patterns, exacerbated by climate change, reduce the availability of fresh water in elephant habitats. Elephants rely on traditional paths to access water sources, but scarcity can lead to dehydration and even death (Bucciarelli *et al.*, 2024).

Illegal logging and land use change

Illegal logging contributes to habitat destruction, often making previously inaccessible areas vulnerable to poaching. Logging can also lead to soil erosion, especially in steep mountain regions, increasing the risk of floods that further endanger both habitats and human settlements (Herse *et al.*, 2024).

Tourism and human disturbance

While tourism provides financial support for elephant conservation, it also introduces stress factors. Of the estimated 550,000 elephants used in the tourism industry, only around 13,000 are maintained under welfare-promoting conditions (Moorhouse *et al.*, 2015; Manning *et al.*, 2023). Close human–elephant interactions can provoke stress responses in both wild and captive populations (Szott *et al.*, 2020). Poorly managed tourism can lead to disruptions in elephant behaviour, increased stress and heightened risk of human–elephant conflict

(Sadashige, 2024). Elephants communicate with each other by trumpeting, rumbling and other sounds. Human activities like mining, construction and traffic contribute to noise pollution, which can disturb elephants' communication and increase their stress levels (Mawatha and Lanka, 2022).

Disease

Elephants are increasingly exposed to diseases transmitted by domestic animals and humans. Notably, tuberculosis has been identified in both captive and wild populations (Pandit *et al.*, 2024; Prudence *et al.*, 2024).

Captive elephant issues

The welfare of captive elephants remains a serious concern. Elephants kept for entertainment, tourism or labour are often subjected to conditions that may lead to physical and psychological distress (Warwick *et al.*, 2023).

Conservation breeding challenges

Conservation breeding programmes face difficulties, including maintaining genetic diversity and ensuring the well-being of elephants in non-natural environments (Budd, 2023).

An Abbreviated History of Human Exploitation of Elephants

Exploitation is defined as 'the act of using someone unfairly for your own advantage' (Cambridge Dictionary, n.d.). Exploitation includes using elephants for commercial gain in ETVs, subsistence, or in the interests of animal welfare, conservation or control.

> The means by which it is carried out can be consumptive, either permanently removing animals from the population by hunting or live-trapping or harvesting products from wild individuals under management regimes, such as musk from captive wild Indian civets. Exploitation also involves non-consumptive (non-lethal) enterprises such as ecotourism. The effects of exploitation on animals in terms of their welfare can be marginal or extreme, but in most cases, improvements are possible, and further research is essential.
>
> (Taylor and Dunstone, 1996)

Elephants have been exploited throughout recorded history by humans for their strength, particularly in battle, in displays of a ruler's power, in dragging trees out of forests, and more recently as entertainers. Accurate assessments of their welfare are crucial in ensuring optimum husbandry practices in captive populations (Turner and Kusters, 2021).

The barbarity of slaughters in the Roman arenas reveals one of the outstanding paradoxes of the Roman people. While being so much alive to the interest and beauty of the animal kingdom, they took pleasure in the suffering and agonizing death of its most impressive species. Cicero, Seneca and Plutarch protested, but unsuccessfully. As for the onlookers, the first and last public protest recorded in the ancient tradition occurred in 55 BC during the great show given by Pompey which turned into the killing of about 20 elephants (Scullard, 1974).

An encyclopedia of elephant care had already been developed in India. Ayurveda has its foundations in the ancient schools of Hindu philosophical teachings (Jaiswal and Williams, 2017). Elephant management, training, illness and healing have been studied throughout elephant captivity. The elephant Ayurveda was written by the sage Palakapya in the fifth century BC, based on Hindu lore dating back to the era of the Mahabharata (*c.*5000 BC) (Jaiswal and Williams, 2017).

Hastyayurveda is one of the more prominent ancient texts on elephant management. Written in Sanskrit, it is based on the fundamental principles of Ayurveda. The book deals with several aspects of the elephant, including its anatomy, behaviour, diseases, surgical treatments, management, breeding, capture, musth and training. The *Hastyayurveda* also describes the characteristic features of a good elephant and a good mahout (Balasubrahmanian, 2014).

Matanga Lila is a treatise in Sanskrit dealing with the life and behaviour of elephants, the taming and training of elephants, and also the anatomy and zoological features of elephants.

Elephants were hunted and traded to Ancient Egypt and to the Classical Greco-Roman world for ivory, entertainment and military purposes.

> The full study of elephants requires diverse multidisciplinary research on their evolution, taxonomy, extinction, climate change, the history of human-elephant interactions, and modern issues relating to elephant and ivory policy. This regional view of the past illuminates some of the deep roots of these modern issues in human-elephant relations.
>
> (Lobban Jr and de Liedekerke, 2000)

Elephants have also been used as symbols of good will, gifted by one country to another as a demonstration of international friendship. In Thai culture, elephants hold deep symbolic and spiritual significance, particularly white elephants, which are viewed as sacred and auspicious. This cultural reverence has extended to diplomatic practices, with Thai monarchs often presenting elephants as diplomatic gifts to strengthen international relationships. Such Thai monarchs, particularly the late King Bhumibol Adulyadej, presented elephants as gifts to other nations; for example in 1960 two white elephants were gifted to Japan. The symbolic gesture of the white elephant carries significant cultural and religious importance in Thailand (Grossman and Faulder, 2011), including the promotion of Thai culture, underscoring the importance of elephant conservation, and fostering diplomatic ties. The exchange of elephants in diplomacy is comparable to China's current 'panda diplomacy', which dates back to the Tang dynasty (618–907 CE; Leira and Neumann, 2017).

More recently captive elephants kept in zoos have also been exploited. For example, Honolulu Zoo, like many others, uses elephants in marketing gimmicks, such as picking the winner of the Super Bowl, and in zookeeper demonstrations. In these demonstrations, the elephants can be observed engaging in stress and trauma behaviours, such as rocking and swaying. Captive elephants are often seen engaging in these 'stereotypic behaviours' to cope with their stress, and these behaviours are not seen in elephants living freely in the wild.

With respect to Honolulu Zoo, the Nonhuman Rights Project has filed a lawsuit seeking to have the rights to liberty of Mari and Vaigai – two female Asian elephants gifted to the zoo – recognized, and for them to be released to an elephant sanctuary where they can exercise their autonomy, have opportunities to make social connections with other elephants, and have their physical and psychological needs met (Holden, 2023). Until a renovation in 2011, when the exhibit was expanded to 1.5 acres, they were held in an area that was less than 0.2 acres. Their exhibit not only restricts their autonomy – it has also been cited for multiple health and safety violations. A 2016 report from the Association of Zoos and Aquariums (AZA) revealed that the exhibit lacked adequate shade to keep the elephants out of direct sunlight, that it had rocks that posed danger to the elephants' feet, and that the elephants' water supply wasn't properly tested. At the time of writing (August 2024) an online petition to free the Honolulu Zoo elephants and move them to a sanctuary had reached 33,414 signatures (Change.org, n.d.).

Development of Modern Concerns About Elephant Welfare

The welfare of animals in intensive farming systems became a focal point of British government concern in the mid-20th century. In 1965 a UK parliamentary inquiry into the welfare of animals in intensive livestock production systems focused attention on the need for all farmed animals to be able to stand up, lie down, turn around, stretch their limbs and groom themselves – criteria that set the initial standards for humane treatment.

In 1979 the Farm Animal Welfare Council (FAWC) extended this concept to encompass both physical and mental needs of animals, such as avoiding fear and distress and being able to express normal behaviour. What emerged were five separate 'freedoms' which together provided a simple yet holistic way of considering an animal's welfare state. The inclusion of psychological needs was a significant step forward in acknowledging animal sentience. In 1993, the original Five Freedoms were updated with explanatory words on how to meet each freedom (see information available at: https://kb.rspca.org.au/knowledge-base/what-are-the-five-freedoms-of-animal-welfare (accessed 26 February 2025)), summarized in Table 1.1. Practical guidelines were added on how each freedom could be met, enhancing their applicability across various animal welfare settings. These freedoms became a cornerstone of animal welfare policies, particularly for farm animals, as they were adopted by organizations such as the Royal Society for the Prevention of Cruelty to Animals (RSPCA) in Australia (RSPCA Knowledge Base).

Table 1.1. Captive animal freedoms. From RSPCA, n.d., data used under licence CC-by 4.0.

1. Freedom from hunger and thirst: by ready access to fresh water and a diet to maintain full health and vigour.
2. Freedom from discomfort: by providing an appropriate environment including shelter and a comfortable resting area.
3. Freedom from pain, injury or disease: by prevention through rapid diagnosis and treatment.
4. Freedom to express normal behaviour: by providing sufficient space, proper facilities and company of the animal's own kind.
5. Freedom from fear and distress: by ensuring conditions and treatment which avoid mental suffering.

The Five Freedoms have been influential in shaping the development of evidence-based animal welfare standards. They are internationally recognized and have been referenced countless times by governments, industries and non-governmental organizations (NGOs) in legislation, policy statements, submissions, standards, codes of practice and quality assurance schemes for farm animals. Their simplicity and applicability to all situations of animal production have been fundamental to their success and continued relevance (Webster, 2001).

Animal Sentience

Animal welfare thinking now recognizes animals' emotional needs. Animals need more than just minimizing negative states for them to have a good quality of life, or at the very least, a life worth living (Mellor, 2016).

Although elephants live in matriarchal herds, young bulls naturally live alone or in small temporary groups. But importantly, even in a herd, each elephant is an individual, sentient and worthy of respect (Plotnik and Jacobsen, 2022). Sentient animals have a range of qualities including being socially intelligent and demonstrating empathy towards their fellows (see the information available at: https://www.discovermagazine.com/planet-earth (accessed 25 February 2025)).

Although the Five Freedoms provide a foundation for animal welfare by addressing basic needs and minimizing negative experiences, they do not differentiate between varying levels of harm or the internal and external conditions that contribute to these experiences. A more nuanced approach to animal welfare is necessary – one that systematically evaluates welfare based on sentient animals' capacity to feel both positive and negative emotions (Duncan, 2006).

As Mellor (2016) remarked:

> We understand that they are capable of experiencing positive emotions like joy and excitement. And we also know that they can feel fear, pain, and distress. Recognizing animal sentience isn't a purely theoretical or abstract concept. Accepting that animals feel pain and distress obliges us to reduce their suffering—especially in contexts like factory farming, wildlife trade, and entertainment industries.
>
> (Mellor, 2016)

Understanding animal sentience alters our priorities regarding animal welfare legislation. Basic animal protections might ban physical mistreatment or violence, but sentient beings require more than just being free from physical pain. Animal sentience legislation requires us to consider the mental and emotional well-being of the animals we share our world with (World Animal Protection, 2023).

International Approaches to Animal Welfare

The following subsection draws on the International Fund for Animal Welfare (IFAW) publication IFAW (2023). IFAW notes that understanding animal sentience requires more than banning physical mistreatment – as already stated above, it demands that welfare laws address animals' mental and emotional well-being, ensuring they can experience positive states and freedom from distress (World Animal Protection, 2023). With these principles in mind, IFAW has implemented initiatives across Africa, China and India to protect elephants and promote coexistence with human communities.

> In Africa, our Room to Roam initiative gives elephants space to roam freely within scientifically identified key habitats and at a distance from people. Our goal is to secure and connect habitat within 12 critical landscapes in East and Southern Africa, where more than 330,000 elephants can roam freely by 2040. A core element of this initiative is involving local communities in conservation efforts, as community engagement fosters sustainable ecosystems and reduces the likelihood of human–elephant conflict.
>
> (IFAW, 2023)

At its core, Room to Roam centres on the understanding that community involvement is key to successful conservation. When communities get involved in natural resource management, ecosystems and incomes both become healthier. When families have reliable incomes and sustainable livelihoods, they become more resilient to financial shocks, such as having their crops raided. That's why IFAW partner with the communities that live alongside elephants to improve their livelihoods and increase their involvement in conservation.

In addition to Africa, IFAW has developed innovative conservation efforts tailored to specific challenges faced by Asian elephant populations in China. In 2000, IFAW launched the Asian Elephant Protection Project in Yunnan Province, covering the last remaining Asian elephant habitats in Xishuangbanna, Pu'er and Lincang. In Xishuangbanna, home to most of the approximately 300 remaining wild Asian elephants in China, IFAW trained community rangers to patrol villages and train communities in elephant safety. In the Pu'er region, they provided micro-credit loans to more than 210 households in seven villages, achieving an average annual income growth of 35%. An important achievement has been the establishment of a community-level early warning system in over 60 villages across Yunnan, allowing communities to anticipate and safely manage encounters with elephants (see Chapter 5, this volume).

In the Greater Manas Landscape of Assam, India, IFAW, in collaboration with the Wildlife Trust of India (WTI), has been working with local authorities and communities since 2009 to address human–elephant conflict. Through the formation of 28 Eco Development Committees (EDCs) with the Assam Forest Department, IFAW has created micro-plans that prioritize conflict mitigation and livelihood support for households dependent on forest resources.

To further promote sustainable practices, IFAW has supported more than 100 families with new LPG (liquid petroleum gas) connections, reducing the need for fuelwood collection from protected areas. Between 2016 and 2021, IFAW-WTI also contributed to upgrading over 77,000 ha of reserved forest to protected status, creating secure habitats for elephants in a landscape where human and wildlife coexist (IFAW, 2023).

From 2016 to 2021, IFAW-WTI played a key role in the entire process of upgrading 77,200 ha of reserved forest areas to a protected areas network for better protection, ecological integrity and a secured habitat for wildlife. The collaborative management approach involved local communities in the Greater Manas landscape. Implementation of various conservation programmes jointly with the Forest Department and Bodoland Territorial Council (BTC) has helped secure a large habitat for Asian elephants in Assam to foster coexistence in a human-dominated landscape (IFAW, 2023).

Elephant Behaviour

Elephants are intelligent, sociable and have a highly developed understanding of their own environment (see Table 1.2). Pardo *et al.* (2024) have reported that wild African elephants address one another with an individually specific call. Moreover, elephants differentially responded to playbacks of calls originally addressed to them relative to calls addressed to a different individual.

Changes in the behaviour of captive elephants, who were used to close interaction with humans, were observed during the coronavirus disease 2019 (COVID-19) pandemic, as Manning *et al.* (2023) commented:

> the COVID-19 pandemic led to global closures of animal tourism venues, and thus a sudden and prolonged absence of tourists. We examined the impact of this abrupt, unique scenario on 10 semi-captive African elephants (8 F, 2 M; aged 12–30 yrs) maintained at the Knysna Elephant Park, South Africa, which offers close human-elephant interactions. We monitored rates of self-directed behaviours (SDBs), a novel indicator of anxiety in this species, to observe differences before, during, and after lockdown … Additionally, we recorded general behaviours to calculate activity budgets, and monitored the elephants' movement patterns and spatial use. … [We] found reduced anxiety-related behaviour due to the absence of tourists, and that the return of tourists perhaps invoked higher levels of anxiousness than before lockdown implementation.
>
> (Manning *et al.*, 2023, p. 106007)

Table 1.2. Things elephants do for fun. Adapted from Tsavo Trust, n.d.

- Socializing: Elephants are highly social animals and enjoy spending time with their herd members. They engage in playful interactions, such as touching, grooming and using their trunks to communicate with each other.
- Bathing and swimming: Elephants love water and often engage in bathing and swimming activities. They use their trunks to spray water on themselves and playfully splash around.
- Dust bathing: Elephants take pleasure in dust bathing, which involves rolling in mud or dry dust to help protect their skin from the sun and insects. It also provides a way for them to cool down and remove parasites.
- Exploring and foraging: Elephants are curious creatures and enjoy exploring their surroundings. They forage for food, using their trunks to search for vegetation and using their tusks to dig up roots and bark.
- Playing with objects: Elephants have been observed playing with objects such as branches, logs or balls. They may use these items to toss, kick or even balance on for amusement.
- Vocalizing: Elephants produce a variety of sounds, including trumpeting, rumbling and growling. These vocalizations serve as a means of communication but can also be a form of play or expressing excitement.
- Scratching and rubbing against objects: Elephants often scratch themselves against trees, rocks or other rough surfaces. They may rub their bodies, particularly their backs, to relieve itchiness or for pleasure.

Problems for Elephant Welfare Policy, Practice and Research

Elephants can provide their owners and ETV managers with lucrative sources of income:

> The incorporation of captive elephants in ecotourism generates value from two layers of interactions between humans and nonhumans. First, captive elephants are trained by *mahouts* for encounters with tourists; then, the production of value takes place through tourists' encounters with the elephants in ecotourism activities (elephant bathing, elephant grazing, and trekking alongside the elephants). We argue that the expansion of the commodification of nature in some cases requires an understanding of the way this encounter value produces a 'captive nature': lively beings that are enclosed, managed, and employed to sell experiences.
>
> (Ni'am *et al.*, 2021)

Recognizing the economic value of elephants in tourism underscores the need for policies that balance financial benefits with ethical considerations for elephant welfare. Shaffer *et al.* (2019) point out that:

> resolution of human-elephant conflict and promotion of peaceful coexistence requires a simultaneous focusing of management efforts on site-specific considerations as well as the formulation and application of strategic plans at the landscape level that directly address underlying anthropogenic drivers and their spatiotemporal variation.
>
> (Shaffer *et al.*, 2019)

They suggest that as wildlife needs are measured and modelled to improve conservation management planning, information about cultural values, norms and decision making regarding the 'use of habitat to support local livelihoods and household production is also valuable' (Shaffer *et al.*, 2019).

Understanding cultural dynamics is crucial for successful coexistence, as attitudes towards elephants are often influenced by historical experiences and benefits derived from elephant-related activities.

> Animal welfare is defined as an area of activism, science, and political action in which activists seek to improve conditions for animals, especially animals reliant on human care (Wood, 2022). … Welfare is the central pillar of scholarly work on animal ethics in tourism and stands as the most rational approach to levelling the playing field on animal-human interactions in an industry bent on pleasure and profit.
>
> (Fennell, 2022)

Cultural rural tourism

Elephant tourism venues are often located in remote jungle areas, which may also be home to tribal people with long-established, Shamanistic traditions of living in these surroundings in harmony with range animals including elephants. Cultural rural tourism supports the community's own traditions, heritage arts, lifestyles, places and values, helping preserve the traditional culture for new generations (MacDonald and Jolliffe, 2003). Barkai (2016) traces evidence for animal humanization back to Paleolithic times. Respecting the cultural and ethical dimensions of animal welfare requires a nuanced understanding of human–elephant relationships, shaped by a blend of economics, ethics and traditional practices.

Attitudes towards elephants are influenced by various factors, including perceived intelligence, emotional connection and past interactions. Van de Water and Matteson (2018) argue that:

> Attitudes towards elephants are determined by complex factors like intelligence and emotion connections of these species with humans. Averse opinions about elephant conservation often come from negative experiences with elephants. Additionally, people who benefited from elephants are more likely to coexist with elephants.
>
> (van de Water and Matteson, 2018)

Increasing awareness and providing compensation may help reverse negative attitudes caused by previous conflicts, at least partially (Pant *et al.*, 2016). Therefore:

> when considering the complex issues of HEC [human–elephant conflict], it will be necessary to understand how local people coexist with Asian elephants and what their needs are in conflict cases, to take measures to ensure the effective conservation of Asian elephants and promote the inheritance of an environmentally friendly culture.
>
> (Phengsrakate and Chamaratana, 2021)

Modelling elephant welfare

Current approaches to elephant welfare often follow a linear, extractive model focused on short-term gains. However, Chami *et al.* (2020) advocate a paradigm shift toward a circular, regenerative approach that emphasizes inclusive well-being for both elephants and communities. This shift requires a broader perspective that recognizes elephants' ecological roles and promotes welfare practices that align with environmental sustainability. This approach may be compared and contrasted to fission–fusion modelling of elephant herd behaviour (Gautam and Vidya, 2023).

A scientific approach to any area of study involves reflecting on current thinking. Argyris and Schön (1996, p. 21) defined double-loop learning as 'learning that results in a change in the values of theory-in-use, as well as in its strategies and assumptions'. Lai *et al.* (2015) suggest that tourism researchers should be challenged to reflect on their understanding of problems (and the methods of studying them).

Prioritizing elephant welfare in policy and practice involves addressing economic, cultural, ethical and ecological factors. From developing sustainable ecotourism to managing human–elephant conflict, each priority problem calls for policies that integrate community involvement, respect traditional knowledge, and promote ecological resilience. Ultimately, a shift towards regenerative and reflective approaches will be essential for long-term, equitable solutions in elephant welfare and conservation.

Conclusion

The editors of *Elephant Welfare in Global Tourism* embarked on the present book in the hope of providing elephant camp owners, national and regional elephant managers, mahouts who work directly with elephants, NGO experts, local and international tourism managers and journalists, and all who are invested in improving welfare standards for elephants in tourism with a deeper understanding of the complexities. This book provides not only an examination of the negative impacts of tourism on elephant welfare but also offers insights into the urgent need for effective policies to manage future disruptions, whether due to pandemics, economic shocks or environmental crises (see Chapter 14 'Afterword', this volume).

Tourism, a complex and competitive industry, relies on fragmented and interconnected distribution channels that are best understood as mosaics of relationships (Laws and Scott, 2015). From the point of view of welfare for animals used to provide tourist experiences this requires guidance, and preferably, destination- (and origin-) based legislation. Trade standards can be developed and set within destinations or at points of tourist origin. While efforts to regulate and improve these standards have made some progress, they remain an ongoing challenge. Henderson (2007) identified a range of problems for tourism generally, including economic shocks, natural disasters, epidemics, acts of war, terrorism, management failures and technological failures – each of which continues to challenge the stability and ethics of elephant-based tourism (Zhang *et al.*, 2022).

The concept of wilderness has evolved as tourism expands into natural spaces once considered wild, remote and free. Short (1991) and Saarinen (2012) remind us that wilderness areas are increasingly transformed into conservation management units, which are often marketed as commodities within the tourism industry. This shift underscores a critical need to protect the integrity of natural habitats as elephants – and other wildlife – find themselves at the centre of human pursuits.

> Endangered Asian elephants (*Elephas maximus*) find themselves at the center of debates involving politics, land use, human–wildlife conflict, and environmental justice. The intensity of such debates has led scholars to label conservation challenges as wicked problems with profound implications on local and global practice. In elephant range states such as Nepal, these debates are made more complex through human 'ownership' of endangered individuals for use in tourism, worship, or co-work.
>
> (Szydlowski, 2024 p. 171)

Szydlowski identified vast differences in the health, welfare, treatment and behaviour of individual elephants who transported researchers into protected areas, served as mounts for anti-poaching patrols, worked with government employees on conservation efforts and forest management, and those who ferried tourists through the national park's protected areas.

The chapters which follow deal with localized and individual problems but taken together they may encourage a broader perspective on elephant welfare. Tourism could become an interface between humans and elephants if organized in a respectful manner.

Note

[1] It should be noted that published data on several aspects of elephant populations and welfare can vary from source to source.

Bibliography

Ahmed, R., Saikia, A. and Robeson, S.M. (2022) Tracks of death: elephant casualties along the Habaipur–Diphu railway in Assam, India. *Annals of the American Association of Geographers* 112(6), 1553–1575. DOI: 10.1080/24694452.2021.2014934.

Albert, C.D. (2024) Introduction to the special issue—COVID-19, international relations, and security studies: has the pandemic altered the study and practice of international security? *Politics and the Life Sciences* 43(1), 4–10. DOI: 10.1017/pls.2023.19.

Alvesson, M. and Sandberg, J. (2011) Generating research questions through problematization. *Academy of Management Review* 36(2), 247–271. DOI: 10.5465/amr.2009.0188.

Argyris, C. and Schön, D.A. (1996) *Organizational Learning II: Theory, Method and Practice*. Addison-Wesley, Reading, UK.

Ba, F., Li, X., Zhang, Y., Shi, W. and Zhang, P. (2023) How human-elephant relations are shaped: a case study of integrative governance process in Xishuangbanna, China. *Forest Policy and Economics* 156: 103051. DOI: 10.1016/j.forpol.2023.103051.

Bai, D., Wan, X., Zhang, L., Campos-Arceiz, A., Wei, F. *et al.* (2022) The recent Asian elephant range expansion in Yunnan, China, is associated with climate change and enforced protection efforts in human-dominated landscapes. *Frontiers in Ecology and Evolution* 10: 889077. DOI: 10.3389/fevo.2022.889077.

Balasubrahmanian, P. (2014) A study on care and protection of elephants (*Hasthyparipalanam*) WSR to Uttarasthana of Palakapyatantram. Doctoral dissertation, Rajiv Gandhi University of Health Sciences, India.

Barkai, R. (2016) Elephants are people, people are elephants: human–proboscidean similarities as a case for cross-cultural animal humanization in recent and Paleolithic times. *Quaternary International* 406, 239–245. DOI: 10.1016/j.quaint.2015.09.084.

Bielański, M., Korbiel, K., Taczanowska, K., Pardo-Ibañez, A. and González, L.-M. (2022) How tourism research integrates environmental issues? A keyword network analysis. *Journal of Outdoor Recreation and Tourism* 37, 100503. DOI: 10.1016/j.jort.2022.100503.

Bodansky, D., Brunnée, J. and Hey, E. (2008) *The Oxford Handbook of International Environmental Law*. Oxford University Press, Oxford. DOI: 10.1093/oxfordhb/9780199552153.001.0001.

Bodson, L. (1983) Attitudes toward animals in Greco-Roman antiquity. *International Journal for the Study of Animal Problems* 4(4), 312–320.

Bucciarelli, J.R., Pimm, S.L., Huang, R.M., Chase, M.J., Leggett, K. *et al.* (2024) Local elephant movements, turning angles, and water access across a rainfall gradient in Southern Africa. *Biological Conservation* 296: 110669. DOI: 10.1016/j.biocon.2024.110669.

Budd, K., Gunn, J.C., Sullivan, L.L. and Eggert, L.S. (2023) Identification of conservation priority units in the Asian elephant, *Elephas maximus*. *Conservation Genetics* 24(6), 827–837. DOI: 10.1007/s10592-023-01549-6.

Cambridge Dictionary (n.d.) Exploitation. Available at: https://dictionary.cambridge.org/dictionary/english/exploitation (accessed 21 February 2025).

Challender, D.W., Cremona, P.J., Malsch, K., Robinson, J.E., Pavitt, A.T. *et al.* (2023) Identifying species likely threatened by international trade on the IUCN red list can inform CITES trade measures. *Nature Ecology & Evolution* 7(8), 1211–1220. DOI: 10.1038/s41559-023-02045-w.

Chami, R., Fullenkamp, C., Berzaghi, F., Español-Jiménez, S. and Marcondes, M. (2020) On valuing nature-based solutions to climate change: a framework with application to elephants and whales. *SSRN Electronic Journal* 297: 47. DOI: 10.2139/ssrn.3686168.

Chanev, M., Dolapchiev, N., Kamenova, I. and Filchev, L.H. (2023) Application of remote sensing methods for monitoring wildlife populations: a review. In: Themistocleous, K., Hadjimitsis, D.G., Michaelides, S. *et al.* (eds) *Ninth International Conference on Remote Sensing and Geoinformation of the Environment (RSCy2023)*, SPIE (International Society for Optics and Photonics) Proceedings Volume 12786, pp. 731–737. DOI: 10.1117/12.2677053.

Change.org (n.d.) Petition: Free the Honolulu Zoo elephants to a sanctuary. Available at: https://www.change.org/p/free-the-elephants-suffering-at-the-honolulu-zoo-to-a-sanctuary (accessed 10 February 2025).

Chase, M.J., Schlossberg, S., Griffin, C.R., Bouché, P.J.C., Djene, S.W. *et al.* (2016) Continent-wide survey reveals massive decline in African savannah elephants. *PeerJ* 4: e2354. DOI: 10.7717/peerj.2354.

Cheney, T., Newman, C., Olsson-Francis, K., Steele, S., Pearson, V. *et al.* (2020) Planetary protection in the new space era: science and governance. *Frontiers in Astronomy and Space Sciences* 7: 589817. DOI: 10.3389/fspas.2020.589817.

Duncan, I.J.H. (2006) The changing concept of animal sentience. *Applied Animal Behaviour Science* 100(1–2), 11–19. DOI: 10.1016/j.applanim.2006.04.011.

Duporge, I., Isupova, O., Reece, S., Macdonald, D.W. and Wang, T. (2021) Using very-high-resolution satellite imagery and deep learning to detect and count African elephants in heterogeneous landscapes. *Remote Sensing in Ecology and Conservation* 7(3), 369–381. DOI: 10.1002/rse2.210.

Fennell, D.A. (2022) An animal welfare literacy framework for tourism. *Annals of Tourism Research* 96: 103461. DOI: 10.1016/j.annals.2022.103461.

Fernando, P., Wikramanayake, E., Weerakoon, D., Jayasinghe, L.K.A., Gunawardene, M. *et al.* (2005) Perceptions and patterns of human–elephant conflict in old and new settlements in Sri Lanka: insights for mitigation and management. *Biodiversity and Conservation* 14(10), 2465–2481. DOI: 10.1007/s10531-004-0216-z.

Flower, E.K., Burns, G.L. and Jones, D.N. (2021a) How tourist preference and satisfaction can contribute to improved welfare standards at elephant tourism venues in Thailand. *Animals* 11(4): 1094. DOI: 10.3390/ani11041094.

Flower, E.K., Burns, G.L., Jones, D.N. and McBroom, J. (2021b) Does the experience make a difference? Comparing tourist attitudes pre- and post-visit towards the elephant tourism industry. *Annals of Tourism Research Empirical Insights* 2(2): 100025. DOI: 10.1016/j.annale.2021.100025.

Franklin, A. (2007) The problem with tourism theory. In: Ateljevic, I., Pritchard, A. and Morgan, N. (eds) *The Critical Turn in Tourism Studies*. Routledge, Abingdon, UK, pp. 131–148. DOI: 10.1016/B978-0-08-045098-8.50014-3.

Gautam, H. and Vidya, T.N.C. (2023) Do food distribution and competitor density affect agonistic behaviour within and between clans in a high fission-fusion species? *Royal Society Open Science* 10(12): 230990. DOI: 10.1098/rsos.230990.

Government of Nepal (2009) *Elephant Conservation Action Plan for Nepal—2009*. Ministry of Forests and Soil Conservation, Department of National Parks and Wildlife Conservation, Kathmandu, Nepal.

Grossman, N. and Faulder, D. (2011) *King Bhumibol Adulyadej: a Life's Work*. Editions Didier Millet, Singapore.

Hallett, B. (2024) *UK COVID-19 Inquiry—Module 1 Report: The Resilience and Preparedness of the United Kingdom*. UK COVID-19 Inquiry, London.

Hankinson, E. and Nijman, V. (2020) Asian elephants: 15 years of research and conservation. *Journal of Physics: Conference Series* 1460(1): 012055. DOI: 10.1088/1742-6596/1460/1/012055.

Hart, L. and Locke, P. (2007) Indian and Nepali mahouts and their relationships with elephants. In: Bekoff, M. (ed.) *Encyclopedia of Human-Animal Relationships*, Vol. 2. Greenwood Press, Westport, Connecticut, pp. 510–515.

Hauenstein, S., Jassoy, N., Mupepele, A.C., Carroll, T., Kshatriya, M. *et al.* (2022) A systematic map of demographic data from elephant populations throughout Africa: implications for poaching and population analyses. *Mammal Review* 52(3), 438–453. DOI: 10.1111/mam.12277.

Henderson, J.C. (2007) *Tourism Crises: Causes, Consequences and Management*. Routledge, Abingdon, UK. DOI: 10.4324/9780080466033.

Herse, M.R., Tantipisanuh, N., Chutipong, W. and Gale, G.A. (2024) Expanding protected areas globally post-2020: a critical perspective from Thailand, with implications for community forestry. *Critical Asian Studies* 56(3), 371–402. DOI: 10.1080/14672715.2024.2120733.

Holden, M. (2023) Nonhuman personhood: recognizing liberty interests for highly sentient animals. *Arizona State Law Journal* 55(4).

International Fund for Animal Welfare (IFAW) (2023) Human-elephant conflict: What it is and why it's a major threat. IFAW, 20 July. Available at: https://www.ifaw.org/uk/journal/human-elephant-conflict-major-threat (accessed 6 February 2025).

International Union for Conservation of Nature (IUCN) (n.d.) The IUCN Red List of Threatened Species. Available at: https://www.iucnredlist.org/ (accessed 6 February 2025).

Jaiswal, Y.S. and Williams, L.L. (2017) A glimpse of Ayurveda: the forgotten history and principles of Indian traditional medicine. *Journal of Traditional and Complementary Medicine* 7(1), 50–53. DOI: 10.1016/j.jtcme.2016.02.002.

Jiang, W., Yang, Y. and Isukapalli, Y. (2021) Elephant-human conflict mitigation: an autonomous UAV approach. *International Telemetering Conference* 56, 2. arXiv preprint, arXiv:2201.02584.

Joshi, B.K. (2020) Agrobiodiversity and its conservation in Nepal. *Journal of Nepal Agricultural Research Council* 6, pp. 14–33. DOI: 10.3126/jnarc.v6i0.28111.

Jue, J., Thant, Z.M. and Shibata, S. (2024) GPS tracking reveals home range and habitat preference of semi-captive elephants in Myanmar. *Landscape and Ecological Engineering* 20(2), 213–221. DOI: 10.1007/s11355-023-00534-6.

Kharel, F. (2002) The challenge of managing domesticated Asian elephants in Nepal. In: Baker, I. and Kashio, M. (eds) *Giants on Our Hands: Proceedings of the International Workshop on the Domesticated Asian Elephant*. Food and Agriculture Organization of the United Nations (FAO), Bangkok. Available at: https://www.fao.org/4/ad031e/ad031e0e.htm (accessed 23 January 2025).

Kiffner, C., Schaal, I., Cass, L., Peirce, K., Sussman, O. *et al.* (2021) Perceptions and realities of elephant crop raiding and mitigation methods. *Conservation Science and Practice* 3(3): e372. DOI: 10.1111/csp2.372.

Kontogeorgopoulos, N. (2009) The role of tourism in elephant welfare in northern Thailand. *Journal of Tourism* 10, 1–19.

Lai, K., Li, J. and Scott, N. (2015) Tourism problemology: reflexivity of knowledge making. *Annals of Tourism Research* 51, 17–33. DOI: 10.1016/j.annals.2014.12.003.

Laws, E. and Scott, N. (2015) Tourism research: building from other disciplines. *Tourism Recreation Research* 40(1), 48–58. DOI: 10.1080/02508281.2015.1005926.

Lee, S., Lee, N., Lee, T.J. and Hyun, S.S. (2024) The influence of social support from intermediary organizations on innovativeness and subjective happiness in community-based tourism. *Journal of Sustainable Tourism* 32(4), 795–817. DOI: 10.1080/09669582.2023.2175836.

Leira, H. and Neumann, I.B. (2017) Beastly diplomacy. *The Hague Journal of Diplomacy* 12(4), 337–359. DOI: 10.1163/1871191X-12341365.

Linchant, J., Lisein, J., Semeki, J., Lejeune, P. and Vermeulen, C. (2015) Are unmanned aircraft systems (UASs) the future of wildlife monitoring? A review of accomplishments and challenges. *Mammal Review* 45(4), 239–252. DOI: 10.1111/mam.12046.

Liu, Y. and Zhang, Y. (2024) Constructing problemology that is symmetrical to methodology: taking computer science as an example. *Bulletin of Chinese Academy of Sciences (Chinese Version)* 39(7), 1264–1275. DOI: 10.16418/j.issn.1000-3045.2024.07.014.

Lo, Y.C. and Janta, P. (2021) Balancing commercialization and sustainability in community-based tourism practices: a qualitative study of factors affecting elephant habitat communities in northern Thailand. *Frontiers in Psychology* 12: 685426. DOI: 10.3389/fpsyg.2021.685426.

Lobban Jr, R.A. and de Liedekerke, V. (2000) Elephants in ancient Egypt and Nubia. *Anthrozoös* 13(4), 232–244. DOI: 10.2752/089279300786999633.

Lohmann, G. and Netto, A.P. (2017) *Tourism Theory: Concepts, Models and Systems*. CAB International, Wallingford, UK. DOI: 10.1079/9781780647159.0000.

MacDonald, R. and Jolliffe, L. (2003) Cultural rural tourism: evidence from Canada. *Annals of Tourism Research* 30(2), 307–322. DOI: 10.1016/S0160-7383(02)00061-3.

Manning, P., Dawson, E., Tholander, C. and Bonato, M. (2023) The effect of COVID-19 lockdown restrictions on self-directed behaviour, activity budgets, movement patterns, and spatial use in semi-captive African elephants (*Loxodonta africana*). *Applied Animal Behaviour Science* 266: 106007. DOI: 10.1016/j.applanim.2023.106007.

Mawatha, C. and Lanka, S. (2022) Investigation of the connection between elephant acoustic communication signals and locomotive-induced airborne noise. In: *Proceedings of the Technical Sessions* 38, 62–71. Institute of Physics, Sri Lanka.

Mellor, D.J. (2016) Updating animal welfare thinking: moving beyond the 'Five Freedoms' towards 'A Life Worth Living'. *Animals* 6(3): 21. DOI: 10.3390/ani6030021.

Menon, I.K. (2002) *The Story of Ayurveda*. Publications Division, Ministry of Information & Broadcasting, Kerala, India.

Moorhouse, T.P., Dahlsjö, C.A.L., Baker, S.E., D'Cruze, N.C. and Macdonald, D.W. (2015) The customer isn't always right: conservation and animal welfare implications of the increasing demand for wildlife tourism. *PLoS ONE* 10(10): e0138939. DOI: 10.1371/journal.pone.0138939.

Natarajan, L., Nigam, P. and Pandav, B. (2023) Impacts of passive elephant rewilding: assessment of human fatalities in India. *Environmental Conservation* 50(3), 186–191. DOI: 10.1017/S0376892923000189.

Ni'am, L., Koot, S. and Jongerden, J. (2021) Selling captive nature: lively commodification, elephant encounters, and the production of value in Sumatran ecotourism, Indonesia. *Geoforum; Journal of Physical, Human, and Regional Geosciences* 127, 162–170. DOI: 10.1016/j.geoforum.2021.07.005.

Pai, C.K., Chen, H., Lee, T.J., Hyun, S.S., Liu, Y. and Zheng, Y. (2024) The impacts of under-tourism and place attachment on residents' life satisfaction. *Journal of Vacation Marketing* 30(4), 694–712. DOI: 10.1177/13567667231164807.

Pandit, A., Thapa, J., Sadaula, A., Suzuki, Y. and Nakajima, C. (2024) Epidemiology and molecular characterization of *Mycobacterium tuberculosis*, including a drug-resistant strain associated with mortality of Asian elephants in Nepal (2019–2022). *Tuberculosis* 148: 102550. DOI: 10.1016/j.tube.2023.102550.

Pant, G., Dhakal, M., Pradhan, N.M.B., Leverington, F. and Hockings, M. (2016) Nature and extent of human–elephant *Elephas maximus* conflict in central Nepal. *Oryx* 50(4), 724–731.

Pardo, M.A., Fristrup, K., Lolchuragi, D.S., Poole, J.H., Granli, P. *et al.* (2024) African elephants address one another with individually specific name-like calls. *Nature Ecology & Evolution* 8, 1353–1364. DOI: 10.1038/s41559-024-02176-7.

Phengsrakate, P. and Chamaratana, T. (2021) Investigating the relationship between social and cultural tourism in Northeast Thailand: a case study of elephant community. *Journal of Contemporary Issues in Business and Government* 27(02), 1266–1280. DOI: 10.47750/cibg.2021.27.02.141.

Plotnik, J.M. and Jacobson, S.L. (2022) A 'thinking animal' in conflict: studying wild elephant cognition in the shadow of anthropogenic change. *Current Opinion in Behavioral Sciences* 46: 101148. DOI: 10.1016/j.cobeha.2022.101148.

Praesri, S., Meekun, K., Lee, T.J. and Hyun, S.S. (2022) Marketing mix factors and a business development model for street food tourism. *Journal of Hospitality and Tourism Management* 52(6), 123–127. DOI: 10.1016/j.jhtm.2022.06.007.

Prudence, K.K.A., Roland, Y., Roland, N.C., Muller, F.D., Alain, K. *et al.* (2024) Update on the situation of tuberculosis in Africa's wildlife. *Advances in Animal and Veterinary Sciences* 12(2), 259–264. DOI: 10.21475/ajvs.12.2.259.

Reid, A. (2022) Humans and forests in pre-colonial Southeast Asia. In: McNeill, J.R. (ed.) *Environmental History in the Pacific World*. Routledge, Abingdon, UK, pp. 217–234. DOI: 10.4324/9781315256313-9.

Reinwald, M., Moseley, B., Szenicer, A., Nissen-Meyer, T., Oduor, S. *et al.* (2021) Seismic localization of elephant rumbles as a monitoring approach. *Journal of the Royal Society, Interface* 18(180): 20210264. DOI: 10.1098/rsif.2021.0264.

Ritchie, H. (2024) The state of the world's elephant populations. Our World in Data, 10 September 2024. Available at: https://ourworldindata.org/elephant-populations (accessed 23 January 2025).

RSPCA (n.d.) What are the Five Freedoms of animal welfare? Royal Society for Prevention of Cruelty to Animals (RSPCA). Available at: https://kb.rspca.org.au/knowledge-base/what-are-the-five-freedoms-of-animal-welfare/ (accessed 23 January 2025).

Saarinen, J. (2012) 'Tourism into the wild': the limits of tourism in wilderness. In: *The Routledge Handbook of Tourism and the Environment*. Routledge, Abingdon, UK, pp. 145–154.

Sadashige, J. (2024) Hands off the herd: negotiating tourist desires and animal welfare at a Thai elephant sanctuary. In: Hooper, J. and Kline, C. (eds) *Emerging Voices for Animals in Tourism*. CAB International, Wallingford, UK, pp. 46–56.

Schell, C.J., Stanton, L.A., Young, J.K., Angeloni, L.M., Lambert, J.E. *et al.* (2019) The evolutionary consequences of human–wildlife conflict in cities. *Evolutionary Applications* 14(1), 178–197. DOI: 10.1111/eva.13131.

Scott, N. and Laws, E. (2013) Whale watching—the roles of small firms in the evolution of a new Australian niche market. In: Thomas, R. (ed.) *Small Firms in Tourism*. Routledge, Abingdon, UK, pp. 153–166. DOI: 10.1016/B978-0-08-044132-0.50013-7.

Scullard, H.H. (1974) *The Elephant in the Greek and Roman World*. Thames & Hudson, London, pp. 250–251.

Shaffer, L.J., Khadka, K.K., Van Den Hoek, J. and Naithani, K.J. (2019) Human-elephant conflict: a review of current management strategies and future directions. *Frontiers in Ecology and Evolution* 6: 235. DOI: 10.3389/fevo.2018.00235.

Short, J.R. (1991) *Imagined Country: Society, Culture and Environment*. Routledge, London.

Smithsonian Institution (2022) Human characteristics: What does it mean to be human? Smithsonian, National Museum of Natural History. Available at: https://humanorigins.si.edu/human-characteristics (accessed 19 November 2024).

Sukumar, R. (2006) A brief review of the status, distribution and biology of wild Asian elephants *Elephas maximus*. *International Zoo Yearbook* 40(1), 1–8. DOI: 10.1111/j.1748-1090.2006.00001.x.

Supanta, J., Brown, J.L., Bansiddhi, P., Thitaram, C., Punyapornwithaya, V. *et al.* (2024) Physiological changes in captive elephants in northern Thailand as a result of the COVID-19 tourism ban-stress biomarkers. *Frontiers in Veterinary Science* 11: 1351361. DOI: 10.3389/fvets.2024.1351361.

Szott, I.D., Pretorius, Y., Ganswindt, A. and Koyama, N.F. (2020) Physiological stress response of African elephants to wildlife tourism in Madikwe Game Reserve, South Africa. *Wildlife Research* 47(1): 34. DOI: 10.1071/WR19045.

Szydlowski, M. (2024) Wicked problems, novel solutions: Nepalese elephant tourism and conservation. *Animals* 14(1): 171. DOI: 10.3390/ani14010171.

Taylor, V.J. and Dunstone, N. (1996) The exploitation, sustainable use and welfare of wild mammals. In: Taylor, V.J. and Dunstone, N. (eds) *The Exploitation of Mammal Populations*. Springer, Dordrecht, the Netherlands, pp. 3–15.

Tchamba, M.N. (1996) History and present status of the human/elephant conflict in the Waza-Logone region, Cameroon, West Africa. *Biological Conservation* 75(1), 35–41. DOI: 10.1016/0006-3207(95)00040-2.

Timothy, D.J. (1999) Participatory planning: a view of tourism in Indonesia. *Annals of Tourism Research* 26(2), 371–391. DOI: 10.1016/S0160-7383(98)00100-4.

Trautmann, T.R. (2015) *Elephants and Kings: an Environmental History*. University of Chicago Press, Chicago, Illinois. DOI: 10.7208/chicago/9780226264530.001.0001.

Tripathy, B.R., Liu, X., Songer, M., Kumar, L., Kaliraj, S. *et al.* (2021) Descriptive spatial analysis of human-elephant conflict (HEC) distribution and mapping HEC hotspots in Keonjhar forest division, India. *Frontiers in Ecology and Evolution* 9: 640624. DOI: 10.3389/fevo.2021.640624.

Tsavo Trust (n.d.) What do elephants do for fun? Tsavo Trust. Available at: https://tsavotrust.org/what-do-elephant-do-for-fun (accessed 19 November 2024).

Turner, D. and Kusters, N. (2021) The paradox of elephant-friendly tourism. In: Laws, E., Scott, N., Font, X. and Koldowski, J. (eds) *The Elephant Tourism Business*. CAB International, Wallingford UK, pp. 259–268. DOI: 10.1079/9781789245868.0259.

van de Water, A. and Matteson, K. (2018) Human-elephant conflict in western Thailand: socio-economic drivers and potential mitigation strategies. *PLoS ONE* 13(6): e0194736.

van de Water, A., Henley, M., Bates, L. and Slotow, R. (2022) The value of elephants: a pluralist approach. *Ecosystem Services* 58: 101488. DOI: 10.1016/j.ecoser.2022.101488.

Veasey, J. (2006) Concepts in the care and welfare of captive elephants. *International Zoo Yearbook* 40(1), 63–79. DOI: 10.1111/j.1748-1090.2006.00063.x.

Wang, J., Chen, Y., Sun, Y., Lyu, Z. and Shi, K. (2023) Inferring human-elephant coexistence based on characteristics of human-elephant interactions in Nangunhe of Yunnan, China. *Chinese Geographical Science* 33(2), 363–376. DOI: 10.1007/s11769-023-1389-3.

Warwick, C., Pilny, A., Steedman, C. and Grant, R. (2023) Elephant tourism: an analysis and recommendations for public health, safety, and animal welfare. *Health* 9(2), 49–66. DOI: 10.3390/health9020049.

Webster, A.J. (2001) Farm animal welfare: the five freedoms and the free market. *The Veterinary Journal* 161(3), 229–237. DOI: 10.1053/tvjl.2001.0577.

World Animal Protection (2023) Encouraging animal sentience laws around the world. World Animal Protection, 27 April 2023. Available at: https://www.worldanimalprotection.org/latest/blogs/encouraging-animal-sentience-laws-around-world/ (accessed 19 November 2024).

Zakaria, N., Juahir, H., Nor, S.M.M., Hanapi, N.H.M., Jusoh, H.H.W. *et al.* (2024) Challenges and realities in Asian elephant research: a global bibliometric analysis highlighting conservation crises and collaborative opportunities. *Ecological Informatics* 82(7): 102662. DOI: 10.1016/j.ecoinf.2024.102662.

Zanuari, A.H., Abidin, K.Z., Mansor, M.S., Wan, H.Y., Afni Syed Abdullah, S.N. *et al.* (2024) Identifying priority corridors and bottlenecks for three threatened large mammal species in the oil palm-dominated landscape of Peninsular Malaysia. *Global Ecology and Conservation* 54: e03092. DOI: 10.1016/j.gecco.2024.e03092.

Zhang, Y., Lee, T.J. and Xiong, Y. (2022) The contribution of animal-based cultural ecosystem services to tourist well-being at cultural heritage sites. *Journal of Travel Research* 61(7), 1631–1647. DOI: 10.1177/00472875211037743.

2 Sustainable Elephant Tourism, Gender Perspectives

Vorakarn Chalermchaikit*

Kasetsart University, Bangkok, Thailand

Abstract

This chapter explores sustainable tourism through the lens of elephant welfare, aligning with the United Nations' Sustainable Development Goals. Adopting a conceptual framework, it explores human perspectives on elephant rights and well-being. This chapter draws from a larger study in 2023 and 2024 involving surveys, interviews and a focus group with some 200 participants comprising tourists, local Thai residents who visited Wat Pho, and hotel employees from Pattaya City. This study presents preliminary findings from the interviews and focus group only, highlighting how empowering communities and integrating gender-sensitive approaches can enhance sustainable tourism via environmental and socio-economic aspects. The findings support policies of humane and gender-sensitive tourism practices advocating for the welfare of animals and local communities.

Introduction

Conflicting conservation views can arise when economic benefits are prioritized over gender equity. Such contrasting conservation perspectives often also embrace economic gain as a trade-off for animal rights. Market-oriented sustainability mainly focuses on monetary value without sufficient recognition of animal well-being, tolerance and equal rights. Additionally, many conservation practices focus exclusively on the welfare of certain species while neglecting marginalized animals, as evidenced by abusive behaviours used in elephant training. Thus, it is necessary to prioritize animal rights by incorporating human ethics such as morals and ideals to ensure a good quality of life for elephants. A good quality of life for elephants means their mental and physical health, as

*vorakarn.ch.@ku.th

DOI: 10.1079/9781836990093.0002

well as the right to refuse to mate. Female elephants must not be forced to mate if they are unwilling to select their partner. Mating should occur based on their willingness, and not through forced arrangements by camp owners (Frederick *et al.*, 2013). Female elephants should have the freedom to choose their mates naturally instead of being forced to mate with assigned male elephants.

Researchers suggest that society depicts gender roles and stereotypes through different expectations based on fundamental premises and traits (Chalermchaikit and Kozak, 2021). In contemporary tourism, researchers and practitioners increasingly acknowledge these differences, particularly in how they influence perspectives and approaches associated with sustainability (Zhang *et al.*, 2022). Hence, understanding gender perspectives remains crucial to promoting sustainable tourism activities by promoting diverse views.

The United Nations (UN) has initiated a major campaign to advance sustainable development (SD) by 2030 (Botchway and Bradley, 2023). This effort aligns with the growing focus on sustainability by governments and businesses around the world. The UN campaign focuses on Sustainable Development Goals (SDGs), which are tied to dimensions of social well-being, economic prosperity and environmental protection (UN, 2024). While balancing social, economic and environmental needs (Chalermchaikit and Kozak, 2021; Alhotali *et al.*, 2023), these dimensions also combine to create value for elephant tourism.

Elephants are highly esteemed and known for their intelligence and social behaviour (Chatterjee and Mandal, 2020), and they share an interconnectedness not only with each other but also with other species. As human settlements expand worldwide, human habitats increasingly overlap elephant range areas, creating both opportunities and challenges. These interactions have led to new employment opportunities for people, particularly through tourism. However, they also increase the potential for conflict and harm to both elephants and humans, requiring new policies and practices to protect all species in these conflicted areas.

Tourism development can lead to the marginalization of certain groups, including Indigenous peoples, rural communities, women and even non-human animals such as elephants (Knight and Cottrell, 2016). This points to the need for empowering elephants through new institutional mechanisms such as conservation policies, working towards win-win scenarios while supporting multi-species livelihoods, and promoting the sustainable development of areas like elephant sanctuaries (Knight, 2022).

Given the important roles that different genders play in elephant conservation, the purpose of this chapter is to explore how characteristics and applications of gendered perspectives can promote the sustainability of elephant tourism by raising awareness and balancing the rights of female elephants. The chapter is organized as follows. First, the subsequent section presents a conceptual framework directing the study. That is followed by an overview of methods and findings. The chapter ends with a closing discussion around the importance and implications of gendered perspectives of elephant welfare for global sustainability.

Conceptual Framework

This chapter proposes a conceptual framework that connects gendered perspectives to sustainable tourism, with the goal of optimizing elephant welfare. It emphasizes the examination of gender perspectives across four contexts that directly impact elephant welfare. These four phases move from broad and general to focused and specific and include: (i) sustainable development; (ii) sustainable tourism; (iii) elephant tourism; and (iv) elephant welfare (as illustrated in Fig. 2.1).

Gendered perspectives for sustainable development

The triple bottom line (TBL) depends on a balance of gender equity in approaching elephants. Adams *et al.* (2013) explore the TBL as a framework for measuring and reporting corporate performance across three critical dimensions: (i) social; (ii) environmental; and (iii) financial. Moreover, they trace the origins of TBL, which John Elkington created in the 1990s, encouraging businesses to extend their focus beyond economic performance and incorporate environmental and social considerations (Adams *et al.*, 2013). This approach aligns with the broader goals of sustainable development, urging companies to balance profit with responsibility towards people and the planet that another study about TBL could apply. For instance, local people in communities remain key contributors to sustainable planning and action while protecting elephants. This kind of involvement should characterize all genders and related perspectives, encouraging stakeholders' involvement while building trust and a sense of belonging in the community (Custódio *et al.*, 2018).

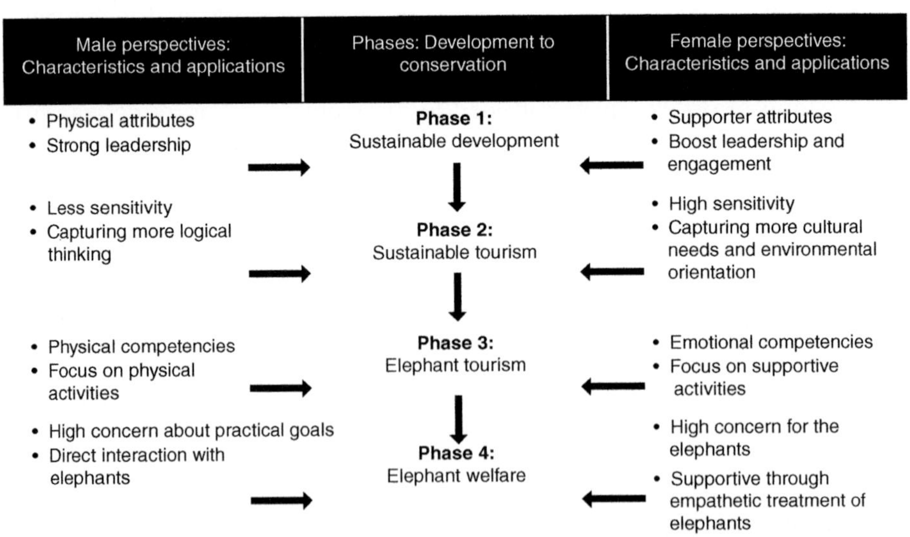

Fig. 2.1. Conceptual framework connecting gendered perspectives and development of sustainable elephant welfare practices.

Gendered perspectives for sustainable tourism

When sustainable elephant tourism is clearly explained to local people, they tend to adopt a more positive view and attitude towards it. Bansiddhi *et al.* (2020) provide supportive information about the positivity through the animal welfare practices in Thailand's elephant tourism industry, focusing on the welfare concerns related to elephants in captivity and highlighting the need for improved management, veterinary care and training programmes for mahouts to ensure better living conditions for elephants. Clearly explaining aspects of sustainable elephant tourism to local people can also foster long-term commitment to higher welfare standards and conservation efforts (Bansiddhi *et al.*, 2020). Additionally, when stakeholders such as local communities, tourists and mahouts are provided with information on sustainable elephant tourism practices, they tend to adopt more supportive actions towards ethical treatment and conservation initiatives (Ashton, 2021; Lee *et al.*, 2024). This underscores the critical role of education and community engagement in promoting sustainable and ethical elephant tourism through collaboration, aligning sustainable interests with humane practices.

Gendered perspectives for elephant tourism

The influence of gender roles on perceptions of elephant tourism is substantial, affecting attitudes and practices in the industry. Many tourists highly value local products in destinations where elephants are a major attraction, such as Thailand, India and South Africa. However, tourists search for destination policies on authenticity and sustainability, where they can express their sensitivity, feeling and emotional concern through the surrounding environment (Chen *et al.*, 2022).

From the perspective of tourists, women ostensibly hold a greater interest than men in sustainable activities as they have a sense of motherhood based on their sense of care. Thus, women visitors are highly conscious that elephants in the wild should live harmoniously with the local community. Also, even though elephants are in captivity, female more than male tourists appear more concerned with whether elephants are well treated by the local community, which represents part of local life.

From the perspective of local residents in Thailand, males often regard elephants as a business achievement in destinations. With less consideration for the environment, men might look for income as a strategic and tactical priority over the balance and well-being of elephants. Meanwhile, female hosts appear to have more sensitivity to environmental sustainability. Local women often hold particular emotional concern for captive more than wild elephants. They tend to express high awareness and a sense of involvement in creating and maintaining sustainable practices. Consequently, women are often passionate about tourism activities and are their main supporters. Also, they experience strong feelings with a high commitment towards attractions and products at particular destinations to promote elephant benefits to all tourists.

Gendered perspectives for elephant welfare

Gendered perspectives associated with elephant welfare can reveal how societal roles and expectations influence the care and management of elephants. Men and women often interact with elephants differently, reflecting broader gender stereotypes. These differences in approach can lead to varying perspectives on elephant welfare.

Men typically focus on practical aspects of conservation while women may place a greater emphasis on empathetic care (Aksatan *et al.*, 2019). Additionally, men appear more oriented to physical and independent behaviour (Patterson *et al.*, 2012). Their approach might be more practical or focused on broader conservation goals. Also, their activities might be more strategic, focusing on long-term sustainability and the role of elephants within broader environmental frameworks.

Meanwhile, women are generally more empathetic towards animals and more likely to support ethical practices that ensure the well-being of elephants. Women's empathetic perspectives often manifest in their preference for supporting sanctuaries, conservation efforts, and tourism practices that prioritize the humane treatment of elephants.

Methodology

This chapter draws from a larger study in 2023 and 2024 involving surveys, interviews and a focus group with some 200 participants comprising tourists, local Thai residents who visited Wat Pho, and hotel employees from Pattaya Cityco. This chapter presents preliminary findings from the interviews and focus group only.

Data collection for the broader study was done in three phases. First, in 2023, a team of graduate students from a research methods course at Siam University issued a survey to assess the tourism industry and gendered perceptions of elephant shows. The sample of 200 survey respondents was divided into three groups: (i) 37 international and Thai tourists who visited the temple of the reclining Buddha (Wat Pho) in Bangkok, Thailand; (ii) hotel employees of a convention hotel in Pattaya; and (iii) Thai residents in the city of Pattaya. For the first group, students issuing the survey at Wat Pho were given permission from the abbot of the temple to conduct the survey with tourists. For the second group, the general manager of 500 hotel rooms in Pattaya invited his staff to do the survey. The students carried out the survey on their own to engage the third group. For the second phase, in October 2024, the second author of the broader study and a team of assistants conducted semi-structured interviews (n = 20) with the students who carried out the elephant survey in 2023. Those interviewed included two students from Nigeria, one from Uganda, and one student from each of the following countries: Germany, Nepal, China and Myanmar. The other 13 students were Thai. The interviews assessed potential differences between genders in their perspectives towards elephant welfare. During the interviews, students were asked what they thought about elephant welfare in the tourism industry after being presented with the following two excerpts:

1. '... elephants possess cognitively complex minds (Marceau and Wiseman, 2020) and advanced abilities akin to human beings, such as insight, awareness of death, self-awareness, intentional and complex communication, memory and theory of mind (Moss *et al.*, 2011; Bates, 2020; Plotnik and Jacobson, 2022) ... . For instance, elephants respond empathetically to other elephants in need or distress; they have preferred friends and cooperate to solve problems (de Silva *et al.*, 2011; Plotnik *et al.*, 2011).'
2. 'Elephants are considered as a higher-order intelligent species and complex social agents.' [author's own statement]

For the third phase, 2 days after the interviews, a focus group was conducted with the same international students ($n = 7$) from Africa, Germany, Myanmar and Nepal to identify any differences in gendered perspectives for elephant welfare. Two video clips were shown to the group: (i) the first focused on the use of electric shock in the training of elephants; and (ii) the second focused on elephant breeding. Students were asked to discuss their opinions and views of the video clips in association with elephant welfare.

Interview and focus-group data were assessed using qualitative analysis to identify key themes associated with gendered perspectives of elephant welfare. These findings are presented in the next section.

Results

Interview findings

Interview and focus-group findings revealed that most of the students were unaware of elephant rights, and they visited the elephant show in Pattaya because the activity was arranged and easily accessible during a field trip. Analysis of interview and focus-group data also revealed that none of the students were aware of the abusive methods being used in the training of elephants in Thailand.

Most of the male students perceived that tourism income was an important sustainable economic strategy. Conversely, female students were against the idea and showed more empathy for elephant conservation rather than economic value. Then, the students were asked to talk about their experience with the elephant tourism. One male African student said, 'Hunting elephants for trophy was one of the legal activities that Botswanan government used in attracting income and controlling the population of wild elephants which destroy crops of residents'.

When asked if it is legal to control human overpopulation with genocide, all interviewees disagreed and said that humans must use the same ethical standard to control elephant populations. Neither male nor female informants supported elephant trophy hunting. Meanwhile, the German female student argued that elephant hunting for trophy must not be legal regardless of the circumstances. Likewise, all female informants disagreed about forced elephant mating for the benefit of elephant conservation. Conversely, the male students perceived that such activity was necessary to select the best genes for animal conservation.

Interview data also revealed a difference between male and female students in conservation practices associated with sustainable elephant welfare. That is, there was a difference in gendered perspectives on elephant welfare. Regarding the elephant show they visited in Pattaya, the informants were asked whether they thought the show was appropriate. Prior to the visit, none of the informants had any views about whether the show was appropriate, and the type of the show had no impact on their decision to attend the show. When asked if they prefer to watch elephants play football or paint, all respondents said that neither was appropriate for the elephant show. They preferred to see the elephants roaming freely instead of being chained, which looked uncivilized and sad for the elephants being captive. The respondents also agreed with the statement that human activities such as greeting by lifting the two front legs of the elephants, playing football and painting were inappropriate for elephants. They also agreed that such activities would harm the elephants during the training. Particularly, the unusual gesture of lifting the front legs would damage the elephants due to the unbalanced weight pressing on the rear legs. They also agreed that such human activities were designed to generate income for the mahouts and the camp owners rather than the elephants. They also agreed that such activities must be banned for the safety and well-being of the elephants.

Focus-group findings

The focus-group discussion revealed differences by gender in perceptions of elephant welfare in the tourism industry. At first, students alluded to the intelligence of elephants as high-order mammals which can communicate with their herds and are self-aware about death. Then, they were asked to discuss elephant welfare and elephant conservation. Notable differences emerged around attitudes towards elephant training for work and tourism. Male students from Myanmar and Nigeria said that the use of a mahout's hook to control elephants was acceptable. They said that elephants have thick skin and do not feel any pain from the hook. When asked how they knew that the elephants felt no pain, the male students said that they saw the elephants during the elephant show and that the elephants did not react to the bull hook.

They also said they had personal experience of riding elephants to mountains and watching elephants greet tourists. Then, the female German student interrupted and showed the class results from her Internet search that elephants have thick skin, but they still feel pain from mahout hooks. However, the male students still believed in their experience and perceived that taming elephants through training was necessary to control the elephants at work. They also said that training elephants in this way is a necessary part of elephant conservation, particularly since the elephants need to work, which makes the need for taming unavoidable. These findings revealed a difference in tolerance between male and female students concerning elephant welfare.

After watching the video about taming wild elephants in Thailand (in which the captive wild elephants were kept in a narrow space and were hit on the head and ears with a sharp hook until their head and ears were bleeding), the focus group was asked about a solution for elephant welfare in the tourism industry. Neither gender was tolerant of the torturing of the elephants at tourist attractions. That is, in the context of taming wild elephants, differences by gender did not appear to characterize tolerance on the issue of animal cruelty.

Assessing male and female views showed considerable change before and after the videos. That is, before watching the video on cruelty used in elephant taming and training, male informants were confident that training elephants was necessary to control the elephants for work. They felt using a mahout's hook in elephant training was necessary and did not think the elephant skin was sensitive to pain. This was based on their previous personal experiences touching elephants and watching them at shows or while riding elephants. However, after being given more information and seeing the cruelty of the elephant taming and training process, they changed their attitude. Neither male nor female informants were tolerant of the torturing process.

When asked about solutions to replace the taming, they said that instead of taming the wild adult elephants, it is better to train the baby elephants so that they would not be forced to be tamed with such cruelty. Moreover, the students believed that a better way for elephant conservation was to keep them in natural parks and allow tourists to watch them in their natural habitats.

The focus group also watched a video about an elephant sanctuary where elephants were kept in the camp but were allowed to bathe with mahouts and tourists. The video suggested an alternative form of elephant tourism in which the elephants were given more freedom to live. To illustrate, a couple of tourists showed the video about their exclusive visit to an elephant sanctuary where they were charged with a combined package of accommodation, meals and access to bathe and play with the baby elephant and her mother at the camp. The video showed the cuteness of a baby elephant and her mother teasing tourists. Yet, no behind-the-scenes views were shown due to a lack of information about the male elephants of the camp. After watching, the students were asked about their opinions about elephant welfare in alternative elephant tourism. The students unanimously expressed a preference for this alternative method and were willing to pay higher fees if they could prevent cruelty.

Overall, the focus group showed that if the informants were aware of the cruelty in taming and training elephants, they would not support such practices. Thus, it is necessary to educate the public about the cruelty of elephant training and provide alternative friendly treatment for elephants in the tourism industry. Based on these findings, alternative elephant tourism should be promoted effectively, which leads to more positive perceptions. An overview of the interview and focus-group results is provided in Table 2.1.

Table 2.1. Overview of interview and focus-group findings before and after watching videos on cruelty in elephant training and conservation.

Theme	Pre-test observations	Post-test observations
1. Elephant welfare	Students discussed elephant intelligence. However, they lacked awareness of cruelty in training.	After watchig a video showng cruelty, both male and female students were intolerant of torturing elephants.
2. Gender views toward hooks	Male students were more tolerant than female of the use of hooks in elephant training, as some of them believed the use of the mahout's hook was acceptable due to thick elephant skin and no visible reaction from elephants.	No students, regardless of gender or nationality, supported the use of hooks after learning about and witnessing cruelty in elephant taming.
3. Elephant training	Male students perceived that elephant training is important for conservation and unavoidable.	Students suggested alternatives for training baby elephants instead of taming wild adult elephants to avoid cruelty while supporting natural park conservation.
4. Attitudes of elephant tourism	Male students tended to have prior experiences of elephant riding and watching elephant shows.	After watching a video about the sanctuary model, students preferred this method and were willing to pay more to prevent cruelty and support elephants' freedom.
5. Sustainable solution	Students discussed elephant welfare and conservation but did not have a consensus on solutions before seeing cruelty.	Students supported keeping elephants in natural parks and promoting alternative tourism that allows tourists to see elephants in natural settings.

Discussion

Based on the findings discussed, gendered perspectives for elephant welfare reveal that societal roles significantly impact both the practices and the outcomes of sustainable tourism and conservation. It can be inferred that men and women approach elephant welfare with different priorities and behaviours shaped by gender stereotypes. Women, who are typically more sensitive to environmental and ethical concerns, are more likely to participate in conservation efforts and support humane treatment practices for elephants. This aligns with their tendency to value emotional connections and prioritize ethical and cultural experiences. In contrast, men often focus on strategic and leadership roles, engaging in logistical decision making with a broader approach to sustainability.

These gender differences highlight the need to tailor conservation strategies to appeal to both groups. For instance, marketing campaigns that emphasize the conservation and ethical treatment of elephants may resonate more with women, while adventure-focused experiences could appeal to men. Involving both genders in decision making and community-based conservation efforts can create a more inclusive and effective approach to elephant welfare, integrating practical expertise with empathetic care. Additionally, gendered perspectives affect local communities and tourists differently. Female tourists, who are more engaged in cultural and environmental activities, often show greater emotional involvement in elephant-related tourism. Conversely, male tourists often prioritize adventure and efficiency, showing less interest in comprehensive sustainability issues. The challenge lies in designing initiatives that bridge these gendered differences, promoting long-term elephant welfare through gender-sensitive policies that harness the strengths and motivations of both men and women.

The results in this study suggest that men often assume roles that involve direct interaction with elephants. Their work involves practical aspects of elephant care and protection, which are crucial for ensuring the animals' well-being towards the direct approach physically. Women, meanwhile, appear more interested in hands-on welfare practices based on supportive dimensions such as educational programmes and operations. Differentiating between types of engagement by gender for different practices can promote diversity and inclusion while increasing destination benefits (Madera, 2018). Therefore, it extends to community-based efforts that promote ethical treatment and raise awareness about elephant welfare issues.

In addition, engagement with policies related to elephant welfare should be inclusive. This means ensuring that both men and women are involved in the decision-making processes and that the policies address the specific concerns and contributions of each gender. Embracing practical diversity and inclusive policy needs in this way can provide value, motivation and encouragement through authenticity (Ashikali *et al.*, 2021). In Thailand, it can also boost women's representation and important perspectives on the ethical treatment of animals and the need for compassionate conservation practices.

Overall, achieving positive outcomes for elephants requires balancing societal, economic and environmental factors for all key stakeholders. Addressing gender issues can further enhance the benefits in these areas. First, individual people respond differently to attitudes and practices (Chalermchaikit and Kozak, 2021). It can be inferred that gender stereotypes refer to the mainstream general reactions, for example individual females and males may express differences in their values and lifestyles but overall adhere to the general gender stereotype. Our research findings showed males are generally outgoing with less sensitivity. Therefore although in some situations some males may be very perceptive and sensitive, on the whole others may be less so. Regarding elephant benefits in sustainable tourism, the concepts might be perceived differently, so the expected behaviours are interpreted in different ways by different genders' perceptions and demographic factors (Redmore *et al.*, 2020).

Second, focusing on the societal aspect can help to create awareness about the benefits of elephants. Both females and males can contribute positively despite using different strategies. The different role is the main key to how each gender comes up with positive impacts (Chalermchaikit and Kozak, 2021). Then, points of view are expressed from different roles of both tourists and local people towards elephants. To explain the general difference, local people are the stakeholders who know about elephants' lives and communities, as they have spent their lives with the daily practices, while tourists are the stakeholders who visit the destination to see elephants or spend time in areas where elephants live. However, when sustainable practices are launched, the interests of tourists and local people may be conflicted (Park *et al.*, 2017). Local people seek to protect their natural resources and elephants, which hold symbolic value in their area, while also ensuring a sustainable income. On the other hand, tourists may prioritize destinations that demonstrate they are environmentally friendly. It is important to note that the priorities of local people and tourists may not always align.

Addressing gender differences can promote more diverse and sustainable practices for elephant welfare by incorporating both male and female perspectives, which often bring different values and approaches. Activities should be effectively promoted and properly implemented to maximize awareness and integration.

Conclusion

The chapter proposes a conceptual framework that integrates gender perspectives into the TBL approach to enhance elephant welfare. For long-term sustainability, human values should guide the management of elephant tourism. Elephant conservation can conflict with economics by using elephants for tourism and labour without considering the animal well-being.

To conclude, this chapter provides and enhances the scope of sustainable tourism via elephant benefits by gender perspectives. Sustainable tourism increasingly incorporates the TBL, focusing on people, profit and planet. With these three dimensions, sustainable practices are effectively implemented and well adapted to generate enhancement for elephants. Thus, it relates to the social context based on gender issues among males and females between local people and tourists.

Based on our research findings, males tended to show less sensitivity towards elephant-related practices such as forced mating. They often believed that forced mating is necessary to select the best genes for elephant conservation. Conversely, female respondents were against such practices regardless of reason. Male tourists reacted based on a sense of masculinity which is less sensitive to sustainable gender practices. On the other hand, our research revealed that female respondents showed higher emotional concern and sensitivity. Therefore, female local people carefully tend to look at the psychological well-being of female elephants. They express warm relations and empathy for elephants' welfare with a strong sense of motherhood. Moreover, they express greater involvement and are easily persuaded by the implementation of female elephant benefits based on societal cooperation compared with males. Thus, female tourists can be effectively targeted with sustainable gender activities and practices for the welfare of female elephants. Female tourists should be a primary target for social marketing to promote female elephant welfare because they react positively.

Persuading male tourists to support elephant welfare presents a considerable challenge. Although some male tourists might be interested in participating in sustainable actions via elephants, such actions may not be well-received understandable practices by most males compared with females, who are often more inclined towards conservation and ethical tourism. This is because females tend to have stronger concerns for animal welfare and environmental sustainability while males tend to focus on economic and adventure activities. Consequently, this stage may take some time to implement effectively. Currently, sustainable tourism is highly promoted, so tourists have more awareness than in the past, but if local people do not collaborate, the action benefiting elephants can fail in the long term. With effective phases, the community can also enhance women's leadership as well as gender equality allowing high standards of elephant tourism.

Sustaining and promoting elephant benefits can empower local people and tourists, creating positive impacts along with the 'Green Movement'. The concept shows the goals for elephants towards sustainable management with the usage of effective resources and adjustable change. As shown in Fig. 2.1, there are some relevant linkages on how sustainable practices can influence sustainable tourism through elephant benefits from gender perspectives. Thus, this study can generate benefits for three reasons.

First, the conceptual framework broadens the scope of sustainable tourism by integrating gender perspectives into elephant welfare practices. Although this issue has been discussed in the past, some implications are not well recognized or emphasized in the tourism field causing actual implementation to be limited, such as the lack of understanding of female elephants' rights. In current trends, gender issues and animal well-being have become a popular topic to be studied and discussed. Therefore, the connection between gender perspectives and elephant welfare practices shown in this framework is the gap of conceptualization (i.e. the discrepancy between a theoretical concept and the ability to accurately measure or operationalize that concept in a practical setting). Great sustainability is carried out from positive practices based on strong motivation and collaboration of local people and tourists. Also, the nature of people (i.e. how they think and behave) should be better understood because elephant welfare practices come from people's attitudes and beliefs which are strongly influenced by gender stereotypes. Even though there are many new sustainable tourism models, they might not be reliable without effective cooperation. Thus, gender perspectives towards elephants should be well recognized as one of the keys to enhancing sustainable practices.

Secondly, gender perspectives directly influence the outcomes of sustainable practices. Because the stereotypes of femininity and masculinity are different, they represent different perceptions via people's actions. Both males and females have different interests impacting how they respond to sustainable actions differently. The conceptual framework of this study divides gender perspectives into two dimensions to obtain the exact differences and general behaviours towards elephants based on the interdisciplinarity of previous studies. The outcome helps readers understand each gender's reaction to different roles which can be more effective at the implementation stage for all stakeholders.

Thirdly, the framework contributes to the literature by highlighting the relevant connection between human and animal rights. Sustainable elephant tourism should use human morals to be applied to tourist animals. Furthermore, the framework demonstrates possible actions to be introduced for the welfare of elephants. It widens gender scope regarding the roles in the tourism destination.

Limitations

This chapter included preliminary findings based on research samples of students. These students were adults aged between 21 and 47 years old. Most participants were African students who had previously encountered abusive elephant treatment practices such as elephant hunting for trophies and the sale of elephant organs. Meanwhile, they are currently studying tourism as their major subject for their degree course and are exposed to the UN SDGs about gender equity. Thus, they have enough expertise and experience in the exploitation of elephants and elephant welfare. This purposive sampling merely initiates a more detailed study into gender perspectives for sustainable elephant tourism. Future studies should involve larger sample sizes in which respondents' numbers can be increased to 400 and the locations can be specified in specific elephant sanctuaries or elephant valleys in Ayutthaya, Chiang Mai and others in order to generalize the findings more effectively.

Bibliography

Adams, C., Frost, G. and Webber, W. (2013) Triple bottom line reporting: a review of the literature. In: Henriques, A. and Richardson, J. (eds) *The Triple Bottom Line: Does it All Add Up?* Routledge, London, pp. 17–25.

Aksatan, M., Gunlu, E. and Kozak, M. (2019) Women academics in tourism: a cross-gender study in Turkey. *International Journal Tourism Research* 22(2), 1–15. DOI: 10.1002/jtr.2367.

Alhothali, G.T., Mavondo, F. and Elgammal, I. (2023) Sustainability of religious travel and tourism: a profile deviation perspective. *Journal of Islamic Marketing* 14(6), 1551–1576. DOI: 10.1108/JIMA-09-2021-0312.

Ashikali, T., Groeneveld, S. and Kuipers, B. (2021) The role of inclusive leadership in supporting an inclusive climate in diverse public sector teams. *Review of Public Personnel Administration* 41(3), 497–519. DOI: 10.1177/0734371X19899722.

Ashton, A.S. (2021) Elephant tourism conservation and the need for a new strategy: Thai stakeholder attitudes. In: Laws, E., Scott, N., Font, X. and Koldowski, J. (eds) *The Elephant Tourism Business*. CAB International, Wallingford, UK, pp. 160–169. DOI: 10.1079/9781789245868.0013.

Bansiddhi, P., Brown, J.L., Thitaram, C., Punyapornwithaya, V. and Nganvongpanit, K. (2020) Elephant tourism in Thailand: a review of animal welfare practices and needs. *Journal of Applied Animal Welfare Science* 23(2), 164–177. DOI: 10.1080/10888705.2019.1569522.

Bates, L. (2020) Cognitive abilities in elephants. In: Workman, L., Reader, W. and Barkow, J.H. (eds) *The Cambridge Handbook of Evolutionary Perspectives on Human Behavior*. Cambridge University Press, Cambridge, pp. 14–22.

Botchway, G.O. and Bradley, O.J. (2023) The diffusion of the sustainable development goals (SDGs): an examination of preparer perceptions. *Sustainability Accounting, Management and Policy Journal* 14(2), 289–312. DOI: 10.1108/SAMPJ-01-2022-0012.

Chalermchaikit, V. and Kozak, M. (2021) The practice of triple bottom line in the sustainability of tourism: a gender perspective. In: Valeri, M. and Katsoni, V. (eds) *Gender and Tourism*. Emerald Publishing, Bingley, UK, pp. 285–300. DOI: 10.1108/978-1-80117-322-320211016.

Chatterjee, N.D. and Mandal, M. (2020) Human-elephant conflict in Panchet Forest Division, Bankura, West Bengal. *Ecofeminism and Climate Change* 51, 10–15.

Chen, X., Hyun, S.S. and Lee, T.J. (2022) The effects of parasocial interaction, authenticity, and self- congruity on the formation of consumer trust in online travel agencies. *International Journal of Tourism Research* 24(4), 563–576. DOI: 10.1002/jtr.2522.

Custódio, M.J.F., Azevedo, A. and Perna, F.P. (2018) Sport events and local communities: a partnership for placemaking. *Journal of Place Management and Development* 11(1), 6–25. DOI: 10.1108/JPMD-02-2017-0019.

de Silva, S., Ranjeewa, A.D.G. and Kryazhimskiy, S. (2011) The dynamics of social networks among female Asian elephants. *BMC Ecology* 11: 17. DOI: 10.1186/1472-6785-11-17.

Frederick, D.A., Reynolds, T.A. and Fisher, M.L. (2013) The importance of female choice: evolutionary perspectives on constraints, expressions, and variations in female mating strategies. In: Fisher, M.L., Garcia, J.R. and Chang, R.S. (eds) *Evolution's Empress: Darwinian Perspectives on the Nature of Women*. Oxford Academic, Oxford, pp. 304–329. DOI: 10.1093/acprof:oso/9780199892747.003.0015.

Knight, D.W. (2022) Empowerment in tourism. In: Buhalis, D. (ed.) *Encyclopedia of Tourism Management and Marketing*. Edward Elgar Publishing, Cheltenham, UK, pp. 84–87.

Knight, D.W. and Cottrell, S.P. (2016) Evaluating tourism-linked empowerment in Cuzco, Peru. *Annals of Tourism Research* 56, 32–47. DOI: 10.1016/j.annals.2015.11.007.

Lee, S., Lee, N., Lee, T.J. and Hyun, S.S. (2024) The influence of social support from intermediary organizations on innovativeness and subjective happiness in community-based tourism. *Journal of Sustainable Tourism* 32(4), 795–817. DOI: 10.1080/09669582.2023.2175836.

Madera, J.M. (2018) Situational perspective taking as an intervention for improving attitudes toward organizations that invest in diversity management programs. *Journal of Business and Psychology* 33(3), 423–442. DOI: 10.1007/s10869-017-9502-0.

Marceau, J. and Wiseman, S (2020) Brief of Habeas Corpus Scholars Justin Marceau and Samuel Wiseman as *Amici Curiae*, Appellate Case No. 2020-02581: The NONHUMAN RIGHTS PROJECT INC., on behalf of HAPPY, *Petitioner Appellant*, against JAMES J. BREHENY, Executive Vice President and General Director of Zoos and Aquariums of the Wildlife Conservation Society and Director of Bronx Zoo, *Respondents*. New York Supreme Court. Available at: https://www.nonhumanrights.org/wp-content/uploads/Marceau-and-Wiseman-Brief.pdf (accessed 10 October 2024).

Moss, C.J., Croze, H. and Lee, P.C. (2011) *The Amboseli Elephants: a Long-term Perspective on a Long-lived Mammal*. University of Chicago Press, Chicago, Illinois.

Park, K., Lee, J. and Lee, T.J. (2017) Residents' attitudes toward future tourism development in terms of community well-being and attachment. *Asia Pacific Journal of Tourism Research* 22(2), 160–172. DOI: 10.1080/10941665.2016.1208669.

Patterson, N., Mavin, S. and Turner, J. (2012) Envisioning female entrepreneur: leaders anew from a gender perspective. *Gender in Management* 27(6), 395–416.

Plotnik, J.M. and Jacobson, S.L. (2022) A 'thinking animal' in conflict: studying wild elephant cognition in the shadow of anthropogenic change. *Current Opinion in Behavioral Science* 46: 101148.

Plotnik, J.M., Lair, R., Suphachoksahakun, W. and de Waal, F.B.M. (2011) Elephants know when they need a helping trunk in a cooperative task. *Proceedings of the National Academy of Sciences of the United States of America* 108(12), 5116–5121. DOI: 10.1073/pnas.1101765108.

Redmore, L., Stronza, A., Songhurst, A. and Mcculloch, P.G. (2020) Where elephants roam: perceived risk, vulnerability, and adaptation in the Okavango Delta. *Ecology and Society* 25(4). DOI: 10.5751/ES-12001-250427.

United Nations (2024) Sustainable development goals. United Nations. Available at: https://www.un.org/sustainabledevelopment/sustainable-development-goals/ (accessed 31 January 2024).

Zhang, Y., Lee, T.J. and Xiong, Y. (2022) The contribution of animal-based cultural ecosystem services to tourist well-being at cultural heritage sites. *Journal of Travel Research* 61(7), 1631–1647. DOI: 10.1177/00472875211037743.

3 The Complexity of Foraging and its Role in Elephant Well-being

Liv Baker,[1,2,3*] Rebecca Winkler,[1,4] Sarah Blaine,[1] Chelsea Greer,[5] Kerri McCrea[6] and Laura Peoples[6]

[1]Mahouts Elephant Foundation, Harran Peopleton, UK; [2]PAN Works, Wilbraham, Massachusetts, USA; [3]Sarah Lawrence College, Bronxville, New York, USA; [4]University of Pennsylvania, Pennsylvania, USA; [5]Raincoast Conservation Foundation, British Columbia, Canada; [6]Kindred Spirit Elephant Sanctuary, Chiang Mai Province, Thailand

Abstract

This chapter presents behavioural and ethnographic insights into the foraging habits of free-roaming Asian elephants living in close relationship with Indigenous Karen communities in Thailand. For elephants, a socially complex and wide-ranging species, foraging involves much more than fulfilling basic nutritional needs; it is a cognitive process intertwined with social interactions, decision making and movement. Through a detailed examination of foraging behaviour, we argue that access to natural foraging opportunities is critical to elephant well-being. Drawing on foraging observations from elephants in northern and western Thailand, this chapter highlights how foraging behaviours are complex and must be understood within a broader – multispecies – ecological and social context. Furthermore, we present ethnographic insights from Karen communities, demonstrating that the knowledge and observations of local mahouts closely align with scientific data on elephant foraging.

Introduction: the Importance of Foraging in Elephant Well-being

Foraging is a cornerstone of elephant life, shaping not only their physical health but also their cognitive, social and emotional well-being. In free-roaming and wild elephants, foraging extends far beyond simply meeting nutritional needs. It is through foraging that elephants exercise their cognitive abilities, make critical decisions, engage in social learning, and maintain their intricate social

*lbaker@panworks.io

 Elephant Welfare in Global Tourism (E. Laws *et al*. eds)
DOI: 10.1079/9781836990093.0003

bonds. These behaviours are essential for the mental and emotional health of elephants, most manifest in environments where they have the freedom to make choices about what and how they forage.

This chapter explores the cognitive, social and emotional dimensions of foraging, drawing on both behavioural research and ethnographic insights from Karen communities. By examining foraging's role in elephant well-being, we gain a deeper understanding of why natural foraging behaviours are essential for elephants' overall quality of life, not just their physical health. This understanding is critical for developing ecological strategies that address the needs of both captive and wild elephant populations.

The Asian elephant (*Elephas maximus*) is classified as endangered by the International Union for Conservation of Nature (IUCN) (Williams *et al.*, 2020) with global population estimates ranging from 48,000 to 51,000 individuals. In Thailand, a key country for Asian elephant conservation, population estimates reflect the complex dynamics of human–elephant relationships. The total elephant population is estimated at 6783–7483 individuals, with approximately 50% living in captive environments (Bansiddhi *et al.*, 2020). This high proportion of captive elephants underscores the long-standing intertwining of elephant and human lives in the region.

A common misconception about Thailand's domestic elephant population suggests a dramatic decline from over 100,000 at the start of the 20th century to just over 3000 today (e.g. Schliesinger, 2015). However, this widely circulated statistic stems from an unverified casual remark in a 1981 US Forest Service trade magazine article by McNeely and Sinha. A more accurate estimate of historical working elephant numbers in present-day Thailand likely falls between the 1904 Siamese census count of 2036 elephants and broader geographic estimates of around 10,000 working elephants (Grabowsky, 1996).

Thailand is home to the world's largest population of captive Asian elephants used in tourism, with over 4000 individuals spread across most provinces, representing approximately 30% of the global captive Asian elephant population (Menon and Tiwari, 2019). Moreover, recent studies focusing on wild populations suggest a higher estimate of 4013–4422 wild elephants in Thailand (Sukmasuang *et al.*, 2024). These significant demographics present both challenges and opportunities for elephant conservation and protection efforts.

For centuries, Indigenous communities, particularly the Karen people in northern Thailand, have coexisted with elephants, developing a profound understanding of their needs, behaviours and well-being. Their traditional practices offer valuable insights into optimal elephant care. Central to these practices is the provision of access to natural habitats and the opportunity for free foraging, elements that are fundamental, rather than peripheral, to elephant well-being.

Cultural and Linguistic Perspectives on Wild and Domestic Elephants

In Thai language and culture, the categorization of animals as wild (*sat paa*) or domestic (*sat baan*) is closely tied to their location. Wild animals are associated with the forest (*paa*), while domestic animals are linked to the village (*baan*) (Tambiah, 1969). This spatial distinction echoes legal categories of wild and domestic/captive, rather than reflecting biological differences.

Karen traditions, however, present a different conceptual framework. Instead of location-based categories, Karen language distinguishes between wild/feral (*mee*) and tamed (*bghah*) animals. This distinction doesn't correspond to specific locations, unlike the Thai concepts (Norton, 2024). In Karen ontology, tamed animals typically roam freely in the forest rather than being confined to the village.

The Karen concept of animal management involves a process where wild animals can be made tame (*ma bghah*) through feeding. Once tamed, these animals are watched (*gwah*) rather than continuously fed (*bu oh ah tha*). This practice of allowing elephants to freely forage has often been misunderstood by outside observers, who have sometimes misinterpreted this as a sign of poverty or lack of knowledge about elephant care, reflecting ethnocentric biases rather than an understanding of Karen cultural practices.

These differing cultural and linguistic perspectives highlight the complexity of human–elephant relationships and the importance of understanding Indigenous knowledge systems in elephant conservation and management.

Karen ecological knowledge: enhancing elephant well-being across contexts

Karen communities have developed a profound understanding of elephant behaviour and preferences, essential for their safe coexistence in shared forest habitats. Winkler's (2023) ethnographic fieldwork revealed how Karen mahouts demonstrate an intricate understanding of elephant foraging patterns, accurately predicting their movements and adapting to seasonal changes in foraging preferences. This knowledge extends beyond mahouts, with villagers using it to navigate forest areas safely, avoiding potential elephant encounters.

Traditionally, Karen mahouts have raised elephants in their natural habitat, allowing them to live, forage and interact with wild elephants. This approach offers valuable insights into elephant well-being. Two key aspects emerge from Karen practices: (i) the importance of access to natural forage and a diverse diet; and (ii) the recognition that restricting elephant movement through forest areas negatively impacts their well-being.

Karen mahouts' methods of tracking free-roaming elephants across vast forest areas have honed their understanding of elephant behaviour. While fewer contemporary Karen communities have access to large enough forest habitats for elephants to freely roam day and night as per traditional practices, this knowledge remains invaluable. Many Karen communities adapt their traditional knowledge to maximize foraging opportunities for elephants in the remaining forest patches surrounding their villages. This approach contrasts with conventional captive management techniques that rely on artificial enrichment within enclosed spaces.

Importantly, mahouts can mobilize this traditional ecological knowledge, particularly around foraging, to improve elephant lives across various contexts. By partnering and collaborating with relevant organizations, researchers and scientists, Karen mahouts can apply their insights to enhance elephant care in diverse settings, from sanctuaries to conservation projects. This collaboration represents a crucial opportunity to integrate Indigenous wisdom with modern conservation practices, potentially revolutionizing approaches to elephant well-being and protection.

These practices align with the concept of rewilding, as they prioritize the expression of natural behaviours and elephant autonomy within environmental constraints. Moreover, they contribute to forest conservation by reinforcing the community's commitment to preserving surrounding forest areas (Zhang *et al.*, 2022).

The lack of attention paid to Karen elephant traditions in Thai elephant scholarship can be, in part, attributed to language barriers and histories of political suppression between Karen and Thai speakers. Addressing this underrepresentation requires increased collaboration with Karen practitioners and scholars proficient in the Karen language, ensuring they and their valuable knowledge are incorporated into broader elephant conservation and management strategies.

Elephant Foraging and Traditional Ecological Knowledge in Context

A study conducted in northern Thailand from 2016 to 2019 examined the foraging behaviour of six semi-free roaming Asian elephants (Schwarz *et al.*, 2020). These elephants, previously living in captive environments without foraging opportunities and used in the tourism industry, roamed in community forests surrounding Karen villages, providing a unique opportunity to monitor their natural foraging habits.

The research team collaborated with Karen mahouts, who care for the elephants in the forest. The mahouts' close bond with the elephants allowed for intimate observation of their eating habits. Leveraging their extensive knowledge of local plant species, the mahouts assisted in identifying plants in the Karen language. Researchers then recorded the plant species and parts consumed, later having a botanical expert provide scientific names.

The study revealed that the elephants consumed over 165 different plant species across 56 families. They showed a strong preference for browsing over grazing, both in terms of species consumed and percentage of time spent foraging (Table 3.1). Table 3.1, derived from Schwarz *et al.* (2020), highlights the dietary habits of elephants in relation to the available plant species. Out of 165 plant species recorded, browse accounted for 87.9% of species, while grasses made up the remaining 12.1%. Correspondingly, elephants spent 87.6% of their total recorded time (N = 17,912 min) browsing and only 12.4% grazing. Notably, bamboo, despite being botanically classified as a grass, was categorized as browse due to its growth characteristics (Schwarz *et al.*, 2020). Seasonal variations were observed: (i) during the wet season, 94% of time was spent consuming browse species; (ii) in the dry season, this figure was 90%; and (iii) in the cold season, it dropped to 73%, with an increase in grazing.

The elephants exhibited highly selective feeding behaviour, with only six out of 165 plant species accounting for 64% of their foraging time (Table 3.2). Table 3.2, derived from Schwarz *et al.* (2020), identifies six plant species that accounted for the highest percentage of feeding time among all 165 species observed. In contrast, the remaining 159 species each contributed to less than 2% of the total foraging time. Bamboo (*Dendrocalamus* spp.) was particularly favoured, comprising 40.3% of their foraging time. The elephants also showed selectivity in the plant parts they consumed. They preferred leaves from trees, climbers and shrubs, while also consuming bark from 47% of observed tree species, probably for important minerals such as calcium to support bone health (Sukumar, 2006).

This study highlights that elephants have strong foraging preferences and consume a diverse range of plant types including trees, climbers, shrubs, herbs and grasses annually. Allowing elephants to forage freely ensures their nutritional needs are met and enables them to express natural behaviours, which is crucial for their overall well-being.

Table 3.1. Elephant time spent foraging. From Schwarz *et al.*, 2020.

Plant classification	No. of species (%)	Time spent foraging (%)
Browse		
Tree	49.1	29.1
Climber	21.2	12.4
Shrub	10.3	1.4
Herb	6.1	0.8
Bamboo[a]	1.2	44
	Total: 87.9%	*Total: 87.6%*
Graze		
Grass	12.1	12.4
	Total: 12.1%	*Total: 12.4%*

[a]Despite being botanically classified as a grass, bamboo was categorized as browse because of its growth characteristics.

Table 3.2. Six species of plants accounted for the highest percentage of feeding time. From Schwarz *et al.*, 2020.

Plant classification	Species name	Time spent foraging (%)
Bamboo	*Dendrocalamus* spp.	40.3
Grass	*Zea mays*	7.9
Climber	*Sphatolobus* sp.	6.2
Bamboo	*Bambusa* sp.	3.7
Tree	*Radermachera* sp.	3.6
Climber	*Pachyrhizus* sp.	2.3
		Total time: 64%

The Concept of Rewilding and its Relevance to Elephant Conservation

Our approach to rewilding is centred on restoring autonomous agents to the landscape. We believe that a state of being wild that is meaningful to elephants can be attained in a landscape where both elephant and human cultures are valued. This perspective aligns with more recent rewilding endeavours that recognize humans as part of nature (e.g. Torres *et al.*, 2018) and seeks to create opportunities for captive elephants to regain psychological wildness while maintaining beneficial relationships with human communities.

In the context of Asian elephants in Thailand, rewilding efforts present a unique opportunity to address the complex entanglement of captive and wild populations, as well as the cultural and economic realities of human–elephant relationships. By focusing on the foraging behaviours of rewilded elephants, we can gain insights into the process of psychological and behavioural restoration, informing both conservation strategies and support for animal well-being.

Foraging as a Cognitive Process

Foraging in elephants is a deeply cognitive process that goes beyond simply seeking food to satisfy hunger. Elephants exhibit decision making, problem solving and memory use while foraging, highlighting their intellectual complexity. In natural habitats, elephants face a dynamic and often unpredictable environment that requires constant evaluation of food sources, nutritional value, and the effort required to obtain them.

Decision making and problem solving in foraging

Elephants regularly make decisions about where to forage based on past experiences, environmental conditions and social factors. Their spatial memory plays a crucial role in recalling the locations of specific food sources, such as waterholes or areas rich in bamboo shoots. This spatial memory is honed over time and passed down through generations within family groups, with the matriarch often guiding the herd to reliable foraging sites.

Elephants' trunks serve as both tools for grabbing food and sensory organs for evaluating potential food items. They use their acute sense of smell to determine if a plant is worth the effort of consumption. This sensory evaluation process, combined with the elephant's memory of past foraging experiences, helps them make informed decisions about what to eat and where to find it.

Observations of free-roaming elephants show that they use their trunks with incredible dexterity, not only to grasp and manipulate objects but also to solve problems in real time. For instance, an elephant might use its trunk to strip bark from a tree or uproot plants by dislodging the soil with its tusks. Additionally, elephants can manipulate tools, such as using rocks or sticks to dig for water or break apart tough vegetation. This level of adaptability allows them to access food sources that would otherwise be unavailable, further emphasizing their problem-solving capabilities.

In Thailand, where seasonal variability creates a shifting landscape of food availability, elephants must constantly assess the changing environment. During the wet season, the abundance of bamboo shoots and fresh grasses allows for more selective foraging. Elephants can afford to focus on high-nutrient plant parts, discarding the less digestible components. However, in the dry season, when food sources become limited, elephants must employ a more energy-efficient strategy, balancing the effort required to obtain food with its nutritional value.

Memory, learning and seasonal changes in foraging

Elephants possess remarkable long-term memory, which allows them to recall specific locations of food and water sources over vast distances and extended periods of time. This spatial awareness is not only critical for individual survival but also for the survival of the herd. Older elephants, particularly matriarchs, act as repositories of knowledge, guiding younger members of the group to known foraging sites during times of scarcity.

Young elephants learn how to forage through social learning, observing older elephants and imitating their actions. Calves and juveniles practise using their trunks to grasp and manipulate food, a skill that takes years to fully master. This learning process is crucial for their development and ensures that knowledge about the local environment and foraging strategies is passed down through generations.

The role of memory in elephant foraging is particularly evident in their ability to navigate to specific food sources during different seasons. For example, elephants may remember the location of fruit-bearing trees that only produce edible fruit at certain times of the year, or recall the locations of water sources that persist through dry seasons. This cognitive map of their environment, built up over years of experience and social learning, allows elephants to make efficient use of available resources and adapt to changing environmental conditions.

Foraging as a Social Behaviour

Foraging is not only a cognitive activity for elephants but also a social one, reflecting their complex social structures and adaptable group dynamics. Asian elephants typically live in fission–fusion societies, where group composition is fluid and can change frequently. While family units often consist of related females and their offspring, these groups may temporarily split or merge with others depending on environmental conditions, resource availability and social factors. This flexible social structure allows for diverse foraging strategies and knowledge exchange across different group configurations, contributing to the adaptability and survival of individuals within the broader elephant population.

Social learning and knowledge transfer

In elephant societies, learning is a social process. Younger elephants, especially calves and juveniles, acquire essential foraging skills through observation and imitation. This social learning begins early in life, with calves closely watching their mothers and older members of the group to understand how to use their trunks, select food and process plants for consumption.

The role of the matriarch in this learning process is crucial. As the most experienced member of the group, the matriarch leads the herd to known foraging sites, teaching younger elephants the locations of food sources and water. This knowledge is passed down through generations, ensuring the survival of the herd even in times of scarcity. Matriarchs also serve as role models, demonstrating advanced foraging techniques that require skill and experience, such as digging for roots or stripping bark from trees.

In Thailand, where some elephants live in close association with certain Karen communities, mahouts observe that elephants will frequently gather in the same areas to forage together. This collective foraging behaviour reflects the importance of social learning, as younger elephants benefit from the guidance of older, more experienced individuals. This behaviour reinforces social bonds within the group and ensures that critical knowledge about the landscape is passed on.

Foraging as a bonding activity

Foraging in Asian elephants serves as a dynamic social activity that both reflects and reinforces their complex social structures. In fission–fusion societies, foraging groups may vary in composition, allowing for diverse social interactions and knowledge exchange. These fluid associations during foraging contribute to the formation and maintenance of social bonds across different group configurations.

Elephants engage in a range of social behaviours while foraging, from subtle tactile communications to more overt cooperative actions. They use their trunks for touching, caressing or playful interactions, which not only serve practical purposes – such as food sharing or guiding younger individuals – but also strengthen social cohesion within temporary or long-term groupings.

Cooperative foraging behaviours further highlight the adaptability of elephant social structures. For instance, elephants may collaborate to access challenging food sources, with individuals assuming different roles based on their size, strength or experience. One elephant might push down a tree while others harvest the leaves, demonstrating their capacity for coordinated action within variable group compositions.

Additionally, foraging is highly linked to complex play behaviour in elephants. Play behaviours in the context of foraging serve as a crucial mechanism for social and cognitive development within their complex fission–fusion societies. Young elephants frequently engage in playful activities during foraging, such as tossing vegetation, mock sparring with trunks, or engaging in brief chases (Lee and Moss, 2012). These behaviours not only refine motor skills essential for effective foraging but also foster social competencies vital for navigating fluid group dynamics.

Play has been recognized as fundamental to Asian elephants' natural behavioural repertoire and has a significant role in maintaining social hierarchies, as observed among orphaned elephants in Sri Lanka (Poole *et al.*, 1997). In both wild and captive environments, play functions as a behavioural catalyst, creating challenges that develop physical and social skills across all age groups (Webber and Lee, 2020).

These spatial associations and high rates of tactile and non-tactile interactions during foraging contribute significantly to bond formation and reinforcement among group members (Lee, 1987; Sukumar, 1989; Moss *et al.*, 2011). In the context of fission–fusion dynamics, these shared foraging experiences become crucial for maintaining social connections across changing group memberships. This flexibility in social foraging strategies is particularly vital for Asian elephants' emotional well-being and survival, as it allows them to adapt their social support networks in response to environmental changes and resource availability.

Seasonal variations in foraging behaviours

Elephants in Thailand exhibit distinct foraging patterns that adapt to the dramatic seasonal changes in their environment. These patterns not only reflect the elephants' cognitive flexibility and ecological knowledge but also illuminate the complex interplay between environmental factors, social dynamics and individual decision making within fission–fusion societies.

Wet season foraging: abundance and selectivity

During the wet season (variably, July through to October), the forests of northern Thailand transform into lush, verdant landscapes, offering elephants a diverse array of foraging opportunities. This period of abundance significantly influences elephant behaviour, social interactions and nutritional strategies. Elephants demonstrate a marked preference for bamboo during this season, allocating substantial time to browsing on shoots, leaves and stems. The rapid growth and dense clustering of bamboo provide an energy-rich food source that aligns well with the elephants' need for efficient foraging in a fission–fusion context. Even amidst abundance, elephants exhibit sophisticated selectivity, discarding tougher plant parts in favour of tender, nutrient-dense portions. This behaviour underscores their cognitive ability to assess food quality and make optimal foraging decisions, a skill crucial for navigating variable group dynamics and environmental conditions. Karen mahouts' observations of elephants vocalizing with excitement upon discovering bamboo patches suggest a deep emotional connection to foraging success. These positive associations may reinforce social bonds within temporary groupings and contribute to the overall cohesion of the fission–fusion society.

Dry season adaptations: resilience and memory

The dry season (variably, November through to June) presents a stark contrast, challenging elephants to adapt their foraging strategies within a resource-scarce environment. This period highlights the elephants' cognitive flexibility and the importance of social learning in fission–fusion societies. As the landscape transforms, elephants pivot to rely more heavily on grasses, shrubs and ground-level vegetation. This shift demonstrates their ability to flexibly adjust foraging behaviours in response to environmental changes, a critical skill for maintaining group cohesion and individual health in variable social groupings. Elephants leverage their extensive spatial memory and past experiences to locate food sources, often revisiting productive areas from previous dry seasons. This behaviour underscores the crucial role of long-term memory and information sharing within fission–fusion societies, where knowledge transfer can occur across various social configurations. The challenges of the dry season may influence temporary group formations, with elephants potentially adjusting their social associations to optimize foraging success. This adaptability in social structure in response to resource availability exemplifies the dynamic nature of elephant societies.

The stark contrast between wet and dry season foraging behaviours illuminates the remarkable adaptability of elephants within their social structure. Their ability to adjust foraging strategies, utilize cognitive skills and maintain social flexibility in response to seasonal changes is crucial for both individual and group survival. These observations have significant implications for conservation strategies. Conservation efforts must prioritize the protection of diverse habitats that support year-round foraging opportunities, including bamboo forests and varied vegetation types critical for dry season survival. Thus, any such practices should account for the fluid nature of elephant social groups, ensuring that conservation areas are sufficiently large and diverse to accommodate changing group dynamics across seasons.

Foraging and Well-being: the Psychological and Emotional Dimensions

The act of foraging extends far beyond mere sustenance for elephants, encompassing crucial psychological and emotional aspects that profoundly influence their overall well-being. Within the context of fission–fusion societies, foraging behaviours intertwine with social dynamics, cognitive processes and emotional experiences, shaping the elephants' daily lives and mental health.

Autonomy and choice in foraging

Central to elephants' psychological well-being is the autonomy afforded by natural foraging. In their native habitats, elephants exercise agency through decisions about food selection, timing and acquisition methods. This freedom of choice allows for the expression of individual preferences and personalities, contributing to the diversity of behaviours observed within fission–fusion groups. The ability to make independent foraging choices not only satisfies immediate nutritional needs but also reinforces the elephants' sense of control over their environment, a crucial factor in maintaining positive mental states.

The contrast between natural foraging environments and captive settings underscores the importance of choice. In tourist camps or zoos, where food is often pre-prepared and presented, elephants may experience a significant reduction in foraging-related decision-making opportunities. This limitation can lead to psychological distress, manifesting in stereotypic behaviours that signal emotional discomfort. The observation of these behaviours highlights the critical need for conservation and management strategies that prioritize natural foraging opportunities, even within controlled environments.

Emotional engagement and cognitive stimulation

Foraging serves as a rich source of emotional and cognitive engagement for elephants. The activity involves complex decision-making processes, memory utilization and problem-solving skills, all of which contribute to the elephants' cognitive health. In fission–fusion societies, these cognitive challenges are further enhanced by the need to adapt foraging strategies to changing group dynamics and environmental conditions.

The emotional aspect of foraging is evident in the elephants' responses to different food sources and foraging experiences. Beyond the excitement observed when encountering preferred foods, elephants demonstrate a range of emotions tied to their foraging activities. The satisfaction derived from successful foraging, the comfort found in familiar feeding grounds, and the anticipation of seasonal changes in food availability all contribute to a complex emotional landscape. These emotional experiences play a crucial role in strengthening social bonds within temporary groupings and contribute to the overall cohesion of elephant societies.

Stress reduction and environmental adaptation

The extensive time elephants dedicate to foraging-related activities in natural settings serves a dual purpose of nutrition and stress management. The rhythmic nature of foraging behaviours, combined with the constant engagement with their environment, provides elephants with a natural mechanism for stress reduction. This aspect of foraging becomes particularly significant in the context of fission–fusion dynamics, where the ability to manage stress through familiar activities can help elephants cope with the social fluidity of their groups.

Moreover, the problem-solving aspects of foraging contribute to the elephants' adaptability to environmental changes. As elephants navigate seasonal variations in food availability, they develop and refine cognitive strategies that enhance their resilience. This adaptive capacity is crucial for survival in dynamic ecosystems and plays a vital role in the elephants' ability to thrive within their fission–fusion social structures.

Conservation Implications of Foraging Behaviour

The intricate relationship between elephant foraging behaviours and their fission–fusion social dynamics carries profound implications for conservation strategies. Recognizing the multifaceted role of foraging in elephant societies is crucial for developing holistic approaches that address both ecological and social needs of these complex beings.

Reframing elephant habitats: historical contexts and conservation strategies

The perception that Thailand lacks sufficient forest for elephants to forage freely is often overstated. Despite significant habitat loss, vast forested areas remain, with potential for reforestation. Recent meta-analyses challenge the assumption that elephants prefer pristine environments, showing they often favour human-disturbed areas over old-growth forests (de la Torre *et al.*, 2021). This preference is often overlooked due to the concentration of wild elephants in Thailand's national parks, leading to misconceptions about their habitat needs.

Historically, areas now considered pristine within protected zones and World Heritage sites, such as Thung Yai and Huai Kha Khaeng national parks, were long inhabited by Karen and other forest-dwelling communities (Vandergeest and Peluso, 1995; Buergin, 2015). This historical context dispels the myth of complete separation between captive and wild elephant populations and highlights a long-standing coexistence of humans and free-roaming elephants in forested areas.

Traditional rotational agriculture practices have created diverse landscapes within these protected areas. Long-fallow rice swiddens and secondary forests resulting from these practices are common, and mahouts often observe elephants preferring these areas. This underscores the need for a more nuanced understanding of elephant habitat preferences and use.

To avoid oversimplified assumptions about population dynamics, human–elephant conflict and habitat use, conservation efforts must consider historical land settlement patterns of Indigenous groups, deepen understanding of environmental history, and pay more complex attention to elephant foraging preferences. These multifaceted approaches are crucial for developing more meaningful and effective conservation strategies that reflect the true complexity of elephant ecology and human–elephant relationships. Conservation strategies should thus prioritize preserving and restoring diverse habitats, including attention to agrobiodiversity (Baird, 2022). This approach goes beyond protecting existing forests to actively restoring degraded areas, focusing on recreating the mosaic of vegetation types that elephants rely on year round.

Moreover, habitat conservation must account for the spatial and temporal variability in elephant group dynamics. Protected areas should be sufficiently large and diverse to accommodate the fluid nature of fission–fusion societies, allowing for natural group formation and dissolution in response to seasonal changes and resource availability. This may involve creating networks of interconnected habitats that mirror the elephants' dynamic use of their environment.

Collaboration with local communities, particularly those with traditional ecological knowledge like the Karen people, is crucial. Their insights into sustainable land management practices and historical elephant movement patterns can inform more effective and culturally sensitive conservation strategies.

Preserving ecological functions in dynamic social contexts

The ecological roles of elephants as seed dispersers and vegetation engineers are intrinsically linked to their foraging behaviours and social structures. Conservation strategies must aim to maintain these functions by ensuring that elephants can engage in natural foraging patterns within their fission–fusion societies.

This involves protecting not just individual feeding sites but entire foraging routes that elephants use as they move between temporary group formations. By preserving these movement corridors, conservation efforts can support the natural flow of genetic material and ecological processes across landscapes, enhancing ecosystem resilience.

Furthermore, recognizing the varied foraging strategies employed by different age and social groups within elephant societies can inform more nuanced habitat management practices. For instance, ensuring the availability of diverse food sources that cater to the nutritional needs of both young and adult elephants supports the health of the entire population.

Ethical Tourism and Research: Supporting Natural Behaviours

Ethical conservation tourism and research initiatives should be designed to respect and support the natural foraging and social behaviours of elephants (Baker *et al.*, 2021). This approach moves beyond simplistic viewing experiences to create opportunities for tourists and researchers to observe the complex interactions among foraging, social dynamics and environmental factors in elephant societies.

Ethical tourism models could incorporate unobtrusive observation areas strategically located along natural foraging routes. This would allow visitors to witness the formation and dissolution of elephant groups in response to seasonal changes, providing valuable educational experiences while minimizing disruption to natural behaviours. Crucially, these models must be informed by principles – with regard to humans and non-humans – of ethically grounded community-based tourism, prioritizing local governance and equitable distribution of economic value.

Research programmes should focus on non-invasive methods that enable the study of elephant foraging and social behaviours in their natural context.

Long-term studies tracking changes in group dynamics, foraging patterns and habitat use over time can provide crucial insights for adaptive conservation management.

By aligning conservation strategies with the intricate realities of elephant foraging behaviours and fission–fusion dynamics, we can develop more effective and ethically sound approaches to elephant protection. This holistic perspective supports not only the physical and psychological well-being of elephants but also enhances the resilience of their ecosystems and fosters more harmonious relationships between elephants and human communities.

The Role of Mahouts in Elephant Well-being

Mahouts in the Karen tradition play a crucial role in maintaining the well-being of elephants – they are not only caretakers but also companions and protectors. This role, often passed down from father to son, involves forming deep bonds with elephants from calfhood through to adulthood. The Karen culture uniquely recognizes aspects of elephant personhood and agency, exemplified by key practices. For example, they perform annual ritual kinship ceremonies for elephants, the only non-human species accorded this honour. Additionally, they conduct a naming ritual where young elephants choose their own names by selecting food items associated with different names (Greene, 2021).

In Karen ontology, elephants occupy a unique spiritual role as intermediaries between humans and the spirit world. They are often described as 'beings that speak for the spirits' or as messengers of truth and higher power. This spiritual significance elevates the status of mahouts within their communities, as their close relationship with elephants grants them a form of spiritual insight. Mahouts' observations of elephant behaviour and moods are considered reflections of the community's spiritual health. As a result, before interacting with their elephants, mahouts often consult with village elders to discuss any community issues that might affect the elephants' demeanor. This practice underscores the interconnectedness of elephant well-being, community harmony and spiritual balance in Karen culture.

The spiritual significance of elephants in Karen culture creates a profound sense of responsibility among mahouts. Mistreating an elephant is considered a spiritually dangerous violation, potentially jeopardizing not only the mahout's spiritual well-being but that of the entire community and future generations (Lee *et al.*, 2024). This belief system reinforces the mahouts' dedication to closely observing and respecting individual elephant personalities, behaviours, moods and preferences.

Most Karen mahouts prioritize natural foraging as essential for elephant well-being, recognizing its importance for both nutritional and psychological health. Unlike in commercial tourist camps where elephants are often fed prepared food on a schedule, the Karen communities ensure that their elephants have the freedom to forage naturally in the forests surrounding their villages.

Moreover, Karen mahouts develop an intimate understanding of their elephants' individual foraging preferences across seasons. For instance, during the wet season, they may guide elephants to bamboo-rich areas, knowing it is often a preferred food source. In the dry season, when natural food is scarcer, mahouts are known to supplement the elephants' diet by cultivating crops like Napier grass on behalf of the elephants, ensuring consistent access to nutritious food.

Karen mahouts have also reported observing how elephants display distinct preferences for certain plant species and even specific parts of plants. For instance, elephants may prefer the shoots or tender leaves of bamboo during the rainy season and might avoid tougher plant material when more nutritious options are available. This nuanced understanding of foraging patterns aligns with scientific observations about the selective feeding behaviour of elephants, highlighting the practical knowledge that has developed through long-term, close relationships between mahouts and elephants.

The Karen people's understanding of elephant behaviour is deeply embedded in their culture and reflects their respect for the intelligence and social complexity of elephants. Mahouts believe that elephants, like humans, have unique personalities and emotional lives, and they adjust their care practices accordingly.

This traditional knowledge, accumulated over generations, is key to successful management of elephants in Karen communities. The mahouts' ability to identify changes in an elephant's behaviour – such as a sudden disinterest in a particular foraging site or a shift in dietary preferences – enables them to provide care that is responsive to the elephants' needs. This is particularly important when the elephants are experiencing stress due to external factors such as habitat degradation, changing weather patterns or interactions with other animals.

This holistic approach to elephant care, rooted in spiritual beliefs and traditional ecological knowledge, demonstrates the depth of the mahout–elephant relationship in Karen culture and its potential contributions to modern elephant conservation and welfare practices.

The Relationship Between Elephants and Karen Communities

Beyond a relationship of transaction, the Karen people view elephants as sentient beings with whom they share a spiritual connection, and this belief informs the way they interact with and care for the elephants.

The unique relationship is also reflected in the way Karen communities manage their natural resources. The forests where elephants forage are also vital to the livelihoods of the Karen people, providing food, medicinal plants and materials for building. As such, the Karen have developed sustainable land management practices that ensure the long-term health of the forest ecosystem. These practices include selective planting of crops that benefit both the elephants and the community, as well as the protection of critical foraging areas from overuse or degradation (Park *et al.*, 2017).

As global pressures on elephant populations intensify, the role of Karen mahouts in protecting and promoting elephant well-being becomes increasingly critical. The traditional knowledge held by mahouts offers valuable insights into coexisting with and protecting elephants in a way that prioritizes their cognitive, social and emotional needs. This expertise is particularly relevant as elephant populations face mounting challenges tied to habitat loss, human–wildlife conflict and the commercialization of elephant tourism.

The Karen communities, with their emphasis on ethical and sustainable practices, provide a counterpoint to exploitative trends, demonstrating that it is possible to care for elephants while respecting their autonomy and cognitive complexity. However, these communities themselves face challenges as modern economic pressures threaten their traditional way of life. Despite these pressures, many Karen communities continue to prioritize elephant well-being, advocating for more ethical and sustainable approaches to elephant management.

The knowledge and practices of Karen mahouts will be essential in shaping future policies and initiatives aimed at protecting both elephants and the communities that depend on them. By integrating this traditional knowledge with modern conservation science, we can work towards a future where elephants thrive in their natural habitats, and the deep bonds between elephants and humans continue to flourish. This collaborative approach offers a path to more effective, culturally sensitive and ethically grounded conservation strategies that benefit both elephants and the communities that have long lived alongside them.

Conclusion: Fostering Elephant Well-being through Natural Foraging

The intricate tapestry of elephant foraging behaviour, woven through the dynamic structure of fission–fusion societies, reveals a profound connection between ecological processes, cognitive development and social cohesion. Our examination of free-roaming elephants living alongside Karen communities in Thailand illuminates the critical importance of natural foraging opportunities not just for individual elephants, but for the resilience and adaptability of their social groups and the multi-species ecosystems they inhabit.

Foraging emerges as a multifaceted activity that transcends mere sustenance. It serves as a cognitive playground where elephants exercise decision-making skills, a social arena where knowledge is shared across fluid group compositions, and an emotional landscape where individual preferences and collective experiences shape group dynamics. The seasonal variations in foraging patterns highlight the remarkable adaptability of elephant societies, underscoring the need for conservation strategies that preserve the full spectrum of their habitat requirements.

The insights gained from studying elephant foraging behaviour in the context of fission–fusion societies and their relationship with Karen communities emphasize the importance of integrating traditional ecological knowledge with scientific research. Karen mahouts' deep understanding of elephant behaviour, rooted in centuries of coexistence, aligns closely with scientific observations on foraging patterns, social dynamics and seasonal adaptations. This synthesis offers a powerful framework for developing conservation strategies that are both ecologically sound and culturally sensitive, addressing the complex challenges facing elephant populations in a rapidly changing world.

Our research challenges common misconceptions about elephant habitat preferences and historical population trends in Thailand. It highlights the need for a more nuanced understanding of elephant–human coexistence, recognizing the long history of interaction between forest-dwelling communities and elephants. This perspective calls for conservation approaches that value both human and elephant cultures, moving beyond simplistic notions of 'wild' versus 'captive' populations.

Moving forward, conservation efforts should prioritize:

1. Protecting and restoring diverse habitats that support year-round foraging opportunities and accommodate the fluid nature of elephant social groups.
2. Developing conflict mitigation strategies that account for the seasonal variations in elephant movement patterns and group formations.
3. Promoting ethical tourism and research practices that respect the natural foraging behaviours and social dynamics of elephants.
4. Fostering collaborations among local communities, particularly Karen mahouts, scientists and conservation organizations to create holistic management approaches that benefit both elephants and humans.
5. Recognizing and incorporating traditional ecological knowledge, especially from Karen communities, in elephant conservation and management strategies.
6. Addressing the psychological and emotional dimensions of elephant well-being through conservation practices that allow for natural foraging and social behaviours.

By embracing the complexity of elephant social structures and foraging behaviours, we can craft more effective and nuanced conservation strategies. These approaches will not only ensure the physical survival of elephants but also preserve the rich tapestry of their social lives and cognitive experiences. In doing so, we protect elephant lives, their species, underpinned by the intricate ecological relationships and cultural values that elephants embody in the landscapes they inhabit.

Ultimately, safeguarding natural foraging opportunities for elephants within their fission–fusion societies is crucial for their well-being and future. Natural foraging is not merely about nutrition; it is integral to elephants' cognitive, emotional and social health. This understanding recognizes elephants as sentient beings with complex inner lives, deserving of environments that support their full behavioural repertoire. Moving forward, conservation strategies must draw from a diverse range of ethically grounded epistemologies, including: (i) scientific research; (ii) traditional ecological knowledge; (iii) Indigenous wisdom; (iv) historical analysis; and (v) anthropological insights. By integrating these varied perspectives, we can develop more comprehensive and culturally sensitive approaches to elephant conservation. This holistic strategy acknowledges the intrinsic value of elephants and their right to flourish in habitats that allow for the full expression of their natural behaviours, including the vital act of foraging. Our goal should be to ensure a future where elephants can live and thrive as elephants, with their well-being at the centre of our conservation and protection efforts.

Bibliography

Baird, I.G. (2022) Political violence, migration, lack of citizenship, and agrobiodiversity loss in the borderlands of Thailand and Laos. *Geoforum* 128, 263–275.

Baker, L., Blaine, S. and Winkler, R. (2021) Community collaboration, elephant conservation and protection. In: Laws, E., Scott, N., Font, X. and Koldowski, J. (eds) *The Elephant Tourism Business*, 1st edn. CAB International, Wallingford, UK, pp. 123–133.

Bansiddhi, P., Brown, J.L. and Thitaram, C. (2020) Welfare assessment and activities of captive elephants in Thailand. *Animals* 10(6): 919.

Buergin, R. (2015) Contested rights of local communities and Indigenous peoples in conflicts over biocultural diversity: the case of Karen communities in Thung Yai, a World Heritage Site in Thailand. *Modern Asian Studies* 49(6), 2022–2062.

de la Torre, J.A., Wong, E.P., Lechner, A.M., Zulaikha, N., Zawawi, A. *et al.* (2021) There will be conflict – agricultural landscapes are prime, rather than marginal, habitats for Asian elephants. *Animal Conservation* 24(5), 720–732. DOI: 10.1111/acv.12668.

Grabowsky, V. (1996) The Thai census of 1904: translation and analysis. *Journal of the Siam Society* 84(1), 49–85.

Greene, A.M. (2021) Speaking with an upside-down tongue: reflections on human-elephant multispecies culture in northern Thailand. *Gajah* 53, 4–19.

Lee, P.C. (1987) Allomothering among African elephants. *Animal Behaviour* 35(1), 278–291.

Lee, P.C. and Moss, C.J. (2012) Wild female African elephants (*Loxodonta africana*) exhibit personality traits of leadership and social integration. *Journal of Comparative Psychology* 126(3), 224–232. DOI: 10.1037/a0026566.

Lee, S., Lee, N., Lee, T.J. and Hyun, S.S. (2024) The influence of social support from intermediary organizations on innovativeness and subjective happiness in community-based tourism. *Journal of Sustainable Tourism* 32(4), 795–817.

Menon, V. and Tiwari, S.K. (2019) Population status of Asian elephants *Elephas maximus* and key threats. *International Zoo Yearbook* 53(1), 17–30.

Moss, C.J., Croze, H. and Lee, P.C. (2011) The Amboseli elephants: a long-term perspective on a long-lived mammal. *Journal of Mammalogy* 93(1), 294–295. DOI: 10.1644/11-MAMM-R-329.1.

Norton, M. (2024) *The Tame and the Wild*. Harvard University Press, Cambridge, Massachusetts.

Park, K., Lee, J. and Lee, T.J. (2017) Residents' attitudes toward future tourism development in terms of community well-being and attachment. *Asia Pacific Journal of Tourism Research* 22(2), 160–172. DOI: 10.1080/10941665.2016.1208669.

Poole, T.B., Taylor, V.J., Fernando, S.B.U., Ratnasooriya, W.D., Ratnayeke, A. *et al.* (1997) Social behaviour and breeding physiology of a group of Asian elephants *Elephas maximus* at the Pinnawala Elephant Orphanage, Sri Lanka. *International Zoo Yearbook* 35(1), 297–310.

Schliesinger, J. (2015) *Elephants in Thailand Vol 1: Mahouts and Their Cultures Today*. BooksMango, Bangkok.

Schwarz, C., Jobocola, A. and Hammer, M. (2020) Foraging ecology of semi-free-roaming Asian elephants in northern Thailand. *Gajah* 52, 4–14.

Sukmasuang, R., Phoonjampa, R., Chutipong, W., Steinmetz, R., Pattanavibool, A. *et al.* (2024) Review: Status of wild elephant, conflict and conservation actions in Thailand. *Biodiversitas Journal of Biological Diversity* 25(4), 1479–1498.

Sukumar, R. (1989) *The Asian Elephant: Ecology and Management*. Cambridge University Press, Cambridge.

Sukumar, R. (2006) A brief review of the status, distribution and biology of wild Asian elephants *Elephas maximus*. *International Zoo Yearbook* 40(1), 1–8.

Tambiah, S.J. (1969) Animals are good to think and good to prohibit. *Ethnology* 8(4): 423.

Torres, A., Fernández, N., Zu Ermgassen, S., Helmer, W., Revilla, E. *et al.* (2018) Measuring rewilding progress. *Philosophical Transactions of the Royal Society B* 373(1761): 20170433.

Vandergeest, P. and Peluso, N.L. (1995) Territorialization and state power in Thailand. *Theory and Society* 24(3), 385–426.

Webber, C.E. and Lee, P.C. (2020) Play in elephants: wellbeing, welfare or distraction? *Animals* 10(2): 305. DOI: 10.3390/ani10020305.

Williams, C., Tiwari, S.K., Goswami, V.R., Silva, S., Kumar, A. *et al.* (2020) *Elephas maximus. The IUCN Red List of Threatened Species 2020.* International Union for Conservation of Nature (IUCN), Gland, Switzerland, p. e.T7140A45818198. DOI: 10.2305/IUCN.UK.2020-3. RLTS.T7140A45818198.en.

Winkler, R. (2023) Multispecies anthropology: fieldwork among human-elephant communities. Paper presented at *Life Ethnographically: Thailand's National Academic Conference on Anthropology and Sociology, Princess Maha Chakri Sirindhorn Anthropology Centre (SAC)*, Bangkok, Thailand.

Zhang, Y., Lee, T.J. and Xiong, Y. (2022) The contribution of animal-based cultural ecosystem services to tourist well-being at cultural heritage sites. *Journal of Travel Research* 61(7), 1631–1647. DOI: 10.1177/00472875211037743.

4 Human Enjoyment of Interaction with Elephants

ANN SUWAREE ASHTON*

National Institute of Development Administration (NIDA), Bangkok, Thailand

Abstract

This chapter analyses the enjoyment humans experience through interactions with elephants. Today, most interactions take place within conservation areas, where there are numerous elephant sanctuaries, especially in Chiangmai Province, Thailand. Other prominent locations include Chitwan National Park in Nepal and various sites in South Africa. Human–elephant interactions have been happening for thousands of years. Elephants are thought to share a special affinity for humans, which is probably due to significant similarities in social behaviour and common aspects of genetic evolution. The chapter discusses current research on elephants, focusing on their potential role in psychological therapy, along with a case study of tourists' experiences at the Elephant Breeding Center in Chitwan National Park. Nestled within the lush greenery of the national park, this centre is a vital hub for conservation efforts and a symbol of Nepal's rich biodiversity.

Introduction

Animals have been used for entertainment activities at tourist destinations, including elephants. Countries well known for elephant tourism include popular destinations in Thailand, Nepal, Sri Lanka and India (Cui and Xu, 2019; Ashton, 2020; de Silva *et al.*, 2023; Szydlowski, 2024).

Numerous aspects of elephant tourism have been investigated, with significant focus on elephant welfare (Lacinak, 2024; Sadashige, 2024; Szydlowski, 2024). For example, research has explored animal ethics in Thai elephant tourism (Cui and Xu, 2019), the impact of tourists' ethical experiences and psychological well-being on travel satisfaction (Lee *et al.*, 2024), and the treatment of elephants by mahouts at a sanctuary (Flower *et al.*, 2021).

*suwareeashton@hotmail.com

DOI: 10.1079/9781836990093.0004

From the stakeholder perspective on elephants, topics such as elephant tourism conservation, the need for new strategies, stakeholder attitudes, and perceptions regarding elephant conservation have been explored (Ashton, 2020; Situmorang *et al.*, 2020). Studies have also examined sustainable management of elephant tourism, including case studies in Botswana and other parts of Africa (Adams *et al.*, 2017; Tickle *et al.*, 2024), as well as the intersection of elephants and ecotourism activities (Tilley *et al.*, 2024).

The emotional story of humans and elephants has been extensively discussed (de Silva *et al.*, 2023; Shakespeare, 2023; Clark, 2024). Elephants are often perceived as exhibiting positive emotions, including friendly behaviour, love, motivation, naturalness, kindness, peacefulness, playfulness, pride, relaxation, safety, satisfaction and overall goodness (Lacinak, 2024). Studies have examined the impact of human–elephant interactions, for instance the relationship between elephants and their mahouts, with a case study from India and Nepal (Rizzolo and Bradshaw, 2018; Hart, 2020).

Hence, this chapter is an attempt to understand the role of human interaction with elephants, and asks if elephants can help to improve human mental health and well-being and if elephants and humans can live in harmony in the natural environment (Kim and Hyun, 2024).

Can Human Interaction with Elephants be Therapeutic?

Human nature is inborn with all the potential of clarity, self-value, power, wisdom, love and wakefulness. People long to discover their spiritual roots and mindfulness which leads humans to be able to focus their attention on the present, moment by moment, noticing sensations such as seeing, hearing, thinking, feeling, touching and tasting. There are several effective ways to relieve human stress, such as spending time in nature, engaging with the environment or being around animals. The relationship between humans and animals has garnered significant scholarly attention (Shakespeare, 2023; Lacinak, 2024; Zhang and Cheng, 2024). It has been observed that human–elephant interactions have received attention, for example in Africa and Thailand (Twine and Magome, 2008).

In Thailand, there is strong belief about the connection between humans and elephants, which are considered to be spiritually protecting and healing. It is noted that the Asian elephant is a powerful animal of steadfastness and mental resilience (Lyons, 2013). In Thailand, elephants are viewed as therapeutic beings, with many Thais forming deep emotional connections with them (Ribó, 2017; Greene *et al.*, 2020). In Buddhism, faith and culture often associate meditation with the image of a pure white elephant. Thai people see elephants as guardians of temples, and the relationship between the King of Thailand and elephants has a long history. Elephants were historically used in battles, and reverence towards them is believed to bring victory over adversaries. Throughout the country, monuments and temples prominently display sculptures and murals adorned with white elephants, which Thai Buddhists consider especially auspicious and sacred, reflecting a tradition that has been passed down through history (Lyons, 2013; Ribó, 2017; Bansiddhi *et al.*, 2020).

Elephants play a crucial role by offering unique experiences for tourists and fostering a feeling of interaction that provides numerous benefits in return. They are highly valued by the public who empathize with these intelligent, social and long-lived creatures (Twine and Magome, 2008). In particular, the psychology of elephants has been extensively discussed, especially regarding animal consciousness, self-awareness, empathy and cultural behaviours (Plotnik *et al.*, 2006; Byrne *et al.*, 2008), making the concept of an animal psyche more accepted (Bradshaw, 2009). Communicating with elephants prompts questions such as, 'What would you say if an elephant were standing right in front of you listening?' and 'What would you say honestly, without feeling ashamed?'. As elephants have been observed exhibiting behaviours akin to humans, it has been discovered that their personalities are as diverse as those found in humans (Bradshaw, 2009).

Observing wild elephants to develop spiritual strategies is a fascinating theme in Buddhist literature (Shainberg, 2001). Elephants exhibit qualities such as loyalty, caring for others and teamwork, demonstrating intelligent decision making to safeguard their herds (Ramanathapillai, 2009).

Elephants exhibit a wide range of emotions; they can be joyful or sorrowful, volatile or calm. They display traits such as envy, jealousy and the ability to throw tantrums, and are fiercely competitive. Elephants experience deep grief for lost loved ones, often shedding tears and showing signs of depression. Their sense of compassion extends beyond their own species. Elephants are loving, nurturing and highly responsive creatures. They are particularly known for their profound grief when a loved one dies or departs, showing an understanding of death and revisiting the bones of relatives (Bradshaw, 2009). Their society structures are complex, with intricate networks of relationships similar to those of humans (Bradshaw, 2009). Moreover, elephants express the intensity of their emotions through vocalizations; both joyful occasions like family reunions and sorrowful moments like the death of a family member evoke behaviours and vocal responses. These reactions can include urination, temporal gland secretion, rumbling and trumpeting (Soltis, 2013).

Several activities emphasize human interaction with elephants (Sawatsky, 2019). For instance, the renowned elephant farm in Surin Province, located in north-eastern Thailand, offers programmes that allow tourists to engage closely with these majestic animals (Sregongsang, 2017). Additionally, elephants are integral to spiritual healing rituals, believed to protect the soul and spiritual well-being, especially during wartime when they were employed on the battlefield (Ramanathapillai, 2009; Roothaan, 2019). Therefore, it is believed that the power of kings depends on their possession of excellent elephants. This intricate relationship with nature, especially emphasized in Buddhist philosophy, underscores the profound philosophical significance and unique spiritual status of elephants among all forest animals (Ramanathapillai, 2009).

From an elephant's perspective, human societies reveal numerous intriguing parallels to their own. This viewpoint highlights the remarkable connection between humans and elephants, especially regarding their shared abilities to heal and promote mental well-being (George, 2024). For example, how do elephants relate to mental health? Both species, human and elephant, experience the impacts of environmental crises, leading to issues like anxiety, stress-related disorders, mood disorders and self-harm. Healing for both involves restoring ecological balance and embracing a sense of interconnectedness; just as humans can heal, so can elephants. Providing elephants with safety and the freedom to choose allows them to recover. Similarly, trauma treatment for humans begins with establishing safety and stability, which is crucial for healing (George, 2024).

Types of healing arising from encountering elephants

Encountering elephants can lead to several forms of healing for humans. First, *emotional connection and empathy* provides emotional support – elephants are known for their strong social bonds and empathy. Their ability to form close relationships and exhibit emotional intelligence can provide humans with a sense of connection and understanding. For example, spending time with elephants can reduce feelings of loneliness and increase feelings of belonging. Moreover, there are elephant–humans therapeutic interactions: programmes like elephant-assisted therapy are designed to help individuals with mental health issues. These therapies leverage the elephants' calming presence and non-judgemental nature to create a supportive environment. The process of grooming, feeding and interacting with elephants can be soothing and help reduce stress, anxiety and depression. Records show that elephants are capable of recognizing animacy and goal-directedness. They can also understand the physical competence, emotional state and intentions of other beings (Byrne *et al.*, 2008).

Secondly, *stress reduction and relaxation* – an encounter with elephants can reduce stress and enhance relaxation as elephants are large, gentle animals whose presence alone can be calming. The interaction with animals, including elephants, can lower the level of cortisol (a stress hormone) and increase the release of endorphins (feel-good hormones). This can lead to a reduction in overall stress and anxiety. In addition, being around elephants encourages mindfulness, as their slow and deliberate movements and calm invite people to be present in the moment. This mindfulness can contribute to improved mental clarity and emotional stability.

Thirdly, *education and inspirational aspects* – observing and learning about elephants can be both educational and inspiring. Understanding their complex social structures and behaviours can offer new perspectives on empathy, cooperation and resilience. This knowledge can foster a deeper appreciation for the natural world and our place within it. Both give purpose and connection, such as engaging with elephants through volunteering, conservation efforts or educational programmes can provide a sense of purpose and fulfilment. This sense of contributing to a greater cause can enhance overall well-being and provide a positive outlet for personal growth.

Finally, personal contact with an elephant can enhance human *mindfulness*. Mindfulness involves fully paying attention to your surroundings and your internal state, your body, heart and mind (Bays, 2011; Moscardo, 2013).

The benefits of mindfulness includes improved mental health and overall well-being as well as a deeper connection to your spiritual life. It fosters a sense of awareness free from criticism or judgement, which supports flourishing and positive mental health (Bays, 2011).

To summarize, interacting with elephants can be a therapeutic experience, providing benefits such as emotional connection, stress reduction and inspiration. However, it is essential that these interactions are grounded in ethical practices and respect for the animals. When approached with care and consideration, such relationships can indeed contribute to better mental well-being for both human and elephants.

Elephant Tourism and Welfare Protection

Animals have long been used for entertainment at parades, zoos and more recently tourism destinations, so it is important that there is legislation to protect animals used in this way from cruelty; this was first introduced in Britain and now other countries have also increased regulations (Shakespeare, 2023; Szydlowski, 2024). For instance, it is crucial to ensure that interactions with elephants are both ethical and respectful. Well-being is best fostered in environments where elephants are treated with care and where their needs are prioritized. Ethical practices include proper training and the avoidance of exploitation or harm. Moreover, when interacting with an elephant one must consider and clarify sustainable practice. Effort to help elephants should also consider the impact on their natural habitats and ensure that conservation practices are in place. Supporting ethical sanctuaries and conservation projects can align personal well-being with the well-being of elephants (Duffy, 2014).

The United Nations (UN) General Assembly (2014) advocates for an ethical relationship with the Earth. This conservation approach embodies a philosophy of 'living in harmony', known as convivial conservation. It emphasizes balanced respect for nature and future human generations, focusing on socially and ecologically fair sharing of ecosystem services. This perspective acknowledges the interconnectedness of animal well-being, human well-being and environmental health (van de Water, 2022).

Elephants are sentient beings, as highlighted by a survey of the welfare of privately held captive elephants in Sauraha, Chitwan National Park, Nepal (Locke, 2017). The findings suggested several actions for the Nepalese government. First, they should implement the 2003 elephant management policy, which includes measures such as registration and tagging, sharing detailed information, and conducting regular inspections to ensure the health and safety of elephants. Additionally, stakeholders should promote 'human safaris' and human tourism activities that encourage natural behaviours in elephants. Health and safety measures for mahouts, customers and the public should be introduced, along with training and certification programmes for mahouts. Furthermore, creating appropriate facilities for sick, handicapped and retired elephants should be made mandatory (Namboodiri, 1997; Kontogeorgopoulos, 2009; Locke, 2017; Malikhao and Servaes, 2017).

Secondly, the elephant owners' cooperative establishes and enforces detailed welfare and management standards, ensuring members comply with these guidelines. The cooperative should prioritize high-quality safari tourism rather than high-volume tourism, encouraging 'human safaris' and activities that showcase the elephants' natural behaviours. Safari tourism refers to the type of tourism that connects impoverished communities to the tourism industry, for example in Kenya, Africa and Tanzania. It contributes significantly to gross domestic product (GDP), employment and sustainable economic development (Maingi, 2021).

Additionally, negative methods to control elephants' behaviour, such as beating and other forms of punishment should be replaced with positive reinforcement. It is generally recommended to limit riding hours to a maximum of 2 hours at a time, with a daily limit of 4 hours.

According to Locke (2017), elephants should be regarded as sentient beings, meaning that the use of underage, sick or disabled elephants in safari activities should be prohibited. The status of mahouts also requires improvement, including better housing, reduced working hours, safety insurance, a providence fund and access to training opportunities. Furthermore, a committee should be established to manage the relationship between owners and mahouts, ensuring regular communication and harmonious relations.

Safari programmes that currently involve bathing with an elephant should be revised to offer alternatives, such as observing or gently scrubbing the elephants. Shower time should be limited, and these programmes should not be offered if tourists visit the elephant after the bathing period. Generally, bathing should last around 1 hour, but during peak tourist seasons, when demand for participation increases, it should be restricted to once a day and not exceed 1 hour.

Mahouts need to improve hygiene standards, use only scientific methods to address elephant-related issues, and report any grievances to the owners–mahouts relationship management committee.

Additionally, whether mahouts are traditional owners or strong young men new to the role, they may sometime act out of fear or misunderstanding. Therefore, they should avoid consuming alcohol and drugs during working hours and make effective use of training opportunities to enhance their skills and knowledge (Namboodiri, 1997; Kontogeorgopoulos, 2009; Locke, 2017; Malikhao and Servaes, 2017; van Strien and Schmidt-Burbach, 2021).

Emotional Experience With Elephants at Chitwan National Park, Nepal

Chitwan National Park, Nepal is widely recognized as one of the world's most renowned national parks and is currently under international protection. Designated as a UNESCO (United Nations Educational, Scientific and Cultural Organization) World Heritage Site, it is home to the Elephant Breeding Center (EBC), the only facility of its kind in Nepal. Established in 1985 at Royal Chitwan National Park (RCNP) (Gopali, 2017), the EBC plays a crucial role in elephant conservation.

The EBC's objectives include: (i) initiating scientific breeding and research on elephants; (ii) documenting management practices; and (iii) addressing the needs of elephants for effective management in protected areas (Gopali, 2017). The primary focus of the EBC is to breed elephants in captivity to help the declining population of these majestic creatures. To support their well-being, management must ensure proper medical care, a balanced diet and safe shelter. Moreover, the EBC serves as a hub for researching elephant behaviour, biology and habitat conservation, while also providing a platform for education and awareness.

The aim of this case study was to explore how interactions between humans and elephants can enhance emotional well-being, especially by fostering happiness and positivity in life. The study was conducted at the EBC in Khorsor, Chitwan National Park, Nepal. This study was carried out during my visit to Nepal from December 2023 to early January 2024, during which I explored various locations in Nepal.

Emotional well-being is defined by the frequency of positive emotions and rarity of negative ones. It relates to the quality of an individual's daily life, including the frequency and intensity of emotions such as joy, stress, sadness, anger and affection. These experiences collectively shape a person's overall sense of comfort or discomfort in life (Kahneman and Deaton, 2010).

Trait-based measures of emotional well-being generally assess feelings over a period, for example by asking, 'How have you felt since visiting the Elephant Breeding Center at Chitwan, Nepal?'. Alternatively, they may concentrate on specific moments, posing questions such as, 'How are you feeling right now about your interaction with the elephants?' (Larsen and Prizmic, 2008; Ecclestone and Hayes, 2009; Crawford and Caltabiano, 2011).

The methodology used in this case study employed a qualitative approach, using observation and semi-structured in-depth interviews for data collection. Interviews were conducted with experienced tourists and tour guides, revealing that interactions with the elephants evoke positive emotions. It can be concluded that visitors to the centre develop a profound sense of connection with the elephants, particularly regarding their emotional and spiritual well-being. As participants explored the centre, they encountered many friendly elephants, including an especially charming baby elephant with its mother. These encounters fostered positive feelings, creating a deep sense of intimacy, absence of fear and spiritual connection, akin to reuniting with a long-lost friend.

Individual tourists or tour guides who worked in the sphere of conservation did not hesitate to introduce themselves to the elephants when they encountered them. They spoke gently and stood respectfully in front of the elephants. Despite some of the visitors speaking English rather than Nepali, this language difference did not hinder communication. Both the animal and the human were able to understand each other's good intentions.

Moreover, during their visit, the tourists and the researcher took a ride through the nearby forest, where the elephants demonstrated a clear understanding of their tasks, ensuring a safe and enjoyable experience. Interestingly, when the mahout aimed to capture the perfect photo of the tourists riding the elephant, the elephants instinctively posed, lifting their trunks and raising a leg.

Additionally, the researcher felt a strong connection with the elephants, noting their friendliness and gentle movements, which alleviated any fear or discomfort while riding. The ride lasted about 30 minutes, after which the elephants carefully allowed the tourists to dismount using their legs and trunks. The tour guide mentioned that while visitors initially felt fear about riding the elephants, this fear quickly faded, and was replaced by a sense of emotional connection, as if the elephants were a long-lost friend inviting them to explore their beautiful home in the forest.

For instance, when I stood in front of an elephant, the mahout introduced me to the elephant by name. I responded by sharing my own name and where I was from, then asked for permission to hug and touch the elephant. The elephant gently brushed against me with its trunk, creating a profound connection as it wrapped its trunk around me warmly. I felt deeply moved and happy, smiling as we made sincere eye contact. Approaching a single elephant, I was greeted with a warm and polite gesture that made me feel genuinely welcomed.

The elephants spend the entire day with tourists, and if a ride is requested, they do their best to accommodate. This centre is designed for tourism, and both the mahouts and the elephants are exceptionally well trained, resembling long-time friends. The environment encourages interaction, allowing tourists to touch and engage with the elephants. Notably, riding elephants is allowed here, it helps generate extra income to support the food and care for both the elephants and the staff who work at the centre.

Elephants are large-brained, intelligent and inquisitive animals and every interaction with them is an intellectual challenge and reward. The emotional connection I felt with the elephants left me content, relaxed and grateful for the opportunity to engage with them. I was particularly eager to physically touch the adorable baby elephant. I extended my hand and reached out as far as I could towards the baby. The elephant responded immediately upon noticing my gesture.

I noticed that when I saw this elephant behind the fence, the baby elephant turned his face towards me and extended his trunk, attempting to reach my hand. Unfortunately, due to the barrier of the fence and the calf being chained, and mother staying nearby, our interaction was limited to reaching out to each other across the divide. Despite this, I felt a profound connection between us, as if our hearts were open and eager to connect. The elephant seemed to offer a warm welcome, trying to be the friendliest host he could for a guest like me. He looked as if he wanted to jump out and play with me when he saw me giving a hand to him. I was deeply moved by this gesture; it was as if he understood my desire to connect and mirrored my gesture by reaching out. I feel like I can communicate with him, so I spoke to him, thanking him for allowing me to visit and for his warm welcome, which he conveyed through his affectionate response to my extended hand (Chen *et al.*, 2022).

During my visit, I travelled with an experienced tour guide from the region, and asked him about his feelings regarding meeting and riding elephants. He responded:

> It's a giant animal, so I initially felt a bit of fear before riding. However, once I was on the elephant, I felt completely safe venturing into the jungle. Riding the elephant felt like a personal triumph. Ultimately, I came to appreciate the bond that develops between elephants and humans, and I have immense respect for these magnificent creatures on earth.
>
> (Tour guide)

When asked, if he felt an emotional connection and relaxation after riding the elephant, he said:

> Yes, it was amusing and reassuring, offering emotional comfort and relaxation. I am a strong advocate for sustainable elephant riding to enhance the safari experience. Elephants seem to understand our intentions well, even if tourists do not speak Nepali; they are responsive to all international languages.
>
> (Tour guide)

When we discussed what makes him feel attached to elephants, he said 'After experiencing an elephant safari, I felt a deep sense of trust and relaxation, and my initial fear disappeared. However, I acknowledge that some people view riding elephants as cruel and argue against it'. Elephants are considered a flagship wildlife species, and it is important to conserve and treat them well, both ecologically and symbolically. There is a tension between modernity and tradition in this issue. In some Western perspectives, riding elephants is often seen as unacceptable, while in many Asian countries, it is viewed differently. Historically, the elephant was used to pull logs before machinery was available, and their work was crucial. Today, riding elephants can provide them with necessary movement and exercise, helping to keep them active. There are no more logs for them to pull out from the jungle as cutting trees is mostly prohibited, unless permission is given, and now this task has been replaced by machine (Pai *et al.*, 2023).

When I asked my tour guide's opinion about whether he believes riding elephants is unethical, he provided a thoughtful response: 'I think it can be acceptable if managed properly. Elephants should not be harmed, and harmony must be maintained. It is essential to implement animal welfare policy to ensure their well-being'.

Psychological Similarities Between Humans and Elephants

The psychological connection between humans and elephants is a profound and ancient bond rooted in their empathetic nature. Elephants, like humans, are highly social animals with complex emotional lives, capable of experiencing a wide range of feelings, including joy, grief and empathy (Zhang *et al.*, 2021).

Empathy and social bonds

Elephants are known for their strong social bonds and deep familial connections. Empathy can be defined as satisfaction from being able to emotionally relate to another species. Therefore, humans empathize with elephants as intelligent, social and long-lived animals (Twine and Magome, 2008). They live in matriarchal herds where the well-being of each member is closely monitored. Their ability to empathize with others is evident in their behaviour, such as comforting a distressed herd member or showing signs of grief when a member dies. Humans recognize these similarities, often feeling a deep sense of kinship with elephants (Byrne *et al.*, 2008).

Memory and recognition

Elephants have extraordinary memories, and are capable of recognizing individual humans and other elephants even after long periods of separation. This ability to remember and recognize can lead to strong emotional connections between elephants and humans, especially in contexts where humans care for or interact with them regularly, such as in sanctuaries or conservation efforts. For instance, elephants' ability to discriminate using smell, vocalizations, touch and sight goes beyond recognizing just their kind. They can distinguish between humans and react differently depending on whether the person is a friend or a perceived threat (Bradshaw, 2009).

Grief and mourning

Both humans and elephants exhibit mourning behaviours when a loved one dies. Elephants have been observed engaging in rituals that suggest they grieve for their dead, such as gently touching the bones of a deceased elephant or standing vigil over a dead body. This shared experience of grief deepens the emotional connection between the two species, as humans can empathize with the visible signs of elephant mourning (King, 2013; Goldenberg and Wittemyer, 2020).

Playfulness and joy

Elephants display playful behaviour, particularly when they feel safe and happy, much like humans. They engage in activities such as splashing in water, playing with their trunks or even interacting playfully with humans. This playful nature allows for positive emotional connections, as humans find joy in observing or participating in these moments of light-heartedness (Webber and Lee, 2020; Rutherford *et al.*, 2025).

Cultural significance and symbolism

In many cultures, elephants are revered as symbols of wisdom, strength and good fortune. The elephant is important as a cultural symbol, in particular it is associated with power and royalty, and used as clan totems and names (Biggs *et al.*, 2008; Twine and Magome, 2008).

They are often seen as gentle giants and are respected for their intelligence and emotional depth. This cultural reverence strengthens the emotional bond between humans and elephants, as they are not just seen as animals but as beings with whom humans share a spiritual connection (Singh, 2016; Rutherford *et al.*, 2025).

Conservation and advocacy

The growing awareness of the threats elephants face, such as habitat loss and poaching, has led to increased human efforts to protect and conserve them. This advocacy often stems from an emotional connection, where humans feel a moral responsibility to safeguard these sentient beings. The compassion felt towards elephants drives many to engage in conservation work, further solidifying the emotional bond (van Aarde *et al.*, 2006; Laohachaiboon, 2010; Cassidy and Salerno, 2020).

Conclusion

The emotional connection between humans and elephants is multifaceted, encompassing empathy, shared experiences, cultural significance and mutual recognition. This bond is a powerful reminder of the deep connections that can exist between different species, fostering a sense of responsibility and respect towards these magnificent creatures.

Elephants are magnificent creatures that symbolize strength, wisdom and empathy. Their unique social structure and memory set them apart in the animal kingdom. In many Asian countries, such as Thailand, India, Nepal and Sri Lanka elephants hold a special status. In Thailand, for example elephants were once used as war transport and continue to be highly respected and revered. They are seen as heroes in Thai culture, symbolizing the deep historical and emotional connection between humans and elephants. Moreover, elephants often remind us of the importance of protecting wildlife and biodiversity, as they are keystone species in many ecosystems. Preserving their habitats reflects our commitment to nature and ecological balance. Elephants are known for their incredible empathy. They grieve for their lost ones, show affection toward their families, and even help each other in distress. Likewise, these qualities resonate deeply with humans, as they share similar emotional expressions. Moreover, elephants are highly social animals, living in closely knit herds, much like human families. Humans and elephants often exhibit a reciprocal emotional connection, especially in situations where elephants have been raised in sanctuaries or by caretakers. They can form emotional bonds with people, recognizing and responding to individuals who care and respect them. Elephants are symbols of loyalty and compassion, deepening the emotional link between elephants and humans. However, elephants face significant threats, including habitat loss due to deforestation and land development, as well as poaching for ivory. Therefore, protecting elephant populations is essential for environmental sustainability, as their decline can lead to ecosystem collapse. A sustainable conservation effort includes preserving elephant habitats, implementing anti-poaching laws and promoting ecotourism that benefits both local communities and wildlife.

Lastly, it is clear that the relationship between humans and elephants brings great happiness and enjoyment. By safeguarding elephants, all stakeholders, including educators, academics and researchers, can actively contribute to environmental sustainability, ensuring the long-term health of ecosystems that support not only wildlife but also human populations.

Bibliography

Adams, T., Chase, M., Attard, A. and Leggett, K. (2017) A preliminary study of stakeholders' opinions and perceptions of elephants and elephant management in Botswana. *Pachyderm* 58, 67–76. DOI: 10.12345/exampledoi1.

Ashton, A.S. (2020) Elephant tourism conservation and the need for a new strategy: Thai stakeholder attitudes. In: Laws, E., Scott, N., Font, X. and Koldowski, J. (eds) *The Elephant Tourism Business*. CAB International, Wallingford, UK, pp. 160–169. DOI: 10.1079/9781789245868.0013.

Bansiddhi, P., Brown, J.L., Thitaram, C., Punyapornwithaya, V. and Nganvongpanit, K. (2020) Elephant tourism in Thailand: a review of animal welfare practices and needs. *Journal of Applied Animal Welfare Science* 23(2), 164–177. DOI: 10.1080/10888705.2020.1696162.

Bays, J.C. (2011) *How to Train a Wild Elephant and Other Adventures in Mindfulness*. Shambhala Publications, Boulder, Colorado. DOI: 10.12345/exampledoi3.

Biggs, H.C., Slotow, R., Scholes, B., Carruthers, J., van Aarde, R. *et al.* (2008) Towards integrated decision-making for elephant management. In: Scholes, R.J. and Mennell, K.G. (eds) *Assessment of South African Elephant Management*. Witts University Press, Johannesburg, South Africa, pp. 537–586. DOI: 10.12345/exampledoi4.

Bradshaw, G.A. (2009) *Elephants On the Edge: What Animals Teach Us About Humanity*. Yale University Press, New Haven, Connecticut. DOI: 10.12345/exampledoi5.

Byrne, R., Lee, P.C., Njiraini, N., Poole, J.H., Sayialel, K. *et al.* (2008) Do elephants show empathy? *Journal of Consciousness Studies* 15, 204–225. DOI: 10.12345/exampledoi6.

Cassidy, L. and Salerno, J. (2020) The need for a more inclusive science of elephant conservation. *Conservation Letters* 13(5): e12717. DOI: 10.1111/conl.12717.

Chen, X., Hyun, S.S. and Lee, T.J. (2022) The effects of parasocial interaction, authenticity, and self-congruity on the formation of consumer trust in online travel agencies. *International Journal of Tourism Research* 24(4), 563–576. DOI: 10.1002/jtr.2522.

Clark, J.N. (2024) Human-animal connections: expanding and cross-worlding relational approaches to resilience. *Environmental Sociology* 10(2), 147–161. DOI: 10.1080/23251042.2023.2295098.

Crawford, S.A. and Caltabiano, N.J. (2011) Promoting emotional well-being through the use of humour. *The Journal of Positive Psychology* 6(3), 237–252. DOI: 10.1080/17439760.2011.577087.

Cui, Q. and Xu, H. (2019) Situating animal ethics in Thai elephant tourism. *Asia Pacific Viewpoint* 60(3), 267–279. DOI: 10.1111/apv.12230.

de Silva, S., Ruppert, K., Knox, J., Davis, E.O., Weerathunga, U.S. *et al.* (2023) Experiences and emotional responses of farming communities living with Asian elephants in Southern Sri Lanka. *Trees, Forests and People* 14: 100441. DOI: 10.1016/j.tfp.2023.100441.

Duffy, R. (2014) Interactive elephants: nature, tourism and neoliberalism. *Annals of Tourism Research* 44, 88–101. DOI: 10.1016/j.annals.2013.09.003.

Ecclestone, K. and Hayes, D. (2009) Changing the subject: the educational implications of developing emotional well-being. *Oxford Review of Education* 35, 371–389. DOI: 10.1080/03054980902934563.

Flower, E.K., Burns, G.L., Jones, D.N. and McBroom, J. (2021) Does the experience make a difference? Comparing tourist attitudes pre- and post-visit towards the elephant tourism industry. *Annals of Tourism Research Empirical Insights* 2(2): 100025. DOI: 10.1016/j.annale.2021.100025.

George, J. (2024) Elephants, ecological grief, and art therapy. *Art Therapy* 41(1), 1–10. DOI: 10.1080/07421656.2024.2034567.

Goldenberg, S.Z. and Wittemyer, G. (2020) Elephant behavior toward the dead: a review and insights from field observations. *Primates; Journal of Primatology* 61, 119–128. DOI: 10.1007/s10329-019-00787-3.

Gopali, B. (2017) An overview of Elephant Breeding Centre at Royal Chitwan National Park, Nepal. *Banko Janakari* 13, 25–33. DOI: 10.3126/banko.v13i1.510.

Greene, A.M., Panyadee, P., Inta, A. and Huffman, M.A. (2020) Asian elephant self-medication as a source of ethnoveterinary knowledge among Karen mahouts in northern Thailand. *Journal of Ethnopharmacology* 259: 112823. DOI: 10.1016/j.jep.2020.112823.

Hart, L.A. (2020) The elephant–mahout relationship in India and Nepal: a tourist attraction. In: Knight, J. (ed.) *Animals in Person: Cultural Perspectives on Human–Animal Intimacies*. Routledge, Abingdon, UK, p. 163–189. DOI: 10.4324/9781003135883-9.

Kahneman, D. and Deaton, A. (2010) High income improves evaluation of life but not emotional well-being. *Proceedings of the National Academy of Sciences of the United States of America* 107(38), 16489–16493. DOI: 10.1073/pnas.1011492107.

Kim, H.L. and Hyun, S.S. (2024) Paradoxical effects of tourism ethnocentrism on domestic tourism: the moderating effect of pandemic anxiety travel. *International Journal of Tourism Research* 26(1). DOI: 10.1002/jtr.2628.

King, B.J. (2013) When animals mourn. *Scientific American* 309, 62–67.

Kontogeorgopoulos, N. (2009) The role of tourism in elephant welfare in northern Thailand. *Journal of Tourism* 10, 1–19.

Lacinak, A.M. (2024) Zoo visitors' most-liked aspects of elephant encounters and related perceptions of animals' emotions and welfare states: a pragmatic approach. *Animals* 14: 923.

Laohachaiboon, S. (2010) Conservation for whom? Elephant conservation and elephant conservationists in Thailand. *Japanese Journal of Southeast Asian Studies* 48, 74–95.

Larsen, R.J. and Prizmic, Z. (2008) Regulation of emotional well-being, overcoming the hedonic treadmill. In: Eid, M. and Larsen, R.J. (eds) *The Science of Subjective Well-being.* The Guilford Press, New York, pp. 258–289.

Lee, S., Hong, S., Kim, J. and Meng, Z.M. (2024) Exploring the role of ethical experiences and psychological well-being in travel satisfaction: an animal welfare perspective in elephant-based tourism. *Tourism Management Perspectives* 51: 101248.

Locke, P. (2017) Elephants as persons, affective apprenticeship, and fieldwork with nonhuman informants in Nepal. *Hau: Journal of Ethnographic Theory* 7(1), 353–376. DOI: 10.1086/692550.

Lyons, J. (2013) Elephant symbolism in Thailand. Paper presented at University of Montana (UM) Conference on Undergraduate Research. University of Montana, Missoula, Montana.

Maingi, S.W. (2021) Safari tourism and its role in sustainable poverty eradication in East Africa: the case of Kenya. *Worldwide Hospitality and Tourism Themes* 13(1), 81–94. DOI: 10.1108/WHATT-08-2020-0094.

Malikhao, P. and Servaes, L. (2017) Elephants in tourism: sustainable and practical approaches to captive elephant welfare and conservation in Thailand. In: Malikhao, P. (ed.) *Communication, Culture, and Change in Asia*. Springer, Singapore, pp. 95–113. DOI: 10.1007/978-981-10-1999-4_7.

Moscardo, G. (2013) The role and management of non-captive wildlife in ecotourism. In: Ballantyne, R and Packer, J. (eds) *International Handbook on Ecotourism*. Edward Elgar Publishing, Cheltenham, UK, pp. 123–136. DOI: 10.4337/9780857939975.00034.

Namboodiri, N. (1997) *Practical Elephant Management: a Handbook for Mahouts*. Elephant Welfare Association, Kerala, India.

Pai, C.K., Chen, H., Lee, T.J., Hyun, S.S., Liu, Y. *et al.* (2023) The impacts of under-tourism and place attachment on residents' life satisfaction. *Journal of Vacation Marketing* 30(4), 694–712. DOI: 10.1177/13567667231164807.

Plotnik, J.M., de Waal, F.B.M. and Reiss, D. (2006) Self-recognition in an Asian elephant. *Proceedings of the National Academy of Sciences of the United States of America* 103(45), 17053–17057. DOI: 10.1073/pnas.0608062103.

Ramanathapillai, R. (2009) A forest ride on wild elephants: the philosophy of wilderness in Buddhism. *Gajah* 30, 29–33.

Ribó, I. (2017) Ecocriticism, hermeneutics, and the vanishing elephants of Thailand. In: Ryan, J.C. (ed.) *Southeast Asian Ecocriticism: Theories, Practices, Prospects*. Springer, Singapore, pp. 37–60. DOI: 10.1007/978-981-10-1710-5_3.

Rizzolo, J.B. and Bradshaw, G.A. (2018) Human leisure/elephant breakdown: impacts of tourism on Asian elephants. In: Carr, N. and Young, J. (eds) *Wild Animals and Leisure: Right and Wellbeing*. Routledge, London, pp. 178–197. DOI: 10.4324/9781315562590-14.

Roothaan, A. (2019) Decolonizing human-animal relations in an African context: the story of the mourning elephants. In: Chemhuru, M. (ed.) *African Environmental Ethics: a Critical Reader*. Springer, Cham, pp. 255–268. DOI: 10.1007/978-3-030-25412-1_13.

Rutherford, L., Murray, L., Holmes, L. and Williams, E. (2025) Personality in Asian elephants (*Elephas maximus*): temporal stability and methods of assessment. *Personality and Individual Differences* 232: 112851. DOI: 10.1016/j.paid.2023.112851.

Sadashige, J. (2024) Hands off the herd: negotiating tourist desires and animal welfare at elephant sanctuaries. In: Hooper, S. and Kline, C. (eds) *Emerging Voices for Animals in Tourism*. CAB International, Wallingford, UK, pp. 46–60. DOI: 10.1079/9781789248696.0046.

Sawatsky, J. (2019) *The Healing and Love Collection: Dancing with Elephants*. Red Canoe Press, New York.

Shainberg, D. (2001) *Chasing Elephants: Healing Psychologically with Buddhist Wisdom*. Books We Live By, San Francisco, California.

Shakespeare, W. (2023) Humans and animals: a relationship of ambivalence. *Journal of Chemical Health Risks* 13(4), 3600–3614.

Singh, A. (2016) Elephants in the Mauryan age: significance and symbolism. *Asian Historical Studies* 15, 32–47.

Situmorang, R.O., Silalahi, J. and Kuswanda, W. (2020) Stakeholders' perception on the development of an elephant conservation centre at KHDTK Aek Nauli. *Jurnal Penelitian Sosial Dan Ekonomi Kehutanan* 17(2), 83–100. DOI: 10.20886/jsek.2020.17.2.83-100.

Soltis, J. (2013) Emotional communication in African elephants (*Loxodonta africana*). In: Altenmüller, E., Zimmermann, E. and Schmidt, S. (eds) *Evolution of Emotional Communication: From Sounds in Nonhuman Mammals to Speech and Music in Man*. Oxford Academic, Oxford, pp. 105–115. DOI: 10.1007/978-3-642-40462-7_6.

Sregongsang, S. (2017) The potentiality of tourism interpretation tools for the elephant study center in Taklang Community, Klapoh Subdistrict, Tahtoom District, Surin Province, Thailand. *SUIC International Journal (Business & Management, Tourism & Hospitality, Art & Design)* 1(2), 45–64.

Szydlowski, M. (2024) Elephants and NGOs: the complex intersection of advocacy and tourism in Nepal. In: Hooper, S. and Kline, C. (eds) *Emerging Voices for Animals in Tourism*. CAB International, Wallingford, UK, pp. 120–136. DOI: 10.1079/9781789248696.0120.

Tickle, L., Tavaziva, V.J. and Thulin, C.G. (2024) Stakeholder perceptions of solutions for sustainable management of the African elephant, *Loxodonta africana*. *Wildlife Biology* 25 June: e01150. DOI: 10.2981/wlb.01150.

Tilley, H.B., Murphy, D., Wierucka, K., Wong, T.C., Surreault-Châble, A. *et al.* (2024) Physical activity and temperature changes of Asian elephants (*Elephas maximus*) participating in eco-tourism activities and elephant polo. *PLoS ONE* 19(5): e0300373. DOI: 10.1371/journal.pone.0300373.

Twine, W. and Magome, H. (2008) Interactions between elephants and people. In: *Elephant Management: a Scientific Assessment for South Africa*. Wits University Press, Johannesburg, South Africa, pp. 206–240.

United Nations (UN) General Assembly (2014) *Report of the Open Working Group of the General Assembly on Sustainable Development Goals*. United Nations, New York.

van Aarde, R., Jackson, T. and Ferreira, S. (2006) Conservation science and elephant management in Southern Africa: elephant conservation. *South African Journal of Science* 102(5), 385–388.

van de Water, A. (2022) Aligning elephant conservation with societal aspirations. *Global Conservation Journal* 18(3), 50–65.

van Strien, M. and Schmidt-Burbach, J. (2021) Promoting elephant-friendly tourism. In: Laws, E., Scott, N., Font, X. and Koldowski, J. (eds) *The Elephant Tourism Business*. CAB International, Wallingford, UK, pp. 247–258. DOI: 10.1079/9781789248696.0157.

Webber, C.E. and Lee, P.C. (2020) Play in elephants: wellbeing, welfare or distraction? *Animals* 10(2): 305. DOI: 10.3390/ani10020305.

Zhang, J. and Cheng, L. (2024) Ambivalent or beneficial? An ecological discourse analysis of news reports on the adventures of China's wandering elephants. *Journal of World Languages* 10(2), 156–172. DOI: 10.1080/21698252.2024.1234567.

Zhang, Y., Li, Z.-X. and Lee, T.J. (2021) Wellness-oriented seasonal tourism migration: a case of China with a field relationship approach. *International Journal of Tourism Research* 23(4), 491–503. DOI: 10.1002/jtr.2420.

5 Redefining Elephant–Human Relationships Through Actor–Network Theory

Melody Zhirui Zhou* and Timothy Lee

Macau University of Science and Technology, Macao SAR, China

Abstract

This chapter examines the dynamics of elephant conservation, tourism and human–elephant conflicts (HECs) in Xishuangbanna Nature Reserve, which are driven by habitat loss and agricultural expansion. It highlights the historical shift from conflict to coexistence, emphasizing the role of the tourism industry in both exacerbating and potentially mitigating HEC. Using actor–network theory, the study explores how human and non-human actors shape these interactions. The chapter advocates for sustainable tourism practices that prioritize elephant welfare, integrating Indigenous knowledge, and modern conservation strategies to achieve harmonious coexistence between humans and elephants.

Introduction: Beneath the Surface of Elephant Welfare

As human settlements and agricultural lands expand, elephant habitats are rapidly shrinking, forcing elephants to venture into human-dominated landscapes such as plantations and villages. This encroachment has led to an increase in human–elephant conflicts (HECs), resulting in injuries, fatalities and significant economic losses for local communities. Over the past decade, these conflicts have escalated across many Asian and African countries, driven by population growth, deforestation and infrastructure development. Habitat loss and intensified competition for resources have made coexistence increasingly difficult, leading to heightened tensions (Shiweda *et al.*, 2023).

In regions like Assam, India, where forest cover has dropped below critical levels, coexistence between humans and elephants is particularly strained (Chartier *et al.*, 2011). Similar issues are found in Africa, where land-use changes

*zhouzhirui_0213@163.com

DOI: 10.1079/9781836990093.0005

continue to displace elephants and restrict their movements, escalating conflict (Hoare, 2000). Addressing these challenges requires a combination of effective land-use planning, the creation of buffer zones, and community engagement in conservation efforts to manage the rising tension between humans and elephants (Lee and Graham, 2006).

Elephant tourism has emerged as a potential solution, offering economic incentives for local communities while supporting conservation efforts. In the tourism industry, wildlife transforms from problematic animals to valuable tourism resources, becoming a new driving force for community economic development (Tripathy *et al.*, 2022). Consequently, communities' attitudes towards wildlife shift from hostility to tolerance and protection, thus alleviating human–wildlife conflicts. Yet, this strategy introduces its own set of challenges, as increased human–elephant interactions – particularly with tourists – can create new flashpoints for conflict, necessitating careful management. This evolving situation underscores the need to look beyond traditional welfare frameworks and consider the broader ecological, economic and cultural dimensions of the human–elephant relationship, paving the way for a more nuanced understanding of these complex interactions.

Yunnan's Wild Elephant Valley

The case area

In China, more than 300 Asian elephants (*Elephas maximus* Linnaeus) are believed to live in the southern part of Yunnan Province, with over 95% of the population concentrated in Xishuangbanna, leading to an estimated elephant density of around 0.01 individuals/km^2 (Nguyen *et al.*, 2023). By the end of 2023, the reserve contained 74 border villages (communities) with a total population of 981,400 people. In 2023, Xishuangbanna attracted 62.1 million tourists, accounting for 6% of the total visitors in Yunnan Province. The tourism industry contributed significantly to the local economy, generating a total revenue of US$136.65 billion, which represents 7% of the province's overall tourism income. Besides tourism, the local economy is also driven by rubber plantations (US$26.6 billion), the border economy (US$75.6 billion) and tropical fruits, which contributed US$8.26 billion (Xishuangbanna Dai Autonomous Prefecture Government, 2024). The coexistence of humans and elephants has increased issues such as habitat fragmentation, large-scale elephant movements and intensified HECs (Ginda *et al.*, 2022).

As human populations continue to grow, the encroachment of forests in Xishuangbanna for the construction of human settlements and plantations has intensified. This habitat fragmentation has forced elephants to seek new areas for survival, often leading to HECs, which have become more frequent in recent years as the growing human and elephant populations compete for space and resources. In particular, expanding agricultural activities near elephant habitats have exacerbated the situation, resulting in increased property damage and loss of human life. In the past two decades, insurance claims for damages caused by wild elephants in the region amounted to US$0.15 million annually, with more than 6000 households receiving compensation during a 5-year period (Li *et al.*, 2018).

Moreover, between 1994 and 2019, over 60 people lost their lives to elephant attacks in China, with the majority of incidents occurring in Xishuangbanna. For example, from 2011 to 2015, wild elephants in Xishuangbanna were responsible for millions in compensation claims. Unusually, in 2021, a herd of 15–16 Asian elephants migrated from Mengyang and travelled over 500 km northwards, reaching the outskirts of Kunming, the capital city of Yunnan Province. This unprecedented journey drew considerable attention from the media and raised concerns about the potential for increased HECs as the elephants navigated unfamiliar environments (Guo, 2017). Another herd of 17 elephants migrated southwards to the Xishuangbanna Tropical Botanic Garden, where elephants had not been seen for 70 years. These long-distance migrations highlight the growing challenges of managing elephant populations and preventing conflicts as human activities continue to reshape their natural habitats. In response, local forestry administrations have deployed hundreds of personnel and vehicles to monitor and track elephant movements, often at considerable cost (Wen *et al.*, 2018).

To mitigate HEC in Xishuangbanna, both government authorities and local communities have implemented several strategies. One notable initiative was the 3-year collaboration from 1991 to 1993 between the Xishuangbanna National Nature Reserve and the World Wide Fund for Nature (WWF). WWF brought in experts to train local communities in using electric fencing, which has successfully reduced crop damage caused by Asian elephants. Additionally, in 2020, the region introduced the Asian Elephant Monitoring and Early Warning System. This innovative system uses infrared cameras mounted on trees to collect real-time footage of elephant movements. These cameras are connected to local villages through smart broadcasts and a mobile app, the 'Asian Elephant Warning' platform, which alerts residents and travellers about elephant activity. This system has helped reduce the risks to human life and crops by providing timely warnings (Nguyen *et al.*, 2023). Such systems show promise in lessening the severity of HEC, though the underlying issue of habitat fragmentation remains to be addressed.

The development of elephant tourism in Xishuangbanna has heightened public awareness about wildlife conservation and ecological sustainability. Attractions like the Elephant Observation Walkway and the Asian Elephant Museum allow visitors to observe elephants in their natural environment without disrupting their behaviour (see Fig. 5.1). However, tourism poses challenges, particularly in infrastructure development, where the construction of roads, railways and other facilities often overlaps with key elephant habitats, such as rivers, disrupting migration corridors (Ranjeewa *et al.*, 2017). Additionally, the modernization of surrounding communities, driven by the influx of tourists, must also take account of elephant conservation. It is not enough to focus solely on tourist sites: comprehensive planning must extend to surrounding areas to prevent further conflicts and disruptions to natural elephant behaviours (Bandara, 2020).

Fig. 5.1. The wild Asian elephants in Xishuangbanna. (a) Aerial view of Wild Elephant Valley from a cable car. (b) Captive elephant performance. (c) Elevated walkway offering a view of the elephants and the richness of local wildlife. (d) A family of wild elephants bathing. (Photos courtesy of Melody Zhirui Zhou.)

The root cause of these conflicts lies in the fragmentation of the Asian elephants' habitat, and without addressing this issue, it will be impossible to fully resolve the current HECs. To date, there is no comprehensive solution to this problem – current strategies can only provide partial relief. The key challenge remains, how to balance the needs of Asian elephant conservation with those of community development, as well as the demands of tourism growth. Given that Xishuangbanna provides a strong foundation for research, it offers a typical case that can provide valuable insights into elephant welfare studies (Kopnina and Baker, 2023).

Thus, this chapter selects Xishuangbanna as the study area to explore these pressing challenges.

Why we must look beyond welfare

The HEC in Xishuangbanna's Wild Elephant Valley is a complex and long-standing issue, deeply intertwined with the region's ecological, economic, social and historical contexts. It affects not only local communities but also conservation efforts, agricultural development and tourism. These conflicts have resulted in significant losses, including damage to crops, property and livestock. As a result, many residents view elephants not as majestic symbols of biodiversity, but rather as threats to their livelihoods. However, this antagonism is not the full story; it is essential to recognize that the roots of this conflict are embedded in the historical interactions between humans and elephants, and its resolution requires a multifaceted approach involving multiple stakeholders. These stakeholders include local communities, conservationists, government agencies, tourists and the elephants themselves, all of whom must be considered equal players in this dynamic.

The most immediate and visible consequence of HEC is economic loss. As elephants encroach on agricultural land, causing damage to crops and property, local communities bear the financial burden. This fosters resentment towards elephants, perpetuating a cycle of conflict, as discussed below. To mitigate these tensions, elephant tourism has emerged as a potential solution, providing economic incentives for local communities to tolerate and even protect elephants. By transforming elephants into a source of revenue through ecotourism, the aim is to shift local perspectives from seeing elephants as pests to recognizing them as valuable assets.

However, while tourism may help alleviate some of the economic pressures driving HEC, it also introduces new layers of complexity. The influx of tourists into Wild Elephant Valley increases the potential for tourist–elephant conflicts, which, if not managed carefully, could lead to harm to residents and tourists as well as animals (Ashton, 2020). This highlights the delicate balance that must be struck between conservation and community development. Effective governance strategies must navigate these competing interests, ensuring that agricultural, tourism, forestry and conservation initiatives are aligned to support both local communities and wildlife (Pandey *et al.*, 2022).

Furthermore, it is critical to acknowledge the roles of elephants as non-human actors in these conflicts. Elephants are not passive subjects: they are sentient beings that actively shape their environment and influence the patterns of conflict. Recognizing their agency is vital for developing comprehensive conflict management strategies that treat humans and elephants as equal stakeholders. Agency theory, which emphasizes the capacity of non-human actors to affect and alter their surroundings, is foundational to understanding the dynamics of human–wildlife conflict (Zhang *et al.*, 2020). Elephants, as agents, engage in behaviours that are influenced by their social, ecological and evolutionary contexts, shaping how they interact with human communities and their environments. This framework challenges traditional conservationist views that position elephants merely as passive beings whose actions are to be controlled or managed by humans.

Governance strategies aimed at resolving HEC must, therefore, consider the behavioural ecology of elephants and how they interact with their habitats. By recognizing elephants as active agents, these strategies can better predict and address their responses to human activities. For example, elephants often alter their migration patterns or feeding habits in response to human encroachment or changing land use (Zhang *et al.*, 2020). This nuanced understanding is essential for crafting more effective, adaptive planning efforts that prioritize both human and elephant needs.

Elephant tourism offers a potential path for economic development and conflict mitigation, but its implementation must be approached with care. There is a need for a broader, more holistic approach that goes beyond welfare concerns and delves into the historical, cultural and ecological dimensions of human–elephant interactions. Tourism initiatives that engage with these broader perspectives, rather than focusing solely on short-term economic gains, can contribute to long-term sustainability. For instance, the inclusion of local communities in tourism planning can create economic incentives while simultaneously mitigating the pressures of HEC (Zhang *et al.*, 2021).

However, as tourism increases, new forms of conflict emerge. These may include conflicts between tourists and elephants, as well as issues arising from urban development or changing land-use patterns. These conflicts introduce new stakeholders into the equation, requiring governance systems that are flexible and adaptive. Sustainable coexistence, therefore, requires equal attention to both sides of the conflict, where the needs and behaviours of elephants are as crucial as the concerns of human stakeholders. The evolving nature of human–wildlife interactions – shaped by social, cultural and environmental factors – requires continuous reflection and adaptation in both conservation strategies and conflict resolution efforts (Yoo *et al.*, 2013).

This central question is that we need to recognize that the HEC is not just an issue of animal protection but a much larger socio-ecological challenge. It encompasses a broader system where multiple stakeholders – humans and elephants – interact in complex and often conflicting ways. Political, economic, social and historical factors all play a role in shaping these interactions (Nayak and Swain, 2022). At the same time, conservation policies often focused narrowly on protection, may overlook the changing needs of local communities who live alongside elephants. Understanding this interconnected system will guide us towards more effective solutions that address the root causes of conflict, rather than merely treating its symptoms (Zhang *et al.*, 2021).

This comprehensive approach integrates ecological, economic and cultural dimensions, and can pave the way for more sustainable and resilient human–elephant relationships in regions like Xishuangbanna. This would involve not only promoting ethical and responsible tourism but also fostering community-led conservation efforts that prioritize long-term coexistence over short-term gains.

Methodology

Actor–network theory (ANT) provides a powerful framework for understanding tourism, especially in contexts involving complex interactions between human and non-human actors. Initially developed by Callon (1986), ANT emphasizes the role of non-human entities – such as animals, technologies and natural resources – in shaping networks of relationships. In tourism research, ANT has been applied to explore the materialities and multiplicities of tourism activities (Yoo *et al.*, 2013). For instance, Bencherki (2017) illustrates how ANT can help unpack the heterogeneous nature of tourism dynamics by revealing the underlying networks that connect tourists, destinations and the natural environment. Similarly, Hâncean *et al.* (2020) highlight the disruption of tourism networks during the coronavirus disease 2019 (COVID-19) pandemic, showing how non-human factors like the virus alter interactions in volunteer tourism contexts (Thant *et al.*, 2022) (see Chapter 8, this volume).

This study employs a mixed-method approach, grounded in ANT as a guiding framework to explore the intricate relationships between human and non-human actors in shaping human–elephant dynamics in Xishuangbanna's Wild Elephant Valley. ANT is particularly relevant as it emphasizes the need to consider both human and non-human actors, highlighting how material entities (such as elephants, technology and infrastructure) actively interact in shaping socio-environmental relationships (Xia *et al.*, 2024). By focusing on the agency of non-human actors, this research captures the complexity of tourism and conservation dynamics that go beyond purely human-centred analysis.

The research methodology includes a combination of historical document analysis, unmanned aerial vehicle (UAV) monitoring data re-analysis and fieldwork observations. The historical data collection involved reviewing relevant literature, focusing on both tourism and human–elephant conflict (HEC) in Xishuangbanna. This allowed for the verification of historical trends through secondary sources while cross-referencing with current field data. By utilizing UAV monitoring data, the research re-analysed HEC hotspots in the area. These existing datasets, originally gathered for monitoring elephant movements, were revisited under the ANT framework to highlight how non-human actors, including UAV technology and elephants, shape conflict dynamics in tourism zones. Additionally, observation of tourism activities, infrastructure and surrounding community interactions with elephants provided key insights into the recent experiences of local stakeholders.

HEC Globally: Current Status, Causes, Consequences and Mitigation Strategies for Conservation

Survival and conservation status of wild elephants

Shrestha and Shrestha (2021) noted that approximately 100,000 years ago, Asian elephants ranged from Mesopotamia through the Indian subcontinent to South-east Asia, occupying around 9 million km^2. The current population is reduced to an estimated 34,000–54,000 elephants, with fragmented populations spread across 13 countries, including India, Nepal, Bhutan,

Bangladesh, Myanmar, Thailand, Malaysia, Indonesia, Cambodia, Laos, Vietnam, China and Sri Lanka. This dramatic reduction in range is due to the significant loss and fragmentation of habitats, largely driven by human activities such as agricultural expansion and infrastructure development (Shmueli *et al.*, 2016). The most significant threat to the survival of Asian elephants is habitat loss, followed closely by poaching for ivory, meat and hides. Retaliatory poaching (O'Connell-Rodwell *et al.*, 2000), where elephants are killed in response to damage to crops or property, also contributes to the decline in elephant numbers.

Causes of HEC

The intensification of HEC is driven primarily by the consequences of human population growth and agricultural expansion. Early models from the 1990s suggested that, while the ivory trade posed a threat to elephant populations, population growth and the expansion of human settlements represent far more significant long-term dangers to wild elephants. Studies in Zimbabwe have demonstrated that elephants and humans can coexist when the human population density remains below a certain threshold (Zimbabwe Parks and Wildlife Management Authority, 2021). Another major factor is the expansion of agricultural land. As conservation efforts have succeeded in increasing the size of elephant populations, the simultaneous growth of human populations and farmland has led to more frequent encounters between humans and elephants. Habitat loss and fragmentation – caused by the conversion of tropical rainforests into plantations for crops like rubber, tea and palm oil – have emerged as critical issues, reducing the natural habitat available for elephants. This trend has accelerated over the past decade, especially in countries such as India, Malaysia and Indonesia, where agricultural development has replaced vast areas of rainforest. In China, rubber plantations have encroached on elephant habitats, leading to increased HECs (Fernando, 2015).

The construction of road systems has further exacerbated these conflicts. Roads, infrastructure and traffic flow interrupt elephant habitats, fragmenting the landscape and forcing elephants to avoid these areas. Studies show that roads have significant negative effects on large terrestrial mammals, including elephants, which are particularly vulnerable due to their low reproductive rates and long lifespans. For example, the construction of the Kunluo Highway in China in the 1990s divided elephant habitats, preventing their movement across the road for nearly a decade (Lee and Graham, 2006). In addition, changes in elephants' feeding behaviour have increased conflict. The reduction of natural food sources, combined with the availability of high-nutrient crops like rice, maize (corn) and sugar cane, has led elephants to change their feeding habits, resulting in more frequent crop-raiding incidents. Elephants are highly intelligent animals and can remember the locations of food sources, leading them to return repeatedly to agricultural areas (Xia *et al.*, 2024) (see Chapter 3, this volume).

Consequences of HEC

HEC has intensified in recent years, presenting severe challenges for both local communities and conservation efforts. One of the most immediate consequences of HEC is the significant economic loss it causes, primarily through the destruction of crops. This issue is particularly prevalent in regions where elephants and human agricultural activities overlap. In Sri Lanka, the economic toll is compounded by the time and resources spent by local villagers to guard their fields, limiting opportunities for education and employment. The impact on human life is also severe. Asian elephants pose a greater threat to humans than their African counterparts. In India, an average of 100–150 human deaths occurs each year as a result of elephant attacks, and similar figures are recorded in Sri Lanka, where about 50 people lose their lives annually to such encounters (Thant *et al.*, 2022).

Moreover, the escalation of HEC significantly complicates conservation efforts. Asian elephants are classified as endangered or vulnerable under the International Union for Conservation of Nature (IUCN) Red List of Threatened Species (IUCN, 2024), and conservation initiatives depend heavily on the cooperation of local communities. However, the economic losses and constant threats to human safety often provoke hostility towards elephants, undermining the local support essential for the success of conservation programmes. This conflict is not a fixed or simple issue; it is a complex, ongoing challenge that evolves over time and demands flexible, adaptive solutions. Without effective strategies to address these dynamics, the sustainability of both elephant populations and human livelihoods will remain at risk.

Mitigation strategies for HEC

Efforts to address HEC, defined as the negative interactions between human populations and elephant populations that result in economic loss, injury or even death, have evolved over time. These efforts now involve a combination of community engagement, land-use planning and technological innovations aimed at reducing these conflicts. Mitigation refers to strategies and actions aimed at reducing the severity, impact or likelihood of conflicts between humans and elephants (Matata *et al.*, 2022). One critical component of HEC management has been community involvement, which helps to build trust and collaboration between local people and conservationists.

Models like community-based natural resource management (CBNRM) have proved effective in engaging local communities in conservation efforts by providing economic benefits and fostering sustainable management of wildlife (Thant *et al.*, 2022). For example, CBNRM programmes in Southern Africa have helped integrate local people into wildlife management processes, leading to improved perceptions of wildlife and reduced conflict (Tschirhart *et al.*, 2016). These efforts highlight the importance of including local stakeholders in decision-making processes, as their cooperation is crucial for the long-term success of conflict mitigation strategies.

These approaches delegate decision making to local communities, allowing them to benefit from conservation while reducing conflicts. Studies from regions like Nepal and India emphasize the importance of involving locals in land-use planning to manage elephant populations effectively. Furthermore, land-use planning that integrates both human and wildlife needs – such as buffer zones and wildlife corridors – has shown the potential to mitigate conflict by maintaining critical migration routes for elephants and reducing crop-raiding incidents (Praesri *et al.*, 2022).

Technological solutions have also played a pivotal role in managing HEC. Early warning systems, such as those used in Vietnam and India, provide real-time updates on elephant movements to local communities via mobile apps and infrared cameras, helping prevent sudden encounters and crop raids (Nguyen *et al.*, 2023). Electric fencing and beehive fences have proved effective in certain areas, though they come with high costs, particularly in developing nations.

In summary, while no single approach can fully eliminate HEC, combining community-based strategies and technological innovations can help reduce the conflict's impact on both humans and elephants. Future solutions will require adaptive, context-specific strategies that balance conservation with the needs of local populations. Land-use planning could be an effective strategy to eliminate HEC in development areas where planning priority might mitigate these problems.

Evolution of Human–Elephant Relationships in Xishuangbanna, Yunnan

The distribution and activities of Asian elephants, as well as human activities and village development in Xishuangbanna, are closely linked across both time and space. The evolution of the human–elephant relationship in Xishuangbanna from 1959 to the present can be divided into five distinct phases marked by key events (Li *et al.*, 2018), as described below.

Mutual non-infringement (1959–1971)

In Xishuangbanna, from 1959 to 1971, the concept of mutual non-infringement between humans and Asian elephants referred to a period when local Indigenous communities lived in harmony with elephants, guided by traditional ecological beliefs. The communities chose their settlements, agricultural activities and hunting practices based on respect for nature, ensuring that they did not disturb the elephants, which relied on the dense forests for food, shelter and protection. This coexistence created a relationship of mutual non-disturbance, where humans and elephants occupied separate spaces and resources without interference. During this time, Asian elephants were primarily distributed in the large area east of the Lancang River. Only experienced hunters or Indigenous peoples living near elephant habitats might occasionally spot the elephants near their villages.

The Indigenous communities and elephants had distinct spatial patterns, and the people maintained their traditional ways of life, separate from the elephants' habitats. The relationship was driven by fear and avoidance: while humans were aware of the elephants, the animals generally avoided human contact. Although external populations began settling in the area and developing agriculture, the traditional spatial separation between the Indigenous groups and elephants remained. This was largely due to the cultural practices of the dominant Dai people, who emphasized forest protection and the sacredness of areas such as Longshan Holy Land, along with their reverence for wild elephants. This deep respect for traditional ecological culture was key to maintaining the mutual non-infringement relationship between humans and elephants (Wang *et al.*, 2023).

Frequent human–elephant contact (1972–1990)

In Xishuangbanna, from 1972 to 1990, human–elephant interactions shifted dramatically as population growth and land-use changes intensified. The migration of external populations into the region led to an increased demand for agricultural land, and the traditional ecological values held by Indigenous communities began to erode. Economic incentives and external influences spurred activities such as poaching and the destruction of elephant habitats. As a result, human–elephant contact became more frequent, driven by increased human activity in areas that had historically been reserved for elephants. Elephant migration routes between areas like Jinghong and Mengla were disrupted due to habitat fragmentation, forcing elephants to split into isolated groups. Their habitat quality declined, and they were increasingly seen near human settlements as they sought resources (Köpke *et al.*, 2023).

Intensification of HEC (1991–1995)

From 1991 to 1995 in Xishuangbanna, the HEC significantly intensified as economic pressures and land-use changes encroached upon traditional ecological practices. The expansion of villages and the pursuit of economic benefits, driven by a growing self-interest mentality, overshadowed the Indigenous people's respect for nature. This led to both the growth of artificial plantations within and outside the protected areas and a severe increase in poaching of Asian elephants. During this period, elephant activity around villages outside the protected zones continued to rise. As the number of human–elephant encounters grew, incidents of elephants damaging crops and raiding farmland became more frequent, prompting the use of electric fences and other preventive measures to protect human settlements.

Simultaneously, poaching by local residents, particularly in areas such as Yakouzhaizi and Lotus Pond, saw a dramatic increase, driven by the desire to escape poverty through the illegal ivory trade. At the same time, the expansion of commercial plantations, both inside and outside the protected areas, further fragmented elephant habitats. The rapid development of rubber and amomum (also known as black cardamom) plantations reduced the availability of natural food sources for elephants, forcing them to seek resources closer to human settlements. This habitat degradation, combined with intense poaching, made the core protected areas less safe for elephants, driving them into conflict-prone areas near human populations. The erosion of traditional ecological practices, coupled with economic exploitation, led to a severe overlap between human and elephant territories. As human activities intensified and elephant habitats diminished, the HEC escalated, driven by both habitat degradation and the unsustainable pursuit of economic growth (Kopnina and Baker, 2023; Li *et al.*, 2023).

Human–elephant stalemate (1996–2005)

Since 1996, the HEC in Xishuangbanna has escalated, largely driven by road construction and the expansion of plantation agriculture. The construction of highways such as the Simao-Xiaomeng Highway has fragmented traditional elephant migration routes, forcing elephants into increasingly fragmented habitats and human settlements. These developments have also fostered economic growth and facilitated communication between local and external communities, but at the cost of exacerbating the conflict between humans and elephants.

As elephants' natural migration routes are blocked, they are now limited to small, fragmented habitats. The growing dependence of local communities on land for rubber plantations has further increased the overlap between human and elephant territories. As a result, elephants often stray into villages, raiding crops and causing significant damage to local livelihoods. The conflict has intensified, with both humans and elephants actively avoiding each other during periods of heightened activity. Villagers take shelter or avoid areas known for elephant activity, while elephants conceal themselves in the forests during periods of human presence (Dundi *et al.*, 2023).

The Xiaomeng Highway and other road networks have significantly altered the natural movement patterns of elephants, leading to irregular behaviours that exacerbate habitat loss and increase the frequency of HECs. As elephants venture closer to human settlements, attracted by the availability of food sources, their feeding schedules have begun to align with local agricultural cycles, resulting in more opportunities for conflict. Villagers, increasingly dependent on agricultural activities for their livelihoods, have been forced to adopt various defensive measures, including electric fences, to safeguard their crops and properties from elephant intrusions. This ongoing struggle underscores the complexities of coexistence, driven by both economic dependencies of local communities and the continuous shrinking of elephant habitats (Matata *et al.*, 2022).

Human–elephant stalemate (2005–present)

Since 2005, HEC in Xishuangbanna has intensified due to habitat fragmentation, agricultural expansion and infrastructure development. As explained above, the construction of roads, such as the Xiaomeng Highway, has obstructed traditional elephant migration routes, forcing elephants into human-dominated areas, increasing crop raiding and damaging property. Agricultural expansion, particularly rubber plantations, has reduced natural habitats, pushing elephants into closer contact with local communities. Recent studies show that elephants alter their movement patterns to avoid humans but are drawn to agricultural lands where food is abundant (Rosner-Katz *et al.*, 2020). As habitats shrink, elephants become more dependent on fragmented land, exacerbating conflict with growing human populations (Hua *et al.*, 2021). Efforts to manage these conflicts include land-use planning, electric fences and compensation schemes, though success depends on integrating these measures with long-term conservation strategies. Continued research into elephant movement and local land use is essential to ensure both human livelihoods and elephant populations can coexist.

Traditional Knowledge and Modern Conservation in Xishuangbanna

The evolving human–elephant relationship in Xishuangbanna offers key insights into wildlife conservation, especially through fission–fusion theory. Fission–fusion theory explains the dynamic and flexible nature of social group structures in animals. This theory highlights the flexible nature of animal group structures in response to environmental changes, making it highly relevant to elephants whose habitats are increasingly fragmented by agricultural expansion. As observed in other species like sheep and Cape buffalo, social groupings are not fixed but adapt based on factors such as resource availability, seasonal variation and environmental pressures (Della Libera *et al.*, 2023).

In Xishuangbanna, the conversion of forested land to rubber plantations has reduced resources for elephants, forcing them to adjust their behaviour. As food sources become scarcer, elephants alter their movement patterns, form smaller subgroups, or expand their ranges to find new resources, mirroring the fission–fusion dynamics seen in other species (Wielgus *et al.*, 2020). These adaptive social shifts are a direct response to habitat fragmentation and human encroachment, emphasizing the need for conservation strategies that account for these changing group behaviours.

As human activities continue to encroach on elephant territories, resource depletion leads to more frequent interactions with human settlements, often resulting in crop damage and heightened conflict (Li *et al.*, 2018). Understanding fission–fusion dynamics – where the elephants' group composition shifts based on resource availability and safety – is essential for developing effective strategies to mitigate HEC and ensure both species can coexist in a rapidly changing environment (Zhang *et al.*, 2021).

The fragmentation of habitats due to infrastructure development further exacerbates this issue. Roads like the Simao-Xiaomeng Highway have restricted elephant movement, forcing them to navigate fragmented landscapes where their mobility is limited. Elephants now rely on cultivated crops for sustenance, which intensifies the conflict with local farmers. Artificial feeding grounds, though intended to mitigate conflict, have been only partially successful. This is because these sites are near human settlements, so elephants frequently pass through villages, damaging property and threatening livelihoods (Praesri *et al.*, 2022).

Xishuangbanna underscores the importance of comprehensive land-use planning in addressing human–wildlife conflicts. The overlap between human land-use and elephant habitats is inevitable as populations grow. A balanced approach is essential, integrating habitat restoration, wildlife corridors and careful management of human activities to ensure coexistence. However, beyond environmental changes, cultural shifts play a fundamental role in shaping human–elephant dynamics. Traditional groups including the Dai people, maintained a respectful relationship with nature, guided by traditional knowledge and cultural values. These practices played a critical role in preserving the elephants' habitats. However, the influx of new populations and economic interests eroded these cultural practices, leading to the fragmentation of habitats and increased HEC (Park *et al.*, 2016).

The transformation from cultural preservation to economic exploitation highlights the dangers of disregarding traditional ecological knowledge. As seen in Xishuangbanna, the shift towards cash crops and deforestation has driven elephants into human settlements, intensifying conflict. This underscores a global conservation lesson: short-term economic gains often lead to long-term environmental degradation and heightened human–wildlife conflict. Despite conservation efforts, including protected areas and stricter laws, human–elephant relationships in Xishuangbanna have continued to deteriorate. Elephants have become more dependent on human-dominated landscapes, leading to increased conflicts. This scenario demonstrates that conservation strategies must integrate local cultural values with modern practices to succeed in the long term (Hoare, 2000).

Figure 5.2 illustrates a framework for managing these human–elephant interactions, transitioning from conflict to coexistence and collaborative action. It highlights the need for balancing economic interests, habitat preservation and local cultural values. Successful strategies, as seen through government, community and public cooperation, must integrate ecological benefits with sustainable development, showing that long-term solutions require both restoration and community-based management. This case demonstrates that ignoring cultural traditions and socio-economic needs leads to persistent conflicts, while inclusive approaches foster harmony (Lee and Graham, 2006; Chartier *et al.*, 2011).

ANT and Human–Elephant Relationships in Tourism Spaces

Human–wildlife conflict presents a significant obstacle to harmonious coexistence between humans and nature. Scholars have extensively studied

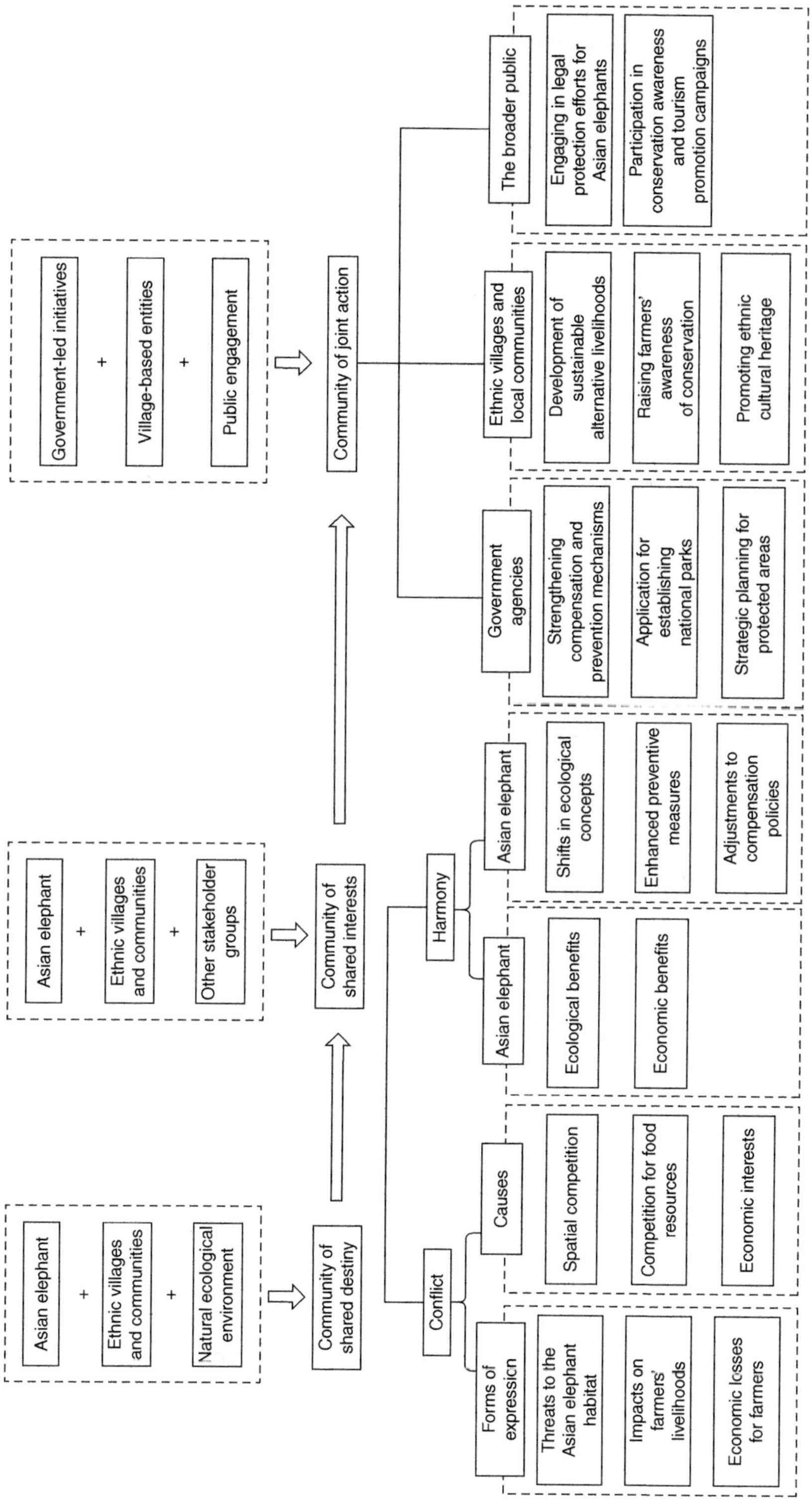

Fig. 5.2. Framework for managing human–elephant relationships. (Adapted from Kopnina and Baker, 2023, drawn by Melody Zhirui Zhou.)

these conflicts, especially those between wildlife and adjacent communities, as seen in HECs in Yunnan, brown-bear incidents in the Sanjiangyuan region, and the spread of wild boars across China. Such conflicts often lead to losses in human safety, property and resources, which foster antagonistic attitudes towards the animals involved.

Wildlife tourism has been suggested as a potential solution, providing economic incentives to encourage local tolerance and conservation awareness (Della Libera *et al.*, 2023). Yet, as tourism grows, new conflicts emerge – particularly between tourists and wildlife – requiring careful management of these tourism spaces (Park *et al.*, 2016). Traditionally, two frameworks have addressed these conflicts: (i) the natural science approach, which attributes conflict to disruptions in animal behaviour due to tourism; and (ii) the social constructionist approach, which posits that 'wildness' is inherently shaped by human influence, highlighting the need to integrate these dynamics into management strategies.

While these frameworks offer valuable insights, they often fail to capture the broader network of influences shaping animal behaviour. This study employs ANT to bridge this gap, viewing human–wildlife conflicts as dynamic interactions between human and non-human actors. ANT assigns agency not only to animals but also to material elements like landscapes and infrastructure, particularly in contexts where urban landscape transformations or ecological interactions mediated by infrastructure play a significant role. Under such conditions, these elements collectively shape the outcomes of interactions, highlighting the interdependence between human and non-human. A notable aspect of ANT is that it redefines animal agency as evolving and responsive rather than fixed. Elephants, for instance, do not merely react to environmental changes but actively shape conservation and management outcomes through adaptive, learned behaviours, indicating a capacity for agency beyond simple behaviour patterns (Lim *et al.*, 2015).

This relational approach – acknowledging both human and non-human actors as active agents – suggests that management strategies should account for these fluid dynamics to improve human–wildlife coexistence (Chen *et al.*, 2022). ANT's focus on interactions among actors highlights that human–wildlife relations are not static but continuously redefined through interactions (Dundi *et al.*, 2023). Effective conflict management thus requires governance strategies that respect the distinct identities and roles of each actor, recognizing the dynamic nature of these relationships.

In Xishuangbanna, tourism has significantly influenced the dynamics of HEC. As the region has become a key destination for wildlife tourism, especially with attractions like Wild Elephant Valley, interactions between humans and elephants have increased. Local stakeholders, including community members and tourism operators, report that the influx of tourists has disrupted traditional elephant migration routes. Interviews with residents near Elephant Valley reveal that elephants, once wary of humans, have become more tolerant as infrastructure developments like roads and hotels increasingly encroach upon their habitats (Ball *et al.*, 2022).

Through the lens of ANT, tourism is seen as a dynamic network of human and non-human elements that mutually shape outcomes. In wildlife tourism, encounters between humans and elephants serve as 'compulsory passage points', essential to tourism's stability and reliant on coordinated interactions between actors, including elephants, tourists and spatial design elements. While WWF and other conservation organizations led initiatives to foster human–wildlife interaction within tourism frameworks to promote environmental consciousness, the role of non-human actors in creating and sustaining these interactions is a key consideration.

HEC within tourism spaces is complex, often arising from elephants' agency, which can counter initial spatial designs intended to facilitate encounters. Elephants, with their strong memories and route-tracking skills, follow 'elephant pathways' shaped by historical experiences, spatial awareness and protective instincts. Static tourism infrastructure alone cannot account for these dynamic behaviours, particularly when past threats lead elephants to avoid human interaction.

However, spatial designs initially meant to attract elephants may inadvertently foster conflict by overlapping tourism spaces with natural habitats. This overlap creates physical spaces where elephant behaviours and human safety expectations conflict, particularly as elephants adapt and confront human presence under strengthened protections. Although proximity-based experiences can enhance visitor engagement, the risks associated with unpredictable elephants are substantial (Lim *et al.*, 2015).

In Wild Elephant Valley, spatial markers like salt licks and treehouses were introduced to stabilize encounters by attracting elephants. Yet, as Hâncean *et al.* (2020) argue, such efforts reflect a commodified approach that prioritizes tourism objectives over welfare. Consequently, tourism managers face complex decisions, balancing visitor satisfaction with safety, often compromising elephant autonomy. WWF's introduction to the controlled form of 'elephant agency' creates a stable tourism product but raises ethical concerns about commodification and animal welfare. The concept of 'elephant agency' can be understood as efforts to create conditions that mimic natural settings, thereby giving elephants more autonomy and reducing stress from human interaction. In Laos' Nam Poui NPA (National Protected Area), regular patrols by local villagers and authorities help monitor elephant habitats and curb poaching, fostering a sense of shared responsibility. Conservation centres in Thailand and Laos offer semi-natural environments where rescued elephants can forage, socialize and explore, giving them a sense of freedom while under care (Kim and Hyun, 2024).

Given these factors, tourism spaces must evolve to integrate animal agency into spatial design and visitor management strategies. ANT shows that wildlife tourism networks are composed of human and non-human actors, with material elements shaping encounters. As elephant behaviours and protections shift, traditional spatial configurations alone are unlikely to ensure coexistence without proactive, adaptive management. Effective human–wildlife conflict management thus requires ongoing reassessment of both physical and relational elements, creating environments where human–elephant interactions are managed ethically and sustainably.

Discussion and Conclusions

This chapter has explored the intricate and multifaceted dynamics of human–elephant interactions in Xishuangbanna, revealing a complex web of ecological, cultural and economic elements that intersect and shape these relationships. A singular, narrowly focused approach cannot adequately address the challenges posed by such intricate networks. Instead, a holistic perspective is essential, one that intertwines conservation efforts with local socio-economic realities.

The persistent issue of HEC, driven primarily by habitat fragmentation and agricultural encroachment, mirrors challenges faced across regions in Asia. While it may be preferable to view conservation through the lens of wildlife protection, this approach often overlooks the deeply rooted socio-economic dependence of local communities on land and resources. As the evidence suggests, any sustainable solution must engage these communities as active participants, encouraging a paradigm shift from perceiving elephants solely as threats to recognizing them as valuable assets that can coexist with human livelihoods (Fernando, 2015; Fernando *et al.*, 2022). This perspective fosters a more resilient and inclusive model of conservation.

Tourism, particularly elephant-based tourism, has emerged as both a challenge and an opportunity in this context. On the one hand, it provides economic incentives that can support conservation by creating value around elephant habitats. On the other hand, the commodification of elephants risks undermining conservation efforts if managed irresponsibly, potentially exacerbating the very conflicts it seeks to prevent. Therefore, the call for sustainable tourism practices is not just an ethical imperative but a pragmatic necessity. Models that prioritize animal welfare while promoting community-based ecotourism have shown promise in reducing conflicts and supporting local economies (Bandara, 2020). However, as argued earlier, tourism must be carefully integrated within broader conservation strategies to ensure that its benefits are truly sustainable.

Infrastructure development, such as the expansion of roads and railways, continues to disrupt traditional elephant migration corridors, leading to habitat fragmentation and heightened conflict. The experiences from other regions indicate that the implementation of wildlife corridors and buffer zones can effectively mitigate these impacts, preserving essential pathways for elephants while reducing the likelihood of encounters with human settlements (Lim *et al.*, 2015). However, the success of such measures depends on comprehensive planning and adaptive governance, which must be flexible enough to account for the dynamic and sometimes unpredictable movement patterns of elephants.

The integration of technology also offers new avenues for managing HECs. Innovations such as real-time early warning systems, utilizing infrared cameras and mobile alerts, have been effective in some regions, helping communities anticipate and avoid dangerous encounters. However, there is little evidence to suggest that technology alone can serve as a definitive solution. It must be seen as part of a larger, integrated approach that addresses underlying issues such as habitat degradation and resource competition.

Throughout this chapter, a recurring theme has been the need for an integrative approach that bridges ecological, socio-economic and cultural divides. Conservation efforts in Xishuangbanna – and indeed, in other regions facing similar issues – must transcend isolated initiatives, embracing a comprehensive framework that respects both human and elephant needs. This includes drawing on traditional ecological knowledge, promoting ethical tourism, and embedding adaptability within governance structures to accommodate shifting environmental and social conditions (Kopnina and Baker, 2023).

Thus, the complex and evolving landscape of human–elephant interactions in Xishuangbanna provides valuable insights into the broader challenges of wildlife conservation. Effective strategies must navigate the delicate balance of competing interests, informed by a nuanced understanding of local contexts. The management of tourism, the strategic deployment of technology and the thoughtful design of infrastructure are all pivotal, yet each must be executed with sustainability at the forefront. Ultimately, the future of human–elephant coexistence will hinge on our ability to see beyond immediate conflicts, recognizing the interconnectedness of all actors within this intricate network. By embracing these complexities, we can pave the way for a future where humans and elephants not only coexist but thrive together, ensuring the preservation of biodiversity and the well-being of local communities.

However it is described, the challenge of human–elephant coexistence in Xishuangbanna requires a multifaceted approach that transcends traditional conservation strategies. While it may be preferable to view it simply as a matter of habitat preservation or conflict mitigation, the reality is far more complex, demanding integrated efforts that encompass ecological, technological and socio-economic perspectives. There remains, however, significant room for innovation in understanding the behavioural ecology of elephants, particularly their responses to fragmented habitats, agricultural cycles and encroaching infrastructure. This evidence suggests that sustainable solutions must prioritize adaptive strategies that balance the needs of elephants and human communities alike.

As argued earlier, technological advancements such as real-time monitoring systems hold great promise, but there is little evidence to suggest that technology alone can resolve the conflict. Instead, such innovations must be embedded within community-led frameworks that address local needs and ensure equitable participation in conservation efforts. One feature that is worthy of note is the potential of ethical tourism practices to transform human–elephant relationships. While tourism offers economic incentives, it may also risk commodifying wildlife if not carefully managed. For the reasons discussed, balancing conservation with community well-being must remain a central objective.

Ultimately, the argument for coexistence hinges on fostering collaboration among governments, non-governmental organizations (NGOs), researchers and local communities. Alternatively, neglecting these intersections risks perpetuating the very conflicts we seek to resolve. Xishuangbanna offers a unique opportunity to serve as a global model for harmonizing conservation and development, demonstrating how inclusive, evidence-based approaches can yield sustainable outcomes. By embracing these complexities, conservation efforts can evolve from mitigating conflicts to nurturing resilience, ensuring a future where humans and elephants thrive together.

Bibliography

Ashton, A.S. (2020) Elephant tourism conservation and the need for a new strategy: Thai stakeholder attitudes. In: Laws, E., Scott, N., Font, X. and Koldowski, J. (eds) *The Elephant Tourism Business*. CAB International, Wallingford, UK, pp. 160–169. DOI: 10.1079/9781789245868.0013.

Ball, R., Jacobson, S.L., Rudolph, M., Trapani, M. and Plotnik, J.M. (2022) Acknowledging the relevance of elephant sensory perception to human-elephant conflict mitigation. *Animals* 12(8): 1018. DOI: 10.3390/ani12081018.

Bandara, T. (2020) Potentiality of ecotourism in enhancing ethno-zoological values of elephant corridors for mitigating human-elephant conflict in Sri Lanka. *International Journal of Scientific and Research Publications* 10(3): 9951. DOI: 10.29322/IJSRP.10.03.2020.p9951.

Bencherki, N. (2017) Actor–network theory. In: *The International Encyclopedia of Organizational Communication*. Wiley, Hoboken, New Jersey, pp. 1–13. DOI: 10.1002/9781118955567.wbieoc002.

Callon, M. (1986) The sociology of an actor-network: the case of the electric vehicle. In: Callon, M., Law, J. and Rip, A. (eds) *Mapping the Dynamics of Science and Technology: Sociology of Science in the Real World*. Springer, New York, pp. 19–34. DOI: 10.1007/978-1-349-07408-2_2.

Chartier, L.A., Zimmermann, A. and Ladle, R. (2011) Habitat loss and human–elephant conflict in Assam, India: Does a critical threshold exist? *Oryx* 45(4), 528–533. DOI: 10.1017/S0030605311000044.

Chen, X., Lee, T.J. and Hyun, S.S. (2022) How does a global coffeehouse chain operate strategically in a traditional tea-drinking country? The influence of brand authenticity and self-enhancement. *Journal of Hospitality and Tourism Management* 51, 176–186. DOI: 10.1016/j.jhtm.2022.03.003.

Della Libera, K., Strandburg-Peshkin, A., Griffith, S.C. and Leu, S.T. (2023) Fission-fusion dynamics in sheep: the influence of resource distribution and temporal activity patterns. *Royal Society Open Science* 10(7): 230402. DOI: 10.1098/rsos.230402.

Dundi, D.B., Praet, I., Marvin, G., Goossens, B., Lee, P. and Chettri, N. (2023) Good, quarrelsome, bad: animal agency and human-elephant interactions in the Western Ghats, India. *Frontiers in Conservation Science* 4. DOI: 10.3389/fcosc.2023.1142333.

Fernando, C., Weston, M., Corea, R., Pahirana, K. and Rendall, A.R. (2022) Asian elephant movements between natural and human-dominated landscapes mirror patterns of crop damage in Sri Lanka. *Oryx* 57(4), 481–488. DOI: 10.1017/S0030605321000971.

Fernando, P. (2015) Managing elephants in Sri Lanka: where we are and where we need to be. *Ceylon Journal of Science (Biological Sciences)* 44(1), 1–11. DOI: 10.4038/cjsbs.v44i1.7336.

Ginda, G.B., Syarifuddin, H. and Hamzah, H. (2022) Pengetahuan dan persepsi masyarakat terhadap konflik gajah Sumatera di Desa Lubuk Mandarsah. *Biodiversitas* 8(1), 29–39. DOI: 10.22437/bio.v8i1.16028.

Gray, A., Roberts, S., Stafford, B. and Broadbent, J. (2024) Editorial: The commodification of the public good—who wins and who loses? *Public Money & Management* 44(4), 277–280. DOI: 10.1080/09540962.2023.2247889.

Guo, X. (2017) Asian elephants research review in China. *Open Journal of Nature Science* 5(1), 31–36. DOI: 10.12677/OJNS.2017.51005.

Hâncean, M.-G., Slavinec, M. and Perc, M. (2020) The impact of human mobility networks on the global spread of COVID-19. *Journal of Complex Networks* 8(6). DOI: 10.1093/comnet/cnaa041.

Hoare, R. (2000) African elephants and humans in conflict: the outlook for co-existence. *Oryx* 34(1), 34–38. DOI: 10.1046/j.1365-3008.2000.00092.x.

Hua, J., Chen, W.Y., Liekens, I. and Cho, F.H.T. (2021) Partial attribute attendance in environmental choice experiments: a comparative case study between Guangzhou (China) and Brussels (Belgium). *Journal of Environmental Management* 285: 112107. DOI: 10.1016/j.jenvman.2021.112107.

International Union for Conservation (IUCN) (2024) The IUCN Red List of Threatened Species. Available at: https://www.iucnredlist.org/ (accessed 12 October 2023).

Kim, H.L. and Hyun, S.S. (2024) Paradoxical effects of tourism ethnocentrism on domestic tourism: the moderating effect of pandemic anxiety travel. *International Journal of Tourism Research* 26(1). DOI: 10.1002/jtr.2628.

Köpke, S., Withanachchi, S.S., Pathiranage, R., Withanachchi, C.R., Gamage, D.U. *et al.* (2023) Human-elephant conflict in the Sri Lankan dry zone: investigating social and geographical drivers through field-based methods. *GeoJournal* 88(5), 5153–5172. DOI: 10.1007/s10708-023-10913-7.

Kopnina, H. and Baker, L. (2023) Conservation, animal wellbeing, and indigenous participation at an elephant sanctuary in Mondulkiri, Cambodia. *Society & Animals* 32(5–6), 560–581. DOI: 10.1163/15685306-bja10126.

Lee, P.C. and Graham, M. (2006) African elephants (*Loxodonta africana*) and human-elephant interactions: implications for conservation. *International Zoo Yearbook* 40(1), 9–19. DOI: 10.1111/j.1748-1090.2006.00009.x.

Li, W., Liu, P., Guo, X., Wang, L., Wang, Q. *et al.* (2018) Human-elephant conflict in Xishuangbanna Prefecture, China: distribution, diffusion, and mitigation. *Global Ecology and Conservation* 16: e00462. DOI: 10.1016/j.gecco.2018.e00462.

Li, W., Liu, P., Yang, N., Pan, H., Chen, S. and Zhang, L. (2023) Spatio-temporal trend and mitigation of human–elephant conflict in Xishuangbanna, China. *The Journal of Wildlife Management* 87(8). DOI: 10.1002/jwmg.22485.

Lim, Y.-J., Kim, H.-K. and Lee, T.J. (2015) Visitor motivational factors and level of satisfaction in wellness tourism: comparison between first-time visitors and repeat visitors. *Asia Pacific Journal of Tourism Research* 21(2), 137–156. DOI: 10.1080/10941665.2015.1029952.

Matata, M.T., Kegamba, J.J., Mremi, R. and Eustace, A. (2022) Electrified fencing as a mitigation strategy for human-elephant conflict in Western Serengeti: community perspectives. *Journal for Nature Conservation* 70: 126271. DOI: 10.1016/j.jnc.2022.126271.

Nayak, M. and Swain, P. (2022) Human–elephant interaction: community perspectives on conflict mitigation and conservation mechanisms. *International Journal of Environmental Research and Public Health* 19(3): 2820. DOI: 10.1002/pa.2820.

Nguyen, V., Nguyen, H.T., Phan, T.T.T. and Lee, C.-H. (2023) Determinants of locals' willingness to participate in human–elephant conflict management: evidence from Dong Nai Biosphere Reserve, Vietnam. *Trees, Forests and People* 8(1): 100435. DOI: 10.1016/j.tfp.2023.100435.

O'Connell-Rodwell, C.E., Rodwell, T., Rice, M. and Hart, L.A. (2000) Living with the modern conservation paradigm: Can agricultural communities co-exist with elephants? A five-year case study in East Caprivi, Namibia. *Biological Conservation* 93(3), 381–391. DOI: 10.1016/S0006-3207(99)00108-1.

Pandey, N., Lurz, P., Anderson, N., Hopker, A., Goswami, J. *et al.* (2022) Impact and mitigation of human-elephant conflict around Kaziranga National Park, Assam, India. *International Journal of Ecology and Environmental Sciences* 48(6). DOI: 10.55863/ijees.2022.6703.

Park, K., Lee, J. and Lee, T.J. (2016) Residents' attitudes toward future tourism development in terms of community well-being and attachment. *Asia Pacific Journal of Tourism Research* 22(2), 160–172. DOI: 10.1080/10941665.2016.1208669.

Praesri, S., Meekun, K., Lee, T.J. and Hyun, S.S. (2022) Marketing mix factors and a business development model for street food tourism. *Journal of Hospitality and Tourism Management* 52, 123–127. DOI: 10.1016/j.jhtm.2022.06.007.

Ranjeewa, A.D., Pastorini, J., Isler, K., Weerakoon, D.K., Kottage, H.D. and Fernando, P. (2017) Decreasing reservoir water levels improve habitat quality for Asian elephants. *Mammalian Biology* 88, 130–137. DOI: 10.1016/j.mambio.2017.10.002.

Rosner-Katz, H., McCune, J.L. and Bennett, J.R. (2020) Using stacked SDMs with accuracy and rarity weighting to optimize surveys for rare plant species. *Biodiversity and Conservation* 29(11–12), 3209–3225. DOI: 10.1007/s10531-020-02018-1.

Shiweda, M., Shivute, F., Sales, A.R. and Pereira, M.J. (2023) Climate change and anthropogenic factors are influencing the loss of habitats and emerging human–elephant conflict in the Namib Desert. *Sustainability* 15(16): 12400. DOI: 10.3390/su151612400.

Shmueli, G., Ray, S., Velasquez Estrada, J.M. and Chatla, S.B. (2016) The elephant in the room: predictive performance of PLS models. *Journal of Business Research* 69(10), 4552–4564. DOI: 10.1016/j.jbusres.2016.03.049.

Shrestha, B.B. and Shrestha, K.K. (2021) Invasions of alien plant species in Nepal: patterns and process. In: Pullaiah, T. and Ielmini, M.R. (eds) *Invasive Alien Species: Observations and Issues from Around the World*. Wiley, Hoboken, New Jersey, pp. 168–183. DOI: 10.1002/9781119607045.ch20.

Thant, Z.M., May, R. and Røskaft, E. (2022) Effect of human–elephant conflict on local attitudes toward the conservation of wild Asian elephants in Myanmar. *Human Dimensions of Wildlife* 28(6), 547–563. DOI: 10.1080/10871209.2022.2134524.

Tripathy, B.R., Liu, X. and Ranga, V. (2022) Demographic circumstances and people's sentiments towards elephants in the human–elephant conflict hotspot villages of Keonjhar Forest Division in Eastern India. *Diversity* 14(5): 311. DOI: 10.3390/d14050311.

Tschirhart, C., Mistry, J., Berardi, A., Bignante, E., Simpson, M. *et al.* (2016) Learning from one another: evaluating the impact of horizontal knowledge exchange for environmental management and governance. *Ecology and Society* 21(2). DOI: 10.5751/ES-08495-210241.

Wang, Y., Liu, Z., Wen, Y. and Wang, Y. (2023) Land use transition and its driving mechanism of 'human–elephant' conflicts zone in Yunnan, China. *Land* 12(5): 1104. DOI: 10.3390/land12051104.

Wen, W., Liu, P., Zhang, X., Wang, L. and Zhang, Q. (2018) Balancing elephant conservation and infrastructure development in Xishuangbanna. *Journal of Ecological Planning* 25(3), 145–158. DOI: 10.1016/j.jepp.2018.e00462.

Wielgus, E., Cornélis, D., de Garine-Wichatitsky, M., Cain, B., Fritz, H. *et al.* (2020) Are fission-fusion dynamics consistent among populations? A large-scale study with Cape buffalo. *Ecology and Evolution* 10(17), 9240–9256. DOI: 10.1002/ece3.6608.

Xia, L., Lee, T.J. and Kim, D. (2024) Relationships between motivation, service quality, tourist satisfaction, quality of life, and spa and wellness tourism. *International Journal of Tourism Research* 26(1). DOI: 10.1002/jtr.2624.

Xishuangbanna Dai Autonomous Prefecture Government (2024) Xishuangbanna Asian elephant rescue and breeding center information disclosure. Xishuangbanna Forestry and Grassland Bureau. Available at: https://www.xsbn.gov.cn/lfw/84137.news.detail.dhtml?news_id=2862470 (accessed 5 September 2023). [in Chinese]

Yoo, I.Y., Lee, T.J. and Lee, C.-K. (2013) Effect of health and wellness values on festival visit motivation. *Asia Pacific Journal of Tourism Research* 20(2), 152–170. DOI: 10.1080/10941665.2013.866970.

Zhang, Y., Lin, Z. and Lee, T.J. (2020) Wellness-oriented seasonal tourism migration: a field relationship study in China. *International Journal of Tourism Research* 23(4), 491–503. DOI: 10.1002/jtr.2420.

Zhang, Y., Lee, T.J. and Xiong, Y. (2021) The contribution of animal-based cultural ecosystem services to tourist well-being at cultural heritage sites. *Journal of Travel Research* 61(7), 1631–1647. DOI: 10.1177/00472875211037743.

Zimbabwe Parks and Wildlife Management Authority (2021) *Zimbabwe National Elephant Management Plan*. Available at: https://www.cms.int/sites/default/files/document/cms_nlp_zwe_plan_elephant_2021.pdf (accessed 15 October 2023).

6 Can Symbolic Value and Religious Beliefs Save Elephants' Lives?

Jing Zhuo,[1*] Timothy Lee[2] and Yuchen Ti[2]

[1]*University of New South Wales, Sydney, Australia;* [2]*Macau University of Science and Technology, Macao SAR, China*

Abstract

In some countries, animals are an important aspect of tourism, such as South Africa and its safari tourism. In this context our topic, elephant tourism, refers to the practice of using elephants for entertainment and other tourism purposes such as elephant rides and shows. Elephants working in tourism have the potential to be injured when being fed or ridden, or risk being abused by mahouts. It is important to note that comments on the elephant tourism industry have raised significant ethical concerns and criticism from animal rights groups. This chapter focuses on the influences of symbolic value and religious belief in cultural customs that support ethical concerns and the rights of elephants particularly in India, Thailand, Sir Lanka and China. It is crucial for tourists and local stakeholders to be well informed and choose activities that promote the well-being and preservation of elephants and focus on observation and non-intrusive interactions with these animals.

Introduction

This chapter explores the reality of elephant abuse, from different perspectives concerning the religious and symbolic values of elephants, which can be used to effectively contribute to conservation and raising awareness about animal protection and animal rights in various human–elephant interactions. In the complex realm of global wildlife conservation, elephants are distinguished by their majestic presence and the symbolic and religious importance they possess in diverse cultures. These magnificent creatures are often revered in religious and cultural narratives, imbued with meanings that transcend their physical existence. The evolution of legal safeguards for elephants in Thailand can be

*JingZhuo.Aidan@outlook.com

 Elephant Welfare in Global Tourism (E. Laws *et al.* eds)
DOI: 10.1079/9781836990093.0006

traced back to the 17th century, a period during which concerns about the dual impact of human livelihoods and elephant conservation emerged (Chaitae *et al.*, 2022).

However, despite their outstanding status in religions and culture, elephants face relentless threats from ivory poaching, habitat loss and potential dangers in human–elephant conflicts. The number of elephants in Thailand, for example, has decreased dramatically in recent years. In 1950, there were about 50,000 living in Thailand, but this population has been decimated to roughly 3500 elephants today. Nowadays, feral elephants can seldom be found in Thailand. There are an estimated 300 elephants in the north of the country, where the Kaeng Krachan National Park is home to approximately 200 elephants. Globally, between 2003 and 2020 the Asian elephant population has declined from an estimated 41,410–52,345 individuals to approximately 4189–6999 individuals (Williams *et al.*, 2020). The International Union for Conservation of Nature (IUCN) Red List shows that the wild Asian elephant is endangered (Nyi *et al.*, 2021).

The major reasons for the decline of elephant population in Thailand are the profit-oriented businesses and continuous forest clearance. Jungle clearing means the destruction of their habitat. At the end of the 19th century, about 70% of Thailand was covered with forest but today this has been reduced to an alarming 20%. The deforestation was stopped in 1989 by a new forest protection law which meant that elephants' habitats were protected by legislation, but on the other hand the elephants that had been used to move logs and tree trunks became useless to their owners.

Moving to China, there are only about 300 Asian elephants left in the wild there, fewer than the panda, so the Asian elephant remains a priority on the list of wildlife under state protection. Asian elephants exist only in Xishuangbanna, Pu'Er and Lincang, southern Yunnan Province, with 95% of the wild population residing in the Xishuangbanna National Nature Reserve. In March 2020, an adult female elephant led a dozen elephants from the Mengyangzi Reserve in Xishuangbanna National Nature Reserve, all the way north to Kunming. The elephants spent 17 months in various places, covering more than 1300 km, before returning to their original habitat in August 2021 (Liu, 2023). The migration of Asian elephant populations in China is thus not uncommon and has attracted the attention of scientists. Wang *et al.* (2021a) found that the drastic reduction of herbaceous and shrub resources in the reserve, caused by extremely hot and dry weather since 2019, has exacerbated elephant food shortages and is likely to be a key factor in the northward migration of Asian elephants. Furthermore, under climate change scenarios for 2021–2030, Asian elephants are forecast to spread north-east from their current range. However, not all elephants are able to make climate and environmental adaptations in time (Liu, 2023). Between March and August 2020, more than 300 African elephants died in Botswana. A study by Wang and a team of researchers (2021b) showed that sustained high temperatures and drought conditions had spurred the growth of blue-green algae in water sources, producing cyanotoxins, which led to the mass death of elephants.

According to Asian religious culture and heritage, elephants are revered animals. Thus, the fascination with elephants is far from a recent development –

throughout history, humans have alternately revered, romanticized, pondered and killed these creatures, but seldom have they been overlooked (Carruthers, 2010). This chapter describes how cultural reverence and religious sanctification of elephants has influenced conservation strategies and policies in the present. Also, it explains how the investigation spans various geographical and cultural landscapes, from the elephant gods of Hindu mythology in India to the iconic status of elephants in Thai and Chinese cultures, assessing how these beliefs shape local and global conservation initiatives. Animal welfare has emerged as a critical concern in wildlife tourism, increasingly influencing the choices made by tourists (Flower *et al.*, 2021). The objective of this chapter is not only to highlight the role of cultural and religious values in animal conservation but also to critically analyse their effectiveness in fostering sustainable practices that protect elephant populations in the future.

The Religious Metaphor of the Elephant

According to historical research, elephants lived in the Yellow River basin during the Yin and Shang dynasties (*c*.1600 BC–*c*.1046 BC). Elephants then had extensive and close relations with the ancient people in the Central Plains and had a sacred status: elephants were not hunted by the ancient people. This was due to the cultural myth of 'Emperor Shun tamed elephant', which was meticulously recorded by Sima Qian in Records of the Grand Historian of China (Annal of the Five Emperors, 109 BC–91 BC) (Yu, 2016). Emperor Shun was the ancestor of the Shang dynasty, and 'Xiang' (elephants) were always depicted in myths as Shun's younger brother. In general, wild elephants are strong and stubborn, and it is difficult to tame them without facing many challenges. Therefore, the myth-makers portrayed Xiang as Shun's younger brother to emphasize the difficulty of taming the stubborn elephant. In actual historical records, Shun was also a famous hunter in ancient times, who subdued wild elephants and domesticated them for work for humans in agriculture, highlighting the courage and determination of ancient people in taming such dangerous and huge animals. This is the true meaning of the legend of Shun and Xiang (Yu, 2016). In the long history of the image of elephants they were sacred animals, used in sacrificial activities, making ritual vessels and in naming emperors (Li, 2018).

From archaeological findings and the records of oracle bones, elephants were used as sacrifices to ancestors. Animal burial pits were found in the archaeological site of Yin Ruins, which is consistent with the record of offering elephants as sacrifices to ancestors (Li, 2018). The ancestors of the Shang dynasty used the elephant in sacrificial activities, so the image of the elephant's huge body has gradually acquired sanctity, enriching the cultural implication of the elephant, so that the word 'elephant' has developed from just referring to the animal to referring to everything in the universe. In addition, the elephant was depicted as an artistic image mainly in bronzeware and ivories engraved with various images of elephants, which stand for holiness, dignity and power (Zhang, 1981).

At the end of the Western Han dynasty (206 BC–AD 24), Buddhism was established in China from India, and elephants began to be revered again. However, the cultural meaning of the elephant in Buddhism was different. The religious significance of elephants was particularly prominent, especially the six-toothed white elephant, which was a symbol of 'the birth of Bodhisattvas', 'the representative of Mahayana Buddhism', 'the giving of gifts' and 'Buddha's treasure'. Buddhism is also known as the 'elephant religion'. As a symbol of Buddha and Bodhisattvas, the image of elephants not only represents the Buddha itself, but also expresses the particular Buddhist sect and Buddhist doctrine, which have the connotation of holiness, nobility, power, auspiciousness and completeness (Song, 2014; Li, 2021).

Elephants and their image are an important feature of religious activities in other Asian countries. Figure 6.1 shows the lead tusker (male elephant with large tusks) of the Esala Perahera ceremony in Sri Lanka. The annual Esala Perahera ceremony is one of the biggest festivals in Buddhism. A pagoda is placed on the back of an elephant and it is paraded through the city, so that people can share the glory of the Buddhist relic. The festival is a well-known Buddhist cultural event in Sri Lanka; it has been held annually in Colombo since 1979. One million free seats are provided for the 2 days of the ceremony, which attracts millions of Buddhists, local people and tourists to participate every year. According to Zhang and Xu (2021), Sri Lankan and Indian visitors who have a specific cultural and religious connection to elephants experience a significantly higher sense of awe than Western visitors, because of their different culture and religious beliefs. Personal interactions with wildlife can inspire a sense of awe (Hicks and Stewart, 2018). So, a visitor's experience of such interactions is an important aspect of the sustainable protection of wild animals and wildlife tourism.

The tourism image of Thailand is shaped by countless temples, mile-long beaches and impressive elephants. It is little known, but elephants even have their own letter in the Thai alphabet. The Chor Chang letter can be found in street names, city names or the names of many Thai people. All in all, elephants embody an important part of Thai society. Elephant sculptures are omnipresent in temples, elephant prints decorate the famous fisherman pants and loads of souvenirs with elephant images can be found in Thai shops. It is thus not surprising that the calm giants can be found in tourism too.

Symbolic Value and Religious Beliefs about Elephants

Religious beliefs about elephants in India

Elephants have a deep religious and symbolic significance in Indian culture. The ancient treatise on statecraft, the *Arthasastra*, which originated during the Mauryan Empire (300 BC–AD 300), advocated the establishment of elephant sanctuaries. The practice of hunting elephants was met with severe penalties, including the death penalty for those who violated the law (Bist *et al.*, 2002). In Hinduism, Ganesha, the god with an elephant's head, is highly revered by local believers. Ganesha is a symbol of wisdom, wealth and good fortune, as

Fig. 6.1. Lead tusker of the Esala Perahera ceremony in Sir Lanka. (Photo courtesy of Yuchen Ti.)

well as a deity who removes obstacles (Grewal, 2009). Devotees often invoke Ganesha's blessings for success and smooth sailing when starting a new venture or journey. The elephant's strength, wisdom and steadfastness are regarded as sacred qualities, symbolizing solidity and enduring power, which reflect the high esteem given to the elephant in Hinduism. Home to more than 60% of the extant wild Asian elephant population, India's elephant numbers are reported to be relatively stable (Government of India, 2020).

In addition, elephants play an important role in other Buddhist traditions. According to Lyons (2013):

> In the Theravada Buddhist tradition, the Asian elephant is a profound symbol of steadfastness and mental perseverance. The uncontrolled mind in the beginning of one's practice of Buddhist meditation is represented by a gray elephant who runs wild. After studying the dharma (the nature of reality regarded as a universal truth in Buddhism), the psyche is represented as a pure white elephant.
>
> (Lyons, 2013, p. 1)

Legend has it that a white elephant in Buddha's mother's dream was seen as a sign of Buddha's birth. The white elephant is thus imbued with auspicious symbolism, representing purity and sanctity. Elephants also symbolize wisdom and steadfastness in Buddhist culture. These qualities are closely related to Buddhist teachings and practices, showing the importance of elephants in Buddhism (Choskyi, 1988).

Symbolic value of the elephant in Thailand

In Thailand, the elephant is not only a national symbol, but also closely associated with the royal family. In the Buddhism of Thailand, Indra is known as the leader of all heavens and gods, and the elephant Erawan means water, rain cloud, rainbow or lightning. Indra used Erawan as a vehicle, flying across the realm, giving rain to the Earth. The ancient myth has it that this was the most important duty of the great Erawan. Erawan was able to assist Indra in helping him bring good things to the world, and he is also a symbolic weapon of good fighting evil (Erawan Museum Official, 2018; Tian, 2023).

In Thai culture, Erawan is considered the master of all elephants in the universe, he is the trusted companion of Indra and is one of the most significant manifestations of Indra: a symbol of abundance and joy. Thai people also believe that elephants are lucky animals, and many images show elephants as animals that bring joy and prosperity to the owners' life. The Thai people believe in an ancient tradition known as crossing under the elephant's belly. Since elephants are extremely big, the people who could cross under the elephant are the brave ones and shall not face any troubles later. In terms of luck for pregnant ladies, going under the elephant's belly was believed to assist them in the process of giving birth; they will give birth more easily (Erawan Museum Official, 2018). In Thai royal tradition, elephants are often used to represent the glory and power of the country. There are also many temples in Thailand where elephants are worshipped, and devotees use these rituals to pray for good luck and prosperity (Zhang *et al.*, 2021).

Elephants in Chinese culture

In Chinese culture, elephants often symbolize good fortune, wealth and longevity. The elephant's symbolic value in China tends to be positive. Its image is widely seen in traditional art and decoration, representing peace and happiness. Images of elephants are often used to decorate good luck charms and New Year's paintings, which signifies a good and peaceful life (Li, 2021). In ancient times, elephants were gradually tamed by people and began to be used in people's lives for hunting, sacrifice and war, and gradually the elephant took on political implications to indicate conquest, power status, naturalized loyalty and so on (Li, 2021). Nowadays, China's concern for elephants focuses more on animal conservation and environmental protection. With the rising concern over their possible extinction, the elephant has become an important symbol calling for the global protection of nature and wildlife. The endangered state of elephants reminds people of the importance of ecological conservation and promotes public awareness and action for environmental protection.

The Impact of Symbolic Value and Religious Beliefs about Elephants

The impacts of symbolic value and religious beliefs about elephants are multi-layered, encompassing both respect for and protection of elephants as well as economic and cultural challenges. It can be helpful to understand how these impacts can assist in developing more effective conservation measures while improving animal welfare based on respect for cultural traditions. Elephants are accorded high symbolic value in many cultures and arts; this value may have a positive impact on conservation measures. Governments and non-governmental organizations (NGOs) devote significant resources to the conservation of these animals in some countries because of their religious and cultural importance. Several NGOs have been established with the specific objective of addressing the issues and improving the welfare of a country's elephants (Ratanakorn, 2002; Cui and Xu, 2019). The symbolic value of culture and religion motivates people to become more active in campaigning against illegal hunting and trying to avoid habitat destruction. For example, the cow is important in the Hindu faith in India. Cows are not just an animal, but also a cultural symbol and religious symbol, deeply influencing the way of life of Indians. In Hinduism, cows are considered sacred animals and have sacred and symbolic meanings. They are believed to be the mount of Shiva, symbolizing life and fertility. Therefore, the respect and protection of cows in India are deeply rooted in people's hearts. Indians believe that cows should not be eaten or harmed, mainly due to religious beliefs and respect for cows. According to the religious doctrine of Hindu, killing cows is an immoral act (Phillips, 2021).

In Thailand, elephants are worshipped by people every day. The Erawan Museum, Samut Prakan, has a statue of the god Indra on his elephant Erawan; they are flying through the atmosphere to oversee all the things that go on in heaven and Earth. Visitors come to pray and worship, believing that the power of Indra can bless good people to fight against bad (Erawan Museum Official, 2018). With education and rising awareness of animal protection, highlighting the cultural and religious significance of elephants can also help raise public awareness of conservation. For example, educational activities to inform people about the religious and cultural importance of elephants can promote support for elephant conservation. The long-term objective is to enhance understanding of the advantages and disadvantages of animal rights and animal welfare for individuals and society (Getz and Baker, 1990). According to Hindu tradition, the image of the 33-headed elephant of the Hindu deity Airāvata has been spread and innovatively developed in the artistic traditions of various South-east Asian and East Asian religions. In practice though, artists often omit the 33 heads in favour of a simplified three-headed elephant image. In China, the Naxi people, who are native to the high-altitude region where the borders of Yunnan, Sichuan and Tibet intersect, attribute to the elephant the same cultural meaning and symbolic values as found in Indian Hindu and Buddhist cultures: the elephant is a holy, celestial and auspicious animal of the divine realm (Mu, 2017).

However, symbolic values and religious beliefs do not always have a positive impact on elephant livelihoods when considered against economic activities and cultural conflict. In some cases, the outstanding status of elephants can also exacerbate cultural conflict and economic pressures. For example, although many cultures and religions venerate elephants, ivory is still seen as a symbol of status and wealth in some areas. The prevalence of elephant poaching and illegal ivory trading in a country is more likely to be associated with the country's lax wildlife management practices, law enforcement and corruption than with the choice of CITES (Convention on International Trade in Endangered Species of Wild Fauna and Flora) appendix listings and the extent of trade restrictions that result from these listings (Stiles, 2004). Whatever the reason, the ivory trade poses a serious threat to elephant populations because despite objections in religion and culture, economic interests often make it difficult to protect these animals completely.

Some other symbolic values of elephants can also lead to damage. In some places, elephants are used in traditional festivals and ceremonies. Despite the cultural significance of these events, these activities can lead to the improper treatment of elephants. In some religious ceremonies, elephants are used for specific celebrations or rituals, and the practical implications of these activities can negatively affect their health and well-being. The British newspaper, *The Sun* reported in 2019 that an emaciated elephant called Tikiri was being maltreated at the Buddhist cultural festival Esala Perahera in Sri Lanka. Tikiri is 70 years old, she has been used for parades and other celebrations since she was 5 years old. Due to her long-term working life and the malnutrition that went with that, she has become so skinny that her bones are visible. Tikiri is responsible for performing in the festival, and when she carries people during the parade, she wears a fancy cover. Therefore, most people couldn't notice her actual body shape. When the cover is removed, Tikiri has no elephant-like body shape at all. Her skin is dull and her bones are clearly visible. Despite this, she is forced to perform high-intensity shows until late at night every day (Awford, 2019; Miller, 2019; White, 2019).

Symbolic values and religious beliefs can, however, raise discussions about animal welfare and ethics. For example, elephants are used for tourist activities such as elephant-back riding. While this activity may have cultural or economic significance, it also raises controversies about the welfare of the animal, as close observation, feeding, touching the trunk and assisted skin scrubbing are all activities that potentially harm the elephant, especially if the animal is mistreated or mismanaged in general.

Elephant Tourism and its Impact on Elephant Conservation

Elephant tourism refers primarily to elephant-themed tourism activities including, but not limited to: (i) elephant taming; (ii) elephant shows; and (iii) elephant-related tourism experiences. Elephant safaris, where elephants are used for tourism activities, remain a popular tourism experience in many places. The development of elephant tourism in Thailand has become a significant socio-economic factor following the implementation of a logging ban in response to serious flooding in heavily logged mountain areas, which resulted in the sudden unemployment of thousands of elephants (Bansiddhi *et al.*, 2020). However, the current status of this activity and its impact on elephant conservation is a controversial topic. Elephant-back riding remains a very popular activity in Asian countries such as Thailand, India and Sri Lanka. Tourists can ride elephants to visit scenic spots. The development and expansion of elephant riding gives rise to significant ethical concerns pertaining to animal welfare, particularly regarding the delineation of acceptable and appropriate standards for working animals (Duffy and Moore, 2011; Zhang *et al.*, 2022). At the same time, in some tourist attractions, elephants are trained to perform various shows such as kicking a ball, painting or performing a complex manoeuvre.

Sintayehu and Kassaw's research (2019) indicates that the expansion of agricultural land and human settlements has become a significant threat to the ecological integrity and viability of elephant habitats. Some tour companies offer 'elephant sanctuary' experiences, which claim to provide a more humane environment where tourists can get up close and personal with elephants while supporting conservation efforts. The establishment of elephant sanctuaries may potentially protect elephants but regulation and animal welfare in those sanctuaries remains a problem. It is claimed that the major impacts of tourism on elephants are health and welfare problems of how living in human-controlled environments influences the behaviour, health and affective states of these animals. This field has expanded to public zoos because good animal welfare is essential to a zoo's mission of promoting connections between animals and visitors and raising awareness of conservation issues. Also, a significant challenge for zoos is to ensure the optimal welfare of a long-lived, highly social species such as elephants (Meehan *et al.*, 2016). The disparate legislative frameworks across countries gives rise to stark contrasts in the legal norms and regulatory frameworks for animal ethics and elephant tourism (Fakfare *et al.*, 2024).

It seems that the involvement of elephants in the economic activities of tourism is a viable and beneficial strategy for generating income for local communities. However, long hours of working, inappropriate training methods and poor living conditions can lead to elephants' health problems causing illness and even death. Under unregulated training, elephants are often subjected to cruel treatment to adapt them to various tourist activities. In a banned Thai documentary called 'Black Elephant' in 2017, the cruel training process that elephants go through in elephant tourism was revealed. In the elephant camp, many elephants have to carry heavy metal chairs on their backs all day long, and also have to bear the weight of at least three people. Their working hours are also far beyond 12 hours, which puts an unbearable burden on their spines which is the weakest part of an elephant's body (Yoo *et al.*, 2015; Suk, 2016).

Ethical Issues of Animal Abuse

Elephants are intelligent and good tempered by nature. Unfortunately, we cannot experience what these majestic animals are all about if they are kept in confinement. In order for them to become a tourist attraction and source of earnings though, elephants have to be trained to obey humans. For this purpose, their will is broken with a cruel process of submission all elephants have to endure, even those born in captivity. This barbaric method, which has been used in Thailand for centuries, is called 'phajaan'. This procedure teaches the elephants submission and obedience (Natasha, 2019). 'Phajaan' is a cruel training process used by mahouts to tame elephants and other smart animals (Gillespie, 2015). The mahout does not participate in the whole process of the 'phajaan' ritual, but he commits the cruel deed of appearing in the last stage of the 'phajaan', pretending to be a saviour. The mahout is the first one to give water and food to the elephant, the one to finally loosen his chains. It is also he who frees the elephant from the crush shed (Gillespie, 2015). After weeks of torture, mental and emotional abuse, loneliness, confusion and isolation, the elephant considers the mahout to be his saviour and starts to trust him. This is an extremely perfidious way of mental and emotional manipulation. But even after their will is finally broken, the maltreatment continues.

Elephant babies are usually taken from their mothers at between 3 and 6 years old, often even younger. The young elephant is now in the hands of his trainer, and the 'phajaan' ritual begins: the animal is kept in a small shed, its legs, painfully stretched, tied up with ropes. In this state of complete motionlessness, the miserable elephant babies are abused by being beaten with sticks and being shouted at. They are not given any water or food during this period of torture. Their heads, ears and skin are constantly stabbed with an iron hook, the fearsome goad without which no elephant could be controlled (Gillespie, 2015; Suk, 2016). At the end of this ordeal, the ropes used for tying up and stretching the legs of the elephant are replaced by tight chains. The terrible 'phajaan' can last for weeks, with no respite from the physical and psychological torture. The frazzled ears and countless scars of the oppressed elephants bear testimony to this cruel tradition.

Nowadays, many mahouts formerly employed in the timber haulage business have switched to a new job because they are attracted by the money in elephant trekking and animal shows for tourists. However, the activities of playing football, doing massage to tourists, painting pictures or carrying tourists are not at all natural for elephants. While adventurous tourists striving for amusement on their holidays struggle to understand the history of the giant animals within a few minutes or hours, having a close look at the body language of the elephants often reveals pure boredom or even post-traumatic behavioural disorders like shaking their heads or walking around in circles. That is the beginning of a vicious circle, since the money the mahouts make is also a sort of life insurance for the elephants: Adult elephants need 150–200 kg of food a day, and their maintenance, including care and medical treatments costs, about US$500 a month (Xia *et al.*, 2024).

Ethical Elephant Sanctuary Practice

Elephant Nature Park (ENP), Chiang Mai

Elephant Nature Park (ENP), a Thai non-profit organization, is dedicated to caring for and assisting Thailand's elephants. ENP is a sanctuary in Thailand that rescues elephants from mistreatment and abuse, protects the environment and promotes their welfare (Lee *et al.*, 2024a). The founder of the sanctuary, Saengduean Chailert, an actress who is also an award-winning conservationist, has devoted her life to the protection of Asian elephants. With the wish for wildlife to live without fear and with dignity, she began rescuing injured, neglected and elderly elephants in the Mae Taeng Valley near Chiang Mai in northern Thailand in 2003 (Chen *et al.*, 2022). Instead of working, performing acrobatics or being ridden, the elephants in the park are allowed to live a more natural life. Saengduan Chailert also started a project where volunteers can have the opportunity to care for elephants (Park *et al.*, 2017; Vitayaveerasuk, 2020).

By implementing better management strategies that consider the individual physiological and psychological needs of elephants, tourist-oriented elephant camps can enhance their welfare, ensuring adequate socialization, nutrition, healthcare and living conditions (Bansiddhi *et al.*, 2020). The sanctuary aims to raise awareness about the mistreatment of elephants and to safeguard their right to natural conservation. They hope visitors will recognize the cruelty inherent in elephant shows by showing them documentary films, providing guided tours, and allowing close encounters with the elephants. It is hoped that visitors will cease to attend tourist shows and instead spread the conservation message, which holds educational and ecological importance for animal protection. To profit from tourism, we have seen that some tour operators in South-east Asian countries still inflict severe harm on local elephant populations through brutal taming methods, including beatings, chaining, bodily mutilations and forcing them to paint (Suk, 2016). The non-profit elephant sanctuary also serves as a great elephant tourism destination, offering elephant-related observation activities for visitors. Visitors can pay for experience activities in the park, and this income can contribute to financing the sanctuary's daily operation expenses and the living costs of elephants. Visitors can choose harmless interaction activities like feeding the elephants, washing and cleaning them (Gorman, 2022).

Both camp and sanctuary models create a work-for-care cycle in which elephants work to generate economic gains, some of which are in turn used to care for the elephants (Cui and Xu, 2019). Morally, sanctuaries serve as a testament to the ethical responsibility humans bear towards the protection and preservation of these majestic creatures. They represent a commitment to ensuring that elephants are allowed to live in environments that mimic their natural habitats, free from the threats of poaching, habitat destruction and human–animal conflict. Practically, such sanctuaries play a crucial role in the preservation of elephant populations by providing a haven where they can breed without interference, thus contributing to the growth and stability of their numbers. They also facilitate research and monitoring, which are essential for better understanding the species' needs, and developing effective conservation strategies.

The Green Elephant Sanctuary Park, Phuket

The Green Elephant Sanctuary Park, Phuket is a shelter for elephant protection on the Phuket peninsula. It stretches over an enormous area of 40,000 m^2 and uses as many natural and renewable resources as possible in an ecological park project. Visitors can enjoy close contact with elephants by touching and feeding them. Traumatized animals are not allowed to be ridden. Four species-appropriate night compounds have been built in the park as well as a 24-hour water-supply system to fulfil the needs of the nocturnal Asian elephants, who sleep during the heat of the day. The park also provides a customized travel programme for tourists. After arriving at the park, tourists have the opportunity to feed the large elephants, while a short presentation in English is provided by the elephant protector covering their vision of the park and providing basic information about Asian elephants. The tourists can rub the elephants and wash mud off them in the freshwater pool (Green Elephant Sanctuary Park, 2024).

Ethics and Morality: Positive Initiatives for Animal Rights in Elephant Tourism

A number of welfare campaigning organizations have expressed significant concerns regarding the treatment and general welfare of elephants involved in various tourism-related activities (Laws *et al.*, 2007; Warwick *et al.*, 2023; Lee *et al.*, 2024b). An increasing number of conservation organizations and tour companies are promoting 'no ride' elephant experiences, which emphasize observation and interaction rather than riding. This approach reduces physical stress on the elephants. Thus, the trend in elephant tourism has shifted from watching elephant shows to encouraging travellers to choose certified sanctuaries that have a genuine focus on animal welfare, and which follow high standards of animal welfare practices. All stakeholders in elephant tourism should consider suitable policies and regulations to strengthen the protection of elephants' rights. Governments and international organizations have obligations to strengthen regulation of elephant tourism activities to ensure that the welfare of elephants is safeguarded and that severe penalties are imposed for abuse. Public education and advocacy can be an important way to increase public awareness. Increased awareness of elephant welfare issues among tourists in turn encourages them to choose more responsible tourism activities, advocating more humane tourism practices and supporting organizations that are committed to elephant conservation and welfare.

Edelblutte *et al.* (2023) defined animal agency, which is the ability of animals to actively influence conservation and management outcomes through their adaptive, context-specific and complex behaviours that are predicated on their sentience, individuality, lived experiences, cognition, sociality and cultures in ways that shape and reshape shared human–wildlife cultures, spaces and histories. They also state that the agency of wild animals cannot be simply summarized by general rules of animal behaviour. Wild animals possess adaptability, evolutionary capacity and individuality, among other forms of agency (Edelblutte *et al.*, 2023). For example, the habituation and luring of animals is basically accomplished through feeding them, which can change the population, dietary structure and behavioural habits of wild animals. That is why some zoos do not allow visitors to feed the animals by themselves.

The important issue of wild animal ethics relates to how to deal with the relationship with human beings and how to manage both sides of this situation.

The relationship between humans and elephants at *Wild Elephant Valley, Xishuangbanna* serves as a further case study that explains how human and non-human actors are interconnected and how they contribute to the emergence of interspecies relationships. The World Wide Fund for Nature (WWF) was an important initiator in the establishment of the Elephant Valley Scenic Area in its early days. In 1986, the WWF began working with Chinese government agencies to protect the tropical rainforests of Xishuangbanna, where elephants were among the protected species. The WWF primarily focused on implementing elephant protection by addressing the relationship between rural and urban residents and elephants. The organization believed that developing elephant tourism projects was an important means of helping urban residents understand and experience elephants. Experiences of visiting elephants in their natural habitat were intended to promote ecological conservation awareness; wildlife tourism could foster positive human–elephant relationships.

Visitor motivations and satisfaction levels have not undergone significant changes at the Wild Elephant Valley, Xishuangbanna. Visitors still come there with the hope of seeing elephants with their own eyes. When wild elephants appear, the valley authorities notify visitors, to allow them to watch the wild elephants first. The wild elephants frequently appear during the Chinese Spring Festival period. In some areas of the valley an elevated boardwalk has been built to reduce the interference of visitors' activities on the wild elephants (see Fig. 5.1 in Chapter 5, this volume). The local government and volunteers of elephant protection at Wild Elephant Valley believe that the management of wild elephants in protected areas and tourist sites should prioritize an equal and analytical approach to human and non-human actors. Attention should be paid to the role of species characteristics, perception, emotional capacity, individuality and group dynamics in shaping cross-species conflicts and their evolution. Also the relationships between heterogeneous actors such as humans, animals and material objects should be coordinated in a targeted and timely manner to address conflicts and their changes, so that humans and wild animals can live in harmony (Cui, 2023).

Conclusions

For global standards to be both viable and agreeable to tour operators, animal welfare organizations, elephant sanctuary proprietors and tourists collectively, it is imperative that efforts to regulate on that scale meaningfully incorporate local practices (Duffy and Moore, 2011). However, the regulation of elephant tourism is still far from what it needs to be, it requires further planning and regulation by local government, elephant keepers and tourists in many situations. Elephants are spiritual beings; thus, elephant tourism should not be an excuse for elephant abuse. While focusing on the economic benefits of elephants' symbolic value, they should not be subjected to external abuse and harm. As Cui and Xu (2019, p. 267) claim, 'As non-anthropocentrism, animal rights ethics are impractical in Thailand because of temporal, spatial, economic and social constraints, sanctuaries offer a direction for a local solution because of their potentially responsible business model'. For communities whose primary source of revenue is derived from elephant tourism, it is challenging to entirely abandon the financial value associated with elephants. Thus, the establishment of a reputable sanctuary may offer a viable solution to enhance elephant welfare while maintaining the feasibility of local tourism attractions (Lim *et al.*, 2016; Praesri *et al.*, 2022).

Overall, the current state of elephant tourism continues to be characterized by a number of challenges. While certain human–elephant interaction activities may have a negative impact on elephants, there are several ways in which this situation can be improved over time. These include: (i) advocating for more humane practices; (ii) supporting genuine conservation and sanctuary projects; and (iii) strengthening policy, regulation and monitoring. This approach will ensure that elephants are treated with the respect and care they deserve during tourism activities.

Bibliography

Awford, J. (2019) LIFE IN CHAINS Tikiri the elephant dies after photos of her skeletal body from '70 years as a slave' shocked the world. *The Sun*. Available at: https://www.thesun.co.uk/news/9999579/tikiri-elephant-dead-70-starved-sri-lanka/ (accessed 10 May 2024).

Bansiddhi, P., Brown, J.L., Thitaram, C., Punyapornwithaya, V. and Nganvongpanit, K. (2020) Elephant tourism in Thailand: a review of animal welfare practices and needs. *Journal of Applied Animal Welfare Science* 23(2), 164–177. DOI: 10.1080/10888705.2019.1569522.

Bist, S.S., Cheeran, J.V., Choudhury, S., Barua, P. and Misra, M.K. (2002) The domesticated Asian elephant in India, giants on our hands. In: Baker, I. and Kashio, M. (eds) *Proceedings of the International Workshop on the Domesticated Asian Elephant*. Food and Agriculture Organization of the United Nations (FAO) Regional Office for Asia and the Pacific, Bangkok, Thailand. FAO, Bangkok, pp. 129–148.

Carruthers, J. (2010) Romance, reverence, research, rights: writing about elephant hunting and management in Southern Africa, *c.*1830s to 2008. *African Protected Area Conservation and Science* 52(1), 1–6. DOI: 10.4102/koedoe.v52i1.880.

Chaitae, A., Gordon, I.J., Addison, J. and Marsh, H. (2022) Protection of elephants and sustainable use of ivory in Thailand. *Oryx* 56(4), 601–608. DOI: 10.1017/S0030605321000077.

Chen, X., Hyun, S.S. and Lee, T.J. (2022) The effects of parasocial interaction, authenticity, and self-congruity on the formation of consumer trust in online travel agencies. *International Journal of Tourism Research* 24(4), 563–576. DOI: 10.1002/jtr.2522.

Choskyi, J. (1988) Symbolism of animals in Buddhism. *Buddhist Himalaya* 1, 259–286.

Cui, Q. (2023) From conflict to harmony: non-human agency and the production of human-asian elephant relations in Yunnan Wild Elephant Valley. *Journal of Guangxi Minzu University* 45(5), 97–106.

Cui, Q. and Xu, H. (2019) Situating animal ethics in Thai elephant tourism. *Asia Pacific Viewpoint* 60(3), 267–279. DOI: 10.1111/apv.12221.

Duffy, R. and Moore, L. (2011) Global regulations and local practices: the politics and governance of animal welfare in elephant tourism. *Journal of Sustainable Tourism* 19(4–5), 589–604. DOI: 10.1080/09669582.2011.566927.

Edelblutte, É., Krithivasan, R. and Nassif, H.M. (2023) Animal agency in wildlife conservation and management. *Conservation Biology* 37(1): e13853. DOI: 10.1111/cobi.13853.

Erawan Museum Official (2018) Available at: https://www.erawanmuseum.com/en/history/ (accessed 3 November 2024).

Fakfare, P., Lee, J.S., Kim, J.Y., Ryu, H. and Han, H. (2024) Animal ethics and tourism: deepening a stimulus–organism–response (S-O-R) framework. *Journal of Travel Research* 63(4), 940–958. DOI: 10.1177/00472875231175079.

Flower, E.K., Burns, G.L., Jones, D.N. and McBroom, J. (2021) Does the experience make a difference? Comparing tourist attitudes pre- and post-visit towards the elephant tourism industry. *Annals of Tourism Research Empirical Insights* 2(2): 100025. DOI: 10.1016/j.annale.2021.100025.

Getz, W.R. and Baker, F.H. (1990) Educational methodology in dealing with animal rights and welfare in public service. *Journal of Animal Science* 68(10), 3468–3474. DOI: 10.2527/1990.68103468x.

Gillespie, E. (2015) Camas woman founds nonprofit to aid elephants. *TCA Regional News*, February 1. Tribune Content Agency LLC, Chicago, Illinois.

Gorman, K. (2022) The elephant in the room: exploring visitor decision, experience, and satisfaction at elephant and community-based sanctuaries in Thailand. MSc thesis, San Diego State University, San Diego, California.

Government of India (2020) Status and distribution of elephants in India. Project Elephant. Ministry of Environment, Forest and Climate Change, Government of India, New Delhi. Available at: https://moef.gov.in/project-elephant-pe (accessed 23 May 2024).

Green Elephant Sanctuary Park (2024) Available at: https://www.green-elephantsanctuarypark.com/ (accessed 3 November 2024).

Grewal, R. (2009) *The Book of Ganesha*. Penguin Books India, New Delhi.

Hicks, J.R. and Stewart, W.P. (2018) Exploring potential components of wildlife-inspired awe. *Human Dimensions of Wildlife* 23(3), 293–295. DOI: 10.1080/10871209.2018.1419518.

Htet, N.N.P., Chaiyarat, R., Thongthip, N., Anuracpreeda, P., Youngpoy, N. *et al.* (2021) Population and distribution of wild Asian elephants (*Elephas maximus*) in Phu Khieo Wildlife Sanctuary, Thailand. *PeerJ* 9: e11896. DOI: 10.7717/peerj.11896.

Hytten, K.F. and Burns, G.L. (2007) Deconstructing dingo management on Fraser Island, Queensland: the significance of social constructionism for effective wildlife management. *Australasian Journal of Environmental Management* 14(1), 48–62. DOI: 10.1080/14486563.2007.9725149.

Laohachaiboon, S. (2010) Conservation for whom? Elephant conservation and elephant conservationists in Thailand. *Southeast Asian Studies* 48, 74–95.

Laws, E., Prideaux, B. and Chon, K.E. (2007) *Crisis Management in Tourism*, 1st edn. CAB International, Wallingford, UK.

Lee, S., Hong, S., Kim, J. and Meng, Z.M. (2024a) Exploring the role of ethical experiences and psychological well-being in travel satisfaction: an animal welfare perspective in elephant-based tourism. *Tourism Management Perspectives* 51: 101248. DOI: 10.1016/j.tmp.2024.101248.

Lee, S., Lee, N., Lee, T.J. and Hyun, S.S. (2024b) The influence of social support from intermediary organizations on innovativeness and subjective happiness in community-based tourism. *Journal of Sustainable Tourism* 32(4), 795–817. DOI: 10.1080/09669582.2023.2175836.

Li, A.Z. (2018) On the sanctity of the elephant in the Shang dynasty. *Journal of Tangshan University* 31, 88–97. DOI: 10.16160/j.cnki.tsxyxb.2018.02.014.

Li, A.Z. (2021) Cultural symbolism of elephants in Ancient China. *Journal of Chongqing Jiaotong University (Social Sciences Edition)* 21, 48–53.

Lim, Y.J., Kim, H.K. and Lee, T.J. (2016) Visitor motivational factors and level of satisfaction in wellness tourism: comparison between first-time visitors and repeat visitors. *Asia Pacific Journal of Tourism Research* 21(2), 137–156. DOI: 10.1080/10941665.2015.1029952.

Liu, L.C. (2023) Why did the Yunnan elephants trek so far north? Dialogue Earth. Available at: https://dialogue.earth/en/nature/why-did-the-yunnan-elephants-trek-so-far-north/ (accessed 10 May 2024).

Lyons, J. (2013) Elephant symbolism in Thailand. Available at: https://scholarworks.umt.edu/umcur/2013/oralpres3f/2/ (accessed 20 August 2024).

Meehan, C.L., Mench, J.A., Carlstead, K. and Hogan, J.N. (2016) Determining connections between the daily lives of zoo elephants and their welfare: an epidemiological approach. *PLoS ONE* 11(7): e0158124. DOI: 10.1371/journal.pone.0158124.

Miller, C. (2019) Tikiri: beloved elephant dies in Sri Lanka after being forced to perform for decades. *Independent*, 25 September. Available at: https://www.independent.co.uk/news/world/asia/elephant-tikiri-sri-lanka-animal-cruelty-kandy-perahera-festival-a9119486.html (accessed 25 October 2024).

Mu, S.H. (2017) The study of the 33 elephant origin songs in the Naxi Dongba religion's Shenlutu. *Journal of Xizang Minzu University (Philosophy and Social Sciences Edition)* 38, 91–102.

Natasha, D. (2019) The wildlife we see, the suffering we don't. *National Geographic* 235, 44–77.

Nyi, N.P.H., Chaiyarat, R., Thongthip, N., Anuracpreeda, P., Youngpoy, N. and Chompoopong, P. (2021) Population and distribution of wild Asian elephants (*Elephas maximus*) in Phu Khieo Wildlife Sanctuary, Thailand. *PeerJ* 9: e11896. DOI: 10.7717/peerj.11896.

Pandey, R.K., Yadav, S.P., Selvan, K.M., Natarajan, L. and Nigam, P. (2024) Elephant conservation in India: striking a balance between coexistence and conflicts. *Integrative Conservation* 3(1), 1–11. DOI: 10.1002/inc3.38.

Park, K., Lee, J. and Lee, T.J. (2017) Residents' attitudes toward future tourism development in terms of community well-being and attachment. *Asia Pacific Journal of Tourism Research* 22(2), 160–172. DOI: 10.1080/10941665.2016.1208669.

Phillips, C.J.C. (2021) Are there lessons from India about the management of cattle? A review of 'Cow Care in Hindu Animal Ethics' by Kenneth R. Valpey. *Animals* 11(8): 2175. DOI: 10.3390/ani11082175.

Praesri, S., Meekun, K., Lee, T.J. and Hyun, S.S. (2022) Marketing mix factors and a business development model for street food tourism. *Journal of Hospitality and Tourism Management* 52, 123–127. DOI: 10.1016/j.jhtm.2022.06.007.

Ratanakorn, P. (2002) The role of NGOs in the management of domesticated elephants in Thailand. Food and Agriculture Organization of the United Nations (FAO). Available at: https://www.fao.org/4/ad031e/ad031e0q.htm (accessed 20 May 2024).

Sintayehu, D.W. and Kassaw, M. (2019) Impact of land cover changes on elephant conservation in Babile elephant sanctuary, Ethiopia. *Biodiversity International Journal* 3(2), 65–71. DOI: 10.15406/bij.2019.03.00129.

Song, F. (2014) Study on elephant culture and strategy of tourism resources development in Thailand. *Tourism Overview* 22, 168–169.

Stiles, D. (2004) The ivory trade and elephant conservation. *Environmental Conservation* 31(4), 309–321. DOI: 10.1017/S0376892904001614.

Suk, H. (2016) The ethics of riding an elephant in Thailand. *Not Without My Passport*, July 5. Available at: https://notwithoutmypassport.com/ethics-of-riding-an-elephant-in-thailand/ (accessed 25 October 2024).

Tian, L. (2023) *History of Thailand*, 1st edn. China Book Press, Beijing.

Vitayaveerasuk, V. (2020) The influences of communications about animals on attitude and behavior changes of social media users. *Journal of Public Relations and Advertising* 13(2). Available at: https://so03.tci-thaijo.org/index.php/jprad/article/view/237658 (accessed 6 March 2025).

Wang, H.J., Wang, P.Z., Zhao, X., Zhang, W.X., Li, J. *et al.* (2021a) What triggered the Asian elephant's northward migration across southwestern Yunnan? *The Innovation* 2: 100142. DOI: 10.1016/j.xinn.2021.100142.

Wang, H., Xu, C., Liu, Y., Jeppesen, E., Svenning, J.C. *et al.* (2021b) From unusual suspect to serial killer: cyanotoxins boosted by climate change may jeopardize megafauna. *The Innovation* 2(2): 100092. DOI: 10.1016/j.xinn.2021.100092.

Warwick, C., Pilny, A., Steedman, C. and Grant, R. (2023) Elephant tourism: an analysis and recommendations for public health, safety, and animal welfare. *International Journal of One Health* 9, 49–66. DOI: 10.14202/IJOH.2023.49-66.

White, D. (2019) HIDDEN TORTURE Harrowing pics expose abused elephant's emaciated body that's normally HIDDEN by a colorful festival costume. *The Sun*, 13 August. Available at: https://baijiahao.baidu.com/s?id=1641831540039472981&wfr=spider&for=pc (accessed 25 October 2024).

Williams, C., Tiwari, S.K., Goswami, V.R., De Silva, S., Kumar, A. *et al.* (2020) *Elephas maximus*, Asian Elephant. The IUCN Red List of Threatened Species 2020: e.T7140A45818198. Available at: https://www.iucnredlist.org/species/7140/45818198 (accessed 6 March 2025).

Xia, L., Lee, T.J. and Kim, D.K. (2024) Relationships between motivation, service quality, tourist satisfaction, quality of life, and spa and wellness tourism. *International Journal of Tourism Research* 26(1): e2624. DOI: 10.1002/jtr.2624.

Yoo, I.Y., Lee, T.J. and Lee, C.K. (2015) Effect of health and wellness values on festival visit motivation. *Asia Pacific Journal of Tourism Research* 20(2), 152–170. DOI: 10.1080/10941665.2013.866970.

Yu, Y.R. (2016) *Research on Mythology History Narration of Records of the Grand Historian*, 1st edn. China Social Science Press, Beijing.

Zhang, G.Z. (1981) Animal patterns on bronze vessels of the Shang and Zhou dynasties. *Journal of Archaeology and Cultural Relics* 60.

Zhang, Q.F. and Xu, H.G. (eds) (2021) Awe experiences of wildlife viewing tourists: an empirical study based on elephant tourism in Sri Lanka. *Journal of Chinese Ecotourism* 11, 705–719. DOI: 10.12342/zgstly.20210064.

Zhang, Y., Li, Z.-X. and Lee, T.J. (2021) Wellness-oriented seasonal tourism migration: a case of China with a field relationship approach. *International Journal of Tourism Research* 23, 491–503. DOI: 10.1002/jtr.2420.

Zhang, Y., Lee, T.J. and Xiong, Y. (2022) The contribution of animal-based cultural ecosystem services to tourist well-being at cultural heritage sites. *Journal of Travel Research* 61(7), 1631–1647. DOI: 10.1177/00472875211037743.

7 Turning Threats into Opportunities for Communities and Elephants in North-eastern Botswana

LIFE MASHUMBA,[1] JOY MOSITI LIFE,[1] GALAMOYO PIJE,[2] STACY J. LYNN[3] AND CYNTHIA S. BROWN[3]*

[1]*Lijoka International Seminary and Bible College, Francistown, Botswana;* [2]*Sustainable Elephant and Ecosystem Community Collaborative, Maitengwe, Botswana;* [3]*Colorado State University, Fort Collins, Colorado, USA*

Abstract

What are communities naive to living with elephants to do when these majestic, yet threatening creatures begin calling their land home? Here we first describe the elephant population in north-eastern Botswana and explain the origins of human–elephant conflict to provide context for our work. Second, we describe solutions that are culturally appropriate and provide benefits to both people and elephants. Third, we investigate how residents are affected by elephants and how they feel the challenges should be handled. We aim to join local knowledge, experiences and perspectives with Western scientific approaches to learn alongside our focal communities. Finally, we explain our vision for sustainable coexistence of human communities and elephant populations and how this might be achieved through combined scientific, educational and economic approaches. Tourism represents new economic opportunity and can be intentionally developed when the safety and livelihoods of community members have been sufficiently ensured through a knowledge-building combination of participatory research and demand-driven educational outreach.

Introduction

Elephants and people have cohabitated across much of Africa for millennia, sharing space and resources, and at times coming into conflict for diverse reasons when overlapping in space. In north-eastern Botswana, elephant movement patterns are shifting, often across international boundaries, introducing new

*cynthia.s.brown@colostate.edu

DOI: 10.1079/9781836990093.0007

communities to the challenges of living with elephants. What are communities naive to living with elephants to do when these majestic yet potentially destructive and dangerous creatures begin calling their land home? That is the question facing people living in five focal villages of interest in Botswana's north-eastern region bordering Zimbabwe: (i) Dagwi; (ii) Maitengwe; (iii) Nkange; (iv) Senete; and (v) Changate (see Fig. 7.1). We call them 'focal villages' because while we are aware other villages nearby are facing challenges with elephants, these five villages are at the centre of these challenges and are the villages that requested help. There are many potential reasons for the changing elephant movement patterns, but here we explore consequences and potential solutions for the five focal village communities based largely on *in situ* conversations with community members and previous work done in other places.

Elephants in North-eastern Botswana

Northern Botswana is home to the largest African savannah elephant population on the continent (Pozo *et al.*,2017). Thus, northern Botswana is a hotspot of human–elephant interaction with negative impacts for both elephants and people a frequent outcome, especially where people and elephants coincide

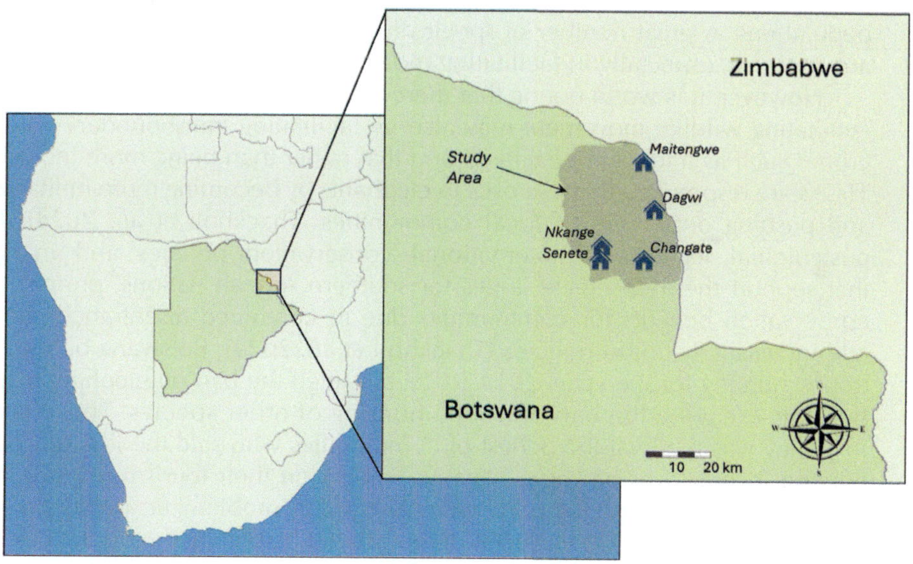

Fig. 7.1. This project's five focal villages – Maitengwe, Senete, Changate, Nkange and Dagwi – are located in the southern African country of Botswana along the northeastern border with Zimbabwe. The study area's approximate area is represented in grey. ESRI ArcGIS Online *World Countries Generalized* Base Map (Sources: Esri; Garmin International, Inc.; U.S. Central Intelligence Agency (The World Factbook); National Geographic Society, updated March 7, 2025). Botswana country boundary source: Michael Bauer Research GmbH, October 2023. Village locations and study area boundary were digitized from World Imagery base layer (Source: Esri, Maxar, Earthstar Geographics, and the GIS User Community). (Created by Stacy J. Lynn (Lynn, 2025)).

in space. A study by Thouless *et al.* (2016) estimated that the elephant habitat in Botswana covers 228,000 km^2 and supports a population of 131,626 ± 12,508 elephants in the northern areas alone. Based on the more recent 2022 Kavango–Zambezi Transfrontier Conservation Area (KAZA TFCA) African savannah elephant survey, Botswana's northern elephant population has remained stable (Chen *et al.*, 2022a; Bussiere and Potgieter, 2023). Despite this stable status, the threat of poaching looms over elephant populations as reports from the 2022 survey indicate a concerning proportion of elephant carcasses among all elephants counted in northern Botswana (12.8%), exceeded only by Angola (16.27%) (Schlossberg and Chase, 2024). Many of those Botswana elephant carcasses were observed in groups of four or more, a likely indication of poaching events (Yoo *et al.*, 2015; Bussiere and Potgieter, 2023).

Botswana is known for its wilderness and rich biodiversity. The country's elephant populations are mainly found in northern regions. As a TransFrontier Conservation Area (TFCA), KAZA TFCA's wildlife management, wildlife and habitat conservation efforts, tourism (especially ecotourism) and resulting economic benefits are ideally shared across international borders (Thackholi *et al.*, 2024). This approach benefits wildlife populations both socially and genetically by encouraging support for elephant populations rather than antagonism. The ecosystem's connectivity allows more natural freedom of movement to adapt to local ecological and resource conditions and other needs to maintain healthy populations. A great number of species including elephants benefit from this arrangement, especially in facilitating movement.

However, it is worth noting that there are suspicions that the open borders facilitating wildlife movement may also be facilitating transboundary wildlife crimes such as trade and poaching, and that rather than being more inclusive, TFCAs are responding to these risks to elephants by becoming more militarized and pushing out voices of local communities (Thackholi *et al.*, 2024). The postcolonial legacies of international conservation policies and markets that support them do create issues for southern African nations' promises of conservation benefits for communities due to continued disenfranchisement and increasingly unjust policies (Thackholi *et al.*, 2024). Botswana banned all trophy hunting for the years 2014–2019 but lifted the ban on elephant trophy hunting – leaving the ban of trophy hunting of other species. This change in policy was made at the behest of communities who said the loss of trophy hunting income was having a negative impact on their tourism revenue and increasing elephant populations were becoming problematic (Mokgalo and van der Merwe, 2022). It has been demonstrated that lifting the trophy hunting ban may have improved resilience of human communities, and improved communication about conservation and livelihood diversification (Mokgalo and van der Merwe, 2022).

The early 21st century saw an increase in elephant populations in regions where they were previously scarce (Junker *et al.*, 2008). More recent aerial elephant population surveys indicate that elephant populations remained relatively constant between 2014/15 and 2020/22 in the region encompassing Angola, Botswana, Namibia, Zambia and Zimbabwe although their distributions are heterogeneous (Schlossberg and Chase, 2024).

Past research suggested that historical southern elephant migration was at least in part due to the ivory trade and its associated hunting and poaching pressures, the expansion of human settlements, and a decrease in available natural water sources (Campbell, 1990; Cumming and Jones, 2005). Botswana's 2014 ban on hunting turned the country into a sanctuary for elephants; research has demonstrated that elephant populations are declining in areas where hunting of the species is allowed and increasing in areas where it is not allowed (Selier *et al.*, 2014). Otisitswe Broza Tiroyamodimo, director of the country's Department of Wildlife and National Parks, recognizes this new situation and refers to it as 'providing shelter for refugee elephants within the nation' (Lindsay *et al.*, 2017).

Residents in the focal villages do not recall seeing elephants transiting through or residing in their villages prior to approximately 2018. However, our recent work in the focal villages indicates elephants first reappeared in Changate in 2002 and have steadily increased with groups of five to 30 elephants now being commonly reported. While it is understood that elephants must have inhabited this area in the distant past, interactions with elephants are not part of the villages' collective living memory. Since 2018, however, elephants have been venturing into the focal villages and surrounding areas, destroying crops, damaging water facilities and posing a direct threat to people during unexpected encounters as they move through people's home spaces. These interactions create potential negative consequences for human health, safety, livelihoods and the community's sense of security. Negative encounters even have potential to cause post-traumatic stress and other psychological and physical scars that impact long-term human mental and physical health (Chen *et al.*, 2022b; Blackie, 2023).

Local news reports in Botswana suggest that while elephants have been seen in the Maitengwe area for several years, they have not been permanent residents but rather have moved in search of seasonal resources like water. These resources attract, or *pull*, elephants into areas that contain desirable resources. Now, elephants are being observed in the focal villages year round (Praesri *et al.*, 2022).

We believe that the tension between pushing drivers of elephant movement, things elephants want to get away from, and pulling drivers, things elephants need to survive or want, is a complex dynamic. If we ascertain through community observations where elephants may be coming from and what conditions they may be avoiding, as well as the areas they favour, this is likely to reveal temporal and spatial patterns of heavy elephant use and transit, and areas where elephants are few and conflict less likely (Zhang *et al.*, 2021). The dramatic change in elephant presence and movement patterns over just half a decade – from absent, to transitory, to potentially resident – combined with community interest in exploring approaches to coexistence has made the five focal villages a prime area for investigating potential solutions.

Climate Change and its Impacts on Elephants

Just like many other regions, Botswana is expected to undergo notable shifts in both temperature and rainfall trends due to global climate change, which will affect wildlife and conservation efforts. Climate change is making droughts in Botswana more frequent, severe and longer lasting (Lekorwe *et al.*, 2024), thus pushing water-dependent animals like elephants to search for resources in regions where people practice agriculture (Marima, 2022). Elephants need to drink 200 l (50 gallons) of water/day, and competition for resources has led to increased conflicts between humans and elephants (Marima, 2022). This is particularly true in dry ecosystems such as the transboundary region of Zimbabwe and Botswana, with at least 20 people being killed by elephants in Zimbabwe alone in the dry first seven months of 2022 (Marima, 2022).

Climate change also impacts elephants through rising temperatures. Despite being adapted to warm climates, savannah elephants are quite sensitive to heat. Studies conducted by Dingle and Drake (2007) revealed that temperatures higher than the critical threshold of 23°C (73.4°F) significantly raise their susceptibility to heat stress, especially among young elephant calves. The central region of Botswana has become hotter in recent years, leading to some elephant deaths due to heat stroke, while other elephants have migrated to cooler parts of Botswana (Specktor, 2020). Experts forecast that African elephants in areas such as Zimbabwe and Botswana could see a 40% reduction in their living spaces by 2050 due to rising temperatures (Mpakairi *et al.*, 2020; Specktor, 2020). This decrease in living space will limit their ability to find water resources for bathing and drinking that they would normally use to regulate their body temperature to stay alive. Unless steps are taken, the projected increase in ambient temperatures in the next three decades may drive elephants over the brink to extinction (Mpakairi *et al.*, 2020).

Drought and its Impact on Elephants

The increasing frequency and duration of droughts in southern Africa are presenting challenges for both people and wildlife. The impact of these droughts is worsened by weather phenomena such as El Niño, which disrupt rainfall patterns and make rainy seasons unpredictable. In recent years, severe droughts have devastated communities and wildlife alike. In 2019, tropical cyclone Idai brought floods and high winds that claimed hundreds of human lives in Zimbabwe, while simultaneously approximately 200 African elephants died from drought-related causes in Hwange National Park. This demonstrates a high level of precipitation variability reaching the two extremes over a relatively small area. A similar loss of 160 elephants occurred in late 2023 – also in Hwange National Park – due to high temperatures, rainfall 50% below the long-term mean and resulting starvation (Karombo, 2024).

At the same time, people are also facing food and water shortages. During such times there is a reported increase in bushmeat poaching as people attempt to meet their food needs (Karombo, 2024). The increasing frequency of such occurrences indicate that such events may become a new normal. The dire conditions in Zimbabwe have forced some elephants to migrate to neighbouring countries like Botswana, particularly to the area surrounding the focal villages located close to the border, in search of water and sustenance.

Notably, recent studies have shown that African savannah elephants can lose up to 10% of their body weight in water in 1 day during hot weather conditions (Barker, 2023), leading some to wonder whether climate change is, or will soon be, killing more elephants than poachers (Ngcobo *et al.*, 2018). This significant 1-day body water loss is the largest recorded among land animals. As water holes dry up, water scarcity not only results in dehydration among elephants but also carries consequences for their reproductive health. Inadequate water consumption can elevate the risk of miscarriages, diminish milk production in nursing females, and lower calf survival rates (Barker, 2023). Ensuring survival of calves until they reach reproductive age is crucial for long-term preservation of elephants as a species.

Experts have proposed solutions to mitigate the impacts of drought on both humans and elephants. One proposed solution involves drilling boreholes within national parks to provide water sources for elephants during drought periods (Barker, 2023). Another suggestion is to close off watering holes near settlements to deter elephants from entering villages, thereby reducing conflicts between humans and wildlife. Drought also results in reduced elephant forage, although drought is not the sole threat to elephant nutrition through loss of vegetation. Dealing with the impacts of food shortages on elephants requires conservation plans that focus on protecting habitats, restoring ecosystems and building climate resilience. By safeguarding food supplies and maintaining ecological relationships, we can reduce climate change impacts on elephant communities to secure their long-term survival. The cascading effects of the climate change phenomenon emphasizes the interconnectedness of ecosystems and stresses the importance of conservation in tackling pressing ecological issues such as habitat deterioration and water scarcity. Given changes in temperature and less predictable water availability, it will be crucial to take proactive steps to fortify ecosystem resilience to climate change and human activities.

Focus Groups in Five Villages

Our team conducted focus groups (i.e. group interviews) with representatives of different social groups and strata, across the five focal villages to gain understanding of local experiences with elephants, perceptions, and thoughts on solutions to conflict. A different mix of village representatives were involved in each focus group. All together a total of 80 people from the five villages participated in focus groups, with focus group sizes ranging from ten to 30 participants. We made an effort towards gender parity, but this was difficult due to the influence of gender roles in Botswana society and our final gender representation was 30 females and 50 males. Our hope is that through these initial conversations with community members, we can better understand the local experience, knowledge and concerns. This place-based and community-engaged grounding and relationship building will create balance between science and local knowledge and experience. It will also facilitate strong collaboration among the communities who solicited our assistance and their new elephant neighbours, and help to conduct locally appropriate, community-led efforts to mitigate human–elephant conflict.

Participant profiles

Participants in the Maitengwe focus groups represented several community roles: youths, farmers, herders, village chiefs, and public servants including police officers, local political leaders and Village Development Committee members (Table 7.1). *Police officers* play a crucial role in ensuring order and safety in areas where elephants are prominent. Their presence helps mitigate conflicts and ensures compliance with regulations governing human–wildlife interactions. Police officers collaborate with wildlife authorities to protect communities and empower them with strategies to coexist harmoniously with elephants.

Village chiefs bring insights into their communities and first-hand knowledge of how residents have been impacted by interactions with elephants. These leaders possess considerable knowledge of their communities and hold valuable historical insights. As guardians of wisdom, they play a crucial role in sharing historical information about elephants with their communities. They are well equipped to advocate for their communities' needs, collaborate with government programmes and agencies, and lead efforts to enhance coexistence with elephants.

The *Village Development Committee* plays a role in supporting community development efforts and safeguarding the well-being of village residents. Through collaboration with farmers and other community members the committee works towards identifying and executing strategies to enhance village livelihoods and address issues arising from conflicts between humans and wildlife. These community members play a role in influencing attitudes and responses to conflicts between humans and elephants in areas where they coexist. *Farmers and herders* produce food for themselves and the community, and are at the front line of elephant interactions, observations of elephant activities and building new knowledge about living with elephants. They therefore contribute important perspectives and information gained through these experiences, and will also be key recipients and participants in our project. *Youths* represent the next generation of rising leaders, and opportunities to share knowledge and perspectives across generations are valuable. Youths will be carrying this community forward, making their observations, concerns and vision for the future very important. Youths also play a vital role in community efforts to mitigate human–elephant conflicts by actively patrolling border gates and locations where electric fences have been installed to deter elephants, contributing to the protection of crops and livelihoods.

Community member perceptions

Focus group participants described some of their perceptions about elephants and their behaviour. Elephants are seen daily, especially near farm fields and

Table 7.1. Overview of focus groups involving participants from five villages in north-eastern Botswana ($N = 80$), representing various community roles and both male and female genders.

		Number of						
Village	Gender	Chiefs	Police officers	VDC[a]	Herders	Farmers	Youths	Total by gender
Maitengwe	Female	0	0	0	0	8	4	12
(30 total)	Male	1	3	0	6	2	6	18
Changate	Female	0	0	3	0	3	0	6
(10 total)	Male	0	0	2	0	2	0	4
Nkange	Female	0	0	0	1	0	0	1
(10 total)	Male	1	0	0	8	0	0	9
Dagwi	Female	0	2	0	0	0	0	2
(10 total)	Male	2	6	0	0	0	0	8
Senete	Female	0	0	7	0	2	0	9
(20 total)	Male	0	0	4	0	7	0	11
Total by group	*30 F* *50 M*	4	11	16	15	24	10	80 total

[a]VDC, Village Development Committee members.

cattle posts outside of villages. They visit villages, but some villages are frequented more than others. In the villages they visit, elephants damage municipal water infrastructure such as tanks and pipes as they can sense the water it contains, and trample field crops, disrupting daily lives of residents. Elephants frequently visit water sources in our focal villages, as well as the Maitengwe Dam, a reservoir situated on the Zimbabwe side of the border. While conflicts between elephants and livestock have not been reported, there are concerns about the safety of both livestock and herders as they take livestock to water.

The elephants travel mostly at night looking for food and water and are not seen as often during the day. Elephants were first reported visiting one of the villages (Dagwi) in small numbers as early as 2002. At first the elephants passed through the villages on their way to other parts of Botswana. They have since taken up residence and occur in groups of up to about 30 individuals in the focal villages. Participants believe elephants are bearing and raising their calves in the area and report that elephants will remain in or return to the place they were born. Thus, many elephants live in the area year round. Participants across villages believe that the elephants originally came from Zimbabwe, moving into Botswana to escape the threat of being hunted for food there (Xia *et al.*, 2024).

In areas heavily populated by elephants, residents report devising preventative strategies to minimize interactions with elephants. These measures include: (i) setting fencing; (ii) noisy deterrents such as vuvuzelas – a horn with an inexpensive injection-moulded plastic shell about 65 cm long that produces a loud monotone note; (iii) gunshots; and (iv) building wildlife corridors to be designated crossing points to prevent elephants from moving further into human settlements. Residents also opt to seek safety on high hills when elephants are roaming nearby since they feel intimidated by the animals' presence; elephants tend to invoke fear in the residents as they are moving through because of earlier encounters they or others have had.

As the primary providers for their families, the impact of elephant-related crop damage is deeply felt by farmers and herders who spend time on the outskirts of the villages and encounter elephants frequently. This is causing distress among affected households and potentially worsening instances of gender-based violence (Zhang *et al.*, 2022).

In rural, drought-prone areas like the focal villages, subsistence farming is prevalent and crop losses due to elephant raids threaten livelihood security and nutrition. Farmers bear the brunt of elephant destruction on their farms, leading to reduced production and increased poverty among households. Participants reported that distress and depression caused by losses due to elephants contributes to heightened levels of gender-based violence.

Elephants are dangerous to people and children who travel around 10 km to school on foot and may come across elephants on the way (e.g. see Box 7.1). Most of the villagers see elephants in their farm fields and at cattle posts and run away in fear (e.g. see Box 7.2). As already mentioned, some villagers report climbing hills to safety because elephants do not climb.

Some participants noted that elephants are a potential source of income as they are natural resources and attract tourists. As such they can create employment

Box 7.1. A boy was attacked by an elephant and narrowly escaped death in Nkange village.

The majority of children in Nkange village walk to school and face the constant threat of encountering elephants on their journey, which can stretch up to 10 km. Unfortunately, a distressing event unfolded when a young boy was attacked by an elephant while making his way home from school in Nkange. The violent encounter with the elephant left the boy deeply shaken and his clothing ripped. These frightening occurrences not only pose risks, but also leave behind emotional wounds that can have a long-lasting impact, potentially disrupting the child's education. Sometimes the mental toll from encounters drives children to abandon their schooling. However, dedicated public servants, like social workers, can step in to provide assistance and emotional support to those affected by such traumatic events.

Box 7.2. The lady who encountered the wrath of an elephant in Changate village.

In the heart of the Central District, a chilling story unfolded in Changate village involving a woman encountering an elephant while working on her farm. The peaceful day was disrupted by the appearance of the elephant as the woman tended to her crops. The aggressive charge of the elephant forced her to retreat to safety on the side of the fields. In a moment of fear, she managed to escape and sought refuge with nearby farmers, with whom she shared her experience. The incident deeply impacted her, causing a lost sense of security, and leaving behind a lasting fear that has continued after the encounter. The trauma from such an event affects all aspects of her life creating unease over even the most everyday of activities. Her beloved farm now holds a sense of dread making her hesitant to return to its fields.

for youth as tour guides employed by the Department of Tourism. All participants agreed it is important for people to be educated about the behaviour of elephants and how to live with them to pave the way for coexistence.

Culturally Appropriate Deterrents to Reduce Human–Elephant Conflict While Minimizing Harm to Elephants

The relationship between farmers and elephants is crucial for ensuring peaceful coexistence and sustainable agriculture to support both human and elephant communities. It is important for elephants to have freedom of movement and access to necessary resources without risk of harm, just as farmers and herders require access to traditionally important places for their livestock, fields and daily activities. The ideal solutions to human–elephant conflict will prioritize safety, affordability and sustainability ensuring that communities can thrive while fostering coexistence with healthy elephant populations (Cooper *et al.*, 2021).

Traditional methods rooted in culture, local resources and capacity have been utilized to divert elephants and other species away from communities. Farmers in Southern Africa commonly use early warning systems to monitor elephant movements and alert others when they approach fields (Gunaryadi *et al.*, 2017). African elephants are notorious for causing damage to farms during the night. Over time, different strategies have been devised to address human–elephant conflicts in Southern Africa such as: (i) loud noises; (ii) repellant and unpalatable crops; (iii) bright lights; (iv) cropland location; (v) olfactory deterrents; and (vi) different types of fences (O'Connell-Rodwell *et al.*, 2000).

Farmers in Kenya learned to employ various strategies to mitigate human–elephant conflict that drew on a combination of traditional knowledge, resources and technology, bringing together local experience and scientific approaches (Sitati and Walpole, 2006). Across Africa, elephant deterrents have included very diverse approaches from noise, to physical barriers such as thornbrush fences, and technologies such as electric fences, beehive fences and even mobile 'virtual fences' composed of items such as bottles and cow bells along with sensory deterrents that make elephants suspicious and turn away before they even reach crop fields (O'Connell-Rodwell *et al.*, 2000; King *et al.*, 2009; La Grange *et al.*, 2022). Here we describe an array of approaches to reducing human–elephant conflict, primarily surrounding crop fields, clustered into three types of deterrents: (i) vegetative; (ii) sensory; and (iii) structural. Recognizing that the lines between the three types are not always clear, this list is meant to demonstrate a variety of approaches, rather than be comprehensive.

Vegetation-derived deterrents

Chilli-pepper-infused fencing flags

Farmers deter elephants by mixing chilli peppers with engine oil and hanging it around the fields in saturated pieces of fabric (sometimes tobacco is included in the mixture) (Von Hagen *et al.*, 2023), or by burning chilli-pepper-infused elephant-dung bricks to create a pungent deterrent smoke.

Crop barriers unpalatable to elephants

Elephants tend to avoid areas where chilli peppers are planted within or alongside field crops (Montgomery *et al.*, 2021) as they cannot tolerate the capsaicin (Chang'a *et al.*, 2016). There are other vegetative species sometimes used to detract elephants, such as deep rings of sunflowers around fields or spiny sisal plants. However, research on these approaches is thin.

Sensory deterrents

Strong flashlights, spotlights, floodlights or strobes

Using flashlights, spotlights or floodlights can help deter elephants from entering crop fields at night (Vollrath and Douglas-Hamilton, 2002). These lights should be bright and numerous enough to make the area appear intimidating to the elephants.

Loud sounds

Using noise as a deterrent has been a method to scare off elephants across regions worldwide. In Africa, farmers utilize sounds such as firecrackers, pipe cannons, vehicle horns, banging objects, shouts and gunshots to deter elephants from damaging crops (O'Connell-Rodwell, 2000). Similarly, villages actively employ these techniques to prevent elephants from encroaching on lands and residential areas. Both human and dog crop guardians are the precursors to all of these loud sounds as elephants need to be detected before being chased away with sound. Guarding of fields is often combined with other approaches presented here.

Elephant urine to mark territory

Osborn (2002) indicated that to mark territory and deter elephants, farmers use elephant urine as these animals are known to recognize markings on tree bark. Spraying collected elephant urine around the perimeter of an area can help keep them at bay.

Structural and fencing deterrents

Thornbrush fencing

Thornbrush fences made from widely available thorny species (e.g. *Acacia* and *Commiphora* species) are commonly used across rural eastern and southern Africa to keep a variety of wild herbivores out of cultivated areas, and to keep predators away from livestock (Muruthi, 2005). Thornbrush fences are generally free of cost. These fences can potentially affect the local environment through shrub and tree removal, but this may be seen as beneficial as well, because it creates a ring free from vegetation that makes it easier to guard (Muruthi, 2005). In places where elephants roam, they can break through thornbrush fences to quickly destroy all crops in their walking path (Lynn, 2010).

Clustered rather than dispersed cropped areas

Cultivating crop fields proximal to each other offers protection against raids from elephants and other species compared with scattering them (Muruthi, 2005; Lynn, 2010). Clustering cultivation provides a more defensible space with a lower edge to area ratio, and maximizes continuity of the non-cultivated matrix, providing space for elephant movement (Lynn, 2010).

Chilli-pepper-infused fencing

As already stated, elephants find the capsaicin in chilli peppers to be an irritant (Chang'a *et al.*, 2016). Farmers can deter elephants by mixing chilli peppers with engine oil and saturating pieces of fabric or sisal string to hang around crop fields (Chang'a *et al.*, 2016; Von Hagen *et al.*, 2023). The recipe used can vary according to what is handy or used locally (Von Hagen *et al.*, 2020). Residents of our focal villages who are dealing with elephants are adopting chilli-pepper fences. This approach is inexpensive and easy for anyone to do.

Beehive fences

Dr Lucy King of the non-governmental organization (NGO) Save the Elephants developed beehive fences as an elephant deterrent (King *et al.*, 2009). This method is founded on elephants' recognized fear of bees. Save the Elephants has tested different approaches to building beehive fences and found that they are most effective on a relatively small scale of up to 3 acres, with hives strung at intervals of approximately 10 m, swinging freely so that if elephants touch the line between the hives it will disturb and activate the bees, scaring the elephants off (King, 2019).

Electric fences

According to Vollrath and Douglas-Hamilton (2002), electric fences are effective in preventing crop-raiding by elephants but are expensive to install and maintain. Increasingly, community elephant fencing projects are being externally funded. Electric fences prove effective in warding off elephants from raiding crops. However, maintenance issues can lead to failure (La Grange *et al.*, 2022). Installation and maintenance costs are not typically affordable without external funding to implement them.

'Virtual' mobile fences

La Grange *et al.* (2022) explored a creative, low-tech and inexpensive approach that acts like a faux virtual fence. This approach entails placing multiple human objects and sensory deterrents in clusters at multiple access pathways to generate suspicion and fear on the part of elephants, spurring them to turn away while still at a distance from crops. The items included are based on local knowledge of what elephants don't like, such as plastic bottles and chilli rags, among others. The locations of deterrents are shifted intermittently to make the elephants more suspicious and fearful so they again turn away and cannot learn patterns in the arrangement of items and their memories accumulate locations where they should not approach. One of the keys to this approach is that deterrents are set up away from the crop fields rather than typical deterrents being set up directly at the edge of fields, reducing temptation. Such mobile deterrents have been found to be up to 95% effective, leading to widespread avoidance of areas now deemed risky.

Striving for Sustainable and Durable Solutions for Communities and Elephants

Conflict between elephants and people arises in the context of complex ecological, social, political and economic systems. Our mission is to affect change that enables both human and elephant communities to thrive, represented by the core of the schematic depicting the holistic vision of our work (Fig. 7.2).

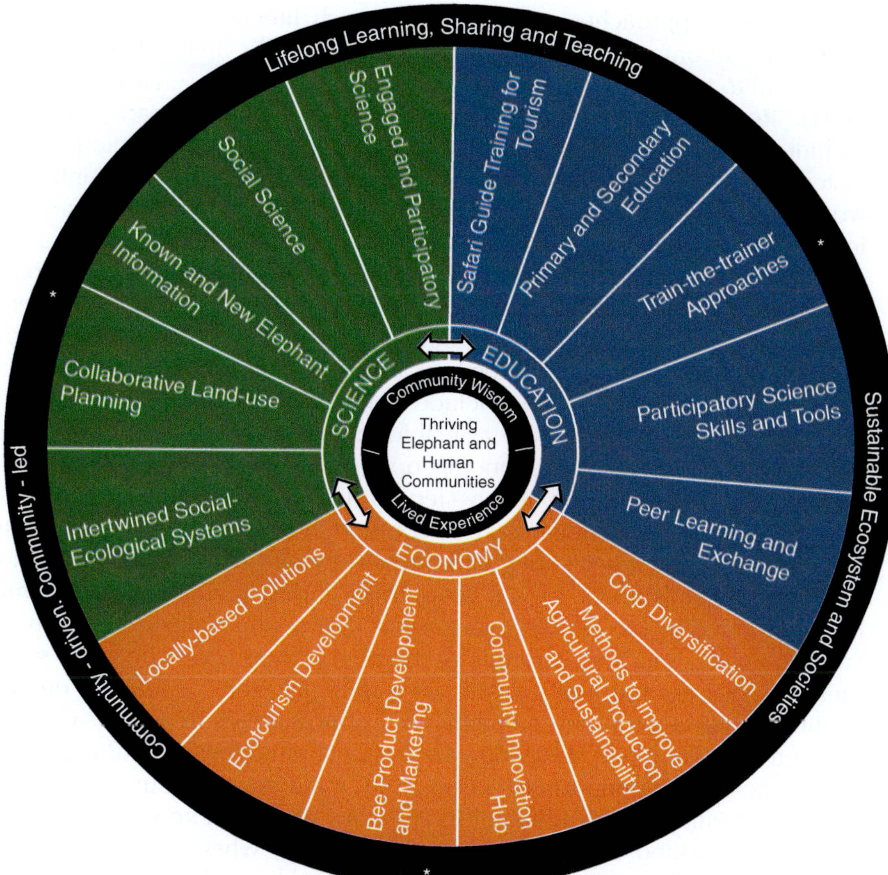

Fig. 7.2. Project conceptual model linking three sectors of science, education and economy to build towards thriving elephant and human communities. (Authors' own diagram.)

We expect the best way to achieve this idealized state is through a three-pronged approach that includes educational, scientific and economic components, each of which can be operationalized through multiple approaches while remaining grounded in community wisdom and lived experiences. In our figure these are represented by the spokes in the wheel, all of which emanate from lifelong learning and teaching, sustainable ecosystems and societies, and community-driven and community-led partnership.

Educational activities include translation of scientific and experiential knowledge to the community, co-creation of new knowledge through project activities within the community, and documenting the lived-experience of community members. This will empower community members with: (i) understanding of elephant behaviour and how to remain safe around elephants; (ii) confidence to implement elephant-safe means of reducing elephant impacts; and (iii) opportunities to share knowledge and experiences with other community members to help the community as a whole reduce conflict with elephants and flourish. Examples of such activities are shown in the blue spokes of Fig. 7.2.

Scientific approaches will harness the rich literature reporting results of studies from communities across the globe generally, and in Southern Africa in particular, to inform community activities and projects (Adams and Hulme, 2001). Research on community-based natural resource management that includes social science tools for learning about complex socio-ecological systems such as those affected by human–elephant conflict will inform our work. Examples of scientific approaches that we strive to incorporate are shown in the green spokes of Fig. 7.2.

Economic well-being is a cornerstone of sustainability (Newmark and Hough, 2000), thus, is an essential component of our work. Solutions that reduce human–elephant conflict through deterrence must be within the economic capacities of the community members if they are to succeed (Newmark and Hough, 2000). Solutions may include compensation to mitigate losses (van Houdt *et al.*, 2021), which are available in Botswana. Some interventions to deter elephants can result in economic opportunity such as production of honey and beeswax products from beehive fences (Taruvinga and Gumpo, 2018).

The presence of elephants also represents economic opportunity despite the direct negative effects they can have. They can draw tourists, which can drive the establishment of an ecotourism industry. Community members can be trained to be wildlife tour guides, dining and lodging establishments can be established and community members hired and trained as staff for these businesses, and artisans can sell traditional crafts to tourists, providing livelihoods for community members and opportunities for youth who are at risk of truancy and bad behaviour when not gainfully engaged (Balogi, 2004). Lack of economic opportunity is one of the main reasons young people leave their home villages in Botswana (Bryant *et al.*, 1978). More recently, McCabe *et al.* (2014) found a similar pattern in Tanzania, where Maasai pastoralists migrate to urban areas in response to poverty and limited resources to improve their livelihoods. Also in Tanzania, Maasai pastoralists migrated to participate in the gem trade, and those who made a profit were able to reinvest in their herds, fields and community (Lynn, 2010). The development of an ecotourism industry in the focal villages would help alleviate the tendency to leave rural communities for employment. Activities that will contribute to the economic well-being of the community are shown in the orange spokes in Fig. 7.2.

The educational, scientific and economic components of our vision are inextricably linked by the activities of our work. Our ultimate goals are: (i) *lifelong learning, sharing, and teaching*; (ii) *sustainable ecosystems and societies*; and (iii) *community-driven and community-led approaches* (Fig. 7.2). We believe that it is through deep community engagement that the most effective and beneficial solutions can be found.

Project Implementation Processes

To implement our project activities, we will employ the adaptive management process, which will be driven by community member input to generate sustainable and durable solutions. Adaptive management was developed to manage natural resources under uncertainty and entails steps of structured decision making and learning (Fig. 7.3).

Adaptive management is appropriate in situations with ecological uncertainty that can be reduced through experimentation (Rist *et al.*, 2013). In our project, there are uncertainties about the spatial and temporal patterns of human–elephant interaction and their underlying causes and about how the needs of elephants can be met while protecting human interests. These uncertainties can be reduced by engaging the community in describing the patterns of interaction and their effects, then identifying and implementing co-created solutions to the observed conflict. Results generated from trials of implemented solutions will be considered in subsequent steps in the adaptive management process.

Adaptive management must be feasible (Rist *et al.*, 2013). The benefits and resources must be sufficient for adaptive management to succeed. There is strong motivation among members of the focal villages and the benefits of resolving the human–elephant conflict will have a big impact. Pilot project funds were applied to build community engagement and deepen the involvement of residents, particularly those who may have been marginalized in the past, and we continue to fundraise. Community members will drive co-creation and implementation of sustainable solutions, laying the foundation for long-term feasibility and successful outcomes.

The final stage of the adaptive management process is to evaluate whether adaptive management was successful (Rist *et al.*, 2013). Evaluation is built into the process in the assessment and adjusting steps of the project's adaptive management process (Fig. 7.3). Thus, our project meets all three criteria put forth by Rist *et al.* (2013) for successful application of adaptive management.

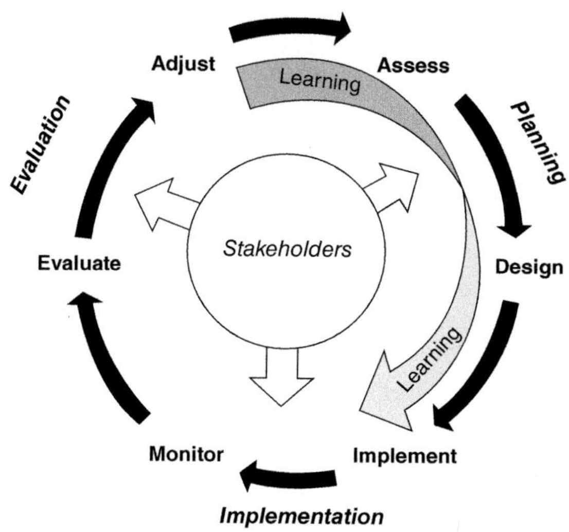

Fig. 7.3. The adaptive management framework is a sequence of steps including planning, implementation and evaluation with input from stakeholders throughout and learning from previous iterations incorporated into subsequent cycles. (Adapted from Williams *et al.*, 2009 and Rist *et al.* 2013, used under license CC-by 4.0.)

Project Activities

Elephant ecology and behaviour handbook

Results from the focus groups held in each of the focal villages indicate that community members are anxious to learn more about how to live peacefully with elephants, a relatively new challenge for the communities. Thus, educational programmes about elephant ecology and behaviour, and non-harmful methods to deter them from farm fields and infrastructure – especially water tanks and pipes – will be an important activity.

A Botswana-based NGO called EcoExist has created an educational elephant handbook, in English and Setswana (the two official languages of Botswana), based on Save the Elephants' Tool Box. One of our first projects will be to translate the handbook into the local Kalanga language. This handbook will be part of a curriculum implemented in training sessions for farmers, elementary and secondary school teachers, parents and other key community members. The curriculum will be interactive and solicit input from community members to generate knowledge that builds on the handbook and is relevant for the local conditions. We will partner with another locally based organization to conduct the training sessions in Kalanga. We believe that conducting train-the-trainers sessions will empower community members to share their knowledge with others in classrooms and community meetings, effectively extending the knowledge to the most vulnerable in the community.

Participatory community science

To institute deep community engagement, our team has initiated a community science project to monitor elephant activity and interactions using the platform CitSci.org to inform future conflict-reduction activities. Community science is an approach to conducting community-driven and community-led research and observations with or without consultation with scientists, particularly grassroots efforts by those typically underrepresented and underserved in science (Cooper *et al.*, 2021). The communities themselves expressed an interest in sharing their observations of elephants and being engaged in devising solutions. Our team is consulting with the communities to create an online project for community members to document all interactions with elephants, including simple sightings, to ensure that the project will meet the explicit interests and needs of the communities, including identifying where elephants are concentrating and moving from and to.

A draft project website has been created and will be finalized and published for use following a comment period with the communities. Once finalized and translated into both languages used locally, Kalanga and Setswana, this site will be used by community members to access co-designed data forms via the CitSci mobile application, using smartphones to document elephant observations and interactions. Alternatively, community members who do not have access to a smartphone can complete an analogous paper form reporting their encounters with elephants and submit it to a trained community-based representative called a *Sentinel* for data entry. Sentinels can also take verbal reports from community members and will be trained by the CitSci team to assist community members as needed. Sentinels will be selected based on minimum criteria of English fluency, technical proficiency, community access, having a smartphone and willingness to take a leadership role. They will also be provided a laptop or tablet device to facilitate this role.

We believe that this project will bring together the best of Western science and technology, and the best of local and traditional knowledge. Our team will honour the important intent of community science projects to: (i) be community driven and controlled; (ii) be founded on local knowledge and collective action; (iii) always actively work towards the dual goals of community and elephant welfare and sustainability; and (iv) respectfully encourage teaching and learning in both directions between researchers and community members, recognizing that each participant has knowledge and contributions of value.

We believe that a community science project is the ideal way to collect both accurate and useful information on elephant interactions. This is a clear way to centre a project on community wisdom and lived experiences. In addition, community project leadership will have full access and ownership of the data and can work on their own to analyse it, or can work with our team or other partners for collaborative interpretation of the data. Approaches to elephant conflict management can be adapted to suit circumstances, such as the types of interactions being recorded, their frequency, and/or their locations and hotspots. If the community science project can identify areas where human–elephant interactions are frequent, where and when elephants concentrate and the conditions of those places, and areas where elephants are few, together we can devise a plan to approach each situation individually and customize solutions for unique place-based circumstances.

Beehive fences

Our team has initiated a beehive fence project modelled after the Save the Elephants' Elephants and Bees Project's design for the dual purposes of keeping elephants out of crop fields and producing local honey (King, 2012; King *et al.*, 2017). A preliminary visual survey of the area indicated that important plant species that contribute to African honeybee success are widely present in the local ecosystem, including flowering mopane trees and various *Acacia* species preferred by African honeybees. A plan has been established for acquiring materials for local woodworkers to create pre-cut beehive kits that can be easily transported to the villages from the nearest town. After setting up a demonstration beehive fence in Maitengwe, we will conduct workshops on hive construction, to share best practices for meeting honeybees' basic needs, and to learn ways to reduce problems with honey badgers.

A secondary benefit of beehive fences is the opportunity to produce honey for use or sale. Communities with beehive fences in countries all over southern and eastern Africa market their honey from beehive fences as 'elephant friendly', thereby facilitating a price markup over traditional honey products. Sale of these products offers diversification of income and further benefit to communities. Based on their research, Save the Elephants has created a guidebook for communities interested in building beehive fences to reduce elephant incursions into cultivated fields (King, 2012, 2019; King *et al.*, 2019), and another Toolbox booklet with a more diverse array of tools (King *et al.*, 2019). The guide both informs communities about elephant behaviour and instructs them on how to construct beehive fences to steer movement away from fields. Once beehive fences are established, we will organize additional training for: (i) extracting honey from honeycombs with an extractor; (ii) honey storage; (iii) sanitary honey packaging; and (iv) marketing for sale.

Long-term objectives

Eventually, we envision co-designing and constructing a community centre to be used for training sessions regarding elephant management as well as community events and educational opportunities to further social and economic development. We believe the presence of elephants can become an economic driver that provides diverse employment and income opportunities. This may enable more community members to make a living in the village without having to move to one of the larger population centres in Botswana or South Africa, as is quite common. This may involve developing elephant water and food sources to draw elephants away from farms and villages and reduce conflict while providing tourism opportunities that can serve to boost local livelihoods (Lee *et al.*, 2024).

Conclusion

Over the past two decades, north-eastern Botswana has seen a dramatic change in elephant movement patterns, sparking concerns among community members and researchers regarding the impact for community safety and livelihoods. People living near wildlife reserves and national parks along the Zimbabwe border, such as the focal villages of Dagwi, Maitengwe, Nkange, Senete and Changate, are experiencing elephants on a daily basis for the first time in living memory.

The arrival of elephants into new areas of Botswana offers both opportunities and challenges for wildlife management and conservation. There are documented challenges being faced by both people and elephants in this region of Africa at the boundary of Botswana and Zimbabwe. Climate change is manifesting as hotter temperature extremes, and increased incidence of drought leading to food and water shortages for both people and elephants, leading people and elephants into conflict where rare life-sustaining resources exist. In addition, as people become hungry, elephants become a source of food. Elephants may have moved into Botswana to avoid these interactions in Zimbabwe, as that country has faced terrible heat and drought in recent years (Lim *et al.*, 2016).

Through community focus groups, we heard about the experiences that community members have faced with elephants and the fear that elephants have brought to the community. However, also we heard about willingness, and even eagerness, to learn about living with elephants to alleviate the tensions between them. Learning more about when and where elephant encounters are happening is the first step to conflict mitigation.

With participatory and co-created approaches we will assist community members with documenting elephant encounters to identify circumstances of elephant interactions and the push and pull forces that are driving new elephant movement patterns. This will help us customize solutions to the circumstances of each location. Through collaborative efforts involving various stakeholders, including youths, farmers, law enforcement agencies and wildlife authorities, communities can develop sustainable solutions to mitigate human–elephant conflict and promote coexistence between humans and elephants in the focal villages.

To address challenges that elephants present to crops more specifically, creative initiatives that have found success elsewhere such as the Elephants and Bees Project have emerged as potential invaluable solutions (King, 2019). By using beehive fences to deter elephants from damaging farmers' crops, we anticipate that these projects will not only safeguard human livelihoods but also will support elephant conservation endeavours. Notably, we observe that several proactive, non-lethal efforts are already being implemented by village residents, actively demonstrating community commitment to establishing dual thriving elephant and human communities. As Botswana strives to navigate complex dynamics of coexistence between humans and elephants, collaborative actions and innovative approaches will play a role in ensuring the welfare of both human and wildlife communities.

Bibliography

Adams, W.M. and Hulme, D. (2001) If community conservation is the answer in Africa, what is the question? *Oryx* 35(3), 193–200. DOI: 10.1046/j.1365-3008.2001.00183.x.

Balogi, K.T.O (2004) At the cross roads: family, youth deviance and crime control in Botswana. *Pula: Botswana Journal of African Studies* 18, 77–87.

Barker, L. (2023) 5 ways climate change is affecting elephants and 1 surprising way they help fight it. WildAid. Available at: https://wildaid.org/5-ways-climate-change-is-affecting-elephants-and-1-surprising-way-they-help-fight-it/ (accessed 26 October 2024).

Blackie, I.R. (2023) Posttraumatic stress and psychological impacts of human wildlife conflict on victims, their families and caretakers in Botswana. *Human Dimensions of Wildlife* 28(3), 248–264. DOI: 10.1080/10871209.2022.2036394.

Bryant, C., Stephens, B. and MacLiver, S. (1978) Rural to urban migration: some data from Botswana. *African Studies Review* 21(2): 85. DOI: 10.2307/523664.

Bussiere, E.M.S. and Potgieter, D. (2023) *KAZA Elephant Survey 2022, Volume I: Results and Technical Report*. Kavango–Zambezi (KAZA) Transfrontier Conservation Area (TFCA) Secretariat, Kasane, Botswana. Available at: https://www.wwf.de/fileadmin/fm-wwf/Publikationen-PDF/Afrika/KAZA-Elephant-Survey-Volume-1.pdf (accessed 5 March 2025).

Campbell, A.C. (1990) History of elephants in Botswana. In: Hancock, P. (ed.) *The Future of Botswana's Elephants: Proceedings of a Symposium*. Kalahari Conservation Society, Gaborone.

Chang'a, A., Souza de, N., Muya, J., Keyyu, J., Mwakatobe, A. *et al.* (2016) Scaling-up the use of chili fences for reducing human-elephant conflict across landscapes in Tanzania. *Tropical Conservation Science* 9(2), 921–930. DOI: 10.1177/194008291600900220.

Chen, L., Lee, T.J. and Hyun, S.S. (2022a) How does a global coffeehouse chain operate strategically in a traditional tea-drinking country? The influence of brand authenticity and self-enhancement. *Journal of Hospitality and Tourism Management* 51, 176–186. DOI: 10.1016/j.jhtm.2022.03.003.

Chen, X., Hyun, S.S. and Lee, T.J. (2022b) The effects of parasocial interaction, authenticity, and self-congruity on the formation of consumer trust in online travel agencies. *International Journal of Tourism Research* 24(4), 563–576. DOI: 10.1002/jtr.2522.

Cooper, C., Hawn, C., Larson, L.R., Parrish, J., Bowser, G. *et al.* (2021) Inclusion in citizen science: the conundrum of rebranding. *Science (AAAS)* 372(6549), 1386–1388. DOI: 10.1126/science.abi6487.

Cumming, D. and Jones, B. (2005) Elephants in Southern Africa: management issues and options. In: *World Wildlife Fund (WWF) SARPO Occasional Paper Number 11*. WWF, Harare.

Dingle, H. and Drake, V.A. (2007) What is migration? *BioScience* 57(2), 113–121. DOI: 10.1641/B570206.

Gunaryadi, D., Sugiyo, D. and Hedges, S. (2017) Community-based human-elephant conflict mitigation: the value of an evidence-based approach in promoting the uptake of effective methods. *PLoS ONE* 12: e0173742. DOI: 10.1371/journal.pone.017374.

Junker, J., van Aarde, R.J. and Ferreira, S.M. (2008) Temporal trends in elephant *Loxodonta africana* numbers and densities in northern Botswana: Is the population really increasing? *Oryx* 42(01), 58–65. DOI: 10.1017/S0030605308000756.

Karombo, T. (2024) More than 160 elephants die in Zimbabwe, with many more at risk. *The Guardian*, 17 January. Available at: https://www.theguardian.com/environment/2024/jan/17/more-than-160-elephants-die-in-zimbabwe-with-many-more-at-risk-aoe (accessed 26 October 2024).

King, L.E. (2012) *Beehive Fence Construction Manual*. Elephants and Bees Project, Save the Elephants' Human-Elephant Co-Existence Program, Sagalla, Kenya. Available at: https://elephantsandbees.com/wp-content/uploads/2013/08/Beehive-Fence-Construction-Manual-2012.pdf (accessed 26 October 2024).

King, L.E. (2019) *Beehive FenceTM Construction Manual: a step by step guide to building a protective beehive fence to deter crop-raiding elephants from small scale farm land*, 4th edn. Elephants and Bees Project, Save the Elephants. Available at: https://elephantsandbees.com/wp-content/uploads/2019/07/LKING-2019-Beehive-Fence-Construction-Manual-4th-edition.pdf (accessed 26 October 2024).

King, L.E., Lawrence, A., Douglas-Hamilton, I. and Vollrath, F. (2009) Beehive fence deters crop-raiding elephants. *African Journal of Ecology* 47(2), 131–137. DOI: 10.1111/j.1365-2028.2009.01114.x.

King, L.E., Lala, F., Nzumu, H., Mwambingu, E. and Douglas-Hamilton, I. (2017) Beehive fences as a multidimensional conflict-mitigation tool for farmers coexisting with elephants. *Conservation Biology* 31(4), 743–752. DOI: 10.1111/cobi.12898.

King, L., Oldenburg, C. and Cookson, L. (2019) *12 Tools to Live in Harmony with Elephants. A toolbox of deterrent methods for small scale rural farmers to reduce elephant crop-raiding, improve yields and enhance quality of life*. Elephants and Bees Project, Save the Elephants. Available at: https://elephantsandbees.com/wp-content/uploads/2019/07/King-2018-HEC-Toolbox.pdf (accessed 5 March 2025).

La Grange, M., Matema, C., Nyamukure, B., Hoare, R.E., Dressel, S. *et al.* (2022) The virtual fence dynamic: a breakthrough for low-cost and sustainable mitigation of human-elephant conflict in subsistence agriculture? *Frontiers in Conservation Science* 3. DOI: 10.3389/fcosc.2022.863180.

Lee, S., Lee, N., Lee, T.J. and Hyun, S.S. (2024) The influence of social support from intermediary organizations on innovativeness and subjective happiness in community-based tourism. *Journal of Sustainable Tourism* 32(4), 795–817. DOI: 10.1080/09669582.2023.2175836.

Lekorwe, M., Molefe, W. and Bogopa, T. (2024) Climate change awareness in Botswana is low, but informed citizens desire action. *AFRO Barometer*, 21 October. Available at: https://www.afrobarometer.org/publication/ad887-climate-change-awareness-in-botswana-is-low-but-informed-citizens-desire-action/ (accessed 26 October 2024).

Lim, Y.J., Kim, H.K. and Lee, T.J. (2016) Visitor motivational factors and level of satisfaction in wellness tourism: comparison between first-time visitors and repeat visitors. *Asia Pacific Journal of Tourism Research* 21(2), 137–156. DOI: 10.1080/10941665.2015.1029952.

Lindsay, K., Chase, M., Landen, K. and Nowak, K. (2017) The shared nature of Africa's elephants. *Biological Conservation* 215, 260–267. DOI: 10.1016/j.biocon.2017.08.021.

Lynn, S.J. (2010) Cultivating the savanna: implications of land use change for wildlife conservation and Maasai livelihoods in East Africa. PhD thesis, Colorado State University, Fort Collins, Colorado.

Lynn, S.J. (2025) Map of Botswana study area villages. Scale not given. Colorado State University, Fort Collins, Colorado. Available at: https://arcg.is/14yjLz5 (accessed 19 March 2025).

Marima, T. (2022) Drought is driving elephants closer to people. The consequences can be deadly. *NPR*, August 15. Available at: https://www.npr.org/2022/08/15/1117076598/drought-is-driving-elephants-closer-to-people-the-consequences-can-be-deadly (accessed 26 October 2024).

McCabe, J.T., Smith, N.M., Leslie, P.W. and Telligman, A.L. (2014) Livelihood diversification through migration among a pastoral people: contrasting case studies of Maasai in northern Tanzania. *Human Organization* 73(4), 389–400. DOI: 10.17730/humo.73.4.vkr10nhr65g18400.

Mokgalo, L. and van der Merwe, P. (2022) A revised CBT strategy for Botswana: reflections from experiences of the ban on trophy hunting. *Cogent Social Sciences* 8(1): 2081109. DOI: 10.1080/23311886.2022.2081109.

Montgomery, R.A., Raupp, J., Mukhwana, M., Greenleaf, A., Mudumba, T. *et al.* (2021) The efficacy of interventions to protect crops from raiding elephants. *Ambio* 51(3), 716–727. DOI: 10.1007/s13280-021-01587-x.

Mpakairi, K.S., Henry, N., Paradzayi, T., Zvidzai, M. and Hilary, M.T. (2020) Futuristic climate change scenario predicts a shrinking habitat for the African elephant (*Loxodonta africana*): evidence from Hwange National Park, Zimbabwe. *European Journal of Wildlife Research* 66(1): 1. DOI: 10.1007/s10344-019-1327-x.

Muruthi, P. (2005) Human wildlife conflicts: lessons learned from AWF's African heartlands. African Wildlife Foundation (AWF) Working Papers. Available at: https://www.awf.org/about/resources/human-wildlife-conflict-lessons-learned-awfs-african-heartlands (accessed 26 October 2024).

Newmark, W.D. and Hough, J.L. (2000) Conserving wildlife in Africa: integrated conservation and development projects and beyond. *Bioscience* 50, 585–592. DOI: 10.1641/0006-3568(2000)050[0585:CWIAIC]2.0.CO;2.

Ngcobo, J.N., Nedambale T.L., Nephawa, K.A., Sawosz, E. and Chwaligob, A. (2018) The future survival of African elephants: implications for conservation. *International Journal of Avian & Wildlife Biology* 3, 379–384.

O'Connell-Rodwell, C.E., Rodwell, T., Rice, M. and Hart, L.A. (2000) Living with the modern conservation paradigm: Can agricultural communities co-exist with elephants? A five-year case study in East Caprivi, Namibia. *Biological Conservation* 93(3), 381–391. DOI: 10.1016/S0006-3207(99)00108-1.

Osborn, F.V. (2002) Capsicum oleoresin as an elephant repellent: field trials in the communal lands of Zimbabwe. *The Journal of Wildlife Management* 66(3): 674. DOI: 10.2307/3803133.

Pozo, R.A., Coulson, T., McCulloch, G., Stronza, A.L. and Songhurst, A.C. (2017) Determining baselines for human-elephant conflict: a matter of time. *PLoS ONE* 12(6): e0178840. DOI: 10.1371/journal.pone.0178840.

Praesri, S., Meekun, K., Lee, T.J. and Hyun, S.S. (2022) Marketing mix factors and a business development model for street food tourism. *Journal of Hospitality and Tourism Management* 52, 123–127. DOI: 10.1016/j.jhtm.2022.06.007.

Rist, L., Felton, A., Samuelsson, L., Sandström, C. and Rosvall, O. (2013) A new paradigm for adaptive management. *Ecology and Society* 18(4), 1029–1037. DOI: 10.5751/ES-06183-180463.

Schlossberg, S. and Chase, M. (2024) *Population Trends and Conservation Status of Elephants in Botswana and the Kavango Zambezi Transfrontier Conservation Area: a Review of Elephant Surveys, 2010–2022*. Elephants Without Borders Technical Report, April. Available at: https://elephantswithoutborders.org/site/wp-content/uploads/Final-EWB-Ele-Pop-Trends-KAZA-report-Mar24.pdf (accessed 26 October 2024).

Selier, S.A.J., Page, B.R., Vanak, A.T. and Slotow, R. (2014) Sustainability of elephant hunting across international borders in southern Africa: a case study of the greater Mapungubwe Transfrontier Conservation Area. *The Journal of Wildlife Management* 78(1), 122–132. DOI: 10.1002/jwmg.641.

Sitati, N.W. and Walpole, M.J. (2006) Assessing farm-based measures for mitigating human-elephant conflict in Transmara District, Kenya. *Oryx* 40(3), 279–286. DOI: 10.1017/S0030605306000834.

Specktor, B. (2020) 350 elephants killed by 'a combination of neurotoxins' in water, Botswana government says. *LiveScience*, September 22. Available at: https://www.livescience.com/mass-elephant-dieoff-botswana-cyanobacteria.html (accessed 26 October 2024).

Taruvinga, A. and Gumpo, N. (2018) Income and conservation dynamics of the biological bee-fence: a bio-economic simulation. *IOP Conference Series: Earth and Environmental Science* 178: 012038. DOI: 10.1088/1755-1315/178/1/012038.

Thakholi, L., Koot, S. and Büscher, B. (2024) Introduction: fallen from grace? The legacy and state of Southern African conservation. *Environment and Planning E: Nature and Space* 7(1), 3–21. DOI: 10.1177/25148486231222145.

Thouless, C.R., Dublin, H.T., Blanc, J.J., Skinner, D.P., Daniel, T.E. *et al.* (2016) African Elephant Status Report 2016: an update from the African Elephant Database. *Occasional Paper of the IUCN Species Survival Commission* No. 60. Available at: https://portals.iucn.org/library/sites/library/files/documents/SSC-OP-060_A.pdf (accessed 26 October 2024).

van Houdt, S., Brown, R.P. and Traill, L.W. (2021) Stakeholder attitudes toward the incentives used to mitigate human-elephant conflict in Southern Africa: a news media content analysis. *Journal for Nature Conservation* 61: 125982. DOI: 10.1016/j.jnc.2021.125982.

Vollrath, F. and Douglas-Hamilton, I. (2002) African bees to control African elephants. *Naturwissenschaften* 89(11), 508–511. DOI: 10.1007/s00114-002-0375-2.

Von Hagen, R.L., Norris, P. and Schulte, B.A. (2020) Quantifying capsaicinoids from chili pepper and motor oil mixtures used in elephant deterrent fences. *Chromatographia* 83(9), 1153–1157. DOI: 10.1007/s10337-020-03934-8.

Von Hagen, R.L., Corde, S.C., Norris, P., Kasaine, S., Githiru, M. *et al.* (2023) Chemical ecology and elephant conservation: examining chili pepper deterrent fences. *Chemical Signals in Vertebrates* 15, 489–506. DOI: 10.1007/978-3-031-35159-4_23.

Williams, B.K., Szaro, R.C. and Shapiro, C.D. (2009) *Adaptive Management: the U.S. Department of the Interior Technical Guide*, 2nd edn. Adaptive Management Working Group, US Department of the Interior, Washington, DC.

Xia, L., Lee, T.J. and Kim, D.K. (2024) Relationships between motivation, service quality, tourist satisfaction, quality of life, and spa and wellness tourism. *International Journal of Tourism Research* 26(1): e2624. DOI: 10.1002/jtr.2624.

Yoo, I.Y., Lee, T.J. and Lee, C.K. (2015) Effect of health and wellness values on festival visit motivation. *Asia Pacific Journal of Tourism Research* 20(2), 152–170. DOI: 10.1080/10941665.2013.866970.

Zhang, Y., Li, Z.-X. and Lee, T.J. (2021) Wellness-oriented seasonal tourism migration: a case of China with a field relationship approach. *International Journal of Tourism Research* 23, 491–503. DOI: 10.1002/jtr.2420.

Zhang, Y., Lee, T.J. and Xiong, Y. (2022) The contribution of animal-based cultural ecosystem services to tourist well-being at cultural heritage sites. *Journal of Travel Research* 61(7), 1631–1647. DOI: 10.1177/00472875211037743.

8 COVID-19 and Elephant Tourism

ERIC LAWS[1]* AND RICHARD BUTLER[2]

[1]*retired Professor of Tourism;* [2]*Emeritus Professor of International Tourism, University of Strathclyde, Glasgow, UK*

Abstract

Pandemics have occurred throughout recorded history, most notably the Black Death or bubonic plague, and the outbreak of influenza (Spanish flu) after World War I. International tourism demonstrated over half a century of continuous growth since figures were first gathered; world economic depression, rapid large rises in energy costs and conflict in various parts of the world failed to stop such growth at the global level. That pattern changed dramatically and unexpectedly at the end of the second decade of the 21st century with the appearance of the virus that caused coronavirus disease 2019 (COVID-19), with tourism numbers not only failing to grow for the first time in decades, but in fact falling drastically in every country. The results were catastrophic for economies in general, and for tourism in particular, resulting in losses of income and of tax revenue, business bankruptcies, large rises in unemployment and many other negative outcomes. Wildlife tourism, including elephant tourism, experienced unique problems relating to both the species involved and the specific local conditions.

Introduction

International tourism demonstrated over half a century of continuous growth since figures were first gathered, and even world economic depression, rapid large rises in energy costs and conflict in various parts of the world failed to stop such growth at the global level. That pattern changed dramatically and unexpectedly at the end of the second decade of the 21st century with the appearance of the virus that caused coronavirus disease 2019 (COVID-19), with tourism numbers not only failing to grow for the first time in decades, but in fact falling drastically in every country. The results were catastrophic for economies in general, and for tourism in particular, resulting in losses of income and of tax

*e.laws@runbox.com

  Elephant Welfare in Global Tourism (E. Laws *et al.* eds)
DOI: 10.1079/9781836990093.0008

revenue, business bankruptcies, large rises in unemployment and many other negative outcomes. While all forms of tourism were affected, the impacts on some segments of tourism were more serious than simply economic losses, and wildlife tourism, including elephant tourism, experienced unique problems relating to both the species involved and the specific local conditions. This chapter reviews the impact of the COVID-19 pandemic on this form of tourism, noting the specific issues which arose, some of which have not yet been fully resolved, the responses of various stakeholders, and the lessons that should be learned from the cessation of tourism in such a catastrophic manner.

Pandemics

Kelly (2011) defined a pandemic as a worldwide epidemic. Pandemics have occurred throughout recorded history, most notably the Black Death or bubonic plague (Glatter and Finkelman, 2021) and the outbreak of influenza (Spanish flu) after World War I (Johnson, 2006). Cantor (2015) described the bubonic plague as the greatest biomedical disaster in history. Nobility and wealth was no defence: Princess Joan of England was struck down on her way to marry in Spain, while the newly appointed Archbishop of Canterbury perished shortly after being ordained by the Pope. The plague even halted (temporarily) the perpetual conflict between the French and English.

Early epidemics such as the first wave of the Black Death, while some eventually became international pandemics, often began and remained relatively local in extent, in part because travel was limited and slow, potentially allowing immunity to develop and an epidemic to decline and disappear before it could spread widely. However, as mobility increased globally and became relatively lower in cost, not only were more people able to travel, but they did so more widely. The outbreak of Spanish flu in 1919 became a true pandemic because of the number of people travelling internationally, in part following the onset of peace and troops returning home after the end of World War I and also because of the rapid contagion rate of the disease, combined with a high and rapid fatality rate. Since then there have been what might be described as minor pandemics, such as severe acute respiratory syndrome (SARS) and related epidemics like Middle East respiratory syndrome (MERS) and bird flu, which had localized, if significant, impacts on travel and tourism but nothing of comparable size and impact until COVID-19 in 2019.

The COVID-19 pandemic, in terms of the rapidity and massive dispersal of the virus and absolute economic impact, was unlike anything that had been recorded before, however, and its effects were felt globally within a few months and the virus is still circulating in variant forms, including long COVID and new sub-variants some 5 years after the initial outbreak. Uncertainty and delays in recording its origins and the distribution of knowledge about the virus, its symptoms and potential levels of fatality and contagion all meant that a considerable number of early victims had travelled internationally, thus spreading the virus to many countries in a very short period of time. By the time this state of affairs was realized and restrictions placed on travel, the virus had become well established globally and the pandemic became a classic case of trying to 'close the stable door after the horse had bolted'.

The typical government response to a pandemic has always been to attempt to break the chain of contact by which diseases are spread. This has generally entailed confining people to their homes, banning travel and isolating communities from each other (Haggett, 2000; Smallman-Raynor *et al.*, 2022) in the hope that immunity would develop and the epidemic disappear as no new victims appeared. The delays in transmission of details about the virus and its high level of dispersal meant that these traditional approaches came into effect too late to prevent the epidemic becoming a pandemic.

COVID-19 was first reported in Wuhan in December 2019 (Tian *et al.*, 2020). The genetic sequence for COVID-19 was provided by a group of Chinese scientists to the World Health Organization (WHO) on 12 January 2020. COVID-19 threatened to cause a global pandemic with about 1% morbidity, meaning that many millions of people might die from the virus. In the last week of January, *The Lancet* (medical journal) published five papers explaining the threat and recommending appropriate responses (Horton, 2020). In addition to all the other consequences for people, society, governments and businesses, COVID-19 had major and rapid consequences for tourism, ending almost all activity and causing immense problems for specific segments such as wildlife and elephant tourism (Laws *et al.*, 2021a, b).

COVID-19, Tourism and Wildlife

Confusion and uncertainty characterized the initial responses to COVID-19 (GOV.UK, 2024). The United Nations World Tourism Organization (UNWTO) forecast on 6 March 2020 that COVID-19 would result in a 2–3% reduction in international travel. But on 26 March 2020 this was adjusted to a 20–30% reduction (Gössling and Schweiggart, 2022), and subsequent data (UNWTO, 2023) shows that overall global international tourism declined to a level of 69% compared to 2019 levels by 2022 and still remains -3% below the 2019 level at time of writing (summer 2024). As an example, Table 8.1 compares international tourist arrivals in Thailand for the period January–May in 2019 and 2020 showing the impact of travel restrictions put in place by the Thai Government to prevent the spread of COVID-19. In addition to constraints and bans on international travel, most countries also imposed restrictions on internal travel, closing hotels, restaurants, bars and tourist venues, with many countries implementing emergency lockdown regulations under which people were only allowed outside their residence for specific purposes such as grocery shopping. Such severe constraints also served to prevent domestic tourism from fulfilling a compensatory role for the drastically depleted numbers of international tourists.

Prior to the COVID-19 pandemic, animal welfare and environmental non-governmental organizations (NGOs) in the tourists' origin countries had begun to circulate videos and stories of cruelty in training elephants through aversive techniques, and the poor quality of the food and accommodation provided

Table 8.1. Comparison of international tourist arrivals in Thailand for January–May 2019 and 2020 indicating the impact on Thai tourism of travel restrictions put in place to reduce the spread of COVID-19.[a] From Thai Ministry of Tourism and Sports, n.d.

Month	Number of tourist arrivals in Thailand	
	2019	2020
January	3,718,504	3,810,155
February	3,603,654	2,061,990
March	3,473,088	819,429
April	3,195,006	No tourists visit Thailand
May	2,726,808	(as of 29 May 2020)

[a]On 1 November 2021, the Thai government commenced a phased reopening of the country, allowing fully vaccinated tourists from 63 low-risk countries to visit with 1 day of quarantine, provided they pass a COVID-19 test upon arrival.

to them in many visitor attractions. The Association of British Travel Agents (ABTA) attempted to set minimum standards at destinations (see Chapter 14, this volume). However, these lacked any compulsion even on ABTA's own members. Nor was there any rigour in monitoring or enforcement. When international tourism stalled in 2020 due to COVID-19, elephant owners and their mahouts were again, suddenly, without income and many were dispersed. Few governments of elephant countries had any effective responses in place to assist elephants or the humans dependent on them.

Thailand has the largest population of captive elephants in the world. Previously used in forestry work, by the mid-2010s their only income-generating capability was from local and international visitors paying to see them in reserves or performing in elephant tourism venues (ETVs) such as elephant camps. Wild African elephant herds also suffered from poaching raids for ivory, and much of the cost of their protection was funded from tourist-generated income. By March 2020 Thai elephant camps were closed to tourists, and many of the elephants, which consume about 150 kg of food/day, were sent back to the areas where their owners lived, although few mahouts could maintain their elephants adequately. Most could not be released into the wild due to lethal rivalry between elephants from different herds, the limited areas suitable to their needs, and the inability of those raised in captivity to cope with wild conditions, as elephants, like most animals, normally learn survival skills in the maternal elephant herds (Laws *et al.*, 2021a, b).

Taweepoke Angkawanish, elephant veterinarian at the National Elephant Institute (NEI) in Lampang, Thailand, provided an insight into the uncertainty of elephant tourism during the COVID-19 pandemic and the changed fortunes of Thailand's elephant tourist camps, the mahouts and the elephant owners. He said: 'Without tourism, these elephants have a real risk that they will again be displaced, without a means to provide their daily care'. He specifically referred to the situation in the late 1980s, when tourism had returned value to the thousands of trained elephants displaced from the timber trade. Tourism had saved those elephants from destitution, but as the pandemic stifled tourism to the region, the future welfare of Thailand's 4700 captive elephants was once again at risk (Gössling *et al.*, 2020).

The business model of many ETVs such as elephant camps is quite simple: they expect to meet their expenses from revenue, and few have a significant cash reserve. Furthermore, most camps do not have sufficient browsing resources to support their elephants on a daily basis, with most buying food in from local farmers as required. There are many reports of elephants being taken by their mahout owners to neighbouring forests where they might have a better chance of foraging for food (Supanta *et al.*, 2022). Apichet Duangdee, the manager of the Elephant Rescue Park, stated: 'We need 1000 baht a day (US$30) for each elephant'. He argued that freeing his own eight elephants that had been rescued from circuses and loggers into the forests would be impossible as they would probably be killed by the resident wild elephants. He was planning to take out a 2 million baht (US$61,000) loan to feed his elephants. 'I will not abandon them', adding that wages for the mahouts who care for the elephants have dropped by 70% (ELEAID, 2020).

An additional and critical aspect of the situation was that poachers of wildlife, including elephants, had easier access to their targets during the COVID-19 pandemic. Maron (2020) reported that ten of the 35 anti-poaching personnel who protected the 450-square-mile Enduimet Wildlife Management Area had become unemployed because of the budget shortfall resulting from the collapse of Tanzania's wildlife tourism industry because of the pandemic. Enduimet, near the Kilimanjaro National Park, is an essential wildlife corridor for elephants, zebras, wildebeest and impalas. 'The prospect of increased poaching because of the coronavirus is a matter of great concern', said John Scanlon, special envoy for African Parks, a non-profit organization that manages 17 national parks and protected areas across 11 African countries.

Although variations on COVID-19 (particularly long COVID) continued to appear, restrictions on international travel had mostly been relaxed by the end of 2022, international tourism began to recover with the development of new vaccines against COVID-19, and the numbers of elephants working in tourism again rose (Albert, 2024). However, conditions for many such elephants had continued to deteriorate because the contexts and constraints were different. Concern with elephant welfare has slipped down the agenda of priorities for many governments, although public awareness about environmental problems, including species survival, ecology and rapid changes to climate, and sea level rises has increased, reflecting in part the pressure from the doubling of the human population to over 8 billion within the last 50 years or so (Statista, n.d.) and the resulting resource depletion and pollution of various kinds.

Pandemic Planning and Recovery

Crises and disasters have received increasing academic and policy attention. Popovski (2018) has identified three key areas:

- first key area – Crisis management and impact mitigation;
- second key area – Providing stimulus and accelerating recovery; and
- third key area – Preparations for tomorrow.

The underlying assumption is that after crises and disasters things will soon return to normal. In contrast, in the early stages of COVID-19 governments began to prepare citizens for 'a new normal' in which a variety of expectations and behaviours would be severely restricted, and a future in which new challenges unrelated to pandemics, including environmental and social concerns, will become more common and urgent, a different new normal to that perceived before COVID-19 (Galbraith, 2015).

A 65% year-on-year drop was reported in international travel for January–June 2020: 'Lufthansa now plans to reduce its fleet by 150 aircraft - 50 more than previously planned - and cut more jobs than the 22,000 full-time equivalent positions already identified as surplus' (Copley, 2020).

In the decades up to 2020 Thai Airways operated two daily flights between Bangkok and London. In late October 2020 they were operating a severely reduced service of only one flight a week.

Discussion

However it is described, whether as a catastrophe or a disaster, the COVID-19 pandemic had massive effects on tourism and every other aspect of the global economy. It may be preferable to view it as a catastrophe, meaning when 'an enterprise ... is confronted with sudden, unpredictable catastrophic changes over which it has little control' (Faulkner, 2001, p. 136), while a crisis often has internal causes; however, tourism researchers have argued that in the case of COVID-19 the terms are interchangeable (Hall *et al.*, 2020). Others note that events of such a magnitude as that of the COVID-19 pandemic have illustrated both external and internal massive impacts and problems (Richie and Jiang, 2019) and revolutionary change in circumstances. Yang *et al.* (2021) recorded over 500 articles on COVID-19 and tourism and since their initial review, that number has increased markedly. It is not necessary to review in detail the global effects of the pandemic again, they have been summarized in many of the above articles and in the case of international tourism by UNWTO (2023). There remains, however, a noticeable absence of comparable details for domestic tourism, which is generally acknowledged to be several times the size of international tourism, at least in terms of numbers of tourists involved.

One feature that is worthy of note is the general agreement that tourism has recovered and is following a similar path of development and regrowth to that of before the COVID-19 pandemic. Such a situation is contrary to expectations and hopes of some academics and interest groups, who argued for a change in approach to tourism, which would see a 'new' tourism emerging from what they saw as an opportunity to reset the pattern of development. The argument was for a more sustainable, just, equitable form of tourism moving from the neoliberal focus of recent decades with its emphasis on growth. Such a scenario did not develop, however, as the results that are now appearing in the literature and reports clearly demonstrate (e.g. Karabulut *et al.*, 2020; Sharma and Nicolau, 2020; Pham *et al.*, 2021).

As tourism continues in its 'old' manner (McKercher, forthcoming), some conclusions can be drawn. One of the common points appearing in the literature in general is the initial widespread failure in all aspects of tourism to anticipate the scale and duration of the pandemic. In that feature, tourism was certainly not alone, few governments and very few tourism operators or agencies were prepared for such a damaging development. Despite the earlier smaller examples of epidemic impacts on tourism, such as SARS, foot-and-mouth disease and bird flu, there was a lack of accurate anticipation of likely effects of the pandemic, which meant that virtually all subsequent responses by most stakeholders and governments were reactive. This was because those concerned with managing and controlling tourism were constantly trying to catch up with an ever-changing situation. This problem resulted in incorrect actions and assumptions held initially, such as one example noted above that domestic tourists would compensate for the lack of international visitors.

A recent study (World Animal Protection, 2023) has revealed that few of the tourism companies engaged in wildlife tourism had policies or resources in place for animal welfare during such a decline in business:

> Possibly due to the impact of COVID-19, companies did not prioritise updating their policy content prior to assessment in 2020. Now, 3 years later and in light of the importance of wildlife friendly tourism and its impact on animal and public health on a global scale, companies have had the growing opportunity to build their business back better, for the benefit of animals, tourists, and their brand.
>
> (World Animal Protection, 2023)

Whether many have done so remains to be explored and will only become clear if and when another similar catastrophe occurs. For the reasons discussed below, few ETVs are likely to have been able to build their businesses back better, or even restore them to their pre-COVID tenuous state of existence.

Many wildlife tourism experiences and opportunities, particularly including elephant tourism, are small in scale, limited in experience and highly locally focused. All of these characteristics made it extremely difficult for many of them to deal with the impacts and massive sudden changes brought about by the pandemic. For many, as expressed in the comments noted earlier, the first and ongoing, and in some cases only, concern was survival, both economically and in terms of their animals, those two factors being inextricably linked. Few such enterprises had sufficient financial reserves to be able to engage in major changes in their methods of operation, nor to be able to make significant financial or technical investments during the pandemic. They had to make do with existing arrangements and resources. This lack of capital, which might have allowed them to make such changes and perhaps recover more quickly after the pandemic, has left many of them still highly vulnerable and not optimistic about surviving after all restrictions and fears are ended.

In some segments of tourism, particularly hospitality, moving to more automated forms of service represented one route to restoring the ability to cater for visitors. However, even if this method of operation was feasible in wildlife tourist enterprises, such alternatives still need significant financial outlay in equipment and training. Ghaderi (2022) noted that moving to untact (i.e. involving no human-to-human contact) operations is very difficult for small-scale and especially family-owner-operated establishments where the personal touch is very much a desired feature of the experience. In the case of elephant tourism such steps are not feasible when dealing with the animals themselves and savings in cost from introducing such features in other aspects of these businesses would be too little to make worthwhile, even if the finances were available. In most cases, provision of such financial support was not forthcoming. Examples of adjustments to operations included in Cakmak *et al.* (2023) illustrated clearly that even when government aid to tourism businesses was available, it was rarely available quickly enough to prevent problems developing. Also, such assistance was often mostly focused on aiding large-scale operations and was not available in ways that assisted small enterprises in remoter locations, such as many elephant tourist businesses.

The level of uncertainty about factors such as the likely duration of the pandemic, its spatial extent, its severity, level of contagion and fatality rate, as well as the possibility of support and assistance from public sector agencies, banks and other institutions meant that businesses had to adapt their operational practices. In many cases, they had to adopt different, sometimes totally new ways and scales of operating, often almost immediately after pandemic-induced restrictions came into effect, without knowledge of the likely duration or scale of those restrictions. Government assistance, when it was offered, varied in its extent, usefulness and availability as well as in its immediacy, significantly affecting the ultimate outcomes for the operations depending on and waiting for such aid.

There is little evidence to suggest that preparing for an almost inevitable future pandemic has proceeded widely, particularly in small enterprises like ETVs. As argued earlier, survival today is still more of a pressing concern than preparing for the future. In reality, that situation is one which exists globally as the problems of anticipation and preparedness remain relatively unaddressed, certainly in the context of tourism in most countries and for almost all businesses, whether in tourism or in other economic activities.

Conclusions

It is still too early to really talk meaningfully about the overall implications of the COVID-19 pandemic on tourism, destinations and tourists, let alone the impacts on specific forms of tourism such as wildlife or elephant tourism. Changes in tourist behaviour, including choice of destination, decisions whether to travel or not, duration of travel and actions while on holiday during the pandemic, were essentially changes forced on them by restrictions and fear and thus reactive. Few appear to have been made from freedom of choice by either hosts or guests. It is unknown at this time to say whether destination choices made during the pandemic will remain in force when all restrictions have been removed and transportation and other services resumed at pre-pandemic levels. Given past reactions to other crises, such as terrorism or natural disasters, tourists are not likely to change their long-term outlook and attitudes and thus their behaviour without considerable thought about perceived benefits and costs.

Whether it is possible to view COVID-19 as simply a blip in what had been a pattern of continual growth of tourism is not clear. If it was only a blip, it was a massive if relatively short-term one, and some of its effects will remain permanently through the absences of closed businesses and the presence of depressed destinations that missed reinvestment and new offerings during COVID-19 and its aftermath. However, whether it has changed or will permanently change tourism appears unlikely, so whether it is appropriate to anticipate a revision in attitudes towards wildlife tourism and elephant tourism in particular is unclear and likely to remain so for some time.

The role of young animals in tourism has been little studied, despite its problematic character. Viewing young wild animals is clearly a valued tourist experience; tourists often enjoy touching or cuddling pups or cubs of wild animals, hence the existence of 'petting zoos' and similar ventures with domesticated and farm animals. However, that fondness can be detrimental to the animals' health and well-being, for reasons of which the tourists might well be unaware. Young animals might find human touch stressful, as well as harmful through the transmission of disease and illness.

At the time of writing (summer 2024) very little empirical work has been published on the specific effects of the COVID-19 pandemic on wildlife tourism or elephant tourism in particular. The brief discussion by Newsome (2021) is one of few papers addressing this problem and his conclusions are worth noting. He suggests two possible situations emerging from the effects of the pandemic. First, 'At the negative end, tourism "players" and protected area managers do not reflect on previous conditions and the way that tourism and the environment were managed and things go on as before' (Newsome, 2021, p. 298). The likely results of this is an increase in negative impacts on environments, a reduction in habitat extent and diversity, wildlife population depletions, and an overall reduction in quality of experience leaving the tourism segment and its components more vulnerable than before. Alternatively, 'At the positive end of the spectrum, post COVID 19, we reach a new awareness of the vulnerability of species and the tourism upon which it is dependent on for survival' (Newsome, 2021, p. 298). This, Newsome (2021) suggests could lead to increased funding and improvements in management, more protection for ecosystems, a better overall experience and more sustainable tourism development. In the context of elephant tourism in particular, however, the COVID-19 pandemic is likely to be viewed as having been entirely negative with little sign of any benefits to that specific segment of tourism.

Bibliography

Albert, C.D. (2024) Introduction to the special issue—COVID-19, international relations, and security studies: Has the pandemic altered the study and practice of international security? *Politics and the Life Sciences* 43(1), 4–10. DOI: 10.1017/pls.2024.2.

Arseault, A. (2020) A timeline of Coronavirus (COVID-19). Available at: https://www.verywellhealth.com/coronavirus-covid-19-timeline-4798671 (accessed 26 February 2025).

Bremner, C. (2020) Accelerating Travel Innovation after Coronavirus: Outlook for Europe & the Americas. *Euromonitor International*. Available at: https://blog.euromonitor.com/accelerating-travel-innovation-after-coronavirus-outlook-for-europe-the-americas (accessed 26 February 2025).

Cakmak E., Isaac, R. and Butler, R. (2023) *Changing Practices of Tourism Stakeholders in Covid-19 Affected Destinations*. Channelview Publications, Bristol, UK. DOI: 10.21832/CAKMAK8755.

Cantor, N.F. (2015) *In the Wake of the Plague: the Black Death and the World it Made*. Simon and Schuster, London.

Chung, L.H. (2015) Impact of pandemic control over airport economics: reconciling public health with airport business through a streamlined approach in pandemic control. *Journal of Air Transport Management* 44, 42–53. DOI: 10.1016/j.jairtraman.2015.02.003.

Cohen, E. (2015) Young elephants in Thai tourism: a fatal attraction. In: Markwell, K. (ed.) *Animals and Tourism: Understanding Diverse Relationships* Volume 1, pp. 163–177. DOI: 10.21832/9781845415051-014.

Copley, C. (2020) Lufthansa steps up cuts to fleet and staff as outlook dims. *Reuters*, 21 September. Available at: https://www.reuters.com/article/business/lufthansa-steps-up-cuts-to-fleet-and-staff-as-outlook-dims-idUSKCN26C1Z8/ (accessed 3 March 2025).

ELEAID (2020) Elephant habitat loss. Available at: http://www.eleaid.com/elephant-conservation/elephant-habitat-loss/ (accessed 26 February 2025).

Faulkner, B. (2001) Towards a framework for tourism disaster management. *Tourism Management* 22(2), 135–147. DOI: 10.1016/S0261-5177(00)00048-0.

Galbraith, J.K. (2015) *The End of Normal: the Great Crisis and the Future of Growth*. Simon and Schuster, London.

Gallego, I. and Font, X. (2021) Changes in air passenger demand as a result of the COVID-19 crisis: using big data to inform tourism policy. *Journal of Sustainable Tourism* 29(9), 1470–1489. DOI: 10.1080/09669582.2020.1773476.

Ghaderi, M. (2022) Public health interventions in the face of pandemics: network structure, social distancing, and heterogeneity. *European Journal of Operational Research* 298(3), 1016–1031.

Glatter, K.A. and Finkelman, P. (2021) History of the plague: an ancient pandemic for the age of COVID-19. *The American Journal of Medicine* 134(2), 176–181. DOI: 10.1016/j.amjmed.2020.08.019.

Gössling, S. and Schweiggart, N. (2022) Two years of COVID-19 and tourism: what we learned, and what we should have learned. *Journal of Sustainable Tourism* 30(4), 915–931. DOI: 10.1080/09669582.2022.2029872.

Gössling, S., Scott, D. and Hall, C.M. (2020) Pandemics, tourism and global change: a rapid assessment of COVID-19. *Journal of Sustainable Tourism* 29(1), 1–20. DOI: 10.1080/09669582.2020.1758708.

GOV.UK (2024) UK Covid-19 Inquiry: Resilience and preparedness (Module 1) Report. Cabinet Office, UK Government, 18 July. Available at: https://www.gov.uk/government/publications/uk-covid-19-inquiry-resilience-and-preparedness-module-1-report (accessed 26 February 2025).

Haggett, P. (2000) *The Geographical Structure of Epidemics*. Oxford University Press, Oxford. DOI: 10.1093/oso/9780198233633.001.0001.

Hall, C.M., Scott, D. and Gössling, S. (2020) Pandemics, transformations and tourism: be careful what you wish for. *Tourism Geographies* 22(3), 577–598. DOI: 10.1080/14616688.2020.1759131.

Hoque, A., Shikha, F.A., Hasanat, M.W., Arif, I. and Hamid, A.B.A. (2020) The effect of coronavirus (COVID-19) in the tourism industry in China. *Asian Journal of Multidisciplinary Studies* 3(1) 52–58.

Horton, R. (2020) *The COVID Catastrophe: What's Gone Wrong and How to Stop it Happening Again*. Polity Press, Cambridge.

Im, J., Kim, J. and Choeh, J.Y. (2021) COVID-19, social distancing, and risk-averse actions of hospitality and tourism consumers: a case of South Korea. *Journal of Destination Marketing & Management* 20: 100566. DOI: 10.1016/j.jdmm.2021.100566.

Johnson, N. (2006) *Britain and the 1918–19 Influenza Pandemic: a Dark Epilogue*. Routledge, London.

Karabulut, G., Bilgin, M.H., Demir, E. and Doker, A.C. (2020) How pandemics affect tourism: international evidence: *Annals of Tourism Research* 84: 102991.

Karl, M., Kock, F., Ritchie, B.W. and Gauss, J. (2021) Affective forecasting and travel decision-making: an investigation in times of a pandemic. *Annals of Tourism Research* 87: 103139. DOI: 10.1016/j.annals.2021.103139.

Kelly, H. (2011) The classical definition of a pandemic is not elusive. *Bulletin of the World Health Organization* 89(7), 540–541. DOI: 10.2471/BLT.11.088815.

Laws, E., Prideaux, B. and Chon, K. (2007) *Crisis Management in Tourism*. CAB International, Wallingford, UK. DOI: 10.1079/9781845930479.0000.

Laws, E., Scott, N., Font, X. and Koldowski, J. (2021a) *The Elephant Tourism Business*. CAB International, Wallingford, UK.

Laws, E., Koldowski, J., Font, X., Scott, N., Angkawanish, T. *et al.* (2021b) Postscript: COVID-19 and elephant tourism, a preliminary analysis. In: Laws, E., Scott, N., Font, X. and Koldowski, J. (eds) *The Elephant Tourism Business*. CAB International, Wallingford UK, pp. 269–275.

Le, T.T., Cramer, J.P., Chen, R. and Mayhew, S. (2020) Evolution of the COVID-19 vaccine development landscape. *Nature Reviews Drug Discovery* 19(10), 667–668. DOI: 10.1038/d41573-020-00151-8.

Li, J., Nguyen, T.H. and Coca-Stefaniak, J.A. (2021) Coronavirus impacts on post-pandemic planned travel behaviours. *Annals of Tourism Research* 86: 102964.

Maron, D.F. (2020) Poaching threats loom as wildlife safaris put on hold due to COVID-19. *National Geographic*, 10 April. Available at: https://www.nationalgeographic.com/animals/article/wildlife-safaris-halted-for-covid-boost-poaching-threat (accessed 30 January 2025).

McKercher, R. (forthcoming) The new normal or same old, same old. In: Butler, R. (ed.) *Future Tourism in Turbulent Times*. Channelview, Bristol, UK.

Miao, L., Im, J., Fu, X., Kim, H. and Zhang, Y.E. (2021) Proximal and distal post-COVID travel behavior. *Annals of Tourism Research* 88: 103159. DOI: 10.1016/j.annals.2021.103159.

Namwat, C., Suphanchaimat, R., Nittayasoot, N. and Iamsirithaworn, S. (2020) Thailand's response against coronavirus disease 2019: challenges and lessons learned. *Outbreak, Surveillance, Investigation & Response (OSIR) Journal* 13(1), 33–37. DOI: 10.59096/osir.v13i1.262858.

Newsome, D. (2021) The collapse of tourism and its impact on wildlife tourism destinations. *Journal of Tourism Futures* 7(3), 295–302. DOI: 10.1108/JTF-04-2020-0053.

PATA Newsletter (2020) Available at: https://mpower.pata.org/ (accessed 21 July 2020).

Pham, T.D., Dwyer, L., Su, J.-J. and Ngo, T. (2021) COVID-19 impacts of inbound tourism on Australian economy. *Annals of Tourism Research* 88: 103179. DOI: 10.1016/j.annals.2021.103179.

Popovski, V. (2018) Crisis management and the concept of resilience: case of the Republic of Macedonia. *International Scientific Journal Contemporary Macedonian Defence/Sovremena makedonska odbrana* 3(4), 83.

Promchertchoo, P. (2020) COVID-19: Jobless Thai elephants make long trek home as tourists disappear. Available at: https://www.channelnewsasia.com/news/asia/elephants-thailand-covid-19-trek-home-tourists-disappear-12747128 (accessed 17 July 2020).

Quarantelli, E.L. (ed.) (2005) *What is A Disaster? A Dozen Perspectives on the Question*. Routledge, Abingdon, UK.

Ritchie, B.W. and Jiang, Y. (2019) A review of research on tourism risk, crisis and disaster management: launching the *Annals of Tourism Research* curated collection on tourism risk, crisis and disaster management. *Annals of Tourism Research* 79: 102812. DOI: 10.1016/j.annals.2019.102812.

Sharma, A. and Nicolau, J.L. (2020) An open market valuation of the effects of COVID-19 on the travel and tourism industry. *Annals of Tourism Research* 83: 102990. DOI: 10.1016/j.annals.2020.102990.

Smallman-Raynor, M., Smallman-Raynor, M.R., Cliff, A.D., Ord, J.K. and Haggett, P. (2022) *A Geography of Infection: Spatial Processes and Patterns in Epidemics and Pandemics*. Oxford University Press, Oxford.

Statista (n.d.) Time taken for global population to double. Available at: https://www.statista.com/statistics/1303469/time-taken-for-global-pop-double (accessed 26 February 2025).

Supanta, J., Brown, J.L., Bansiddhi, P., Thitaram, C., Punyapornwithaya, V. *et al.* (2022) Effect of the COVID-19 pandemic and international travel ban on elephant tourist camp management in Northern Thailand. *Frontiers in Veterinary Science* 9: 1038855. DOI: 10.3389/fvets.2022.1038855.

Tian, H., Liu, Y., Li, Y., Wu, C.-H., Chen, B. *et al.* (2020) An investigation of transmission control measures during the first 50 days of the COVID-19 epidemic in China. *Science* 368(6491), 638–642. DOI: 10.1126/science.abb6105.

Tourism Authority of Thailand (2022) Homepage. Available at: https://www.thaiwebsites.com (accessed 17 July 2020).

United Nations World Tourism Organization (UNWTO) (2020) *World Tourism Barometer*, no. 18. Available at: https://www.unwto.org/world-tourism-barometer-n18-january-2020 (accessed 17 July 2020).

United Nations World Tourism Organization (UNWTO) (2023) *International Tourism Highlights 2023*. UNWTO, Edition, Madrid.

Winston, A. (2020) Is the COVID-19 Outbreak a Black Swan or the New Normal? *MITSloan Management Review*, March 16. Available at: https://sloanreview.mit.edu/article/is-the-covid-19-outbreak-a-black-swan-or-the-new-normal/ (accessed 26 February 2025).

World Animal Protection (2023) Encouraging animal sentience laws around the world. World Animal Protection, 27 April 2023. Available at: https://www.worldanimalprotection.org/latest/blogs/encouraging-animal-sentience-laws-around-world/ (accessed 19 November 2024).

World Health Organization (WHO) (2020) WHO Coronavirus Disease (COVID-19) Dashboard. WHO. Available at: https://covid19.who.int/ (accessed 24 August 2020).

World Travel and Tourism Council (2020) Available at: https://wttc.org/News-Article/WTTC-now-estimates-over-100-million-jobs-losses-in-the-Travel-&-Tourism-sector-and-alerts-G20-countries-to-the-scale-of-the-crisis (accessed 26 February 2025).

Wut, T.M., Xu, J.B. and Wong, S.-M. (2021) Crisis management research (1985-2020) in the hospitality and tourism industry: a review and research agenda. *Tourism Management* 85: 104307. DOI: 10.1016/j.tourman.2021.104307.

Yang, Y., Zhang, C.X. and Rickly, J.M. (2021) A review of early COVID-19 research in tourism: launching the *Annals of Tourism Research*'s curated collection on coronavirus and tourism. *Annals of Tourism Research* 91: 103313. DOI: 10.1016/j.annals.2021.103313.

Yang, Y., Zhang, H. and Chen, X. (2022) Coronavirus pandemic and tourism: dynamic stochastic general equilibrium modeling of infectious disease outbreak. *Annals of Tourism Research* 83: 102913. DOI: 10.1016/j.annals.2020.102913.

Yu, L., Zhao, P., Tang, J. and Pang, L. (2023) Changes in tourist mobility after COVID-19 outbreaks. *Annals of Tourism Research* 98: 103522. DOI: 10.1016/j.annals.2022.103522.

Zenker, S. and Kock, F. (2020) The coronavirus pandemic – a critical discussion of a tourism research agenda. *Tourism Management* 81: 104164. DOI: 10.1016/j.tourman.2020.104164.

9 Regulating and Monitoring the Asian Captive Elephant Industry

GEORGINA ASHBY*

Asian Captive Elephant Standards (ACES), London, UK

Abstract

This chapter explores the current state of tourist venues in South-east Asia, examining factors such as the presence of on-site veterinary care, the extent of elephant freedom (and other welfare factors such as diet, enrichment and exercise). The chapter underscores the importance of robust monitoring and independent auditing mechanisms including use of Asian Captive Elephant Standards (ACES) and the Elephant-First Policy in ensuring adherence to welfare standards.

Introduction

The human–elephant relationship is complex and multifaceted, with debates surrounding the political, economic, social and ethical considerations of animal-based industries, especially tourism where humans come in constant and close contact with the animals. Identified as a prime tourist motivator, wildlife tourism is a highly profitable industry, and elephant-based tourism is considered one of the leading destination experiences for visitors.

The popularization and economic magnitude of elephant-based tourism, particularly in Thailand, has prompted calls for sustainable and ethical management and the welfare of these elephants has been questioned by animal activist groups, international tour operators and the public (Rizzolo and Bradshaw, 2018; Bansiddhi *et al.*, 2020b). The upkeep and care of elephants often depend on the knowledge and skills of mahouts. For some tourists visiting elephant tourism venues (ETVs), it is the mahout's methods of training and control – and the activities involving elephants – that underlie the welfare debate (Flower *et al.*, 2021). Conclusions that captive elephants are abused are

*georgina@elephantstandards.com

DOI: 10.1079/9781836990093.0009

often based on anecdotal evidence and not solid science. Hence, it is difficult to tease apart emotion, opinion and fact regarding which practices are good or bad for elephant welfare.

ETVs vary widely in terms of the quality of care and welfare they provide for elephants. While some ETVs prioritize ethical treatment, offering enriched environments, veterinary care and opportunities for natural behaviours, others fall short, subjecting elephants to poor living conditions, inadequate nutrition and stressful activities such as constant riding or forced performances. The welfare of elephants in these venues is directly influenced by management practices, with significant differences observed across South-east Asia (Bansiddhi *et al.*, 2020a).

Ensuring the well-being of captive elephants requires a balanced approach, integrating economic interests with ethical and scientific considerations. This chapter reviews current regulations in Thailand and other range countries, addressing enforcement challenges and regulatory gaps. It introduces the Asian Captive Elephant Standards (ACES), an independent organization that audits elephant venues in South-east Asia, ensuring the welfare of Asian elephants. ACES offers a certification system with over 190 science-based requirements, aimed at improving elephant welfare in tourism through rigorous guidelines and continuous monitoring. The Elephant-First Policy will also be discussed, emphasizing mahout education and standardized care practices. By analysing current practices and future directions this chapter contributes to the evolving conversation about elephant welfare regulation (Godfrey and Kongmuang, 2009).

Current State of Elephant Tourism

Elephant tourism in South-east Asia has become a significant aspect of the region's tourism industry, attracting millions of visitors each year. The allure of interacting with elephants in a natural setting or observing them perform various tasks has led to the proliferation of numerous elephant camps across Thailand, Cambodia, Laos, Myanmar and Nepal. In Thailand alone, there are approximately 223 ETVs, housing around 2600 elephants (Bansiddhi *et al.*, 2019). Importantly, there are few other ways in which elephants are able to generate any income for their owners.

The landscape of elephant tourism has evolved considerably over the past decade. Elephant riding or trekking was once a popular activity, promoted extensively by the travel industry and seen as a quintessential part of the South-east Asian experience. One study reported that 40% of tourists surveyed in Thailand had ridden, or planned to ride, an elephant during their visit, equating to approximately 12.8 million elephant rides in 2015. However, increased media scrutiny and growing public awareness about the ethical concerns surrounding such activities have led to significant changes. In 2016, TripAdvisor banned ticket sales to attractions involving physical encounters with captive wild animals, including elephant rides and swimming with elephants (Original Travel, 2021). Following this, in 2016 and 2017, major tour operators like

STA Travel, TUI Group, G Adventures and Intrepid Travel publicly denounced elephant trekking, eliminating it from their itineraries. The Association of British Travel Agents (ABTA) also released industry-wide guidelines for elephants in tourism, further denouncing practices which they deem 'unethical' (Original Travel, 2021). Elephant riding, in particular, is a much-debated topic and is one of the many controversial subjects when discussing captive elephant welfare.

Management Practices Within Elephant Camps

Management practices within elephant camps are crucial to the welfare of the elephants and vary significantly across South-east Asia. Studies have shown that key aspects, such as veterinary care and extent of elephant freedom, and various welfare factors, such as diet, enrichment and exercise, are critical for maintaining physical health and reducing stress-related behaviours in captive elephants (Bansiddhi *et al.*, 2019). The implementation of welfare standards, such as ACES certification, aims to improve welfare by setting and enforcing guidelines for elephant care in tourism venues.

Veterinary care

The presence of on-site veterinary care is essential for the health and well-being of captive elephants. However, not all camps have the resources to offer consistent veterinary care, particularly smaller or less financially stable venues. These disparities can lead to significant variations in the health and welfare of the elephants. In Thailand only 18% of camps have a veterinarian on site and 36% have an elephant clinic equipped with basic medical supplies (Bansiddhi *et al.*, 2018). In contrast, most large or affluent camps have at least one full-time veterinarian and some have built on-site clinics. To bridge the gap, mobile clinics funded by the National Elephant Institute (NEI), Chiang Mai University (CMU) and/or the Department of Livestock Development (DLD) provide free health-care services, which include routine health exams and deworming (Bansiddhi *et al.*, 2020a). Additionally, there are two elephant hospitals in Lampang Province, Thailand which offer free veterinary care, one private and one government managed.

One proposed solution is the formation of consortia among several camps to share the costs of veterinarians and health-care supplies. An example of such an initiative is the Thai Elephant Alliance Association (TEAA), which today has members from 15 camps in northern Thailand, with hopes to expand to elephant camps throughout the country (Bansiddhi *et al.*, 2020a). This alliance brings camp owners together to: (i) improve veterinary care, including sharing veterinarians and supporting mobile clinics; and (ii) discuss issues faced by camp owners, such as how to address criticisms by animal activist groups and ensure elephant welfare is a top priority.

A broader study of veterinary care across Asia revealed challenges and deficiencies in basic husbandry and diagnostic capabilities as significant concerns (Miller *et al.*, 2015). This showed that there is not a cohesive and consistent level of veterinary expertise for captive elephants in the region. For example, in Indonesia the Veterinary Society for Sumatran Wildlife Conservation (VESSWIC) initiated the Elephant Health Care Program (EHCP) in 2006 to address the health-care needs of captive Sumatran elephants. This programme, funded by the UK-based charity Elephant Family, employs three full-time veterinarians who provide regular health care in North Sumatra, Aceh and Lampung. The EHCP collaborates with provincial and national conservation agencies to ensure coordinated care. However, due to funding limitations, the programme can only offer veterinary support in other areas upon formal request from government departments (Stremme *et al.*, 2007).

Extent of elephant freedom

Ideally, elephants should have the opportunity to roam freely, socialize and engage in natural behaviours. However, for elephants in captivity the extent to which they can roam freely will depend on the amount of land and resource a specific camp may have. This is why many ETVs utilize chains to keep their elephants from leaving the premises or getting into dangerous situations with mahouts, tourists and local landowners. However, chains are often a controversial topic in elephant welfare.

Studies have shown that different restraint methods can lead to varying levels of stereotypic behaviours, which are repetitive, invariant behaviours with no apparent goal or function and are often indicative of poor welfare. For instance, Gruber *et al.* (2000) conducted a study of circus elephants and found that stereotypies and social interactions were more likely to occur in elephants restrained by chains compared with those in electric-wire pens. Elephants in chains exhibited significantly more stereotypic behaviours, such as weaving and head bobbing, and had reduced opportunities for comfort, ingestion and locomotion activities (Kontogeorgopoulos, 2009).

However, tethering is neither inherently evil nor necessarily injurious to elephants when done in the correct manner with enough length and with adequate tools and time without the tether (Fowler and Mikota, 2006). Ashby (2023b) emphasized that while chains and bull hooks may be viewed as cruel, they can be essential for maintaining control and ensuring safety especially when elephants are in close contact with tourists. Mahouts interviewed about chaining and tethering maintained that these tools are used judiciously and only when necessary (Ashby, 2023a). It is desirable to have the elephant free of tethers as much as possible, but only when the elephant is being closely monitored by its mahout and in an environment where safety is prioritized for both the elephants and the people around it (Collicott, 2019).

Standards around chaining have been provided to ensure tethering is done safely and with minimal harm to the elephants. According to the Thailand National Bureau of Agricultural Commodity and Food Standards (2021), resting areas for elephants during off-service periods or night-time should be in natural or plantation forests, open areas under trees or buildings. Each elephant should have a space of at least 16 m^2, with chains or ropes no shorter than 1.5 m. Additionally, providing enclosures that allow elephants to roam freely, with considerations for shade, water supply and safety, can significantly enhance their well-being.

ACES provide more stringent guidelines, emphasizing that the total camp surface per elephant should be greater than 3000 m^2. During the day, chains used should measure at least 2 m from the foot to the anchorage, allowing elephants to be comfortable and unchained for at least 4 hours. At night, chains should measure at least 10 m with only one foot tethered, and alternatives to chains should be implemented when compatible with the elephants and available space (Varadharajan *et al.*, 2016).

These standards underscore the importance of providing captive elephants with environments that allow for natural behaviours, with a balance between safety for the elephant and those around them (Shell, 2019). Opportunity for socialization and enough tethering length for adequate movement with significant time off-tether provides an ideal balance for welfare of elephants, safety for mahouts and safety for tourists.

Diet and physical welfare

The diets of captive elephants are limited compared to wild elephants, with a lack of the variety of food choices that would be naturally available (Koirala *et al.*, 2016). Elephants in the wild spend a significant amount of time foraging, thus captive elephants are often fed roughage regularly by mahouts and supplemented with treats like bananas and sugar cane. Elephants require large quantities of food daily and managing a diverse and adequate diet is a significant logistical challenge (Hart and Sundar, 2000; Romain *et al.*, 2014).

An unintended consequence of the push to stop riding activities has led towards the popularization of elephant feeding, primarily involving bananas and sugar cane, as a replacement tourist activity. However, this activity has had adverse effects; these foods have high concentrations of sucrose and other soluble sugars that can increase body fat and weight, and lead to insulin resistance, and eventual exhaustion of endocrine pancreatic function and insulin release (Norkaew *et al.*, 2019). A recent study revealed that the average body condition score (BCS) of elephants in northern Thailand generally was high, between 4 and 5 (out of five), meaning most were overweight; none had a BCS of 1 (too thin) (Bansiddhi *et al.*, 2019).

Guidelines for feeding provided by the Central Zoo Authority of India suggest that concentrates should not be fed as the first meal of the day and instead elephants should be provided cultivated cereal fodder. However, concentrates may be fed at noon/during the afternoon (Menon and Tiwari, 2019; Dhairykar and Singh, 2020). For young elephants the proportion of concentrates should be higher in their diet as growing animals require more protein and other nutrients in comparison to adult animals. As elephants are prone to obesity their body condition should be regularly monitored and each animal should be fed individually. Additionally, to manage the weight of captive elephants, grasses should be the main component of their diet (Dhairykar and Singh, 2020).

The certification system developed by ACES (2024) provides further guidance, such as food should be accessed from clean ground (or e.g. from a hanging basket) to avoid it getting dirty and that elephants should be given the opportunity to forage for food in addition to their provided diet. Maintaining a healthy and happy environment for elephants in captivity requires careful planning and regular monitoring of their dietary intake.

Enrichment, psychological priorities and mental welfare

The psychological well-being of captive Asian elephants is as critical as their physical health. Elephants are highly intelligent and social animals, living in large, fission–fusion matriarchal family groups with multimodal sensory perception and communication capabilities. They exhibit complex behaviours such as problem solving, targeted helping and empathy, which underscores the importance of their mental enrichment (Plotnik and Jacobson, 2022).

Results from a recent survey found that few camp managers and owners consider the importance of the mental health and psychological needs of elephants as part of welfare standards (Bansiddhi *et al.*, 2020a). Newer camps that have made changes for the psychological needs of their elephants did so by moving away from scheduled, primarily solitary activities to allowing more free time for elephants to interact and play, especially around bath time and other social activities, such as foraging.

A recent study identified drinking and browsing/grazing as the most important behaviours for Asian elephants in captivity, not only for satisfying the physical needs but also psychological needs (Veasey, 2020). For example, providing browse may meet nutritional needs but does not fulfil behavioural or cognitive needs. Foraging involves social interaction, information gathering, decision making and locomotion. Thus, it is preferable for elephants to engage in motivated behaviours themselves rather than having these needs met through human provisioning.

Sociality is a critical factor in the mental welfare of elephants. Studies have shown that social variables are significant predictors of welfare indicators, including stereotypic behaviours and endocrine dysfunctions like hyperprolactinaemia (Meehan *et al.*, 2016). Social interactions with conspecifics and human caretakers can buffer stress and reduce the risk of developing stereotypic behaviours. For example, the development of positive elephant–keeper relationships may buffer stress, thereby protecting against stereotypic behaviour rate risk (Greco *et al.*, 2016). Transferring elephants between zoos also has major social implications, including separation from herd mates and known caretakers and introduction to unfamiliar elephants and humans. These conclusions for zoo elephants and their caretakers can be extended to elephants in tourist camps and their mahouts (Raviv *et al.*, 2023).

Mahouts play an important role in the life of elephants, both positive and negative. They can incite fear or promote strong, caring bonds over time. This is further supported by findings that positive mahout–elephant relationships can facilitate trauma recovery, highlighting the role of prosocial mahout interactions in the overall well-being of elephants (Rizzolo and Bradshaw, 2016). Positive mahout–elephant bonds undoubtedly have welfare benefits for both mahouts and elephants (Bansiddhi *et al.*, 2020a).

Enrichment activities are designed to stimulate the elephants mentally and physically, preventing boredom and promoting natural behaviours. These activities can include providing: (i) varied terrain; (ii) access to water bodies for bathing; and (iii) objects like logs or tyres for elephants to manipulate. Engaging in such activities helps reduce stress and improve overall welfare (Mumby, 2019). Exercise is another crucial aspect, with camps encouraging elephants to walk long distances daily, mimicking their natural behaviour in the wild. This practice benefits their physical health and supports mental well-being by allowing them to explore and interact with their environment (Bansiddhi *et al.*, 2018).

The industry's evolution towards more ethical practices is also evident in the adoption of the Elephant-First Policy in some camps. This policy emphasizes education and training for mahouts, accreditation for ETVs, and prioritizing the elephants' physical, physiological and psychological needs. Despite these advancements, challenges remain in balancing economic interests with the ethical imperative to ensure the well-being of captive elephants (Zeder *et al.*, 2012).

Regulatory Landscape Concerning Captive Asian Elephants

Thailand

Thailand is home to a significant population of captive Asian elephants and the country has implemented various regulations and guidelines to safeguard their welfare. There has been success in regulation of captive elephants with the Beasts of Burden Act (1939), which requires the certification and identification of ownership of all privately owned elephants aged 8 years and older (Office of the Council of State – Thailand, 1939). This act regulates the domesticated elephant trade aiming to stop the poaching of wild elephants or illegally obtained elephants.

Efforts to improve the welfare of captive elephants have varied in their comprehensiveness and effectiveness. The National Elephant Institute (NEI) of Thailand, established in 1993, plays a key role in conserving elephants sustainably while supporting tourism. The NEI, in collaboration with the Forest Industry Organization (FIO) of Thailand and the Food and Agriculture Organization of the United Nations (FAO), published an elephant care manual to educate mahouts and camp managers on improving welfare standards (Phuangkum, *et al.*, 2005; Bansiddhi *et al.*, 2020b). This manual is available in Thai, English, Lao and Sinhala to ensure broader accessibility.

In 2002, the Department of Livestock Development (DLD) of the Ministry of Agriculture and Cooperatives introduced standards for elephant camps covering aspects like elephant shelters, health care, food and water provisioning, mahout management, environmental and waste management, tourist services and safety (Bansiddhi *et al.*, 2020b; Xia *et al.*, 2024). These standards were expanded in 2009 by the Department of Tourism with a camp scoring and certification system. Despite these efforts, compliance has been low due to the non-enforceable nature of the standards and the lack of incentives for camps to participate (Ghimire *et al.*, 2024).

The Cruelty Prevention and Welfare of Animals Act of 2014 was enacted to prevent animal cruelty and promote welfare. The law stipulates that no person shall perform any act of cruelty without justification and that animal owners must provide proper welfare in accordance with prescribed rules and procedures (Bansiddhi *et al.*, 2020b). However, the efficacy and enforcement of this law remain largely untested, and specific criteria for ensuring welfare are yet to be fully defined.

Most recently, the Thailand National Bureau of Agricultural Commodity and Food Standards launched camp standards where all elephant camps in Thailand will have to apply and be audited and accredited (Ghimire *et al.*, 2024). These standards were released in 2021 with the goal that all camps are to apply these standards by August 2024 (Thailand National Bureau of Agricultural Commodity and Food Standards, 2021). However, the process has moved quite slowly and only a handful of camps have since applied and have been audited.

Cambodia

In Cambodia, regulations concerning captive elephants are less developed compared with Thailand. The primary legal framework is the Forestry Law of 2002, which includes provisions for the protection of wildlife, including elephants (Kingdom of Cambodia Nation Religion King, 2002). Owners of captive elephants in Cambodia are required by law to register their animals with the Forestry Administration. There is consensus that although most captive elephants have been registered, declarations of all ownership may be difficult to achieve as the majority of captive elephants are privately owned by individuals. These are often members of ethnic minority groups in the north-east provinces of Mondulkiri and Ratanakiri, where communities are more isolated and hence it is more difficult to enforce regulation (Dany *et al.*, 2002; Maltby and Bourchier, 2011).

Nepal

Nepal regulates captive elephants under the National Parks and Wildlife Conservation Act of 1973. This act provides protections for wild elephants and governs their capture and use (Gairhe, 2012). Chitwan National Park (CNP) is the busiest protected area in Nepal and is home to several wild bull elephants and one of Nepal's four remaining matriarchal herds (Szydlowski, 2024). Unlike governmentally held elephants, privately owned individuals lack any legal protections regarding their treatment, nutrition or usage (Shrestha and Shrestha, 2021; Szydlowski, 2022).

Sri Lanka

Sri Lanka has a structured approach to elephant management under the Fauna and Flora Protection Ordinance of 1937 and its subsequent amendments. The Department of Wildlife Conservation oversees the welfare of both wild and captive elephants. It is clearly stated that owners of captive elephants are required by law to register any elephant in their custody (Department of Wildlife Conservation, Sri Lanka, 1938). Many elephants in the country are held by temples for use in religious ceremonies, such as The Kandy Esala Perahera also known as the Festival of the Tooth, or are privately owned where they may be used in tourist activities or in logging (Fernando *et al.*, 2011).

India

India has a comprehensive legal framework for elephant protection, including the Wildlife Protection Act of 1972 and the Prevention of Cruelty to Animals Act of 1960. Elephants receive the highest level of protection under Schedule I of the Wildlife Protection Act (1972) and are listed in Appendix I of the Convention on International Trade in Endangered Species of Wild Fauna and Flora (CITES), highlighting their critical conservation status (Sharma, 2020).

The Ministry of Environment, Forest and Climate Change oversees elephant welfare, providing specific guidelines for their care and addresses welfare issues, with an aim to ensure sustainable management of captive elephants (Rangarajan *et al.*, 2010). When elephants are owned illegally, the State Forest Department has the authority to seize the animals immediately and rehabilitate them in recognized elephant camps where they receive long-term care and treatment. In cases where legally owned elephants are reported to be ill-treated, Forest Officers conduct thorough inspections and medical examinations to decide on their confiscation and rehabilitation (Sharma, 2020).

Laos

In Laos, the regulatory framework for elephants is still developing. The country has a small population of both wild and captive elephants, mainly used in logging and tourism, which makes them important for the rural Laos economy (Khounboline, 2011). As all elephants are privately owned, new requirements from the government have been introduced to register domesticated elephants. However, due to lack of knowledgeable and experienced staff its implementation has been slow with little success thus far (Norachack, 2002).

Efforts to improve elephant welfare have been supported by non-governmental organizations (NGOs), which are organizations that are independent of the government and are typically non-profit, and international organizations, such as the Elephant Conservation Center, which focuses on sustainable tourism, veterinary care and mahout training. However, the lack of a robust legal framework and weak enforcement continue to pose challenges (Tomson, 2020).

Indonesia

Indonesia's regulations for elephants are embedded within broader wildlife protection laws, particularly the Conservation of Living Resources and their Ecosystems Act of 1990 (Kuswanda *et al.*, 2022). The Ministry of Environment and Forestry oversees the management of both wild and captive elephants, primarily used in tourism and conservation centres. Despite these regulations, challenges in enforcing anti-poaching laws and ensuring the welfare of captive elephants, especially in remote areas, remain significant (Kuswanda *et al.*, 2022).

The legal status of captive Sumatran elephants is that they are government property and cannot be privately owned. Indonesian law treats captive elephants, along with other protected species, as if they were wild. Consequently, the Directorate General of Nature Protection and Conservation (PKA) mandates the official registration of all captive elephants and requires yearly updates on their status, including transfers between people responsible for their care and/or transfer in location, births and deaths.

Myanmar

Myanmar has a significant population of both wild and captive elephants, primarily used in the logging industry. Domesticated elephants, both privately and state-owned, must be registered with the Forest Department under the Essential Supplies and Services Act, the Burma Act XLVII of 1974, and the Elephant Registration Act of 1951 (Aung and Nyunt, 2002). Elephants owned by the Myanmar Timber Enterprise (MTE) are registered with the Forest Department starting at the age of 5 years old, and their registration must be renewed every 3 years. Additionally, if an MTE elephant gives birth, personnel must notify the nearest Forest Department office within 3 months (Aung and Nyunt, 2002).

Government-owned elephants, approximately 3000 in total, are managed under a set of standards that dictate work hours, activities, mandatory retirement age and access to veterinary care (Bansiddhi *et al.*, 2020b). These elephants are assigned a registration number and a logbook after taming and training. This logbook includes detailed information such as sex, name, age at acquisition or birth, age of training, trainer's name, date of registration, reproductive history, veterinary records, musth periods for males, camp locations, temperament, prescribed workloads and the nature of work (Bansiddhi *et al.*, 2019). This extensive documentation, which is rare in Asia and similar to Western studbooks, allows for detailed analysis of demographic and health data, providing insights into population fecundity, morbidity and mortality (Bansiddhi *et al.*, 2019).

Challenges in Enforcement and Gaps in Regulation

While the existing regulations provide a foundation for elephant welfare, several challenges hinder their effective enforcement. One significant issue is the discrepancy between legal provisions and on-the-ground realities. Many elephant camps, particularly smaller or less financially stable ones, struggle to meet the prescribed standards due to limited resources or lack of knowledge about best practices in elephant care (Bansiddhi *et al.*, 2020b). Additionally, corruption and lack of transparency within the regulatory bodies can impede the implementation of these regulations, allowing non-compliant camps to operate with minimal repercussions.

The registration and tracking of elephants also present significant challenges. Although elephants must be registered with, for example, the DLD in Thailand, inaccuracies and inconsistencies in records are common. This lack of reliable data complicates efforts to monitor and manage the population effectively. Moreover, the existing legal framework does not adequately address the nuances of elephant welfare, such as the psychological well-being of elephants or the specific needs of elephants used in different industries, such as tourism versus logging (Bansiddhi *et al.*, 2020a).

The gaps in regulation also extend to the oversight of training and handling practices. Traditional methods of training, which often involve the use of force or restraint, are still prevalent in some areas, despite being contrary to modern welfare standards. The absence of clear guidelines and training programmes for mahouts exacerbates this issue, leading to variations in handling practices that can negatively impact elephant welfare (Ghimire *et al.*, 2024).

Importance of Robust Monitoring and Independent Auditing Mechanisms

Enforcement challenges and regulatory gaps make robust monitoring and independent auditing vital to improving the welfare of captive elephants. Regular inspections by trained professionals, such as veterinarians or experienced mahouts, are essential to assess camp conditions and suggest improvements (Das *et al.*, 2015).

Independent third-party audits ensure transparency and accountability by providing unbiased evaluations of welfare standards. These audits help identify systemic issues and ensure recommended changes are implemented (Ghimire *et al.*, 2024).

The introduction of ACES represents a positive step. ACES outlines comprehensive criteria for assessing elephant welfare, including health care, diet, housing and social interaction. Regular audits of elephant camps are essential to verify their adherence to these standards and ensure continued compliance (Bansiddhi *et al.*, 2020a, b).

Asian Captive Elephant Standards (ACES)

Created in 2019, the Asian Captive Elephant Standards serve as a reliable and transparent link between the tourism industry and captive elephant welfare by providing independent auditing and certification of elephant camps. The certification was developed by experts Nicolas Dubrocard, a senior advisor in sustainable tourism, Peter Kulmapijit, a specialist in elephant camp management, and Dr Ingrid Suter, an academic who has published studies on elephants in Laos. The certification process involves rigorous assessments and continuous monitoring to ensure compliance with established welfare standards (Suter *et al.*, 2013; Suter, 2020).

ACES welfare standards: auditing and certification

There are ten categories designed to provide a comprehensive evaluation of elephant tourist camps. These categories cover a spectrum of vital aspects, including legal requirements, facility management, elephant welfare and community relations. This framework was developed based on expert findings, science-based research and best practices in camp management.

Challenges for ACES and future direction of elephant-based tourism

One of the biggest challenges ACES faces is resistance to change. Some camps are not ready or willing to allow a deeper look into their operations. However, there has been a gradual improvement in openness, with more businesses seeking certification (Dubrocard, 2024).

Another challenge is navigating the balance between elephant welfare and the economic needs of communities that rely on elephant-based tourism. ACES strives to support mahouts and local communities, acknowledging that tourism is currently the primary source of income for maintaining elephants, especially given their long lifespan and substantial daily food requirements.

The future of elephant-based tourism in South-east Asia is evolving, and it is essential to find a balanced approach that empowers mahouts while promoting intelligent and respectful interactions between tourists and elephants (Dubrocard, 2024).

The Elephant-First Policy

The Elephant-First Policy aims to prioritize the welfare of elephants in tourism by relying on expert guidelines and standards rather than solely on tourist opinions (Ashby, 2022). This approach ensures that the expertise of veterinarians and mahouts inform best practices for elephant care and utilization, addressing both animal welfare and the socio-economic well-being of those who work closely with elephants (Moorhouse *et al.*, 2015).

Expert-based guidelines and standards

The need for expert-based guidelines and standards is crucial for managing domesticated elephants in tourism. According to Ashby (2023a), semi-structured interviews and observations are valuable tools for researchers and policy makers to gather insights from mahouts, veterinarians, tour guides and managers of ETVs. These insights can help refine policies and best practices for elephant welfare.

Tourists' perceptions often differ from veterinary best practices and mahout knowledge. For example, while tourists may view the use of hooks and chains as cruel, these tools are essential for controlling elephants and ensuring safety (Bansiddhi *et al.*, 2020a; Ashby, 2022). Thus, using tourist opinions as the primary driver of guidelines and standards is unsuitable.

Implementing the Elephant-First Policy

The Elephant-First Policy proposes two initial steps: (i) formalized education and training for mahouts; and (ii) standardized accreditation for ETVs. Education and training for mahouts are essential to provide necessary skills and knowledge for elephant husbandry, thus improving both mahout and elephant welfare. Accreditation for ETVs should include stipulations for minimum wage payments, working hours and conditions for employees, as well as adherence to veterinarian guidelines for elephant care (Ashby, 2022).

The objectives of mahout training focus on the promotion of humane handling techniques, reducing reliance on physical punishment and encouraging the use of positive reinforcement. Mahouts are also trained in the nutritional requirements of elephants, ensuring they can provide balanced diets that support health and longevity. In addition, they receive basic veterinary knowledge, allowing them to recognize signs of illness or injury and administer first aid while seeking professional veterinary assistance (Ghimire *et al.*, 2024).

Standardized accreditation for ETVs ensures that venues adhere to strict welfare standards, providing safe and nurturing environments for elephants. Accreditation criteria include the provision of spacious and clean enclosures that promote natural behaviours, regular health check-ups and mandatory access to veterinary care. Venues are also required to offer ethical tourism activities that do not harm the elephants, such as observation-based experiences rather than elephant rides or performances. Organizations like ACES and the Global Federation of Animal Sanctuaries (GFAS) play a key role in enforcing these accreditation standards across Asia (Ghimire *et al.*, 2024).

While the Elephant-First Policy offers a forward-thinking approach to elephant welfare, its implementation faces challenges, particularly financial. Smaller ETVs may struggle to fund necessary training and facility upgrades to meet accreditation standards. This issue can be alleviated through government subsidies, grants from conservation organizations, and partnerships with ethical tourism operators (Yoo *et al.*, 2015).

Another challenge is maintaining consistency across regions, as local regulations, economic conditions and cultural attitudes vary. A centralized body to oversee accreditation and provide ongoing support can help ensure uniform enforcement.

Despite these challenges, the policy offers key benefits, including supporting mahout communities and preventing the mislabelling of poor welfare venues as sanctuaries, allowing tourists to make more informed decisions (Lee *et al.*, 2024). It also enforces stricter welfare regulations and promotes ethical conservation, reducing the risk of captive populations being restocked from the wild (Duffy and Moore, 2011; Williams *et al.*, 2019).

Challenges and Future Directions

Regulating captive elephant welfare presents several challenges, with significant inconsistencies in standards across countries. While some enforce strict regulations, others lack comprehensive frameworks, leading to substandard conditions (Sukumar, 2006). Even where laws exist, enforcement is often hindered by limited resources, inadequate training and corruption, allowing illegal captures and abuses to continue unchecked (Schmidt-Burbach *et al.*, 2015; Park *et al.*, 2017). Public awareness further complicates matters, as tourists may demand welfare changes based on perceptions rather than expert advice.

Future research should focus on creating standardized welfare assessment tools with clear metrics for health, psychological well-being and social interaction (Veasey, 2020). Understanding the long-term impacts of captivity on elephants, considering factors like age and sex, will further inform management practices (Clubb and Mason, 2002; Chen *et al.*, 2022). Policies should also make mahout training mandatory and incentivize accreditation from recognized welfare bodies (Ghimire *et al.*, 2024).

Collaboration between governments, NGOs, researchers and the tourism industry is essential. International cooperation, particularly through organizations like CITES, is vital for addressing issues such as the illegal wildlife trade (CITES, 2021). Engaging diverse stakeholders ensures more comprehensive, culturally sensitive solutions, while public–private partnerships can help mobilize the necessary resources for welfare initiatives.

In conclusion, protecting captive elephant welfare requires science-based guidelines, enforced through collaboration and continuous updates. By prioritizing welfare, we can strive towards ethical, sustainable elephant tourism that benefits both elephants and human communities.

Bibliography

Ashby, G. (2022) An 'elephant-first' policy to aid in the management of elephants used in tourism in Thailand. MSc thesis, University of Kent, Canterbury, UK.

Ashby, G. (2023a) From elephant activist to elephant pragmatist: Navigating the complex reality of animal welfare. Asian Captive Elephant Standards (ACES). Available at: https://www.

elephantstandards.com/post/from-elephant-activist-to-elephant-pragmatist-navigating-the-complex-reality-of-animal-welfare (accessed 14 June 2024).

Ashby, G. (2023b) Tourists care, but they don't always know best. Asian Captive Elephant Standards (ACES). Available at: https://www.elephantstandards.com/post/tourists-care-but-they-don-t-always-know-best (accessed 14 June 2024).

Asian Captive Elephant Standards (ACES) (2024) Asian Captive Elephant Standards. Available at: https://www.elephantstandards.com/ (accessed 14 June 2024).

Aung, U.T. and Nyunt, U.T. (2002) The care and management of the domesticated Asian elephant in Myanmar. Available at: https://www.fao.org/4/ad031e/ad031e0d.htm (accessed 14 July 2024).

Bansiddhi, P., Brown, J.L., Thitaram, C., Punyapornwithaya, V., Somgird, C. *et al.* (2018) Changing trends in elephant camp management in northern Thailand and implications for welfare. *PeerJ* 6: e5996. DOI: 10.7717/peerj.5996.

Bansiddhi, P., Nganvongpanit, K., Brown, J.L., Punyapornwithaya, V., Pongsopawijit, P. *et al.* (2019) Management factors affecting physical health and welfare of tourist camp elephants in Thailand. *PeerJ* 7: e6756. DOI: 10.7717/peerj.6756.

Bansiddhi, P., Brown, J.L. and Thitaram, C. (2020a) Welfare assessment and activities of captive elephants in Thailand. *Animals* 10(6): 919. DOI: 10.3390/ani10060919.

Bansiddhi, P., Brown, J.L., Thitaram, C., Punyapornwithaya, V. and Nganvongpanit, K. (2020b) Elephant tourism in Thailand: a review of animal welfare practices and needs. *Journal of Applied Animal Welfare Science* 23(2), 164–177. DOI: 10.1080/10888705.2019.1569522.

Chen, X., Lee, T.J. and Hyun, S.S. (2022) How does a global coffeehouse chain operate strategically in a traditional tea-drinking country? The influence of brand authenticity and self-enhancement. *Journal of Hospitality and Tourism Management* 51, 176–186. DOI: 10.1016/j.jhtm.2022.03.003.

CITES (2021) Convention on International Trade in Endangered Species of Wild Fauna and Flora. Available at: https://cites.org/eng/disc/text.php (accessed 14 June 2024).

Clubb and Mason (2002) *A Review of the Welfare of Zoo Elephants in Europe*. Report commissioned by the RSPCA (Royal Society for the Prevention of Cruelty to Animals). Available at: https://science.rspca.org.uk/documents/1494935/9042554/A+review+of+the+welfare+of+zoo+elephants+in+Europe.pdf/8dd529a1-5f5b-e713-fcac-4a99c7b90489?t=1553171443018 (accessed 14 June 2024).

Collicott, H. (2019) Elephants in Thai Culture by Holly Collicott - Phang Nga Elephant Park. Available at: https://phangngaelephantpark.com/elephants-in-thai-culture-2-by-holly (accessed 14 June 2024).

Dany, C., Weiler, H., Tong, K. and Han, S. (2002) The status, distribution and management of the domesticated Asian elephant in Cambodia. Available at: https://coin.fao.org/coin-static/cms/media/9/13171049401100/2002_30_high.pdf#page=89 (accessed 16 June 2024).

Das, A., Smith, M.L., Saini, M., Katole, S., Kullu, S.S. *et al.* (2015) Effect of concentrates restriction on feed consumption, diet digestibility, and nitrogen utilization in captive Asian elephants (*Elephas maximus*). *Zoo Biology* 34(1), 60–70. DOI: 10.1002/zoo.21194.

Department of Wildlife Conservation, Sri Lanka (1938) *Fauna and Flora Protection Ordinance*. Available at: https://citizenslanka.org/wp-content/uploads/2016/02/Fauna-and-Flora-Protection-Ordinance-No-02-of-1937-E.pdf (accessed 14 June 2024).

Dhairykar, M. and Singh, K. (2020) Management of nutrition in captive Asian elephants. *International Journal of Veterinary Sciences and Animal Husbandry* 5, 160–163.

Dubrocard (2024) Advancing ethical elephant tourism: an interview with Nicolas Dubrocard of ACESMekong. Mekong Tourism Coordinating Office. Available at: https://mekongtourism.org/advancing-ethical-elephant-tourism-an-interview-with-nicolas-dubrocard-of-aces/ (accessed 16 June 2024).

Duffy, R. and Moore, L. (2011) Global regulations and local practices: the politics and governance of animal welfare in elephant tourism. *Journal of Sustainable Tourism* 19(4–5), 589–604. DOI: 10.1080/09669582.2011.566927.

Fernando, P., Jayewardene, J., Prasad, T., Hendavitharana, W. and Pastorini, J. (2011) Current status of Asian elephants in Sri Lanka. *Gajah* 35, 93–103. DOI: 10.5167/uzh-59037.

Flower, E.K., Burns, G.L. and Jones, D.N. (2021) How tourist preference and satisfaction can contribute to improved welfare standards at elephant tourism venues in Thailand. *Animals* 11(4): 1094. DOI: 10.3390/ani11041094.

Fowler, M.E. and Mikota, S.K. (2006) *Biology, Medicine, and Surgery of Elephants*, 1st edn. Blackwell Publishing, Oxford.

Gairhe, K. (2012) Veterinary care and breeding of elephants in Nepal. *Gajah* 37, 27–30.

Ghimire, R., Brown, J.L., Thitaram, C. and Bansiddhi, P. (2024) Comparison of animal welfare assessment tools and methodologies: need for an effective approach for captive elephants in Asia. *Frontiers in Veterinary Science* 11: 1370909. DOI: 10.3389/fvets.2024.1370909.

Godfrey, A. and Kongmuang, C. (2009) Distribution, demography and basic husbandry of the Asian elephant in the tourism industry in northern Thailand. *Gajah* 30, 13–18.

Greco, B.J., Meehan, C.L., Hogan, J.N., Leighty, K.A., Mellen, J. *et al.* (2016) The days and nights of zoo elephants: using epidemiology to better understand stereotypic behavior of African elephants (*Loxodonta africana*) and Asian elephants (*Elephas maximus*) in North American zoos. *PLoS ONE* 11(7): e0144276. DOI: 10.1371/journal.pone.0144276.

Gruber, T.M., Friend, T.H., Gardner, J.M., Packard, J.M., Beaver, B. *et al.* (2000) Variation in stereotypic behavior related to restraint in circus elephants. *Zoo Biology* 19, 209–221. DOI: 10.1002/1098-2361(2000)19:33.0.CO;2-7.

Hart, L. and Sundar, S. (2000) Family traditions for mahouts of Asian elephants. *Anthrozoös* 13(1), 34–42. DOI: 10.2752/089279300787000055.

International Elephant Foundation and Wildlife Alliance (2016) *Direct Protection to Asia's Last Intact Elephant Corridor: Southwest Elephant Corridor, Cardomom Rainforest, Cambodia.* Available at: https://elephantconservation.org/wp-content/uploads/2022/10/2019_WILDLIFE_ALLIANCE_PROJECT-SYNOPSIS_ACTION-PLAN-AND-BUDGET_IEF.pdf (accessed 16 June 2024).

Khounboline, K. (2011) Current status of Asian elephants in Lao PDR. *Gajah* 35, 62–66.

Kingdom of Cambodia Nation Religion King (2002) *Law on Forestry*. Forest Administration. Available at: https://faolex.fao.org/docs/pdf/cam50411.pdf (accessed 16 June 2024).

Koirala, R.K., Raubenheimer, D., Aryal, A., Pathak, M.L. and Ji, W. (2016) Feeding preferences of the Asian elephant (*Elephas maximus*) in Nepal. *BMC Ecology* 16(1): 54. DOI: 10.1186/s12898-016-0105-9.

Kontogeorgopoulos, N. (2009) Wildlife tourism in semi-captive settings: a case study of elephant camps in northern Thailand. *Current Issues in Tourism* 12(5–6), 429–449. DOI: 10.1080/13683500903042873.

Kuswanda, W., Garsetiasih, R., Gunawan, H., Situmorang, R.O.P., Hutapea, F.J. *et al.* (2022) Can humans and elephants coexist? A review of the conflict on Sumatra Island, Indonesia. *Diversity* 14: 420. DOI: 10.3390/d14060420.

Lee, S., Lee, N., Lee, T.J. and Hyun, S.S. (2024) The influence of social support from intermediary organizations on innovativeness and subjective happiness in community-based tourism. *Journal of Sustainable Tourism* 32(4), 795–817. DOI: 10.1080/09669582.2023.2175836.

Maltby, M. and Bourchier, G. (2011) Current status of Asian elephants in Cambodia. *Gajah* 35, 36–42.

Meehan, C.L., Mench, J.A., Carlstead, K. and Hogan, J.N. (2016) Determining connections between the daily lives of zoo elephants and their welfare: an epidemiological approach. *PloS ONE* 11(7): e0158124. DOI: 10.1371/journal.pone.0158124.

Menon, V. and Tiwari, S.K.R. (2019) Population status of Asian elephants *Elephas maximus* and key threats. *International Zoo Yearbook* 53(1), 17–30. DOI: 10.1111/izy.12247.

Miller, D., Jackson, B., Riddle, H.S., Stremme, C., Schmitt, D. and Miller, T. (2015) Elephant (*Elephas maximus*) health and management in Asia: variations in veterinary perspectives. *Veterinary Medicine International* 2015(1): 614690. DOI: 10.1155/2015/614690.

Moorhouse, T.P., Dahlsjö, C.A.L., Baker, S.E., D'Cruze, N.C. and Macdonald, D.W. (2015) The customer isn't always right – conservation and animal welfare implications of the increasing demand for wildlife tourism. *PLoS ONE* 10: e0138939. DOI: 10.1371/journal.pone.0138939.

Mumby, H.S. (2019) Mahout perspectives on Asian elephants and their living conditions. *Animals* 9: 879. DOI: 10.3390/ani9110879.

Norachack, B. (2002) The care and management of domestic Asian elephants in Lao PDR. Available at: https://www.fao.org/4/ad031e/ad031e0j.htm (accessed 16 June 2024).

Norkaew, T., Brown, J.L., Bansiddhi, P., Somgird, C., Thitaram, C. *et al.* (2018) Body condition and adrenal glucocorticoid activity affects metabolic marker and lipid profiles in captive female elephants in Thailand. *PLoS ONE* 13: e0204965. DOI: 10.1371/journal.pone.0204965.

Norkaew, T., Brown, J.L., Bansiddhi, P., Somgird, C., Thitaram, C. *et al.* (2019) Influence of season, tourist activities and camp management on body condition, testicular and adrenal steroids, lipid profiles, and metabolic status in captive Asian elephant bulls in Thailand. *PLoS ONE* 14(3): e0210537. DOI: 10.1371/journal.pone.0210537.

Office of the Council of State – Thailand (1939) Beasts of Burden Act. Available at: http://report.dopa.go.th/laws/document/2/223.pdf (accessed 16 June 2024).

Original Travel (2021) The nuances and complexities of elephant riding. Available at: https://www.originaltravel.co.uk/travel-blog/the-nuances-and-complexities-of-elephant-riding (accessed 16 June 2024).

Park, K., Lee, J. and Lee, T.J. (2017) Residents' attitudes toward future tourism development in terms of community well-being and attachment. *Asia Pacific Journal of Tourism Research* 22(2), 160–172. DOI: 10.1080/10941665.2016.1208669.

Phuangkum, P., Lair, R.C. and Angkawanith, T. (2005) *Elephant Care Manual for Mahouts and Camp Managers*. Food and Agriculture Organization of the United Nations (FAO), Regional Office for Asia and the Pacific, Bangkok. Available at: https://www.fao.org/4/ae943e/ae943e00.htm (accessed 16 June 2024).

Plotnik, J.M. and Jacobson, S.L. (2022) A 'thinking animal' in conflict: studying wild elephant cognition in the shadow of anthropogenic change. *Current Opinion in Behavioral Sciences* 46: 101148. DOI: 10.1016/j.cobeha.2022.101148.

Rangarajan, M., Desai, A., Sukumar, R., Easa, P., Menon, V. *et al.* (2010) *Gajah. Securing the Future for Elephants in India. The Report of the Elephant Task Force, Ministry of Environment and Forests.* Ministry of Environment and Forests, New Delhi. Available at: https://www.environmentandsociety.org/sites/default/files/key_docs/Gajah.pdf (accessed 16 June 2024).

Raviv, L., Jacobson, S.L., Plotnik, J.M., Bowman, J., Lynch, V. *et al.* (2023) Elephants as an animal model for self-domestication. *Proceedings of the National Academy of Sciences of the United States of America* 120(15): e2208607120. DOI: 10.1073/pnas.2208607120.

Rizzolo, J.B. and Bradshaw, G.A. (2016) Prevalence and patterns of complex PTSD in Asian elephants (*Elephas maximus*). In: Bandara, N., Wickramaarachchi, T. and Zoysa, H. (eds) *Asian Elephants in Culture and Nature*. Centre for Asian Studies, University of Kelaniya, Sri Lanka, pp. 291–297.

Rizzolo, J.B. and Bradshaw, G.A. (2018) Human leisure/elephant breakdown: impacts of tourism on Asian elephants. In: Carr, N. and Young, J. (eds) *Wild Animals and Leisure: Rights and Wellbeing*. Routledge, London, Chapter 7. DOI: 10.4324/9781315457413.

Romain, S., Angkawanish, T., Bampenpol, P., Pongsopawijit, P., Sombatphuthorn, P. *et al.* (2014) Diet composition, food intake, apparent digestibility, and body condition score of the captive Asian elephant (*Elephas maximus*): a pilot study in two collections in Thailand. *Journal of Zoo and Wildlife Medicine* 45(1), 1–14. DOI: 10.1638/2011-0261R3.1.

Schmidt-Burbach, J. (2017) Taken for a ride: thousands of elephants exploited for tourism are held in cruel conditions. *World Animal Protection*, 7 July. Available at: https://www.worldanimalprotection.org/latest/news/taken-ride-thousands-elephants-exploited-tourism-are-held-cruel-conditions/ (accessed 16 June 2024).

Schmidt-Burbach, J., Ronfot, D. and Srisangiam, R. (2015) Asian elephant (*Elephas maximus*), pig-tailed macaque (*Macaca nemestrina*) and tiger (*Panthera tigris*) populations at tourism venues in Thailand and aspects of their welfare. *PLoS ONE* 10(9): e0139092. DOI: 10.1371/journal.pone.0139092.

Sharma, M. (2020) Indian laws protecting elephants - Wildlife SOS. Available at: https://wildlifesos.org/elephant/indian-laws-protecting-elephants/ (accessed 16 June 2024).

Shell, J. (2019) Elephant convoys beyond the state: animal-based transport as subversive logistics. *Environment and Planning D: Society and Space* 37(5), 905–923. DOI: 10.1177/0263775818805491.

Shrestha, S. and Shrestha, J. (2021) Asian elephants and their status in Nepal: a review. *Journal of Agriculture and Natural Resources* 4(2), 227–237. DOI: 10.3126/janr.v4i2.33828.

Stremme, C., Lubis, A. and Wahyu, M. (2007) Implementation of regular veterinary care for captive Sumatran elephants (*Elephas maximus sumatranus*). *Journal of the Asian Elephant Specialist Group* 27, 6–14.

Sukumar, R. (2006) A brief review of the status, distribution and biology of wild Asian elephants *Elephas maximus*. *International Zoo Yearbook* 40(1), 1–8. DOI: 10.1111/j.1748-1090.2006.00001.x.

Suter, I. (2020) Rewilding or reviewing: conservation and the elephant-based tourism industry. *Animal Sentience* 5(28). DOI: 10.51291/2377-7478.1556.

Suter, I.C., Hockings, M. and Baxter, G.S. (2013) Changes in elephant ownership and employment in the Lao PDR: implications for the elephant-based logging and tourism industries. *Human Dimensions of Wildlife* 18(4), 279–291. DOI: 10.1080/10871209.2013.788235.

Szydlowski, M. (2022) Elephants in Nepal: correlating disease, tourism, and welfare. *Journal of Applied Animal Welfare Science* 25, 1–13. DOI: 10.1080/10888705.2022.2028628.

Szydlowski, M. (2024) Wicked problems, novel solutions: Nepalese elephant tourism and conservation. *Animals* 14(1): 171. DOI: 10.3390/ani14010171.

Thailand National Bureau of Agricultural Commodity and Food Standards (2021) *Good Animal Practices for Elephant Facility*. Available at: https://www.acfs.go.th/files/files/commodity-standard/20230403155849_967676.pdf (accessed 16 June 2024).

Tompson, L. (2020) A look into the last 12 months at the Elephant Conservation Center. Elephant Conservation Center. Available at: https://www.elephantconservationcenter.com/the-last-12-months-at-ecc/ (accessed 3 March 2025).

Varadharajan, V., Krishnamoorthy, T. and Nagarajan, B. (2016) Prevalence of stereotypies and its possible causes among captive Asian elephants (*Elephas maximus*) in Tamil Nadu, India. *Applied Animal Behaviour Science* 174, 137–146. DOI: 10.1016/j.applanim.2015.10.006.

Veasey, J.S. (2020) Assessing the psychological priorities for optimising captive Asian elephant (*Elephas maximus*) welfare. *Animals* 10(1): 39. DOI: 10.3390/ani10010039.

Williams, C., Tiwari, S., Goswami, V., Silva, S., Kumar, A. *et al.* (2019) IUCN Red List of Threatened Species: *Elephas maximus*. Available at: https://www.iucnredlist.org/species/7140/45818198 (accessed 16 June 2024).

Xia, L., Lee, T.J. and Kim, D.K. (2024) Relationships between motivation, service quality, tourist satisfaction, quality of life, and spa and wellness tourism. *International Journal of Tourism Research* 26(1): e2624. DOI: 10.1002/jtr.2624.

Yoo, I.Y., Lee, T.J. and Lee, C.K. (2015) Effect of health and wellness values on festival visit motivation. *Asia Pacific Journal of Tourism Research* 20, 152–170. DOI: 10.1080/10941665.2013.866970.

Zeder, M.A., Famula, T.R., Gepts, P., Bettinger, R.L., Brush, S.B. *et al.* (2012) Pathways to animal domestication. In: Zeder, M.A. (ed.) *Biodiversity in Agriculture*. Cambridge University Press, Cambridge, pp. 227–259.

10 The UK Animals (Low Welfare) Act

Eric Laws[1]* and Gary Akehurst[2,3]

[1]*retired Professor of Tourism;* [2]*Emeritus Professor of Management, University of Winchester, UK;* [3]*Emeritus Professor of Marketing, Aberystwyth University, UK*

Abstract

Chapter 10 investigates how origin-based legislation may enhance elephant welfare in elephant tourism venues (ETVs) at destinations overseas. The traditional positive influencers particularly marketing, tourism journalism, nature and cultural TV programmes, previous experiences and recommendations from friends are still active in encouraging elephant tourism. But a new constraint has been added by the Animals (Low-Welfare Activities Abroad) Act 2023. This has the effect of ending the right of UK-based tourism companies to advertise activities which might harm animal welfare in overseas destinations. The chapter also presents verbatim extracts from Hansard, the official record of debates in the UK Parliament in which members discuss their constituents' views of this new law.

The editors of *Elephant Welfare in Global Tourism* wish to acknowledge Duncan McNair's leading role in devising and pioneering the Animals (Low-Welfare Activities Abroad) Act into law, and for his assistance in discussion about the problems for elephants in tourism. Duncan McNair is CEO of Save The Asian Elephants.

Introduction

Early academic models of tourism were interested in synthesizing theory and practice; Burkhart and Medlik (1974) had focused attention on the dynamic nature of tourism, stressing that it was a demand-led industry. The flows of international tourists from a specific origin country to a given destination vary through time. Factors in the origin country that have added to demand for tourism include: (i) increased paid holidays; (ii) increasing disposable

*e.laws@runbox.com

DOI: 10.1079/9781836990093.0010

incomes; (iii) improvements in the tourism industry such as efficiencies leading to reduced package holiday prices; (iv) marketing by competing destinations; and (v) changing propensities for alternative spending such as to upgrade a home.

Factors which attract tourists to a destination include:

- relative cost;
- ease of access;
- the range of interests and activities offered;
- conditions in the destination including safety, quality of accommodation and meals, etc.; and
- competition from alternative destinations.

The traditional positive influencers particularly marketing, tourism journalism, nature and cultural TV programmes, previous experiences and recommendations from friends are still active in encouraging elephant tourism. But a new constraint has been added in the UK by the Animals (Low-Welfare Activities Abroad) Act 2023. This has the effect of ending the right of UK-based tourism companies to advertise activities which might harm animal welfare in overseas destinations. A further effect may be to strengthen those non-governmental organizations (NGOs) which campaign to end harmful activities such as elephant riding, or unnatural 'entertainment' performances in which elephants paint, play football or play musical instruments for the amusement of visitors. The sale of such opportunities will also be banned by UK tour operators in destinations, although locally based organizers and camps will not be restricted because that would be construed as interfering with the destination's rights.

This chapter presents the verbatim debates on the Animals (Low-Welfare Activities Abroad) Act in both the House of Commons and the House of Lords which reveal members' concerns about animal species including elephants. The House of Commons is the democratically elected lower house of the UK Parliament, comprising members of Parliament (MPs) while the House of Lords is the upper house of the UK Parliament which, among other functions, scrutinizes legislation. In contrast to many parliamentary debates, when this act was debated party lines were overridden by shared concern for animal welfare, reflecting the attitudes of many constituents around the UK.

On any day when either legislative chamber is sitting, a 'rolling' version of Hansard publishes what a member has said within 3 hours. In this chapter the detailed discussion in both Houses of the UK Parliament is presented, but with minor editing excluding some of the parliamentary routines. MPs may be Conservative (Con), Labour (Lab) or from one of the minor parties, or they may be independent (i.e. not affiliated to any political party). In debates they generally refer to each other as Honourable Member, followed by the name of their constituency (i.e. the electoral district they represent). The full text of all Parliamentary debates can be found online from Hansard (available at: https://hansard.parliament.uk (accessed 20 February 2025)).

How Law Is Enacted in the UK

Bills are introduced in either the House of Commons or the House of Lords, as a Public Bill, or, as in this case, as a Private Member's Bill. Each bill goes through a number of stages that generally involve members of both Houses examining the bill.

After the second reading the bill proceeds to committee stage, where each clause (part) and any amendments (proposals for change) to the bill are debated. Every clause in the bill is agreed to, changed or removed from the bill, although sometimes this may occur without debate.

Once the committee stage is finished, the bill returns to the floor of the House of Commons for its report stage, where the amended bill can be debated and further amendments proposed.

The report stage is normally followed immediately by the bill's third reading. Debate on the bill at this stage is usually short, and limited to what is actually in the bill, rather than, as at the second reading, what might have been included.

When a bill has completed all its parliamentary stages in both Houses, it must receive royal assent before it can become an Act of Parliament (law) (UK Parliament, n.d.).

The following sections include Parliamentary information licensed under the Open Parliament Licence v3.0. More information on the Open Parliament Licence is available at: https://www.parliament.uk/site-information/copyright-parliament/open-parliament-licence/ (accessed 20 February 2025).

The Commons Committee Debate of 8 March 2023

This is an excerpt from the Commons Committee debate held on Wednesday 8 March 2023 concerning the Animals (Low-Welfare Activities Abroad) Bill (UK Parliament, 2023a).

Angela Richardson (Guildford) (Con)

It is a pleasure to serve under your chairmanship, Mr Stringer. I am grateful to you, and to everyone who has joined the Committee to consider this important Bill once again.

I thank officials at the Department for Environment, Food and Rural Affairs who have supported me throughout this process, and the Ministers at DEFRA, the Under-Secretary of State for Environment, Food and Rural Affairs, my hon. Friend the Member for Copeland (Trudy Harrison), and my hon. Friend the Member for Taunton Deane, who is answering today, for speaking up for the Bill along its journey so far.

I welcome the Government's support for this legislation. Currently, there is no statutory provision in England or Northern Ireland to regulate the advertising or sale of animal activities abroad. This Government are well intentioned on the subject of animal welfare, and I know that this legislation has been a long time coming. The Government's ambitious "Action Plan for Animal Welfare" states:

> "we also want to make sure that businesses do not benefit from selling attractions, activities or experiences to tourists involving the unacceptable treatment of animals;"

and the Bill will deliver just that.

I will not repeat everything I said in the Chamber on Second Reading a few weeks ago, but it is important to break down the clauses and their effect. Clauses 1 and 2 establish the framework of offences that would involve the sale and advertising of animal experiences abroad that are considered to be low welfare. One section of particular note is subsection (3) of clause 1, which sets out the test for assessing whether an activity would be considered low welfare under the Animal Welfare Act 2006 in England, and the Welfare of Animals Act (Northern Ireland) 2011 in Northern Ireland.

Clause 3 is about penalties, prosecution and liabilities under the legislation. The clause also disapplies section 127 of the Magistrates' Courts Act 1980 and article 19 of the Magistrates' Courts (Northern Ireland) Order 1981. That will ensure that the more complex cases that arise as a result of this legislation can be dealt with in a longer period than six months, which is the regular limit for a summary offence.

Clause 4 establishes the authority of the relevant departments in England and the Department for the Economy in Northern Ireland to investigate any allegations resulting from the offences created under the legislation. Clause 5 outlines the procedures for making regulations under the new legislation, both in this Parliament and in the devolved Administration in Northern Ireland. Clause 6 defines the terms commonly used throughout the Bill, including "activity regulations", "animal", "appropriate national authority", "appropriate national legislation", "offering" and "vertebrate".

Finally, clause 7 details the territorial extent of the Bill—it applies to England and Northern Ireland—the commencement of the Act, which is due to take effect two months following Royal Assent from His Majesty the King, and the short title of the Act.

Animals cannot speak up for themselves, but we can speak for them. Charities including Save The Asian Elephants and World Animal Protection have highlighted the plight of many animals, including elephants and dolphins, which suffer in appalling conditions behind the scenes before being paraded around for visiting tourists. World Animal Protection estimates that up to 550,000 wild animals are suffering in poor conditions for the entertainment of tourists worldwide.

While we cannot outlaw those practices overseas, the Bill goes a long way to ensuring that we do our bit. Once enacted, it will prohibit the advertisement in England and Northern Ireland of tourist activities abroad that infringe on animal welfare standards. By reducing the visibility and prevalence of advertisements for such activities on high streets across England and Northern Ireland, the Bill will lead to more welfare-conscious offers being made to tourists who wish to go abroad.

Mrs Flick Drummond (Meon Valley) (Con)

I thank my hon. Friend for promoting this incredibly important Bill. Do those advertisements include those for swimming with dolphins?

Angela Richardson

It does. I will come on to talk about dolphins and other animals later in my speech.

A briefing note circulated by a number of animal welfare charities to members of the Committee highlighted 12 recurring themes in the keeping of animals in low-welfare attractions and facilities. It is prudent to bring them to the attention of the Committee to show the difference that the legislation could make. Animals are taken from the wild, which harms the animal, local wildlife populations and people. Mothers are killed, injured or harmed simply so that their infants can be captured. Breeding mothers are kept and forced to raise their young in low-welfare facilities, as opposed to in the wild. Infants are taken from their mothers far too young. There is a high mortality rate among animals that are in transit or traded.

Animals are kept in situations that are unnatural to them, including close captivity, which can be particularly harmful to long-lived species and to those accustomed to a large range in the wild. Animals are forced to perform unnatural behaviours. The use, or threat, of fear, pain, or drugs is used to control or train animals, and methods of domination are used to traumatise or subdue them. Animals are closely handled by several untrained people, and are often given no option to retreat. There is a risk of zoonotic disease transmission from animals, particularly when they are used as photo props and handled by large volumes of people. Finally, animals who are no longer used for exhibition are kept in cruel surroundings or killed before they have reach the natural end of their life. Those 12 themes paint a picture of a experiences [sic] that none of us would wish on an animal in the wild. This legislation will result in fewer animals being treated in that way by bringing about less consumer demand for experiences based on low-welfare treatment.

Let me mention some of the experiences that feature poor conditions for animals, as well as the species that the Bill could have an impact on. I will start with the Asian elephant, used as a tourist attraction for rides, particularly in South-east Asia. Animals from that precious species are brutally taken in the wild at a young age—sometimes their mothers are killed right in front of them—and then subjected to a breaking of their spirits by isolation, starvation, stabbings and beatings to make them submissive when engaged in activities with tourists.

Another experience used in tourist activities around the world is the use of animals as photo props. That can include primates, reptiles and avian life being used for selfies; and big cats, such as tigers, lions and leopards, being used in public interaction.

Katherine Fletcher (South Ribble) (Con)

I would like to add to that list. I have worked as a field guide, a safari ranger, in Africa, and cheetahs are especially vulnerable. I have seen cheetahs in particularly shocking conditions—tigers, cheetahs and others. Does my hon. Friend agree that they need protecting as much as all the other big cats?

Angela Richardson

I thank my hon. Friend for her timely intervention. It is right to add to the list. In fact, if I went through a list, it would be a lot longer than I have time for this morning—I do not want to keep everyone in a cold Committee Room longer than is necessary. Yes, cheetahs are affected as well, as is marine life, including dolphins, which are used for feeding and swimming experiences, as was mentioned by my hon. Friend the Member for Meon Valley.

Many of us and our constituents will have seen such experiences advertised in the shop windows of travel agents or online, but were not aware of the animal welfare consequences. When we think about low-welfare activities abroad, we first think of the conditions of the animals, but it is important to note that there is a human impact, too. For example, research from Save the Asian Elephants has shown that at least 700 tourists and others have been killed, and more than 900 have suffered sustained injuries, such as crushed chests and internal organs, broken limbs and ribs, and serious head injuries. More widely, experiences involving big cats, marine life and reptiles carry a risk to public safety through the threat of injury and of the zoonotic transmission of disease. The Bill will improve the safety of both the animals involved in tourism abroad and the tourists themselves.

I appreciate that some will be disappointed that the legislation will not cover the whole of the United Kingdom, notably Scotland and Wales. I hope that our colleagues in the Scottish and Welsh Parliaments will be able to introduce legislation in their devolved assemblies that provides a similar framework. Today, we must focus on the first step on that journey, and put the Bill through to the next stage.

Everyone on the Committee and in the House represents a constituency where animal welfare is valued and cherished, as it is in my constituency of Guildford. The Bill will be roundly supported by our constituents. I was pleased to see, both on Second Reading and in an Adjournment debate on the subject in the House in January, that the legislation had cross-party support. There were contributions from Conservative, Labour and SNP Members. I hope that we continue in that cross-party spirit. I look forward to hearing from the Minister and Members on their further views on the Bill.

(From UK Parliament, 2023a; reproduced under Hansard Open Parliament Licence v3.0)

Debate in the House of Lords of the Animals (Low-Welfare Activities Abroad) Bill

These are excerpts from the second reading of the Bill from Hansard Volume 831: debated on Friday 14 July 2023 (UK Parliament, 2023b).

Second Reading
Moved by

Lord Black of Brentwood (Con)

My Lords, noble Lords will know of my long-standing interest in and commitment to animal welfare. I believe, like all colleagues here today I have no doubt, that the way we treat animals is a mark of our humanity. Traditionally, I have campaigned more often on issues relating to domestic animals, such as cats and dogs, as we did yesterday, but today I turn my attention to animals of a somewhat bigger variety, and certainly on a more global scale, by introducing this important Bill. It is a privilege to do so.

As this Bill relates to advertising, I declare an interest as a director of the Advertising Standards Board of Finance and note my other interests. I am grateful to all noble Lords who will take part in this important debate. I much look forward to it, especially to the contribution of my noble friend the Minister. My noble friend Lady Fookes had wanted to take part to support the Bill, but regrettably she is unable to be here today.

I am indebted to Angela Richardson MP, who piloted the Bill through the other place with passion, eloquence and skill. I hope its journey in this House will be just as smooth, reflecting its overwhelming public backing. The Bill has government and cross-party support, and it has incredibly strong public support. An Opinion Matters poll just a few months ago showed that 82% agreed that the Government should use their influence to bring an end to overseas activities which involve animal cruelty.

The Bill also has the powerful backing of many of the charities involved in this field of work, among them Save the Asian Elephants, the RSPCA, World Animal Protection and Four Paws UK. I am particularly indebted to Save the Asian Elephants for the comprehensive briefing it has provided to me and others, as indeed I am to our Library for its background document. I am also very grateful to officials at Defra [sic], who have been generous in their time and expertise working on this Bill.

This Government have done a great deal in recent years to protect and enhance animal welfare, yet it is a never-ending battle. There is always more to be done, and this excellent Bill rises to the challenge, fulfilling the commitment in the 2021 *Action Plan for Animal Welfare* to ensure that "businesses do not benefit from selling attractions, activities or experiences to tourists involving the unacceptable treatment of animals".

The Government's intention, which this Bill delivers on, is to steer tourists away from so-called attractions which rely on cruel and brutal practices to ensure the obedience of animals, towards visits to places where animals are cared for and treated properly, with dignity and humanity. This includes Asian elephants, about which I will say more in a moment, big cats such as tigers and lions, baby monkeys, dolphins and much other marine life. Many of these animals are subjected to unimaginable cruelty in the name of so-called entertainment.

The pattern, whatever the species, is often horribly the same. Taken from their own habitat, on land or sea, infants' mothers are often killed to capture them. They are kept in incredibly harmful close captivity. They are forced through traumatising fear, pain or drugs into a state where they can be dominated and made to perform unnatural behaviours. They are often callously slaughtered when they are no longer needed for exhibition.

Take Asian elephants as an example of the sort of species that might be helped by this enabling legislation. These magnificent animals—now an endangered species, which is incredibly dangerous in view of their crucial role in boosting biodiversity, rejuvenating forests and helping combat climate change—are treated with indescribable viciousness to prepare them for tourist activities such as elephant rides and washing. They are snatched from the wild, with their protective mothers often butchered in front of them, subjected to the brutal "breaking of the spirits" through isolation and starvation, then stabbed and beaten with repulsive hooks and sticks before being restrained by tight wire ties that bite the flesh, prevent movement and cause sepsis—all actions that would clearly be punished with the utmost severity if committed in the UK. They are also things of which the tourists who go to see them are almost always unaware ...

This is about not just animal welfare but human welfare too, as animals treated with such abject cruelty can often themselves become highly dangerous. Asian elephants, when provoked, can attack, often fatally. According to Save the Asian Elephants, at least 700 tourists and others have been killed in the past generation, and 900 more have sustained catastrophic injuries.

While preparing for this debate, I was privileged to meet Helen Costigan, whose 20-year-old sister Andrea died tragically on a visit to Thailand in 2000 when an elephant, which had been trained in the barbaric way I described, charged her at the Nong Nooch resort. Nearly a quarter of a century on, this cruel and dangerous resort, still with no safety measures in place, is still promoted to unsuspecting tourists by 120 UK-based entities. Helen supports the Bill and is working with Save the Asian Elephants not just to help bring an end to animal cruelty but to save human lives too.

We cannot do this on our own. This is a global problem, but it is incumbent on us to do all we can to lead the way. The Bill is not a magic wand, but it will do a huge amount to tackle the problem at source by ending in England and Northern Ireland the sale and advertising of tourism to places abroad where wildlife is cruelly exploited in the way I described, and because of the size of the UK market that will make a real impact. ... 2 million UK tourists visited India and Thailand, with nearly a third of those visiting Thailand reporting having ridden or tried to ride an elephant, unaware of the cruelty, and indeed the danger to human life, involved in it. More than 1,200 companies in the UK market currently promote almost 300 overseas so-called attractions which often make their money from the barbaric treatment of Asian elephants. We sit on top of an awful, unchecked market, feeding violence against animals, malnutrition, overwork, loneliness and despair.

Along with the work being done by the industry on a voluntary basis, the Bill will make a significant difference by dampening demand. How will it work? Clauses 1 and 2 set up a framework of offences involving the sale and advertising of low-welfare animal activities abroad. Clause 3 outlines the penalties, prosecutions and liabilities for offences under the legislation. Clause 4 provides relevant enforcement powers. Clause 5 establishes procedures for making regulations in the UK Parliament and the Northern Ireland legislature, while Clauses 6 and 7 deal with interpretation and the territorial extent of the Bill. Noble Lords will have noted that the Bill relates only to England and Northern Ireland. The devolved Administrations in Scotland and Wales have the power to choose what UK government legislation they wish to consent to, and I hope they will look carefully at the Bill, particularly in view of the huge public support for action across all parts of the UK, including Scotland and Wales. …

Baroness Hodgson of Abinger (Con)

My Lords, I stand to speak in support of this Private Member's Bill and to congratulate Angela Richardson MP in the other place and my noble friend Lord Black on ensuring its introduction and safe passage through Parliament. I am delighted to support the Bill, which will ban the promotion and sale of activities abroad where animals are ill treated and harmed for tourism.

Charles Darwin wrote:

"The love for all living creatures is the most noble attribute of man."

I am a pet owner and feel strongly that we should ensure that animals in our care are treated with kindness. Like my noble friend, I believe that animal welfare is one of the litmus tests of a civilised society, and I hope others agree that it is intolerable that animals should be subjected to trauma, fear and pain.

As has already been highlighted, the scale of animal cruelty in wildlife tourism cannot be overestimated. More than 500,000 animals are currently known to be involved in tourist entertainment in low-welfare establishments where cruel and inhumane training methods are often used to force animals into submission. World Animal Protection's 2016 report found that three in four wildlife tourist attractions involve some form of conservation concern or animal abuse. These ratings were based on animals' ability to experience five freedoms that we take for granted: freedom from hunger and thirst; freedom from discomfort; freedom from pain, injury and disease; freedom from fear and distress; and freedom to behave normally. We should not and must not stand by.

This legislation will prevent UK travel companies profiting from and fuelling the problem. While I understand that there has been guidance from the Association of British Travel Agents, it is only voluntary and has not been taken up widely enough. We need to ensure that tourists are informed so that they choose not to buy holidays involving animals that have been treated cruelly. While I am proud that this country has one of the highest animal welfare records in the world, and I was pleased to read the cross-party and government support this Bill had as it passed through the other place, we must not be complacent. Exploitation and unethical methods of training should not be used to force animals into submission.

Like my noble friend, I was sent horrific and sickening photos by organisations lobbying for the Bill. My noble friend described how Asian elephants, in particular, suffer from extreme cruelty. They are often snatched in the wild, with their mothers killed in front of them, and then their spirit is broken by isolation, starvation, stabbings and beatings to make them easy to use for tourism. The captive trade in primates is threatening some species with extinction, all for an Instagram cuddle. Many big cats in captivity, such as tigers, lions and leopards, may have been deliberately separated from their mothers just days after being born, depriving them of the nutritious milk necessary for their growth and development, as well as maternal care. As we heard, when they become too dangerous to handle, they are often killed or sold. Many lions in South Africa cuddled by paying tourists when they were cubs may end up being shot by paying trophy hunters. There are around 3,500 whales and dolphins languishing in small concrete tanks around the world, deprived of their natural habitat.

It is not just the horrific treatment of the animals involved in tourist entertainment. We also need to consider the wider risks that low welfare standards bring. For example, Save the Asian Elephants research reports that the number of Asian elephants engaged in tourism in Thailand has increased by 70% in recent years, yet the global population has crashed from millions in the 19th century to barely 40,000 today, with an estimated 40% of them in captivity. Asian elephants are now considered an endangered series, and there are wider biodiversity, ecosystem and environmental impacts as the megagardeners of the forests are being enslaved. Unethical tourism has contributed to too many species suffering dramatic decline.

Before I finish, I too pay tribute to my noble friend Lady Fookes, who has spoken so often and is such a powerful advocate for animal welfare. We hope to see her back in the House soon.

To conclude, UK travel companies should not sell wildlife holidays that involve animal cruelty, and we should encourage other nations to do likewise. As it is so powerful, I beg the indulgence of the House to use Mahatma Gandhi's quote again:

> "The greatness of a nation and its moral progress can be judged by the way its animals are treated".

I support the Bill and wish it a speedy passage through our House. …

The Minister of State, Department for Environment, Food and Rural Affairs (Lord Benyon) (Con)

My Lords, I am grateful to all who have spoken in this debate. I am pleased to be speaking in support of the Bill and to see such interest in this legislation from across the House. I pay tribute to my noble friend Lord Black and his colleague in the other place, Angela Richardson, for the eloquence and passion that they have put into this and the excellent work they have done with a variety of different organisations to make sure that we have some legislation here that will be effective and will reflect both the need and what our public demand, which is ever higher animal welfare standards.

This legislation is welcome, as domestic travel agents are currently able to advertise and sell unacceptably low-welfare activities abroad to tourists without any regulation. The Bill will prohibit the advertising and offering for sale in England and Northern Ireland of tourist-related activities abroad involving animals. The Bill will provide a framework under which secondary legislation may be used to implement bans on specific low-welfare activities abroad, examples of which include riding, bathing and taking selfies with animals. The animals used in such practices are often trained using, as my noble friend said, brutal methods that allow tourists to get within touching distance of them. For any activity to be deemed within scope of a specific ban will involve animals that are kept in conditions or subject to treatment that would not be permitted under the Animal Welfare Act 2006 or the Welfare of Animals Act (Northern Ireland) 2011.

Throughout the Bill's passage it has been made clear that low-welfare activities involving Asian elephants are likely to fall within the scope of this legislation. There has been especially strong support for a ban to be introduced in this area. Asian elephant rides, bathing and other similar activities are extremely popular with tourists. However, aside from the suboptimal conditions that the elephants are often kept in, what is not seen is the cruel training methods that they are subject to in order to make them a safe tourist attraction.

While close interactions with captive wild animals are seen by many as a once-in-a-lifetime experience, surely it would be far more fulfilling to observe these animals displaying natural behaviours in natural environments in just the way that nature intended. The Bill aims to encourage tourists to visit high-welfare attractions where animals are free to display more natural behaviours and cruel practices are not used to train them for human entertainment.

World Animal Protection's 2022 report *The Real Responsible Traveller* states that sanctuaries that are certified by the Global Federation of Animal Sanctuaries, and which do not breed for commercial purposes, are likely to offer the highest standards of care to their animals. An example of a high-welfare attraction is ChangChill in northern Thailand, which has become one of the first elephant attractions to transition to an observation-only model. The venue has become a popular tourist attraction, demonstrating that there is a demand for animal-friendly, observation-only tourism.

A scant look at what is being advertised as we sit here today shows quite the opposite in other locations. From the comfort of the UK you can

> "pre-book your joy ride on the back of an elephant"

without any knowledge of what that elephant went through in order for you to have an experience that you might think was trouble-free but, clearly, so often is not.

It has been predicted that, as the travel industry picks up following the pandemic, the UK's outbound travel figures will surpass pre-pandemic levels. It has been estimated that by 2024 up to 86.9 million outbound travel bookings could be made per year. In 2019, 79% of travellers who witnessed animal cruelty said they would pay more for an activity where they knew that the animals did not suffer. However, it is often difficult for tourists to make that judgment [sic] on whether the animals they are interacting with are, or have been, subject to cruelty.

I join the noble Baroness in paying tribute to Save the Asian Elephants for the endless work that it has done on this and so many other areas in protecting this extremely at-risk species. Today I also remember my late friend Mark Shand, who set up and ran Elephant Family, which continues to do noble work in trying to create the wildlife corridors that will allow that extraordinary species to survive in its own environment at a time when there is huge human pressure on it, as there is on so many species.

I shall address some of the questions that were put to me by the two noble Baronesses who represent their parties on the Front Bench. The Bill focuses on advertising and sales taking place in England or Northern Ireland, not those taking place abroad. If an advert is distributed by means of electronic transmission and the person does not carry on business in England or Northern Ireland, we could not prevent that from happening—that has to be said. However, we hope that, if we bring in a domestic ban, awareness-raising will influence potential tourists and dissuade them from pursuing unacceptable activities abroad.

The guidance that we are giving to enforcement bodies will be developed for trading standards in England and the Department for the Economy in Northern Ireland so they will be able to effectively enforce the Bill. The guidance will be produced as and when specific bans are introduced. ...

(From UK Parliament, 2023b; reproduced under Hansard Open Parliament Licence v3.0)

These are excerpts from the third reading of the Bill from Hansard Volume 832: debated on Monday 18 September 2023 (UK Parliament, 2023c).

Third Reading
Motion
Moved by

Lord Black of Brentwood (Con)
That the Bill do now pass.

My Lords, as this Bill relates to advertising, I declare an interest as a director of the Advertising Standards Board of Finance and note my other interests.

I thank all those in this House and beyond who have been involved in the passage of this extremely important piece of animal welfare legislation. It is a world first, and underlines yet again the shining commitment of the UK and this Government to the protection of animals, not just within our own shores but internationally. The Bill started in another place, and I want to record my deep thanks to Angela Richardson MP for stewarding it so effectively there. I am in her debt. …

I want to single out Save the Asian Elephants and its indefatigable CEO [chief executive officer], Duncan McNair, who has campaigned long and hard for this legislation with great skill and energy. Indeed, he devised the original concept of the Bill and has worked tirelessly on it; we would not be here without him. To all those who have been involved and who have campaigned, I say: this is your day, and you deserve it. …

Bill passed.

(From UK Parliament, 2023c; reproduced under Hansard Open Parliament Licence v3.0)

Royal Assent

Royal assent is the monarch's agreement to make a Bill into an Act of Law. The Animals (Low-Welfare Activities Abroad) Act was granted royal assent by the new monarch, His Majesty King Charles III of the United Kingdom of Great Britain and Northern Ireland, immediately after the third reading, on 18 September 2023.

The full text of the Animals (Low-Welfare Activities Abroad) Act 2023 can be read at: https://www.legislation.gov.uk/ukpga/2023/45/introduction/enacted (accessed 20 February 2025).

Bibliography

Burkart, A.J. and Medlik, S. (1974) *Tourism: Past, Present and Future*. Hienemann, Hamburg, Germany.

UK Parliament (n.d.) Royal Assent. Available at: https://www.parliament.uk/about/how/laws/passage-bill/lords/lrds-royal-assent (accessed 20 February 2025).

UK Parliament (2023a) Animals (Low-Welfare Activities Abroad) Bill: debated on Wednesday 8 March 2023. Hansard. Available at: https://hansard.parliament.uk/commons/2023-03-08/debates/aab91687-2917-453c-bc43-7cdc12dca64d/Animal(Low-WelfareActivitiesAbroad)Bill (accessed 20 February 2025).

UK Parliament (2023b) Animals (Low-Welfare Activities Abroad) Bill. Hansard Volume 831: debated on Friday 14 July 2023. Available at: https://hansard.parliament.uk/Lords/2023-07-

14/debates/3650A99C-4D35-4EFE-A6E3-2D17052FF2E7/Animals(Low-WelfareActivitiesAbroad) Bill (accessed 20 February 2025).

UK Parliament (2023c) Animals (Low-Welfare Activities Abroad) Bill. Hansard Volume 832: debated on Monday 18 September 2023. Available at: https://hansard.parliament.uk/lords/2023-09-18/debates/485939E2-68A1-4B21-BE68-92A8EF2ACCB3/Animals(Low-WelfareActivitiesAbroad)Bill (accessed 20 February 2025).

World Animal Protection (2022) *The Real Responsible Traveller.* Report by World Animal Protection. Available at: https://www.worldanimalprotection.org/our-campaigns/wildlife/commercial-exploitation/travel-tourism/the-real-responsible-traveller/ (accessed 20 February 2025).

11 The UK Trophy Hunting Import Ban, Hansard

Eric Laws*

retired Professor of Tourism

Abstract

Archaeological investigation shows that humans have hunted large animals including elephants for meat for thousands of years. This chapter presents excerpts from the UK Parliament's House of Commons debate on the Hunting Trophies (Import Prohibition) Bill 2023–2024 during which a range of views were put forward, mainly in support of the Bill. However, a national election was held in July 2024, consequently this Bill has not been passed into UK law at the time of writing.

Introduction

Archaeological investigation shows that humans have hunted large animals including elephants for meat since 125,000 years ago (Ben-Dor and Barkai, 2020).

Hunting continues, usually under a licence from local or central government agencies. Palmer, a dentist from Minnesota, is said to have paid US$54,000 to bow-hunt Cecil, a magnificent, black-maned, 13-year-old lion who lived in Zimbabwe's Hwange National Park and was well known to visitors (World Animal Protection, 2022). On 1 July 2015 he shot Cecil with an arrow on a farm outside the park. The team of fellow hunters tracked the famed cat and shot him again 11 hours later. Two years later, Cecil's son Xanda, a 6-year-old lion with several young cubs, was shot dead by a trophy hunter, outside the same national park where his father died (University of Oxford, 2017).

African hunting is controversial because the species involved (lions, elephants, giraffes, etc.) are iconic, highly anthropomorphized and sometimes endangered. Both species extinction and species overpopulation are issues in

*e.laws@runbox.com

 Elephant Welfare in Global Tourism (E. Laws *et al.* eds)
DOI: 10.1079/9781836990093.0011

Table 11.1. The true cost of trophy hunting a lion. Adapted from World Animal Protection, 2022.

- Trophy hunting disrupts the social bonds important for a pride – removing one member causes stress.
- When a dominant male is killed, the pride becomes vulnerable to attacks from other males looking to take over.
- Hunting may increase the killing of cubs within prides, that could be the offspring of the deceased dominant male.
- When females are targeted, if they have young, they are likely to fall victim to starvation or be killed by predators.

Africa. Corruption, poverty, poaching and imposing Western wildlife ideals on Africa are also important factors.

McCubbin (2020) argued that the 'Cecil Moment' operated through a more-than-human network which served to channel agency unleashed by Cecil's death to the already empowered lion conservation actors, as well as mutable meanings that shifted Cecil Moment focus away from trophy hunting and towards lion conservation in general.

Every wild animal contributes to the interactions and dynamics of the population and ecosystem they live in. That is especially true of lion prides (see Table 11.1).

Attempts are underway to provide an alternative source of funds to hunting (Moorhouse *et al.*, 2023).

> Trophy hunting treats wild animals as resources to be exploited for commercial gain, rather than respecting them as the sentient beings they are. It is outdated and inhumane. Lions are not trophies; they are not medicine; they are not entertainers. They are wild animals with the right to a wild life.
>
> (Kabisiime, 2022)

This chapter now presents excerpts from the UK Parliament's House of Commons debate on the Hunting Trophies (Import Prohibition) Bill 2023–2024 (UK Parliament, 2024), during which a range of views were put forward, mainly in support of the Bill. However, a national election was held in July 2024, consequently this Bill has not been passed into UK law at the time of writing.

House of Commons Debate on the Hunting Trophies (Import Prohibition) Bill 2023–2024

These are excerpts from the Hunting Trophies (Import Prohibition) Bill, Hansard Volume 747: debated on Friday 22 March 2024 (UK Parliament, 2024). They are reproduced here under the terms of the Open Parliament Licence v.3.0 (available at: https://www.parliament.uk/site-information/copyright-parliament/open-parliament-licence/ (accessed 26 February 2025)).[1]

Second Reading

John Spellar (Warley) (Lab [Labour])

I beg to move, That the Bill be now read a Second time.

Often in debates that have had a long genesis and been considered many times in the House, there is that hackneyed phrase: everything that needs to be said has been said, but not everyone has said it. One cannot even use that phrase now, because everyone has said what they need to say many times over. Of course, that is not true in this case, not least because of the Bill tabled and pioneered very ably by the hon. Member for Crawley (Henry Smith) in the last Session of Parliament. The clear and overwhelming view of this House was that the legislation should go forward. …

Dr Thérèse Coffey (Suffolk Coastal) (Con [Conservative])

About this time last year, on Report, we reached somewhat of a compromise consensus on the Bill that left this place and went to the Lords. Am I right in thinking that the right hon. Gentleman has reintroduced the exact same Bill on which this House reached consensus last year? The Bill technically does not stop hunting; it simply stops the import into this country of any animal protected by the convention on international trade in endangered species of wild fauna and flora.

John Spellar

I thank the right hon. Lady for those comments, and for the work that she undertook as the Secretary of State to support this legislation. Given that we wish to speed the progress of this legislation, I hope that colleagues will not be prone to making long speeches on this issue—indeed, possibly not even medium or short speeches. Subject to Madam Deputy Speaker, I intend to be very generous with my taking of interventions, because right hon. and hon. Members want to ensure that the strong feelings of their constituents—which are made very clear every time this issue comes up—are expressed in this House, so that those constituents know that Parliament is listening and undertaking a course of action.

Justin Madders (Ellesmere Port and Neston) (Lab)

…

I wanted to make the point that he has just made—namely, that there is overwhelming public support for this measure. A number of constituents have contacted me to express their support; as he said, time and again surveys show huge public demand for this. Does he agree that it is important that we get the Bill through as swiftly as possible, so that those in the other place are able to do as much as they can as quickly as they can?

John Spellar

I make no apologies for being regularly re-elected to this place over a number of decades. I am sure that my hon. Friend speaks effectively for his constituents in Ellesmere Port, and I suspect residents in Bebington probably hold similar views. That is important. Sometimes issues come before the House that reflect views from certain parts of the country—there are often arguments that reflect the views of those in the metropolis, or the inner metropolis and the metropolitan elite—but this issue runs across parties, across classes and across regions. This is a universal view across the country. People want this country to have no part in this vile trade.

Kim Leadbeater (Batley and Spen) (Lab)

My right hon. Friend makes an important point. Like many hon. Members, I have received hundreds of emails from my constituents in Batley and Spen, who are appalled at the vile trade of trophy hunting. Does he agree that the Bill will not only prevent the importation of hunting trophies to the UK, but it will also send a powerful message to countries around the world that hunting and killing endangered animals for trophies is always unacceptable, and that much more must be done to prevent that atrocious act wherever it occurs?

John Spellar

I thank my hon. Friend for that contribution, and for the work she has been undertaking on this issue, quite apart from the Bill. She is absolutely right. Other countries, including Australia, France and Belgium—I think there are a couple of others—have already shown the way by banning the trade in hunting trophies, and I hope that what we decide here will start to send a message to other countries that this is an international movement. As we always realise, society and opinions evolve. This country has the Bullring in Birmingham, but we no longer torment bulls with dogs in a public arena, or engage in bear baiting or cock fighting. We have moved on from that and we need to move on from trophy hunting, not least because of the decline in species.

Some of the arguments relate very much to Africa, but I remind colleagues—I pay tribute to the campaign by the *Daily Express* on this—that other regions of the world are also involved, such as polar bears in Canada. The Bill demonstrates that the public do not want those magnificent creatures to be slaughtered not only for a bizarre form of pleasure, but to decorate people's houses. They do not understand it.

Lilian Greenwood (Nottingham South) (Lab)

I congratulate my right hon. Friend on bringing this Bill forward. Is it not the case that this legislation is supported by campaigners in many countries, including in Africa? They love their animals and recognise that there is much more to be gained and it is much more profitable to keep these animals alive, rather than to allow this barbaric practice.

John Spellar

My hon. Friend is clearly speaking on behalf of her constituents in Nottingham in expressing those strong views. In a number of programmes yesterday, I pointed out that for the long-term sustainable future of tourism in these countries, it is much better to have tourists shooting animals with cameras rather than with rifles and crossbows. We need to look towards a future of sustainable species and people being able to enjoy these animals not just through historical videos from David Attenborough, but by visiting themselves. That gives rise to a great and long-term industry.

Tim Loughton (East Worthing and Shoreham) (Con)

I agree with everything that the right hon. Gentleman has said, as well as paying tribute to my Sussex colleague, my hon. Friend the Member for Crawley (Henry Smith), for having persevered with this issue for so long. We should not be here; this legislation should have gone through already. I have been struck by the number of emails I have had from my constituents about how important this matter is, so may I make a practical offer to Members of the House of Lords who are minded to try to sabotage the Bill again? I speak as the chairman of the all-party parliamentary group for photography, and we will have a special category in the exhibition this year for wildlife photos, so that those Members can show how brave and manly they are by getting up close with cameras rather than guns. Is that a deal?

John Spellar

I am not sure their knees could take it, but that is a further matter. I absolutely take the point that the hon. Gentleman makes, and he is right about expanding the scope so that people can show their skill in photography and show these magnificent creatures in their natural environment. That is the record they should have—not some grisly trophy on the wall. I fully understand his point. ...

Theresa Villiers (Chipping Barnet) (Con)

I think it was the distressing case of the killing of Cecil the lion that alerted many people to what is happening. I, too, have many constituents in Chipping Barnet who want this Bill to go through. That is why I am here today to support it. ...

Dean Russell (Watford) (Con)

I thank the right hon. Gentleman for giving way, and I pay tribute to my hon. Friend the Member for Crawley (Henry Smith). Today feels a bit like déjà vu. We are back here again, but that sends a message to our friends in the Lords that we will not give up. This legislation is the right thing to do. It is an abhorrent act to go to another country and kill an endangered animal in order to stick its head on a wall. It seems like something from a totally different century. The fact that we are back again, fighting for the right cause and standing on the shoulders of the giants who have gone before us sends an important message to both the House of Lords and the country. ...

John McDonnell (Hayes and Harlington) (Lab)

There has in the past been the argument that trophy hunting performs the role of culling for protected species. We have always been able to negate that argument. There are times when there is a strategy for culling certain species, but that is done on the basis of scientific fact rather than inhumane delight at the killing of animals. ...

John Spellar

My right hon. Friend is absolutely right, but there is another factor to consider. The elephants taken out are the big leaders of the tribe. That has a significant effect on the gene pool. There is already some evidence that elephants with smaller tusks are surviving and therefore, contrary to natural selection, changes are taking place to their appearance. Also, some hunters do not seem to accept that, although some are solitary, many animals live in social structures. We saw that with the death of Cecil the lion and we see with elephants that the social structure and cohesion of elephant herds are completely disrupted. That applies to other creatures as well. Hunting is to the detriment of gene selection and the development and maintenance of groups of species.

Clive Efford (Eltham) (Lab)

I wholeheartedly support my right hon. Friend's Bill. As in the title of the Bill, these people are after trophies. They will not select the weakest in the herd or the pride. They will go for the one that looks the most magnificent on their wall or wherever they want to display it. Therefore, they are taking out the strongest, weakening the gene pool and having exactly the opposite effect on conservation. ...

John McNally (Falkirk) (Scottish National Party)

I totally agree with the right hon. Member on that point. I support the Bill because I stand with many of my Falkirk constituents who have written to me on the issue. He mentioned many of the non-governmental organisations [NGOs].

I have been heavily involved with FOUR PAWS in the UK, which has provided so much useful information to me on the subject over a long while. As we all know, this is a non-partisan issue. MPs from all corners of the House have spoken at great length and passionately on the totally incomprehensible nature of this brutal sport. Enough talking—the time is to make this actually happen. …

John Spellar

…
There is one particular aspect that I want to highlight. We have talked a lot about hunting in the wild, but there is the even more deplorable business of so-called canned hunting, where animals, especially lions, are bred in an enclosure to be shot by depraved individuals who want a trophy. I pay tribute to Lord Ashcroft—again, someone with whom I might disagree on other issues—who has spent a considerable amount of time campaigning on and instigating research into that appalling trade. I hope the Bill will help reduce the attraction to such trade. One firm involved in that dreadful trade advertised that

> "Your hunt is never complete, until you receive your animals at home for you to reminisce and re-call your experiences for the rest of your life."

Do we really want to be associated with people who take that sort of attitude? …

Sir Christopher Chope (Christchurch) (Con)

Will the right hon. Gentleman take us through the clauses of the Bill? Clause 4 was incorporated as a result of the acceptance of one of my amendments when this Bill was last debated. Clause 4 has not yet been explained, and I would be interested to know whether the right hon. Gentleman supports it, and how he thinks it will work in practice.

John Spellar

I thank the hon. Gentleman, who sits with me on the British-American Parliamentary Group; we are joint officers. I consider him a parliamentary friend. I thank him for highlighting the fact that the Bill was amended to take account of various views. It was carried forward without dissent in this House, and was forwarded to the Lords. That is precisely why the Bill should be voted on again, sent back to the other House, and incorporated into the laws of this land.

Henry Smith (Crawley) (Con)

…
As the right hon. Member for Warley said, the practice that we are discussing is not unique to Africa. Claims have been made that somehow this is racist legislation that tells countries around the world how to act and conduct their hunting policy. Let us just remind ourselves that this Bill is import legislation; it says that we in this country, by a clear majority, choose not to allow the importation of body parts of endangered species slaughtered by hunters to Great Britain; that is the territorial extent of this Bill and what it is designed to do. Nevertheless, it would send a strong signal that these practices are deeply damaging to conservation, as he eloquently said. Damage is done to the gene pool by taking out the top animals in a pride of lions, or the big tuskers from a herd of elephants. That is beginning to damage the ability of those animals to survive. Let us remind ourselves of what this Bill is about. It is not about banning hunting, although I might have a view on that; it is about protecting endangered species before it is too late.

Sir Christopher Chope

In my hon. Friend's tour of Africa, did he have the opportunity to meet President Masisi of Botswana, who has described western interventions as "a racist onslaught"? He has said:

> "It's racism. They talk as if we are the grass the elephants eat. It startles me when people sit in the comfort of where they are and lecture us about the management of species they don't have."

Henry Smith

I have not met the current President of Botswana, but I have met the previous one, President Khama, on a number of occasions. He is passionate about ending trophy hunting, because it is not typical African communities who benefit from it, but the big industry that supports it. Botswana is a good example, because in such countries there is a huge difference of opinion over whether trophy hunting should go ahead.

Clive Efford

I pay tribute to the hon. Gentleman for the work he has done on this issue. Is not the answer to the point made by the hon. Member for Christchurch (Sir Christopher Chope) that the Bill deals with the import of trophies to the UK, and says nothing about Botswana?

Henry Smith

The hon. Gentleman is absolutely correct. As I said, this is import legislation; its territorial extent is Great Britain. It is about what we choose to import to this country, and a clear majority of the British people do not want the body parts of endangered species imported here, because they care about these majestic species and want them to continue to exist, for the sake of their children, grandchildren and many generations to come. The idea that killing an endangered species saves an endangered species is absurd and should be called out for what it is.

Dean Russell

I, too, pay tribute to my hon. Friend for the work that he has done on this issue. I reiterate that it is absurd that we are back here, because this House agreed unanimously to take this Bill through. My constituents, who are very far away from many of the countries in which this practice happens, are absolutely passionate about ending it. However, as has been stated, this Bill is not about the practices in those countries; it is about what we import to our country. If we do anything, we should make sure that we end this abhorrent act of importing the carcases of endangered animals for people to stick on their wall.

Henry Smith

I am grateful to my hon. Friend, who has been stalwart in supporting me in this campaign. He is absolutely right to remind us again about what the legislation does; it is about what we choose to import or not to this country.

The Bill applies to the importation of endangered species' body parts, no matter where in the world the animals were hunted, so it would also prohibit the importation of trophies hunted from polar bears in Canada, as the right hon. Member for Warley said. We do not hear people claiming that we are being racist against the Canadians because we choose not to import endangered polar bears. We need to remind ourselves what the legislation does. …

Rosie Duffield (Canterbury) (Lab)

All of us here are familiar with the term "trophy hunting". We have come to recognise the evil acts that those two harmless-sounding words represent, but for those watching who may be less familiar with the term, animal welfare organisations such as SPCA [Society for the Prevention of Cruelty to Animals] International define it as

> "the hunting of...animals for sport, not for food. Usually, the animal is stuffed or a body part is kept for display."

They go on:

> "Many hunters claim that trophy hunting isn't bad for animals. They say they are supporting animal conservation. The opposite is true, live animals support the population of their species."

The League against Cruel Sports says:

> "We believe this multi-million pound industry is unjustifiable from an animal welfare point of view, but also for conservation, as it is responsible for endangering several species around the world."

As for "sport", that word is usually reserved for activities that revolve around the more positive aspects of life: fitness, healthy competition, teamwork, friendship, personal achievement, endeavour and endurance. Not a single one of those could be attributed to an activity that involves an individual choosing to photograph themselves grinning triumphantly as they celebrate killing a once gentle and graceful giraffe, whose lifeless body now lies slumped and twisted at their feet, pumped full of deadly bullets. My good friend the vet and animal welfare campaigner Dr Marc Abraham OBE agrees. He says:

> "Anyone with an ounce of compassion and kindness despairs at seeing these images of cowardly, pathetic trophy hunters grinning over their still-warm kill. Exploited animals used as pathetic props to maintain, even elevate, an online self-image of superiority, without any shred of guilt or conscience."

He describes those taking part in these killings as having

> "a tragic lack of empathy and the highest form of narcissism",

and says that

> "to be complicit in this most extreme, callous form of animal cruelty, plus then to harvest the body parts and ship them back home to the UK, couldn't be a clearer indicator of violent antisocial behaviour."

Every Member of this House will have had emails and letters from, and meetings with, constituents who love and value animals, and loathe those who exploit, harm or kill them. There are so many British people who show such kindness—who campaign on behalf of animal charities, who volunteer, who make donations or fundraise, and who share a love for our planet and the incredible, breathtaking wildlife that we are so fortunate to benefit from. How dare a few wealthy individuals decide that they have the right to buy and cause the death of a lion, polar bear or elephant.

Alongside our constituents, there are those who use their fame and public platforms to fight for the protection of animals. Those campaigners include frequent visitors to Parliament whose passion is infectious—people such as the wonderful Peter Egan, friend to many in this place, who for years has fought hard to raise awareness and keep a ban on trophy hunting imports at the top of MPs' agendas. Peter works with the fantastic campaigner Eduardo Goncalves, who we talked about earlier, and who is supported by many across this House, including my right hon. Friend the Member for Warley (John Spellar), who has never given up fighting to protect animals during his time here. He steps down at the next general election, but it is vital that we carry on his compassionate work. I absolutely pledge to do that to the best of my ability.

No speech about animal welfare should leave out top animal champion Ricky Gervais. He could spend his days polishing his many awards, but instead he chooses to condemn trophy hunting and shame those who consider the murder of animals to be a hobby. He supports the ban and has called trophy hunting

> "humanity at its very worst".

The murder of animals for fun is also condemned by Chris Packham, Bill Bailey, Joanna Lumley and Sir Ranulph Fiennes, as well as MPs and activists across the political divide and those with no political affiliation whatsoever. The legendary Jane Goodall said:

> "Trophy hunting is utterly cruel, utterly unnecessary and utterly disastrous from a conservation perspective. It inflicts pain and suffering on animals for no other reason than to boast of some ephemeral 'prowess'. There is no material human need met by it; it is a hobby, pure and simple, and a deeply wrong one at that."

I urge colleagues to support the Bill. I sincerely thank my right hon. Friend the Member for Warley for bringing it forward. I echo the words of the Humane Society and say that there is "no excuse" for trophy hunting, so let us get the ban done.

Sir Bill Wiggin (North Herefordshire) (Con)

The one thing that unites the House is that we all want to see successful conservation, but this Bill has always been about racism and neocolonialism. This Bill is questioned by science and by African countries. If anybody, no matter how much they think they love animals, is thinking about writing to me or contacting me about trophy hunting, I insist that they seriously consider what African representatives have said about both the Bill and the people who support it.

Over the last 22 years, 73 CITES-listed species of animal have been imported as hunting trophies. In the same period, the pet industry has traded in over 560 listed species. If hon. Members care about CITES [Convention on International Trade in Endangered Species], then perhaps the Bill should include pets as well.

I do not believe anybody in the House intends to be racist, but this Bill crosses the line. The Namibian Environment Minister, Pohamba Shifeta, has written to our Environment Secretary denouncing the Bill as

> "regressive step towards neo-colonialism... Your bill implies that your judgments supersede our insights and expertise... Such unilateral actions, made without consultation and collaboration with us...challenges the sovereignty of nations like Namibia."

We have talked about Botswana and I will quote what President Masisi says. It is worth remembering that Botswana had 50,000 elephants; it now has 130,000 elephants. The population increases year on year by about 5,000 elephants. Some 400 trophy hunting licences are issued, but those licences have never all been taken up. When President Masisi describes intervention in Africa's wildlife as "a racist onslaught" ... the Namibian Environment Minister, Pohamba Shifeta, says this is

> "regressive step towards neo-colonialism"—

whether it is meant that way or not. He goes on to say,

> "Your bill implies that your judgments supersede our insights"—

those of the people who actually look after these animals. He says:

> "Such unilateral actions, made without consultation…challenges the sovereignty".

President Masisi said that this is "a racist onslaught" from people who "sit in the comfort of where they are and lecture us about the management of species they don't have".

He was not just speaking for himself. Last November, *The Times*, *The Telegraph* and the *Daily Mail* reported that ordinary Africans share the President's view. The paper quoted from a survey of 4,000 people in Botswana, Malawi, Mozambique, Namibia, South Africa, Tanzania, Zambia and Zimbabwe who said that the UK legislation was "racist" and "neocolonial". That is what they are saying about us. Although I respect the sovereignty of this House, I would not like it if they said things like that about us, and I am astonished that the hon. Gentleman does.

Peter Dowd (Bootle) (Lab)

I do not read *The Times* very often, but the hon. Member said that the African community leaders and conservationists he referred to rightly argue that it is not for us in the west [sic] to decide how they should manage their wildlife, and that that is why he cannot endorse the Bill. I am not telling them how to manage their wildlife, or demanding that they do it in a certain way. What I and many Members in this House are saying is that we do not want those disgusting trophies in this country. It is simple.

Sir Bill Wiggin

…

In 2016, briefings from the International Union for Conservation of Nature stated that

> "legal, well regulated trophy hunting programs can, and do, play an important role in delivering benefits for both wildlife conservation and for the livelihoods and wellbeing of indigenous and local communities".

In a letter to the Secretary of State for Environment, Food and Rural Affairs, Namibia's Minister for Environment and Tourism said:

> "We are most concerned about how this proposed law would undermine the finances of our Protected Areas and Conservancies… The lack of dedicated land and the protection which protected hunting pays for would critically undermine the survival of species which we all love."

He went on to say:

> "The implications of this legislation, therefore, extend far beyond what has become known as 'trophy' hunting, potentially impacting the livelihoods of rural communities that rely on the revenue it generates."

A joint statement from southern African Government representatives in the UK opposed the Bill.

Peter Dowd

I think the hon. Gentleman indicated that only 1% of trophies have come to this country. If it is only 1%, enacting this piece of legislation will not make that much difference to those countries, will it?

Sir Bill Wiggin

It would make enough difference for the hon. Gentleman to turn up for the debate, and for me to do so. It would also make enough difference for all the representatives of those southern African countries who care about the creatures that we all purport to care about to say that the Bill is wrong. In fact, they said:

> "If income streams from trophy hunting were substantially reduced—as would be the outcome of this Bill—land would be abandoned and subject to poaching, or converted to less biodiversity-friendly uses, such as agriculture and livestock production. Local communities who live near and with wildlife would suffer."

I think it is pretty clear that they do not think that the hon. Gentleman is right. The statement ends:

> "Southern Africa's track record on conservation is world-leading, and we use trophy hunting to do it. Let us continue to do so."

I recognise that that is awkward for Opposition Members who care about animals, but the people who are responsible for those animals are telling us that we are wrong.

Botswana is the top country in the world for large animals, with Namibia second and Tanzania third. All three countries have paid hunting, which finances protected space and armed guards for those animals. The country that is 123rd in the world—that is us—is, in the words of David Attenborough, one of

> "the most nature depleted countries in the world".

We got rid of the last brown bear 1,000 years ago and our last wolves 264 years ago.

Africa's human population has risen eightfold during our lifetimes, causing immense pressure on the land available for wildlife. That means that Africans increasingly come into conflict with big animals, which may eat their goats, threaten their children or trample their villages. Last year, Botswana's Minister for Environment and Tourism started an article published in the *Daily Mail* by saying:

> "Last month, I attended the funeral of two villagers in my homeland, Botswana. Both were in their teens, tragically killed by charging wild buffalo as they travelled to school and work. Sadly, this was not an isolated incident." …

she says, we

> "all too often…focus solely on animal welfare at the expense of human life in Africa." …

Ruth Jones (Newport West) (Lab)

I am pleased to speak on this important Bill. The importation to the UK of trophies produced during the barbaric sport of trophy hunting should have ended a long time ago. I thank my right hon. Friend the Member for Warley (John Spellar) for introducing the Bill, following the earlier Bill from the hon. Member for Crawley (Henry Smith). We need to get this sorted today, because we have had Warley and Crawley, and I am not sure there is another constituency that rhymes.

I thank animal welfare charities nationwide, including FOUR PAWS, Humane Society International, World Animal Protection and Ban Trophy Hunting. They have worked tirelessly for years to ensure that this legislation is passed, and have produced the most helpful briefing note for this debate. I also pay tribute to the former President of Botswana, Ian Khama, who has been a tireless and passionate campaigner on these issues. …

The Bill will prevent people from bringing into Great Britain hunting trophies from the species listed in annex A, which are the most endangered species, or annex B, which are species threatened by commercial trade, of the principal wildlife trade regulation. Those lists largely correspond to equivalents in CITES, which is an important international agreement protecting endangered plants and animals, and the UK is a party to it. The Bill also creates an advisory board on hunting trophies, as some Conservative Members highlighted, which will advise the Secretary of State on any issues relating to the legislation, or any matter relating to the import to Great Britain of hunting trophies derived from species that are, or are likely to become, endangered.

I cannot emphasise enough how crucial this legislation is. Trophy hunting is not only barbaric, but wholly unnecessary. In this country, as in most others, we have long recognised that animals should not be subjected to unnecessary suffering. That principle is reflected domestically in our Animal Welfare Act 2006, and aligns with our understanding, supported by animal welfare science and enshrined in legislation, that animals are sentient beings. As such, they deserve to be treated with dignity and humanity.

There is nothing dignified or humane about the sport of trophy hunting. It involves killing innocent animals for the sole purpose of turning their bodies into trophies. The animals often experience immense pain, fear and distress in the moments before they die. Some may be shot by inexperienced hunters using less efficient weapons, such as crossbows or spears, which do not deliver a rapid death. We saw this with Cecil the lion in 2015, who suffered for several hours following his wounding by crossbow in a beautiful part of southern Africa before he was finally put out of his misery. His death quite rightly caused outrage around the world, including here in Britain.

Other practices that trophy hunting can involve raise further welfare concerns. I was horrified to learn of the practice of canned hunting—the captive wildlife farming of animals for hunting. It often involves inflicting extremely poor welfare conditions on the captive wild animals, mostly lions, who may have to suffer from unsatisfactory enclosures, a lack of enrichment, and insufficient provision of shelter and vet treatment, all so that part of their body may eventually become somebody's trophy. Let us not forget the negative impact that trophy hunting can have on other animals, such as the harm to offspring, who may be unable to survive on their own after their parent is left for dead. That was highlighted earlier, as was the weakening of the gene pool. These are important factors to consider.

Trophy hunting can have a negative impact on wildlife. Trophy hunters tend to target the world's most iconic animals, including endangered wild animal species such as lions, polar bears, giraffes and rhinos. Hunters selfishly kill these vulnerable animals so that they can display their body parts as some sort of perverse prize. World Animal Protection notes that British hunters have brought home approximately 25,000 hunting trophies since the 1980s, and approximately 5,000 of these came from species at risk of extinction. The public are right to find this absolutely abhorrent, and to want to increase the protection afforded to these species, which are already under pressure from habitat loss, climate change, poaching and the illegal wildlife trade, by passing this important legislation. My hon. Friend the Member for Canterbury (Rosie Duffield) eloquently outlined those issues earlier.

Let us not forget how unnecessary these horrors are. Compared with the overall revenue that local economies gain from tourism, income from trophy hunting is insignificant. A 2017 report by Economists at Large that analysed eight African countries found that while overall tourism was between 2.8% and 5.1% of GDP [gross domestic product] in the eight countries, the total economic contribution of trophy hunters was, at most, about 0.03% of GDP, in stark contrast to the claims made by some Conservative Members.

There are more ethical and sustainable alternatives to trophy hunting for conservation. A recent study showed that 84% of previous or potential tourists to South Africa, including those visiting from within Africa, would be willing to pay a daily "lion protection fee" for wildlife conservation. Photographic safaris, which, as the Born Free Foundation puts it, involves shooting an animal

"with a camera, not a gun",

is another welfare-friendly alternative to hunting trophies. These alternative activities have the potential to generate income equalling or even exceeding the income generated from trophy hunting without causing pain and suffering to wild animals. My hon. Friend the Member for Eltham highlighted that when he mentioned the amazing experience he had on his photographic safari.

Supporting global efforts to promote humane tourism is consistent with recent legislation passed in this House, namely the Animals (Low-Welfare Activities Abroad) Act 2023. However, I note that the Secretary of State for Environment, Food and Rural Affairs is yet to even consult on the activating regulations that are necessary for the 2023 Act to have any impact, or to give any indication of when such consultation will begin. I encourage him to do so as a matter of urgency, because wild animals deserve protection, and that requires regulatory action.

On this and so many animal welfare issues, the Government are letting animals and the public down by failing to act. As the shadow Secretary of State, my hon. Friend the Member for Croydon North (Steve Reed), pointed out last Friday when another private Member's Bill containing a broken Conservative party promise was before the House, the Government have completely abandoned an extraordinary number of the animal welfare pledges they had made. The Government like to tell the public that they have progressed world-leading animal welfare commitments, but Compassion in World Farming ranked the UK only ninth among European countries by percentage of cage-free farm animals, trailing Luxembourg, Austria, Sweden, the Netherlands, Germany, Slovenia, Denmark and Belgium. ...

The Parliamentary Under-Secretary of State for Environment, Food and Rural Affairs (Rebecca Pow)

...

It is clear that the issue of hunting trophies continues to divide opinion. We have witnessed some of that today from my hon. Friends the Members for Christchurch (Sir Christopher Chope) and for North Herefordshire (Sir Bill Wiggin). There is disagreement over the scientific, social, economic, moral and ethical rationales for trophy hunting, and that will no doubt continue for some time. There are those who point to evidence of the potential benefits of well-managed hunting—we heard a great deal about that from my hon. Friend the Member for North Herefordshire. We also heard the other side of the argument, with evidence of the harm caused by poor practice.

I want to stress something critical: we face the triple planetary crisis of biodiversity loss, climate change and pollution. Those are the greatest threats we face globally and, as the nature Minister, they are in my inbox every day. I am only too aware of all those threats and of how we need to tackle them. About 1 million animal and plant species face extinction. Much of that has occurred very recently—in our lifetime. The abundance, diversity and connectivity of species is declining faster than at any time in human history, and that includes the species targeted for trophy hunting. We all know and love them: elephants, rhinos, lions, leopards and polar bears, to name just a handful.

There are those who argue that banning the import of trophies from those animals will do nothing to improve their conservation status, and I am certainly listening to my hon. Friends on that, but we have to ask ourselves whether importing into Great Britain trophies from endangered animals helps to tackle biodiversity loss. Does this trade really help to secure a sustainable future for species on the brink of extinction? Many animals are under terrible threat anyway because their habitats are shrinking. That is happening for a range of social and economic reasons, but climate change is certainly part of it. Ultimately, the aim of the Bill is to ensure that imports of hunting trophies to Great Britain do not put additional pressure on already threatened species. That is what should concentrate our minds, and that is why I am pleased to confirm that the Government will support the Bill. In doing so, we signal our continued determination to fulfil our manifesto commitment in this regard.

I have heard the argument that a ban will have implications for local communities and conservation efforts globally, which is definitely something we must consider carefully. We must be alive to the unintended consequences. However, the Bill is about imports into Great Britain, as many have said in the debate—my right hon. Friend the Member for Suffolk Coastal reminded us of that. This is about listening to the British public. There is a clear, strong and consistent message that we need to bring to an end the imports of endangered animals taken as hunting trophies. The winds of change are blowing us in that direction, and a number of countries have already put restrictions in place. …

It is important to recognise that the import ban will not prevent a UK resident or citizen from participating in hunting while they are overseas. Trophy hunting can and will continue around the world. It is right that each country should be able to decide how best to manage its own wildlife, and the Bill does not change that. That point was highlighted vociferously by my hon. Friends the Members for Christchurch and for North Herefordshire, but it has to be remembered that we are not preventing that. Countries around the world on both sides of the debate have had regular opportunities to discuss this issue and raise their points. Indeed, we have had letters from the Presidents of Botswana and Namibia—the high commissioner was written to just yesterday.

It is important to keep in mind the contribution that the UK trade in hunting trophies makes. Annual imports of hunting trophies to the UK are very few in number—on average, there have been 73 a year over the last 10 years. Even so, it is essential that we play our part to ensure that communities around the world benefit from conserving the wildlife that they live alongside. That was reflected in the agreement of the hugely important global biodiversity framework. There is now a strong and essential focus on how, as a global community, we finance biodiversity, conservation and restoration work. Members will be aware of just how much the Government are doing on that front, with our huge £93 million Darwin initiative and our £30 million Darwin Plus initiative. All of that focuses on biodiversity and conservation, working with locals and indigenous peoples.

Penultimately, let me run through some of the provisions in the Bill. The Bill will ban the import of hunting trophies from specific species, with the explicit aim of ensuring that imports into Great Britain do not place unnecessary pressure on species that are at risk. For those species, an import ban without exemptions will be the most effective protection, as it will provide clarity and address the conservation concerns arising from trophy hunting.

Clauses 1 and 2 make provision for the import ban, which will cover trophies brought into Great Britain from animals hunted after the legislation comes into force—there are strict, clear lines about anything that happens before that. The definition of a hunting trophy in clause 1 is:

> "the body of an animal, or a readily recognisable part or derivative of an animal, that…is obtained…through hunting…for the hunter's personal use."

That is how hunting trophies are defined in our current controls under CITES.

(From UK Parliament, 2024; Hunting Trophies (Import Prohibition) Bill; © Parliamentary copyright House of Commons; reproduced under the terms of the Open Parliament Licence v.3.0)

Current Controls under CITES and Situation to Date

Through Resolution Conf. 10.10 (Rev. CoP12), CITES Parties have been obligated to report the details of elephant product seizures to the CITES Secretariat or to TRAFFIC directly for inclusion in the Elephant Trade Information System (ETIS) since 1997 (Milliken *et al.*, 2004). As of 15 April 2008, the ETIS data set for Thailand comprised 55 seizure cases, but most of these cases were received from credible NGO sources in the country rather than from reports submitted directly by the government agencies themselves. Further, since 2004, no seizure cases have been reported by any sources at all. Consequently, the rate of reporting elephant product seizure data to ETIS remains rather poor. In the meantime, over the period 1989–2006, Thailand was identified as either a source country (the exporter or re-exporter), or the destination country in 314 other ivory seizure cases that were made in other countries around the world. Collectively, these seizures represent 15,660 kg of ivory, most of which is believed to have originated from African elephants.

The Hunting Trophies (Import Prohibition) Bill has not passed into law as an election was called in the UK in 2024.

Note

[1]Information on the Hunting Trophies (Import Prohibition) Bill can be found in the following places:

- The debate transcript is available on the Hansard website at: https://hansard.parliament.uk/Commons/2024-03-22/debates/24032280000001/HuntingTrophies(ImportProhibition)Bill (accessed 7 May 2025).
- Progress of the Hunting Trophies (Import Prohibition) Bill, Hansard Volume 747, debated on Friday 22 March 2024 is available at: https://bills.parliament.uk/bills/3547 (accessed 7 May 2025).

Bibliography

Ben-Dor, M. and Barkai, R. (2020) The importance of large prey animals during the Pleistocene and the implications of their extinction on the use of dietary ethnographic analogies. *Journal of Anthropological Archaeology* 59. DOI: 101192. 10.1016/j.jaa.2020.101192.

McCubbin, S.G. (2020) The Cecil moment: celebrity environmentalism, Nature 2.0, and the cultural politics of lion trophy hunting. *Geoforum* 108, 194–203. DOI: 10.1016/j.geoforum.2019.10.015.

Milliken, T., Burn, R.W., Underwood, F.M. and Sangalakula, L. (2004) The Elephant Trade Information System (ETIS) and the illicit trade in ivory: a report to the 13th meeting of the Conference of the Parties to CITES. *TRAFFIC East/Southern Africa* 20.

Moorhouse, T.P., Elwin, A., Ntuli, H. and D'Cruze, N.C. (2023) Assessing the potential for a levy-based system to replace revenue from trophy hunting in South Africa. *Global Ecology and Conservation* 47: e02656. DOI: 10.1016/j.gecco.2023.e02656.

Stiles, D. (2004) The ivory trade and elephant conservation. *Environmental Conservation* 31(4), 309–321. DOI: 10.1017/S0376892904001614.

UK Parliament (2024) Hunting Trophies (Import Prohibition) Bill, Hansard Volume 747: debated on Friday 22 March 2024. Available at: https://bills.parliament.uk/bills/3547 (accessed 26 February 2025).

University of Oxford (2017) Cecil the lion's son Xanda also shot dead in Zimbabwe. *University of Oxford, News & Events*, 21 July. Available at: https://www.ox.ac.uk/news/2017-07-21-cecil-lion%E2%80%99s-son-xanda-also-shot-dead-zimbabwe (accessed 26 February 2025).

World Animal Protection (2022) Cecil the lion: a tragic tale of trophy hunting. World Animal Protection Blog, 1 July. Available at: https://www.worldanimalprotection.org/latest/blogs/cecil-lion/ (accessed 1 July 2022).

12 UK Zoos Captive Elephants Regulations, DEFRA

Eric Laws*

retired Professor of Tourism

Abstract

Chapter 12 presents in detail the current regulation by the Department for Environment, Food and Rural Affairs (DEFRA) for keeping captive elephants in the UK. There are currently 49 elephants in ten UK zoos.

Introduction

The UK is not an elephant range country, but many people are very interested in elephants, and in the decade preceding the coronavirus disease 2019 (COVID-19) pandemic elephant viewing and elephant activities became a major motivator for outbound tourism to range countries in Asia and Africa. The Association of British Travel Agents (ABTA) has recently published best practice guidance to its member outbound tour operators, giving a quick reference table with examples of best practice and supporting information (ABTA, 2013). The full guidance is available at: https://animalnepal.wordpress.com/wp-content/uploads/2013/12/abta-manual-elephants-in-captive-environments.pdf (accessed 21 February 2025).

In response to my queries Chris Lewis, Captivity Research and Policy Manager, Born Free Foundation, provided the following information on 24 September 2024, concerning elephants held captive in Britain:

> There are currently 49 elephants in ten UK zoos (23 *Elephas maximus* Asian and 26 *Loxodonta africana*).
>
> It is our view that it is impossible to meet the complex physical, psychological and social needs of elephants in a zoo environment. The currently recommended minimum enclosure size for an elephant in a UK zoo is less than half the area of a

*e.laws@runbox.com

DOI: 10.1079/9781836990093.0012

> rugby pitch (0.3 ha). There are plans by the UK government to increase this minimum enclosure size to 2 ha, but these minimum sizes are wholly inadequate when compared to the home ranges elephants utilise in the wild or the functional and behavioural needs of elephants. In 7 of the 10 UK zoos keeping elephants, the zoo's visitor car park is bigger than its elephant enclosure. It is time for the keeping of elephants in UK zoos to be phased out.
>
> The revised UK elephant regulations can be seen at https://consult.defra.gov.uk/animal-health-and-welfare/1d5d9f40/ (accessed 21 February 2025). They include amendments to the elephant appendix, including a slight increase in minimum enclosure size, an end to free-contact and the use of the bullhook/ankus. These were consulted on in 2022 and it remains unclear when they will be coming into force.
>
> (Chris Lewis, Captivity Research and Policy Manager, Born Free Foundation, 2024, personal communication)

The current UK zoo regulations for captive elephants held in the UK now follow.

Current UK Zoo Regulations for Captive Elephants Held in the UK

These regulations are from Appendix 8 of the Department for Environment, Food and Rural Affairs (DEFRA) *Secretary of State's Standards of Modern Zoo Practice* (2017). 'Appendix 8 – Specialist exhibits, Elephants' is reproduced in full here under the terms of the Open Government Licence v.3.

Department for Environment, Food and Rural Affairs Secretary of State's Standards of Modern Zoo Practice

Appendix 8 – Specialist exhibits, Elephants

June 2017

8.8 Elephants

8.8.1 All elephant facilities will be inspected by at least one nominated Defra-appointed elephant inspector. If only one elephant inspector is present, the elephant inspectors may confer on elephant-related aspects of individual zoo inspection reports, including any recommendations or conditions, to ensure consistency of inspections. In addition to the Standards in this Section (8.8), the inspectors will refer to the current Management Guidelines for the Welfare of Zoo Animals: Elephants (BIAZA) and current recommendations of Defra/ZEC [Zoos Expert Committee]-endorsed elephant management groups such as the UK Elephant Welfare Group, and will use these to inform any recommendation or suggested conditions. Institutions will be expected to provide evidence in support of achieving these standards.

Where facilities do not meet these standards, the inspectors will assess the justifications and mitigations.
8.8.2 All elephant holding institutions must produce a documented Long Term Management Plan (LTMP) for the elephant collection and an Individual Welfare Plan for each elephant (IWP).

Long Term Management Plan (LTMP)
8.8.3 It is recognised that zoo masterplans are generally designed to cover a 10-15 year time-frame and thus will not cover the expected lifespan of elephants. The LTMP should aim to cover at least 30 years and account for necessary flexibility needed when keeping and/or breeding elephants. It must cover the following:

- Purpose of collection; e.g. breeding herd, bachelor group, retirement facility for non-breeding animals
- Herd compatibility details
- Financial provision for animal care
- Long term enclosure development planning
- Management systems adopted
- Elephant training programme
- Staff training programme
- Zoo management structure relative to elephants
- Exit strategy should the collection choose to no longer hold elephants

Individual Welfare Plan (IWP)
8.8.4 This document must be produced for each individual elephant and contain, as a minimum, the following;

- Healthcare plan (see 8.8.39)
- Diet plan (see 8.8.33)
- Training plan
- Welfare monitoring data produced by Defra/ZEC-endorsed elephant management groups e.g. UK Elephant Welfare Group Health pack data and behavioural monitoring tool
- Behaviour profile
- Details of any behavioural issues and mitigation plan
- Exercise plan

In addition, bulls over four years old must have a bull profile (see 8.8.15).
All plans must be reviewed and updated regularly as appropriate, and in agreement with inspectors.
8.8.5 Elephants are long-lived, highly intelligent animals with large natural ranges and a complex social life. Meeting their needs in captivity is challenging. These standards should help inspectors and others in assessing the extent to which these welfare needs are being met, and in particular, in assessing the welfare needs of individual elephants and the measures being taken to secure good elephant welfare.
8.8.6 Inspectors, local authorities and zoos must consult the current Management Guidelines for the Welfare of Zoo Animals: Elephants (BIAZA). Elephant-keeping zoos must be aware of the function and current recommendations of Defra/ZEC-endorsed elephant management groups such as the UK Elephant Welfare Group (EWG) and engage constructively with such groups.
8.8.7 Health and welfare monitoring indices identified through Defra/ZEC-endorsed management groups must be implemented within each institution and data on their implementation made available to inspectors.

The captive environment

Social Grouping

8.8.8 Appropriate social grouping is key to successful elephant management and must be pre-eminent in all aspects of care. This must be reflected in the LTMP. The transfer of elephant (cows and bulls) between institutions must be minimised in line with this. Regular behavioural profiles must be made for all elephants and form part of the Institutional Collection Plan (ICP) – these should be used to inform herd compatibility within the LTMP.

8.8.9 Breeding collections should aim for stable matriarchal herds wherever possible. Calves have a long learning period and must be brought up in a matriarchal group. Female elephants must learn calf care and benefit from the presence of a young animal. Cows should remain with their maternal herd, bulls also benefit from maximising the opportunity for socialisation with the matriarchal herd. The age for removal of bulls will vary with individuals, herd structure and facilities. Zoos must demonstrate through behaviour profiling and behaviour monitoring, evidence to inform decisions for the removal of bulls. The social development of young bulls is increasingly recognised as being very important, benefiting from the presence of older, adult males; this must not be overlooked, especially regarding acceptable patterns of aggression within the herd (see 8.8.14).

8.8.10 The zoo should maximise opportunities for every elephant to have unrestricted physical contact with other members of the herd for as many hours each day as possible (see also 8.8.12 for cows). It is recommended that this should be not less than 16 hours in any 24 hour period. Zoos should minimise the time that individuals within the herd are physically separated through management.

8.8.11 African and Asian elephants should never be mixed in the same social grouping.

Cows

8.8.12 Female elephants must have social contact with other elephants at all times. If herds are kept, groups should contain at least four compatible females over 2 years old. All elephants must have the option to get away from other elephants if so desired, through use of space and visual or physical barriers in the enclosure. Where evidenced compatibility problems arise, the zoo must keep records of the steps taken to try to resolve these issues, and plans (with time frame) should these steps prove unsuccessful. Such records must be made available to zoo inspectors upon request.

Bulls

8.8.13 Bull elephants can be difficult to manage (particularly in musth) and are not always compatible with cows. Provision must be made for them to be separated from cows and other bulls when necessary.

8.8.14 Bulls must be given the option to be in social contact with other elephants if they choose. Acceptable social situations for bulls are:

a) housing bulls so they can mix regularly with the family herd, ideally with another bull present, to facilitate social learning (1 older bull, 1 younger); or
b) bachelor herd with other bulls of varying ages.

Bachelor herd size should reflect best practice in current guidelines. All elephants must have the option to get away from other elephants if so desired, through use of space and visual or physical barriers in the enclosure.

8.8.15 A bull profile must be drawn up and documented for each animal from the age of four and should be reviewed (in combination with a risk assessment) at least every six months. This profile will inform the management regime of the bull which should be modified in light of the development of the elephant's character.

8.8.16 All collections keeping bulls must have the facility to carry out any essential veterinary procedures in such a way that is safe for all staff and the elephant concerned. An Elephant Restraint Device (ERD) is recommended. All collections keeping bulls must be able to demonstrate evidence that staff are adequately trained to work with bulls (see current BIAZA Guidelines).

Enclosures

8.8.17 Requirements and justification for the size of indoor and outdoor enclosures in an individual zoo remains with the Defra-nominated elephant inspectors (see also 8.8.1), taking into consideration sections 8.8.20 and 8.8.23 and any other relevant factors such as complexity of the environment and social dynamics of the herd.

8.8.18 Indoor and outdoor accommodation must be provided and, other than in exceptional weather conditions, zoos must aim for all elephants to have access to both over a 24 hour period throughout the year with the ability to choose where they spend their time. Justification must be given if this cannot be achieved. Enclosure design must enhance the social dynamics of the group.

8.8.19 A complex and variable enclosure is essential (see also 8.8.34). The indoor and outdoor environment should be positively challenging and stimulating to the animals and contain devices, structures and terrain which provide variety and complexity to enrich the environment and encourage natural behaviour including, for example moving around, grazing, dustbathing, bathing, scratching, digging and exploration. Zoos must be able to demonstrate evidence that facilities provided to the elephants are being used and, if not, demonstrate plans to mitigate this.

8.8.20 It is recommended that all indoor cow/herd facilities provide at least 300 sq. m for four (or fewer) animals and increase by at least 80 sq. m for each additional animal over two years of age. It is recommended that indoor bull facilities provide at least 160 sq. m for each bull.

8.8.21 Indoor enclosures must allow elephants to move freely as a group, turn and lie down. Indoor enclosures must be well ventilated but at sufficiently low velocity to avoid draughts and must be well lit, preferably with natural skylights and the ability to fade the lighting to minimise disturbance to the elephants. The inside temperature should be no less than 16°C with an area able to be maintained at 21°C for sick or debilitated animals.

8.8.22 Concrete flooring for indoor enclosures can cause foot and joint problems for elephants so enclosures should use alternative substrates. There is increasing evidence that deep sand is the preferred substrate. The depth of sand should enable good drainage and allow for building of sand mounds to enhance recumbent sleep as well as other natural behaviours such as digging (i.e. no less than 1m). A range of other manipulable natural substrates (e.g. mud, clay, bark chip) can also be provided.

8.8.23 Outdoor enclosures must be as large and complex as possible and encourage walking and also exploration, grazing, foraging, social interaction and maintenance behaviours (e.g. dust-bathing). Outdoor areas for bulls and cows (i.e. over two years) must provide all animals with a minimum shared space of 3,000 sq. m (0.3ha) throughout the year, unless the current BIAZA guidelines exceed this. There is evidence that much larger spaces (e.g.>2 ha (20,000 sq. m) for five or fewer adults are required to achieve suitable exercise levels, and development plans are strongly recommended to aim for larger spaces. Inspectors must be satisfied that all animals have sufficient space and access throughout the year. Enclosures must be flexible and allow for animals to get away from each other if they choose, and for separation where needed.

8.8.24 The outdoor area must provide all elephants with access to sufficient areas of shelter and protection from extremes of sunlight, wind and rain.

8.8.25 Outside substrates must be primarily natural e.g. soil, sand or grass with good drainage. Provision for all weather outdoor access must be available.

8.8.26 Elephants must be provided with the opportunity to bathe and enclosures must incorporate a variety of options including a pool, dust bath, and mud wallow, large and deep enough for the needs of all the animals. Sprinklers/showers can also be used. Opportunities for bathing should be provided both indoors and outdoors, particularly if animals spend the majority of their time indoors.

Boundaries

8.8.27 Barriers must prevent escapes and direct contact with the public and must also ensure the safety and well-being of both the elephants and staff. Methods of quick escape must be provided for keepers.

8.8.28 Barriers and gates should not have horizontal bars, which would allow elephants to climb. The minimum height is 1.9m for cows and 2.5m for bulls. A large bull may require a 3m barrier. Designated safety areas for keeping staff must be clearly identified in line with the management system employed. Stand-off areas must be designed to ensure no contact between elephants and public.

8.8.29 Gates should be robust and any hydraulic system should have manual back-up and/or alternative power. Hydraulic gates must be capable of being operated remotely by staff i.e. outside the area within elephant reach, and must be able to be opened and closed quickly with a stop facility to ensure trunks/tails are not crushed. The safe operation of any manual gates must be able to be demonstrated to inspectors, including safe systems of work for scenarios where direct access in free contact (FC) situations (see 8.8.51) is not possible.

8.8.30 Electric fences used as a secondary barrier must be of sufficient voltage to deter elephants and must have a failsafe alarm system. Fences should be checked daily and recorded. Electric fences should not normally be used as a main barrier, but where they are, such as to allow access to large grassed areas, suitably trained staff must be present, directly supervising the animals. Moats are not suitable as barriers and should not be used.

Feeding and nutrition

8.8.31 Feeding should match natural feeding activity as much as possible, where browse and grass accounts for the majority of the diet and feeding time budget. Food presentation should be varied to encourage a full range of natural foraging behaviour and cognitive stimulation.

8.8.32 Elephant diet must be high in fibre and low in nutrients with forage (browse, grass, hay and straw) comprising no less than 80% of the diet with the remainder comprising pellets and other foodstuffs. All forage must be of appropriate quality and analysed annually by appropriate laboratories to ensure it remains within nutritional guidelines. Such analysis must be made available to inspectors on request. Pellets must be high in fibre and low in protein, fed to provide adequate levels of vitamins and minerals in the diet – in general, feeding pelleted food significantly over 2-3kg per adult animal per day is not advised. Other items e.g. vegetables should be used in minimal amounts as needed for training and enrichment activities. High sugar fruits or bread should be avoided or their use carefully limited.

8.8.33 Individual diet plans must be detailed in the IWP and be tailored to individual needs based on body condition score (BCS) and weight. If optimum BCS is not achieved, collections must demonstrate evidence of a plan to achieve optimum BCS and progress made.

8.8.34 Complexity and variation in food presentation is required. Food must be presented to maximise foraging time. Grazing allows elephants to spend significant amounts of time consuming a small amount of forage, and should be encouraged. All facilities should provide some grazing access. Forage, including browse, should be available at all times to all elephants. Food presentation should be at unpredictable intervals, throughout the day and night and methods should be varied, time consuming and include intellectual challenge (e.g. puzzle feeders). Food should be placed throughout the exhibit to provide psychological stimulation, avoid competition and encourage movement.

8.8.35 Animals must have access to clean drinking water at all times from the indoor and the outdoor areas.

Behavioural management

8.8.36 The individual behaviour of elephants must be continually monitored and assessed, (including overnight behaviour) using welfare monitoring tools produced by Defra/ZEC-endorsed elephant management groups. Monitoring tools require cameras to monitor overnight behaviour. Video footage must be stored for a reasonable amount of time to allow easy access and review to follow up any normal [sic] behaviour or concerns noted outside the formal use of the assessment tool.

8.8.37 Extensive and varied enrichment must be provided in both the inside and outside environments and be part of the daily management plan. Evidence must be provided of the implementation of a goal driven enrichment plan with clear aims and evaluation methods. The enrichment plan must be made up of activities from all of the five enrichment categories; social, cognitive, physical habitat, sensory and food.

Healthcare

8.8.38 General health must be assessed regularly and must form part of the daily management routine.

8.8.39 The documented healthcare plan forms part of the IWP. It must be reviewed/updated quarterly (but the appropriate frequency to be established in light of the individual health needs), for each elephant. The plan must contain health monitoring data gathered using methods recommended by Defra/ZEC-endorsed elephant management groups e.g. UK EWG health pack, and show evidence of the steps taken to address any issues and improvements achieved. It must also include: (i) baseline information on the elephant's state of health (ii) any behavioural issues, including stereotypy (iii) exercise plan (iv) weight and body condition score.

Health monitoring

8.8.40 To achieve optimum healthcare of captive elephants it is necessary to be able to achieve safe access to the elephant through training techniques without the need for anaesthesia.

Evidence must be provided to inspectors on request that keepers/vets can do the following:
Calves (1-8 years)

1. Examination of integument, mouth, ears, eyes, feet
2. Body weight and body condition scoring in line with monitoring protocols produced by Defra/ZEC-endorsed elephant management groups
3. Health monitoring photographs (e.g. body and feet) and scoring following protocols of Defra/ZEC-endorsed elephant management groups
4. Intravenous access
5. Rectal access
6. Acceptance of intramuscular injections
7. Acceptance of ultrasound examination
8. Trunk washes for disease screening and clinical monitoring e.g. tuberculosis, herpes virus

Adults (over 8 years)

1. Examination of integument, mouth, ears, eyes, feet
2. Ability to perform foot care as required
3. Body weight and body condition scoring in line with protocols from Defra/ZEC-endorsed elephant management groups
4. Health monitoring photographs (e.g. body and feet) and scoring following protocols of Defra/ZEC-endorsed elephant management groups
5. Intravenous access
6. Rectal access (including for ultrasonography)
7. Acceptance of intramuscular injections
8. Acceptance of ultrasound examination
9. Trunk washes for disease screening and clinical monitoring e.g. tuberculosis, herpes virus

Staff management

8.8.41 There must be a recognised team of elephant handlers. This team must have a structure that includes a team leader, who is responsible for ensuring that agreed protocols, procedures and training are correctly carried out and implemented. Inspectors will assess that adequate staff are available of appropriate training as well as the collection's staffing levels contingency plan (to cover sickness, holiday etc.). There must be a clear decision-making pathway and protocol up to senior management.

Risk

8.8.42 All aspects of elephant management must be risk assessed and a comprehensive system of Safe Working Practices (SWP) implemented. There should be evidence of communication to, and training of, staff in risk management. All risk assessments and SWPs should be regularly reviewed. Risk assessments and SWPs must reflect the elephant management systems identified in the LTMP and IWP with particular reference to "Restricted contact" scenarios (see section 8.8.51 Management Systems).

Staff training

8.8.43 The collection must have a monitored and written staff training programme which is reviewed annually. This must encompass training of new staff and training reviews of existing staff and must also include the outcomes from the risk assessments that have been carried out.

8.8.44 The staff training programme should include an evaluation component suitable for each level of training. Institutions must support all their elephant keepers to continuously update their training to ensure continued professional development (CPD) and that best practice is adopted. CPD records should be available to inspectors on request.

Use of physical restraint

8.8.45 Consequences of bad practice in restraint are significant and severe. Physical restraint of elephants through the use of, for example, chains and shackles must be minimised. There is justification for limited periods of physical restraint for certain husbandry and veterinary procedures which must be documented and included in the IWP.

8.8.46 All restraint equipment must be maintained to the highest standard and replaced immediately if damaged or showing signs of wear and tear to ensure it is not causing physical harm to the elephant or safety risk to staff. The most appropriate equipment must always be used.

8.8.47 Elephants must not be physically restrained for periods in excess of one out of 24 hours except in exceptional circumstances under direct veterinary guidance, such as during specific procedures e.g. AI [artificial insemination] or during transport. All uses of restraints, over one hour must be documented and made available to inspectors on request.

8.8.48 Only named, trained persons may carry out physical restraint. This may include external elephant experts brought in for staff training and/or elephant transportation.

8.8.49 Keepers must be adequately trained in the use of restraint equipment and procedures, and safety aspects followed. Evidence of training must be demonstrated to inspectors upon request.

Elephant training

8.8.50 Each institution must have an elephant training programme (documented in the LTMP) and individual tailored goals for each animal (documented in the IWP).

Management systems

8.8.51 There are two recognised elephant management systems: free contact (FC) and protected contact (PC).

- Free Contact: The direct handling of an elephant, when the keeper and the elephants share the same unrestricted space (without any solid elephant-proof barrier in between them).
- Protected Contact: The elephant and the keeper never share the same unrestricted space. Management of the animal or contact is undertaken through a protective barrier. In situations, in a PC management system, where direct contact with an elephant in restraints (referred to as Restricted Contact) is undertaken then this must be risk assessed in a similar fashion as per an elephant managed in 'Free Contact'.

Institutions must clearly state and describe their management systems in their LTMP and IWPs. This should be reflected in risk assessments and Safe Working Practices (see section 8.8.42).

Ankus or hook

8.8.52 The ankus is a tool used to cue the elephant to maintain commands and train them. It is intended to produce a light physical contact. The ankus must not hit, injure, damage or break the skin or be used in any other way that could cause physical or mental injury. The consequences of bad practice are significant and severe. All injuries caused by an ankus must be recorded, in conjunction with the situation and circumstances of its use, reviewed by management and be made available to inspectors on request. Justification for ankus use and evidence of ongoing staff training in the ankus use must be available to inspectors on request. All staff using the ankus must participate in continued professional development (CPD) and training to ensure best practice is maintained.

Electric goad

8.8.53 Electric goads must only ever be used to protect human safety in extreme situations (such as an imminent threat to human life) and never as a way of controlling the animal to ensure compliance. Goads may be used only by staff that have had appropriate training. Establishments must have a written policy on electric goad use, approved by senior management, and available to inspectors. This must include named persons and parameters of use. In all cases where an electric goad has been used, a full report must be produced detailing the situation and circumstances of its use. The report must be reviewed by management and be made available to inspectors. Discussion must occur surrounding how use could be avoided in the future.

(From DEFRA, 2017; © Crown copyright 2017. Contains public sector information licensed under the Open Government Licence v3.0 (available at: https://www.nationalarchives.gov.uk/doc/open-government-licence/version/3/ (accessed 21 February 2025))

This publication is available at: www.gov.uk/government/publications (accessed 21 February 2025).

Bibliography

Association of British Travel Agents (ABTA) (2013) *Specific Guidance Manual: Elephants in Captive Environments*. ABTA. Available at: https://animalnepal.wordpress.com/wp-content/uploads/2013/12/abta-manual-elephants-in-captive-environments.pdf (accessed 21 February 2025).

Department for Environment, Food and Rural Affairs (DEFRA) (2017) Appendix 8 – Specialist exhibits, Elephants. In: *Secretary of State's Standards of Modern Zoo Practice*. DEFRA. Available at: https://assets.publishing.service.gov.uk/media/5a81f6ec40f0b62305b91c0e/zoo-practice-elephants.pdf (accessed 21 February 2025).

13 Conclusion: Exploring New Frontiers: Research Priorities for Enhancing Elephant Welfare

Kom Campiranon*

College of Innovation, Thammasat University, Thailand

Abstract

Elephants are iconic and intelligent animals with complex needs, yet their welfare remains a critical issue in both wild and captive settings. Despite advancements in research, significant gaps persist, especially in tourism contexts where elephants often face stressful human interactions. This chapter delves into emerging research priorities that aim to enhance elephant welfare, with a focus on the impacts of tourism, conservation efforts and human–elephant relationships, particularly concerning captive elephants. Currently, key research themes include: (i) human–elephant interactions; (ii) tourist perceptions of welfare in elephant tourism; (iii) elephant care; and (iv) overall elephant welfare, especially in regions like Asia where elephant tourism is widespread. To address the growing and complex challenges that elephants face in captivity, this conclusion recommends five interdisciplinary research areas that focus on improving welfare and supporting conservation initiatives.

Introduction

Elephants, being one of the most iconic, intelligent and emotionally complex species on our planet, demand a highly nuanced approach to their welfare that goes beyond basic care and considers their intricate social structures, cognitive capacities and natural behaviours. Despite significant strides in understanding the needs of elephants, particularly in captivity, there remains an urgent need to further explore and address the evolving challenges they face. Factors such as animal welfare, human–wildlife conflict, and the ethical considerations surrounding their use in tourism underscore the importance

*kom@citu.tu.ac.th

DOI: 10.1079/9781836990093.0013

of continuing to push the boundaries of research in this field. The conclusion to *Elephant Welfare in Global Tourism* delves into the emerging frontiers of elephant welfare research, examining innovative methodologies, technologies and interdisciplinary approaches aimed at enhancing both the physical and the psychological well-being of these majestic creatures.

To start with, elephants have long been exploited for public entertainment tourism across Asia and Africa, with varying types of human–elephant interactions ranging from observational experiences to high-contact activities such as elephant riding and bathing. In Asia, particularly Thailand and India, direct engagement with elephants is common, often leading to concerns over animal welfare, public health and species conservation. In contrast, African elephant tourism focuses more on free-range ecotours (Warwick *et al.*, 2023) but also includes hunting, while poaching is also prevalent.

Globally, up to 550,000 animals are used in the tourism industry, with only a small fraction receiving adequate care. Elephants, frequently exposed to tourists, are particularly vulnerable to stress, which can negatively impact both their behaviour and their physiology (Manning *et al.*, 2023). Therefore, animal welfare has become a significant factor in tourism, influencing decisions made by both tourists and operators. In order to examine such an issue, it is crucial to understand the concept of animal welfare which focuses on improving conditions for animals under human care, including those used in tourism (Fennell, 2022), as well as elephants in the tourism context. This is especially important in the case of captive elephants, who face unique welfare challenges due to their size, intelligence and social needs, which are often unmet in tourist settings (Manning *et al.*, 2022).

As Bansiddhi *et al.* (2019) have pointed out, a new trend in elephant tourism in recent years is camps that offer no riding or shows, in part a response to increasing concerns about welfare. Instead, tourists observe elephant behaviour, sometimes with opportunities to feed, bathe or walk alongside them. As shown in Fig. 13.1, the Asian Captive Elephant Standards (ACES) (2023) addressed this issue by introducing the Performance Dashboard, an innovative tool that transforms how the performance of elephant tourist camps is monitored and measured, establishing a new benchmark for responsible and ethical practices in the tourism industry. The goal is to also provide advice on responsible travel at elephant tourism venues and ensure that elephant care and welfare are maintained at accredited elephant venues which follow a set of stringent rules surrounding the health, well-being and social enrichment of elephants.

According to ACES (2023), categories are required for the auditing and certification standards. This comprehensive framework has been developed based on expert findings, science-based research and the best practices in camp management. The guidelines encompass ten key areas for responsible elephant tourism operations:

1. *Legal requirements*: Ensure compliance with laws and regulations for lawful operations.
2. *Facility management*: Evaluate infrastructure and management practices for worker support.

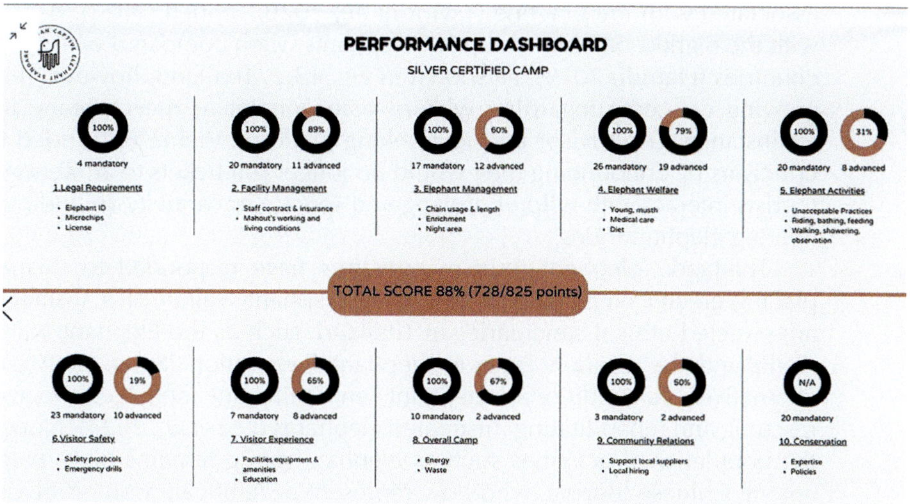

Fig. 13.1. Example of the assessment Performance Dashboard. N/A, not applicable. (Used with permission from Asian Captive Elephant Standards (ACES), 2023.)

3. *Elephant management*: Focus on the care, training, and living conditions of elephants to enhance their well-being.
4. *Elephant welfare*: Prioritize humane treatment, health, and living conditions for elephants.
5. *Elephant activities*: Assess activities to ensure they enrich the elephants' lives without causing distress.
6. *Visitor safety*: Implement safety measures to protect visitors during interactions with elephants.
7. *Visitor experience*: Measure the quality of visitor experiences, emphasizing education and responsible engagement.
8. *Overall camp*: Provide a comprehensive evaluation of camp operations and responsible practices.
9. *Community relations*: Promote positive engagement with local communities for mutual development.
10. *Conservation*: Highlight contributions to conservation efforts aimed at protecting elephant populations.

The Performance Dashboard adopts a holistic approach, thoroughly examining every aspect of a camp's operations. While the primary focus is on elephant welfare, it is equally essential to ensure that the working and living conditions of the mahouts, who are directly responsible for the elephants, meet the highest standards. This consideration is crucial, as the well-being of the mahouts directly influences the welfare of the elephants (ACES, 2023). By adhering to these standards, elephant camps can join the responsible elephant venue movement and achieve international certification.

As a country widely studied and debated for its role in elephant tourism, Thailand, a popular destination for such activities, offers a compelling backdrop for discussions on animal welfare literacy, highlighting the moral dilemmas associated with the practice (Taylor *et al.*, 2020; Fennell, 2022). As a country with the highest number of captive elephants when compared with other Asian countries (Hamdi, 2019), as shown in Fig. 13.2, Thailand, however, has faced growing concerns regarding welfare management in recent years. In 2016, for instance, TripAdvisor and its booking platform, Viator, responded to these criticisms by announcing they would no longer sell tickets to attractions where tourists interact with wild or endangered species in captivity, including venues offering elephant rides.

Thailand's elephant tourism operators have responded to this issue by placing greater emphasis on improving elephant welfare. For instance, there are selected ethical sanctuaries in Thailand, such as the Elephant Nature Park (ENP) and the Golden Triangle Elephant Foundation (Suter, 2020), offering alternatives to traditional elephant entertainment activities, focusing on rescuing and rehabilitating mistreated elephants (Lee *et al.*, 2024). Nonetheless, the popularity of activities such as elephant riding remains high, particularly among Chinese tourists, who now represent a significant portion of visitors to Thailand (Flower *et al.*, 2021).

From an academic perspective, studies on animal welfare in tourism is growing, yet there remains a gap in understanding the ethical dimensions of tourists' experiences with elephants (Lee *et al.*, 2024). Interactions with captive elephants often lead to unexpected emotional responses from tourists, especially when they witness stressful training methods or circus-like performances (Flower *et al.*, 2021). These experiences have the potential to shift perceptions and foster pro-environmental behaviour. However, the complex nature of elephant welfare, coupled with ongoing debates about humane treatment, presents challenges in ensuring their well-being (Winter, 2020).

Thailand has the highest number of captive elephants

Country	Wild elephants	Captive elephants
Thailand	2500–3200	4400
India	30,711	3000–4000
Laos	600–800	< 500
Nepal	100–200	300–400
Sri Lanka	5000–6000	120–200
Cambodia	300–600	< 100

Fig. 13.2. Number of wild and captive elephants in Asia. (From Hamdi, 2019, with permission.)

The next section will focus on the current areas of research related to elephant tourism welfare, aiming to provide a comprehensive understanding of the existing landscape. By examining the studies and findings in this field, it becomes possible to identify key trends, gaps and challenges. This exploration is critical not only for assessing the progress made in ensuring elephant welfare within tourism but also for anticipating and shaping future research directions. Gaining insight into the current state of knowledge will help guide scholars, policy makers and practitioners towards more informed and sustainable practices in elephant tourism, ultimately contributing to enhanced welfare standards.

Current Landscape of Elephant Tourism Welfare Research

Understanding the current state of elephant welfare is crucial for setting new research priorities. Recent studies reveal a growing interest in sustainable and ethical approaches to managing elephants in tourism. This shift emphasizes the need for interdisciplinary strategies that balance animal well-being with tourism demands, ensuring humane and sustainable practices in captive environments.

Global research on elephant welfare and conservation has experienced significant growth over the past decades, with increasing attention towards the Asian elephant. According to Zakaria *et al*. (2024), an analysis of 1780 articles published between 1914 and 2022 reveals a notable rise in research output, particularly since the year 2000. In 2022 alone, 142 articles were published, marking a clear upward trend in the study of elephants. While there was a slight decline in publications between 2014 and 2015, research activity rebounded shortly afterwards, reflecting heightened awareness and concern for Asian elephants.

The research landscape is dominated by a few key journals, with the *Journal of Zoo and Wildlife Medicine* leading in publication volume (5.7% of total articles), followed by *Zoo Biology* and *PLoS ONE*. Elsevier, along with other leading publishers such as Wiley-Blackwell and Springer Nature, plays a pivotal role in disseminating knowledge on Asian elephant research (Zakaria *et al*., 2024).

Analysis of author keywords indicated that 'human–elephant conflict', 'conservation' and 'animal welfare' are central themes, highlighting the intersection between ecological issues and human interaction. Topics such as 'herpesvirus', 'tuberculosis' and other diseases have also garnered attention, reflecting growing concern over elephant health. Additionally, research methodologies such as 'microsatellite analysis', 'camera traps' and 'phylogenetic analysis' are prevalent, illustrating the advancement of scientific techniques in elephant studies.

Such key themes collectively contribute to the current landscape of elephant tourism welfare research, which can be categorized into four main areas: (i) human–elephant interactions; (ii) tourist perceptions of elephant tourism welfare; (iii) elephant care; and (iv) elephant welfare. Each of these categories plays a vital role in understanding the multifaceted challenges and opportunities within the realm of elephant tourism. Details are discussed as follows.

Human–elephant interactions

Regarding studies on human–elephant relationships, Warwick *et al.* (2023) conducted an extensive review of over 500 scientific publications on public health, safety and animal welfare in elephant tourism. Their findings indicate that close contact experiences with elephants pose unmanageable risks for both humans and elephants, leading to significant mistreatment and abuse. They recommend regulatory measures such as legal bans on close contact tourism, continuous monitoring and the promotion of non-interactive wildlife observation. Moreover, Carlstead *et al.* (2019) investigated the relationship between keeper attitudes and elephant welfare, emphasizing the importance of strong keeper–elephant relationships (KERs) for improving welfare outcomes in captivity. Good KERs were found to enhance welfare and provide reciprocal benefits for both keepers and elephants.

Tourists' perceptions

Lee *et al.* (2024) explored the role of ethical experiences and psychological well-being in tourist satisfaction by comparing reviews from rescue centres and general tour sites. Their analysis revealed that tourists at rescue centres experienced greater ethical and emotional satisfaction, underscoring the link between well-being, personal growth and travel satisfaction. Flower *et al.* (2021) surveyed 132 tourists at various elephant venues in Thailand, finding that age, home location and welfare standards influenced post-visit attitudes. Their research suggests that public awareness of elephant welfare can drive positive behavioural changes and encourage tourists to prioritize ethical venues. In addition, Worwag *et al.* (2019) investigated demographic differences in tourists engaging in animal-based tourism and found varying levels of concern for ethical treatment based on factors such as age and background. This points to the need for further research on how tourist responsibility influences animal welfare.

Elephant care

Regarding studies on elephant care, Manning *et al.* (2023) examined the impact of the coronavirus disease 2019 (COVID-19) lockdown on semi-captive African elephants, finding that the absence of tourists reduced stress-related behaviours. This suggests that tourist interactions may provoke anxiety in elephants, contributing to welfare concerns. Supanta *et al.* (2022) surveyed 30 elephant camps caring for over 400 elephants in northern Thailand during the COVID-19 pandemic (April 2020–2022). Results showed reduced mahout-to-elephant ratios, decreased activities and food intake, and increased chaining times compared to pre-pandemic conditions. These changes in management are likely to have impacted elephant welfare, affecting nutrition, health and exercise.

As shown in Fig. 13.3, elephant care includes, but is not limited to, physical health, safety, shelter, food, clean water and clean living conditions (Hamdi, 2019). Fuktong *et al.* (2021) assessed elephant welfare through physiological and

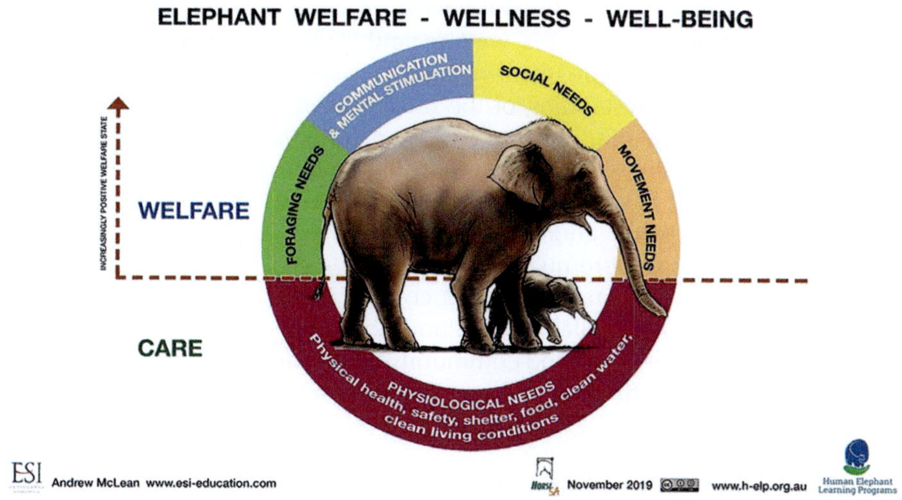

Fig. 13.3. Elephant welfare. (From Hamdi, 2019; H-ELP (Human Elephant Learning Programs) Foundation, with permission.)

physical health measures, highlighting the need for better management practices in camps, such as improving diet, exercise and care for foot health and wounds. Furthermore, Szydlowski (2024) highlights that welfare and health issues in captive elephant management remain contentious among stakeholders.

Elephant welfare

Finally elephant welfare studies examine elephants' foraging needs, communication and mental stimulation, social needs and movement needs (Hamdi, 2019). Although a number of authors (e.g. Flower *et al.*, 2021; Fennell, 2022; Zakaria *et al.*, 2024) have emphasized the need for stakeholders to prioritize animal welfare literacy as part of a responsible tourism agenda (Fuktong *et al.*, 2021; Fennell, 2022), only a few studies have critically examined the welfare of captive elephants in Asia (Bansiddhi *et al.*, 2019).

As discussed above, recent studies on elephant tourism welfare highlight the need for interdisciplinary approaches, focusing on human–elephant interactions, tourist perceptions of welfare, and the complex social, physiological and ecological factors influencing wild elephant conservation. These areas emphasize the importance of integrating diverse perspectives to create sustainable solutions for elephant welfare.

Emerging Research Priorities

The existing research outlined above has yielded valuable insights into the complex dynamics of elephant tourism welfare; however, it also reveals significant gaps and opportunities for further investigation. A number of authors (e.g. Zakaria *et al.*, 2024) emphasize the need for interdisciplinary approaches to effectively address the welfare and conservation of elephants in tourism contexts. They argue that integrating perspectives from various fields can enrich our understanding of the multifaceted issues at play and lead to more comprehensive solutions.

In light of these considerations, this section will delve into emerging research priorities that have been suggested by various authors as recommendations for future studies. By addressing these emerging priorities, future research can contribute to a more nuanced understanding of elephant tourism welfare and pave the way for more effective conservation strategies. Ultimately, fostering interdisciplinary collaboration and focusing on the interconnectedness of welfare, conservation and community engagement will be essential for ensuring a sustainable future for elephants in tourism.

Tourist behaviour, education and ethical awareness

A vital area for future research in elephant tourism welfare lies in understanding how tourists perceive and engage with elephant welfare at tourism venues. Although many tourists partake in activities such as riding or bathing elephants, there is often a significant lack of awareness regarding the ethical implications and welfare consequences of these interactions. As noted by Flower *et al.* (2021), minimal research has been conducted on tourist behaviour within elephant tourism settings, highlighting an urgent need for further investigation.

Future studies should focus on exploring tourists' perceptions of animal welfare, aiming to identify specific areas where targeted education could foster better welfare practices. This could involve examining the various factors that influence tourist choices and their understanding of the ethical dimensions of their interactions with elephants.

Moreover, the diversity of wildlife tourism attractions and their impacts on individual animals warrant further exploration. Research should investigate the effectiveness of different educational interventions—such as on-site information displays, ethical tourism campaigns and online resources—in shaping tourist behaviour and encouraging more responsible decision making. Understanding which types of educational initiatives resonate most with tourists could inform the development of best practices for elephant tourism venues.

Additionally, future studies could compare the impacts of wildlife tourism attractions that offer minimal interaction with those that involve hands-on activities. By examining how these different experiences influence tourists' attitudes towards animal welfare, researchers can gain valuable insights into how to promote more humane practices within the industry. Investigating tourist motivations, their willingness to pay for ethical experiences, and how their attitudes evolve over time will provide critical data for shaping tourism models that prioritize animal welfare.

In summary, by addressing these research areas, we can enhance our understanding of tourist behaviour and its implications for elephant welfare, ultimately leading to more ethical and responsible tourism practices.

Animal welfare literacy among tourism operators

Public concerns regarding elephant welfare are increasingly shaping perceptions about the acceptability of using elephants for entertainment and economic purposes, especially within the tourism sector. The practices and standards for managing elephants in captivity vary significantly; some operations are well regulated and adhere to comprehensive welfare standards, while others lack proper oversight or established guidelines (Bansiddhi *et al.*, 2019). In this context, Fennell (2022) emphasizes the need for research to compare animal welfare literacy among operators managing the same species and across different species, such as elephants and cetaceans. This comparative analysis could help benchmark current welfare conditions and evaluate the impact of interventions on improving literacy over time.

Future research should focus on the considerable variability in management practices, identifying and contrasting those camps that are welfare conscious and well regulated with those that operate with minimal oversight. By establishing benchmarks for current welfare standards, studies can assess how targeted interventions—such as training programmes, certification initiatives and ongoing education—can enhance operators' knowledge and ultimately improve conditions for captive elephants.

Additionally, there is a pressing need to investigate whether tourists become desensitized to welfare concerns after repeated visits or through prolonged exposure to elephant attractions. This potential desensitization may hinder efforts to instill ethical tourism values over time. Understanding how both operators and tourists evolve in their perspectives and practices concerning animal welfare will provide valuable insights into fostering more humane tourism experiences.

By addressing these research priorities, the tourism industry can better align its practices with public expectations and ethical standards, ultimately contributing to the welfare of elephants in captivity and enhancing the overall integrity of elephant tourism.

Keeper–animal relationships (KARs) and human–animal interaction

The well-being of elephants is intricately linked to the experiences and compassion exhibited by their mahouts. However, reports indicate a worrying decline in this quality across Asia. Existing research in the livestock industry has long underscored the significance of positive human–animal relationships (HARs) for enhancing animal welfare and productivity. This research has led to recommendations for implementing cognitive-behavioural training for handlers and incorporating HAR assessments into welfare audits (Supanta *et al.*, 2022).

In the realm of elephant tourism, evidence suggests that captive elephants which regularly interact with their mahouts and engage in daily exercise—such as riding—exhibit lower stress levels compared to those in camps that focus solely on passive viewing (Hamdi, 2019). To further explore this connection, Carlstead *et al.* (2019) propose that future research should examine species-specific variations in the quality of KARs, taking into account critical factors such as housing, management practices and social dynamics. Additionally, cognitive-behavioural training for staff could enhance these relationships, and further investigations should assess how the attitudes of keepers influence the welfare of the elephants.

Hurst and Grimwood (2023) have suggested that future studies should critically analyse how animal welfare theories are applied within the context of tourism, ensuring a balance between theoretical frameworks and practical implications for fostering ethical human–animal interactions.

In summary, nurturing positive relationships between elephants and their mahouts is vital for ensuring their welfare, especially in tourism contexts. However, the quality of these relationships can be inconsistent, affected by the mahout's experience, training and the management practices of the camp. Future research should delve into how these human–animal relationships impact both the physical and the psychological health of elephants.

Studies could examine how cognitive-behavioural training for mahouts, with a focus on promoting compassion and empathy, can enhance elephant welfare by mitigating stress and encouraging healthier behaviours. Furthermore, comparative research could investigate the welfare differences between elephants in high-interaction tourism settings—such as those involving riding or bathing—and those in more passive observation-only environments. Such research would help identify the most beneficial and sustainable types of KARs for the long-term well-being of these magnificent animals.

Impact of tourism on captive elephants and welfare standards

The impact of tourism on the welfare of captive elephants is profound, often resulting in stress for the animals due to the high frequency of human interactions and the physical demands imposed by tourist activities. Worwag *et al.* (2019) argue that, despite a growing interest in animal welfare within tourism, academic literature examining tourist attitudes remains limited. Future research should investigate how tourists' awareness and behaviours are shaped by existing welfare standards, as well as how ethical codes of conduct can be effectively promoted within tourism venues.

Moreover, establishing a theoretical framework to evaluate welfare practices is essential for fostering consensus on best practices, particularly given the sensitive nature of this topic. Manning *et al.* (2023) emphasize the need for research to gain a deeper understanding of how tourism affects the welfare of captive animals, which could yield valuable insights into maintaining welfare standards for elephants used in tourism.

To further advance this area of research, studies should focus on understanding the impacts of tourism on captive elephants in greater depth. Developing evidence-based welfare standards specifically tailored to elephants in tourism settings is critical. Research could explore various factors, including the health consequences of daily tourist interactions, the psychological toll of captivity, and the environmental conditions that most effectively support elephant well-being. This inquiry is particularly urgent in countries like Thailand, where elephant tourism represents a major industry.

In addition, creating adaptable guidelines that can be implemented globally may be essential for ensuring high welfare standards across tourism venues. This will not only promote the well-being of elephants but also contribute to the sustainability of tourism practices, striking a balance between economic benefits and ethical responsibilities towards these magnificent creatures.

Consensus on ethical practices and conservation strategies

The elephant tourism industry is characterized by a spectrum of often conflicting opinions regarding the treatment of elephants. While some advocate ethical, observation-only ecotourism, others continue to offer high-interaction experiences. As highlighted by Worwag *et al.* (2019), despite the growing interest in animal welfare within tourism, there remains a significant gap in the academic literature concerning tourist attitudes. Future research should investigate how tourists' awareness and behaviours are shaped by welfare standards and explore strategies for effectively promoting ethical codes of conduct in tourism venues.

Moreover, Zakaria *et al.* (2024) emphasize the need to address critical knowledge gaps in Asian elephant conservation, including issues related to genetic diversity, human–elephant conflict, disease management, habitat loss and community-based conservation efforts. Targeted research in these areas could inform more effective conservation strategies and enhance welfare outcomes for elephants.

The welfare of captive elephants continues to be a contentious issue among tourists, scientists and stakeholders, largely due to the wide range of working conditions and management practices encountered in the industry (Bansiddhi *et al.*, 2019). While research conducted in Western countries has identified key factors influencing elephant welfare and led to improved care for zoo elephants, similar studies are essential for elephants in the tourism sector in Asia, particularly in Thailand. Such research could facilitate the development of evidence-based standards and guidelines, addressing how tourist activities impact elephant well-being and identifying optimal management practices that promote their health and welfare.

An important focus for future research should be the creation and dissemination of ethical codes of conduct for tourists, such as the Animal Welfare in Tourism Code of Conduct. It is vital to assess how these codes influence tourists' enjoyment and the welfare standards of the facilities they visit (Worwag *et al.*, 2019).

Additionally, developing a consensus on best practices for elephant welfare is crucial. Establishing a unified theoretical framework can guide operators, policy makers and tourists, ensuring that ethical considerations are integral to the future of elephant tourism. This research should aim to bridge existing knowledge gaps in Asian elephant conservation, focusing on the aforementioned issues while investigating how community-based conservation efforts can be effectively integrated into elephant tourism to benefit both local communities and elephant welfare.

Furthermore, examining the implementation and impact of ethical codes of conduct on tourist behaviour and facility welfare standards will contribute to a more standardized approach to welfare in the industry. By centring ethical considerations in future elephant tourism practices, we can work towards a more humane and responsible framework that benefits both elephants and the communities involved in their care.

Elephant Tourism Welfare Studies Across Timeframes

The focus of research has shifted over time. From 2005 to 2010, studies emphasized biological aspects like reproduction, nutrition and morphology. Between 2010 and 2015, the focus shifted towards animal welfare issues, wildlife management and epidemiology. More recently, from 2015 to 2020, social and environmental issues such as climate change, deforestation and human–elephant conflict have gained prominence. These shifts demonstrate an increasing recognition of the multifaceted challenges elephants face in both wild and captive environments and the need for interdisciplinary approaches to address their welfare and conservation (Zakaria *et al.*, 2024). Each period reveals evolving themes and priorities that reflect the changing landscape of elephant tourism and welfare concerns. To achieve the objectives outlined in this chapter, emerging research priorities have been explored alongside key themes from various time periods.

Over the years, research focus has evolved, highlighting significant developments and emerging trends that have shaped the current understanding of elephant welfare in tourism. By addressing these interdisciplinary research directions, the field can progress towards more ethical, sustainable and welfare-conscious practices.

Conclusion

The current key research themes in elephant tourism welfare discussed above are the basis for recommending five interdisciplinary research areas aimed at improving welfare and supporting conservation efforts. These areas include: (i) tourist behaviour, education and ethical awareness; (ii) animal welfare literacy among tourism operators; (iii) KARs and human–animal interaction; (iv) the impact of tourism on captive elephants and welfare standards; and (v) consensus on ethical practices and conservation strategies. These research priorities address the complexities of managing elephant welfare in tourism settings, contributing to more humane and sustainable practices.

Over the past two decades, interest in Asian elephants has grown significantly. This aligns with Zakaria *et al.* (2024) in emphasizing the need for further research on elephant welfare to analyse global trends in scientific publications and identify areas that require interdisciplinary approaches to improve welfare and conservation efforts. When managed appropriately, elephant-based tourism does not have to compromise the health, safety or well-being of elephants (ACES, 2023). More importantly, with better education, training and camp management, such tourism has the potential to foster positive changes for elephants in human care.

The problem lies not in the existence of the camps but in the quality of care provided, which includes attention to the well-being of mahouts. Rather than being an obstacle to conservation or elephant welfare, elephant-based tourism should be viewed as a catalyst for positive change (Suter, 2020).

Bibliography

Asian Captive Elephant Standards (ACES) (2023) Elephant Tourism & Responsible Travel. *ACES*, 8 February. Available at: https://www.elephantstandards.com/post/elephant-tourism-responsible-travel (accessed 5 October 2024).

Bansiddhi, P., Brown, J., Thitaram, C., Punyapornwithaya, V. and Nganvongpanit, K. (2019) Elephant tourism in Thailand: a review of animal welfare practices and needs. *Journal of Applied Animal Welfare Science* 23(2), 164–177. DOI: 10.1080/10888705.2019.1652804.

Carlstead, K., Paris, S. and Brown, J. (2019) Good keeper-elephant relationships in North American zoos are mutually beneficial to welfare. *Applied Animal Behaviour Science* 211, 103–111. DOI: 10.1016/j.applanim.2018.12.009.

Fennell, D.A. (2022) An animal welfare literacy framework for tourism. *Annals of Tourism Research* 96: 103461. DOI: 10.1016/j.annals.2022.103461.

Flower, E., Burns, G., Jones, D. and McBroom, J. (2021) Does the experience make a difference? Comparing tourist attitudes pre- and post-visit towards the elephant tourism industry. *Annals of Tourism Research Empirical Insights* 2(2): 100025. DOI: 10.1016/j.annale.2020.100025.

Fuktong, S., Yuttasaen, P., Punyapornwithaya, V., Brown, J.L., Thitaram, C. *et al.* (2021) A survey of stereotypic behaviors in tourist camp elephants in Chiang Mai, Thailand. *Applied Animal Behaviour Science* 243: 105456. DOI: 10.1016/j.applanim.2021.105456.

Hamdi, R. (2019) The Complicated Business of Saving Elephant Tourism: a Skift Deep Dive. Skift Research, 12 December. Available at: https://skift.com/2019/12/12/the-complicated-business-of-saving-elephant-tourism-a-skift-deep-dive (accessed 9 October 2024).

Hurst, C.E. and Grimwood, B.S.R. (2023) Posthumanism and the sentient elephant in the room. *Annals of Tourism Research* 101: 103604. DOI: 10.1016/j.annals.2023.103604.

Lee, S., Hong, S., Kim, J. and Meng, Z.M. (2024) Exploring the role of ethical experiences and psychological well-being in travel satisfaction: an animal welfare perspective in elephant-based tourism. *Tourism Management Perspectives* 51: 101248. DOI: 10.1016/j.tmp.2024.101248.

Manning, P., Hauff, L., Padfield, C., Olivier, L., Ganswindt, A. *et al.* (2022) Can stress and anxiety be assessed in African elephants (*Loxodonta africana*) using self-directed behaviour? *Applied Animal Behaviour Science* 256: 105746. DOI: 10.1016/j.applanim.2022.105746.

Manning, P., Dawson, E., Tholander, C. and Bonato, M. (2023) The effect of COVID-19 lockdown restrictions on self-directed behaviour, activity budgets, movement patterns, and spatial use in semi-captive African elephants (*Loxodonta africana*). *Applied Animal Behaviour Science* 266: 106007. DOI: 10.1016/j.applanim.2023.106007.

Supanta, J., Brown, J., Bansiddhi, P., Thitaram, C., Punyapornwithaya, V. *et al.* (2022) Effect of the COVID-19 pandemic and international travel ban on elephant tourist camp management in northern Thailand. *Frontiers in Veterinary Science* 9: 990811. DOI: 10.3389/fvets.2022.990811.

Suter, I. (2020) Rewilding or reviewing: conservation and the elephant-based tourism industry. *Animal Sentience* 5(28). DOI: 10.51291/2377-7478.1556.

Szydlowski, M. (2024) Wicked problems, novel solutions: Nepalese elephant tourism and conservation. *Animals* 14(1): 26. DOI: 10.3390/ani14010026.

Taylor, M., Hurst, C., Stinson, M. and Grimwood, B. (2020) Becoming care-full: contextualising moral development among captive elephant volunteer tourists to Thailand. *Journal of Ecotourism* 19(2), 113–131. DOI: 10.1080/14724049.2019.1686585.

Warwick, C., Pilny, A., Steedman, C. and Grant, R. (2023) Elephant tourism: an analysis and recommendations for public health, safety, and animal welfare. *International Journal of One Health* 9(2), 49–67. DOI: 10.14202/IJOH.2023.49-67.

Winter, C. (2020) A review of research into animal ethics in tourism: launching the *Annals of Tourism Research* curated collection on animal ethics in tourism. *Annals of Tourism Research* 84: 102989. DOI: 10.1016/j.annals.2020.102989.

Worwag, S., Varga, P. and Zizka, L. (2019) Tourists' ethical concern for Dumbo: elephant tourism in Thailand. *Journal of Travel, Tourism and Recreation* 1(2), 11–27. DOI: 10.22259/2642-908X.0102002.

Zakaria, N., Juahir, H., Muhammad Nor, S., Mohamad Hanapi, N., Jusoh, H. *et al.* (2024) Elephant research challenges and opportunities: a global bibliometric analysis. *Ecological Informatics* 82: 102662. DOI: 10.1016/j.ecoinf.2023.102662.

14 Afterword

Daniel Turner*

ANIMONDIAL, Brighton, UK

The Problems Facing Elephants – Where Do We Go From Here?

For anyone like me who has been working to improve the welfare of elephants for decades, we already know the problems they face. Through research, investigations and discussions, and even arguments, we have considered and explored the threats they face. Although we better understand the reasons behind them, their problems remain largely unresolved.

A historical issue

I started out as a researcher working for the Wildlife Protection Society of India – that's when I first saw elephants in the wild. It was there that I also had first-hand experience meeting elephant poachers and ivory dealers, as part of a scouting exercise. Elephant welfare became my focus at the Born Free Foundation, and in those 17 years of service, I met countless elephants in hundreds of zoos, circuses and sanctuaries, meeting their carers and gaining valuable insights into elephant husbandry. This would come in use, years later, when I was asked to co-create the tourism industry's animal welfare guidelines and carry out elephant welfare assessments. Unfortunately, in all those years, not much has changed. Elephants continue to be captured, killed and exploited. Like you, I want to see change.

*daniel@animondial.com

 Elephant Welfare in Global Tourism (E. Laws *et al.* eds)
DOI: 10.1079/9781836990093.0014

The opportunity for change

We established ANIMONDIAL, the specialist tourism consultancy, in 2018, with the objective of influencing positive change for animals and nature through tourism. Since then, we have worked with hundreds of tourism businesses, guiding each through the complexities, empowering their decision making, and helping them define the activities they offer. Unsurprisingly, elephants, and tourist activities that involve them, are often at the top of the agenda with operators wanting to do the right thing but struggling to know which suppliers to engage and what activities to sell. In the last decade, this has become something of a minefield. Non-governmental organization (NGO) scrutiny over the products operators sell, among other factors, has driven many of the elephant tourism venues to become evasive about the activities they offer.

In an ideal world, all elephants should be in the wild and allowed to roam free. The reality is that elephants are still hunted for their ivory, they are persecuted for damaging property, many are captured, traded and kept in restrictive conditions, and elephants are still being trained to perform circus-style tricks. The abundance of wild elephants is also on the decline. Threatened by habitat loss, climate change and illegal hunting, the latest assessments indicate that the population of African forest elephants (*Loxodonta cyclotis*) fell by more than 86% over a period of 31 years, while the population of African savannah elephants (*Loxodonta africana*) decreased by at least 60% over the last 50 years (IUCN, n.d.). Asian elephant (*Elephas maximus*) populations are in the same precarious position, now occupying only 5% of their historic geographic range (Sukumar, 2008). Thailand, for example, has fewer than 3500 wild elephants, as compared to an estimated 4000 elephants in private ownership, with the majority involved in tourism.

These are the realities from which we must strive for change, but this can only happen if human stakeholders work together to focus on the root causes of elephant strife, as opposed to battling against each other. This requires a pragmatic approach, fundamental to ANIMONDIAL's operations, whereby solutions to problems are identified through accurate, clear and comprehensive communications, positive engagement, transparent reporting and collaboration. The adoption of applied animal welfare science into tourism practice, such as through the Association of British Travel Agent's (ABTA) *Animal Welfare Guidelines* (ABTA, 2019), involves expert stakeholders from multiple disciplines which would be impossible without that collaborative approach.

Valued by tourism

Few industries value individual elephants more than the tourism sector. In Thailand, where elephants have been a major part of the country's tourism industry for decades, pre-pandemic revenues for elephant-based entertainment were estimated at more than US$500 million/year (Cowan, 2022). Botswana's tourism economy grew by 70%, to exceed US$2.5 billion in 2018, the same year that the country announced its ban on elephant hunting (WTTC, 2019). Elephants are clearly a major source of tourism revenue, and their conservation can be a wise investment for range countries. A single African elephant can apparently generate around US$22,966/year from ecotourism, and the lost economic benefits from elephants not being available for tourism are estimated to be around US$25 million (van de Water *et al.*, 2022). According to the World Travel & Tourism Council, wildlife presents the primary motivator for nature tourism, with wildlife tourism contributing US$343 billion annually and 21.8 million jobs globally (WTTC and ANIMONDIAL, 2022). Tourism also contributes millions of dollars per annum to protected areas and nature conservation, supports sustainable development and local community empowerment, and drives environmental stewardship (Spenceley, 2021). In Africa, where nature and national parks are considered some of the most important tourism assets, wildlife tourism generates around US$142 million in entrance fees for protected areas (UNWTO, 2015; African Leadership University School of Wildlife Conservation, n.d.). Elephant tourism generates substantial economic benefit for both local communities and the range countries that have embraced it.

Elephants are evidently good for tourism and range country destinations, but is tourism good for elephants? There is unequivocal evidence that tourism can be harmful to elephants, particularly if profits are prioritized over their welfare. The rapid growth in elephant tourism venues in Asia in the 1990s, resulting in the capture, trade and abusive training of thousands of wild elephants, was certainly driven by tourism (Hamdi, 2019). Studies on the effects of tourism activities on free-roaming elephants show increases in stress-related flight response and conspecific-directed aggressive behaviour corresponding with an increasing number of tourist vehicles (Ranaweerage *et al.*, 2015; Szott, 2020).

However, if elephant welfare is prioritized as a crucial factor for profit and sustainability, then tourism could be good for elephants too. That is why I chose to help the industry establish its animal welfare guidelines. Since their inception, tourism has influenced significant change in the way animals are used and treated in tourism, correcting historical issues and improving practices by considering the welfare needs of animals, along with the protection of the environment and the support of host communities (Kontogeorgopoulos, 2009; Jenkinson and Felton, 2018; Dell'Eva *et al.*, 2020; Lo and Janta, 2021; Statista, 2024).

So, where do we go from here?

My extensive experience across multiple disciplines has shown me that a positive future for elephants can only be possible through encouraging multi-stakeholder engagement and a resulting integrated approach (Box 14.1). Many of those contributing to this publication follow that approach and will likely succeed in improving the prospects for elephants in tourism, but those that don't, won't.

Box 14.1. Examples of multi-stakeholder engagement and an integrated approach, resulting in positive outcomes.

- *Effective regulation*: clear guidance + robust enforcement + penalties for non-compliance;
- *Welfare improvements*: comprehensive guidance + tourist code of conduct + supplier auditing + mahout training + elephant-welfare fund (to provide for elephant care in the event of no tourism); and
- *Elephant-friendly viewing practices*: tour operators + tour guide collaboration + tourist code of conduct + review of minimum distance recommendations + guide training to monitor elephant behaviour.

My hopes for a better future for elephants are pinned on the potential of Nature Positive Tourism, a recently developed concept that encourages the travel and tourism sector to commit to sustainable practices and, further, to invest in improving the state of nature in destinations to compensate for their unavoidable environmental impacts (through greenhouse gas (GHG) emissions, food sourcing, etc.). Tourism is already critical to conserving elephants by both encouraging range countries to invest in their protection and requiring captive animal facilities to comply with best practice in animal care. But there remains potential for the sector to do much more. A growing sector, it provides one in ten jobs globally, empowering local people and small businesses, it generates significant revenues, contributing more than 9% of the world's gross domestic product (GDP) (WTTC, 2023; UNWTO, 2023). Conservationists agree that international tourism can help to influence local people and governments to better protect their cultural and natural heritage (UN, 2016; Deutz *et al.*, 2020; Nature Positive Tourism Partnership and ANIMONDIAL, 2024).

The need for localized elephant protection measures is now clear, as is the need for local people, in consultation with national, NGO and academic experts, to be involved in improving conditions for themselves and for elephants. If mobilized through positive engagement, and directed by science-based guidance, tourism could help deliver national biodiversity action plans and advocate for and finance protected and conserved areas, ensuring the survival of elephants, and all other species, for future generations.

Bibliography

African Leadership University School of Wildlife Conservation (n.d.) The state of the wildlife economy in Kenya. Country case study for the state of the wildlife economy in Africa. Available at: https://sowc.alueducation.com/ (accessed 3 March 2025).

Association of British Travel Agent's (ABTA) (2019) *Animal Welfare Guidelines*, 2nd edn. ABTA. Available at: https://www.abta.com/industry-zone/abta-shop/abta-animal-welfare-guidelines (accessed 21 February 2025).

Cowan, C. (2022) Thai tourism elephants are 'far better off' in forests: Q&A with photographer Adam Oswell. Mongabay, Menlo Park, California.

Dell'Eva, M., Nava, C.R. and Osti, L. (2020) Perceptions and satisfaction of human-animal encounters in protected areas. *Worldwide Hospitality and Tourism Themes* 12, 441–458. DOI: 10.1108/WHATT-05-2020-0024.

Deutz, A., Heal, G.M., Niu, R., Swanson, E., Townshend, T. *et al.* (2020) *Financing Nature: Closing the Global Biodiversity Financing Gap*. The Paulson Institute, The Nature Conservancy and the Cornell Atkinson Center for Sustainability. Available at: https://www.nature.org/content/dam/tnc/nature/en/documents/FINANCINGNATURE_FullReport_091520.pdf (accessed 4 March 2025).

Hamdi, R. (2019) The Complicated Business of Saving Elephant Tourism: a Skift Deep Dive. *Skift Research*, 12 December. Available at: https://skift.com/2019/12/12/the-complicated-business-of-saving-elephant-tourism-a-skift-deep-dive/ (accessed 3 March 2025).

International Union for Conservation of Nature (IUCN) (n.d.) IUCN Red List of Threatened Species. Available at: https://www.iucnredlist.org/ (accessed 18 November 2024).

Jenkinson, C. and Felton, H. (2018) Animal welfare - driving improvements in tourism attractions. In: Carr, N. and Broom, D.M. (eds) *Tourism and Animal Welfare*. CAB International, Wallingford, UK, pp. 135–137.

Kontogeorgopoulos, N. (2009) The role of tourism in elephant welfare in northern Thailand. *Journal of Tourism* 10, 1–19.

Lo, Y.C. and Janta, P. (2021) Balancing commercialization and sustainability in community-based tourism practices - a qualitative study of factors affecting elephant habitat communities in northern Thailand. *Frontiers in Psychology* 12: 685426. DOI: 10.3389/fpsyg.2021.685426.

Nature Positive Tourism Partnership and ANIMONDIAL (2024) *Nature Positive Travel & Tourism in Action*. Available at: https://animondial.com/resources/reports/nature-positive-travel-tourism-in-action/ (accessed 3 March 2025).

Ranaweerage, E., Ranjeewa, A.D.G. and Sugimoto, K.(2015) Tourism-induced disturbance of wildlife in protected areas: a case study of free ranging elephants in Sri Lanka. *Global Ecology and Conservation* 4, 625–631. DOI: 10.1016/j.gecco.2015.10.013.

Spenceley, A. (2021) The future of nature-based tourism: impacts of COVID-19 and paths to sustainability. *Luc Hoffmann Institute*. Available at: https://luchoffmanninstitute.org/wp-content/uploads/2021/04/luchoffmanninstitute-future-nature-based-tourism-report-2021.pdf (accessed 3 March 2025).

Statista (2024) Sustainable tourism worldwide - statistics & facts. Statista Research Department. Available at: https://www.statista.com/topics/1916/green-tourism/#:~:text=Traveler%20awareness%20of%20social%20and,than%20referenced%20in%20the%20text (accessed 3 March 2025).

Sukumar, R. (2008) Elephants in time and space: evolution and ecology. In: Wemmer, C. and Christen, C.A. (eds) *Elephants and Ethics: Toward a Morality of Coexistence*. Johns Hopkins University Press, Baltimore, Maryland, pp. 17–39.

Szott, I. (2020) The impact of wildlife tourism on African elephants, *Loxodonta africana*, in South Africa. Doctoral thesis, Liverpool John Moores University, Liverpool, UK.

United Nations (UN) (2016) *Cancun Declaration on Mainstreaming the Conservation and Sustainable Use of Biodiversity for Well-being*. UN Convention on Biological Diversity. Available at: https://www.cbd.int/cop/cop-13/hls/cancun%20declaration-en.pdf (accessed 3 March 2025).

United Nations World Tourism Organization (UNWTO) (2015) Towards measuring the economic value of wildlife watching tourism in Africa—Briefing paper. Available at: www.e-unwto.org/doi/book/10.18111/978928441675247 (accessed 3 March 2025).

United Nations World Tourism Organization (UNWTO) (2023) *World Tourism Barometer*, Volume 21(2).

van de Water, A., Henley, M., Bates, L. and Slotow, R. (2022) The value of elephants: a pluralist approach. *Ecosystem Services* 58: 101488. DOI: 10.1016/j.ecoser.2022.101488.

World Travel & Tourism Council (WTTC) (2019) *The Economic Impact of Global Wildlife Tourism*. The World Travel & Tourism Council & Oxford Economics. Available at: https://wttc.org/

Portals/0/Documents/Reports/2019/Sustainable%20Growth-Economic%20Impact%20of%20Global%20Wildlife%20Tourism-Aug%202019.pdf (accessed 3 March 2025).

World Travel & Tourism Council (WTTC) (2023) Travel & Tourism Economic Impact Research (EIR). Available at: https://wttc.org/research/economic-impact# (accessed 3 March 2025).

World Travel & Tourism Council (WTTC) and ANIMONDIAL (2022) *Nature Positive Travel & Tourism*. WTTC. Available at: https://wttc.org/Portals/0/Documents/Reports/2022/Nature-Positive-Travel-And-Tourism.pdf (accessed 3 March 2025).

Index

Note: Page numbers in bold type refer to figures
Page numbers in italic type refer to tables
Page numbers followed by 'B' refer to Boxes

Printed and bound by CPI Group (UK) Ltd, Croydon, CR0 4YY

13/09/2026

14961084-0002